D1525324

Tonality and Transformation

OXFORD STUDIES IN MUSIC THEORY

Series Editor Richard Cohn

Studies in Music with Text, David Lewin

Music as Discourse: Semiotic Adventures in Romantic Music, Kofi Agawu

Playing with Meter: Metric Manipulations in Haydn and Mozart's Chamber Music for Strings, Danuta Mirka

Songs in Motion: Rhythm and Meter in the German Lied, Yonatan Malin

A Geometry of Music: Harmony and Counterpoint in the Extended Common Practice, Dmitri Tymoczko

In the Process of Becoming: Analytic and Philosophical Perspectives on Form in Early Nineteenth-Century Music, Janet Schmalfeldt

Tonality and Transformation, Steven Rings

Tonality and Transformation

STEVEN RINGS

OXFORD
UNIVERSITY PRESS

Oxford University Press, Inc., publishes works that further
Oxford University's objective of excellence
in research, scholarship, and education.

Oxford   New York
Auckland   Cape Town   Dar es Salaam   Hong Kong   Karachi
Kuala Lumpur   Madrid   Melbourne   Mexico City   Nairobi
New Delhi   Shanghai   Taipei   Toronto

With offices in
Argentina   Austria   Brazil   Chile   Czech Republic   France   Greece
Guatemala   Hungary   Italy   Japan   Poland   Portugal   Singapore
South Korea   Switzerland   Thailand   Turkey   Ukraine   Vietnam

Published by Oxford University Press, Inc.
198 Madison Avenue, New York, New York 10016

www.oup.com

Oxford is a registered trademark of Oxford University Press

Library of Congress Cataloging-in-Publication Data
   Rings, Steven.
   Tonality and transformation / Steven Rings.
      p. cm.—(Oxford studies in music theory)
   Includes bibliographical references and index.
   ISBN 978-0-19-538427-7
   1. Music theory.   2. Tonality.   3. Musical intervals and scales.   4. Musical analysis.
I. Title.
   MT6.R682T66 2011
   781.2—dc22   2010019212
**Publication of this book was supported by the AMS 75 PAYS Publication Endowment Fund of the American
Musicological Society.**

3 5 7 9 8 6 4

Printed in the United States of America
on acid-free paper

CONTENTS

	Acknowledgments	vii
	Note to Readers	ix
	A Note on Orthography	xi
	Introduction	1

PART I

Theory and Methodology

Chapter 1:	Intervals, Transformations, and Tonal Analysis	9
Chapter 2:	A Tonal GIS	41
Chapter 3:	Oriented Networks	101

PART II

Analytical Essays

Chapter 4:	Bach, Fugue in E major, *Well-Tempered Clavier*, Book II, BWV 878	151
Chapter 5:	Mozart, "Un'aura amorosa" from *Così fan tutte*	171
Chapter 6:	Brahms, Intermezzo in A major, op. 118, no. 2	185
Chapter 7:	Brahms, String Quintet in G major, mvt. ii, Adagio	203
	Afterword	221
	Glossary	223
	Works Cited	231
	Index	239

ACKNOWLEDGMENTS

Thanks are due first to my wife Gretchen, for her prodigious patience and grace; though she remains blissfully innocent of this book's contents, she has been a limitless source of inspiration. My son Elliott served as a sort of inadvertent quality control: this volume would have been completed at least a year sooner had he not come along. I hope my thinking is a year more refined than it would have been without him; my life is certainly immeasurably richer. The book is dedicated to them. I also thank my mother Linda, my father Dale, and my brother Mike for their unwavering love and support.

My *Doktorvater* Daniel Harrison oversaw the first iteration of many of these ideas; his spirit imbues this work. David Clampitt introduced me to this style of music theory and offered trenchant observations on ideas new to this book. My other teachers at various stages in my graduate work—in particular, Pat McCreless, Allen Forte, James Hepokoski, Leon Plantinga, Craig Wright, Michael Cherlin, and David Damschroder—all played crucial roles in shaping my theoretical and critical outlook. Ian Quinn saved me from myself at one very early stage, pointing out a rather hilarious, exhaustion-induced slip (I had decided for several pages that there were only 11 chromatic pitch classes). Ramon Satyendra and Julian Hook both read the manuscript and provided invaluable comments on matters large and small. Henry Klumpenhouwer offered critical perspectives on the conceptual foundations of Lewinian theory, while Peter Smith and Frank Samarotto lent insight into matters Schenkerian. Dmitri Tymoczko has been a valued sparring partner and friend; this book has benefited greatly from his critical perspective. The anonymous readers for Oxford challenged me on several important points and forced me to clarify my thinking. Lucia Marchi answered questions on Da Ponte's verse. My assistant Jonathan De Souza has done yeoman work as a design consultant, typeface expert, punctuation cop, indexer, and editor extraordinaire (his passion for the *Chicago Manual* almost exceeds my own). All of these individuals helped improve this book. The errors that inevitably remain are mine, not theirs.

Richard Cohn has been a supporter of this work from the beginning—he has in many ways opened the theoretical space within which my ideas have unfolded. As the editor of this series, he also helped acquire the book for Oxford. I cannot thank him enough. Suzanne Ryan has been a model editor, enthusiastic and patient in equal measure; her confidence and understanding helped me weather a couple rough patches. Norm Hirschy and Madelyn Sutton at Oxford have also been a delight to work with, making the whole process run more smoothly than I could have hoped. I would also like to thank the Mrs. Giles Whiting Foundation for supporting the year's research leave necessary to complete the book, and the American Musicological Society for a generous subvention from the AMS 75 PAYS Publication Endowment Fund.

My scholarly home during this book's writing has been the University of Chicago. I would like to thank the chairs of the music department during this time—Robert Kendrick and Martha Feldman, as well as interim chairs Anne Robertson and Larry Zbikowski—for providing unstinting support and helping to create the ideal intellectual environment for a junior faculty member. My fellow theorists at Chicago—Larry Zbikowski and Thomas Christensen—are the best professional and intellectual role models I could hope for; they are also good friends. My colleagues in historical musicology, ethnomusicology, and composition have at once inspired me with their own achievements and helped to keep my thinking productively unsettled. The same can be said for the remarkable cohort of graduate students that I have had the pleasure to work with over the last five years. Finally, I would like to thank Berthold Hoeckner for many hours of stimulating conversation and for his valued insights into the balance between work and family. While I cannot imagine a better personal home than the one I described in the first paragraph of these acknowledgments, I cannot imagine a better intellectual home than the one created by my friends and mentors in the University of Chicago Department of Music.

NOTE TO READERS

I have sought to make this book both accessible and formally substantive. It is a tricky balance: one risks disappointing both specialists (who wish there was more math) and nonspecialists (who wish there was less). The latter readers may indeed wonder why any math is needed at all.[1] While I hope that the book will speak for itself in this regard, I will answer here that statements in transformational theory gain their musical suggestiveness in significant part from the formal structures that support them. Those structures situate each musical interval or gesture within a richly developed conceptual space; the algebraic contours of that space contribute in important ways to the character of the interval or gesture in question. This underlying formal context is sometimes operative only "behind the scenes"; at other times it is thematized in the foreground of an analysis. In either case, an awareness of the pertinent underlying structure adds considerably to the allusiveness of any observation made in the theory, sensitizing us to the expressive particularity of a given musical relationship. Moreover, the theory's formalism can act as a generator of insights: once a basic musical observation has been rendered in transformational terms, the technology can lead the analyst toward new observations. The formal precision of the apparatus assures that the new insights will be related to the old, often in compelling ways.

I have nevertheless limited the amount of formalism in the book, and not only out of ethical concerns for accessibility. The simplicity of the book's math results from my conviction that much of the fascination in this style of music theory resides in the reciprocal interaction that it affords between formal ideas and musical experience. One does not need to delve very far into the math to explore that interaction. My interest has thus been to employ only as much formalism as needed, and to expend somewhat greater effort seeking out the ways in which the resulting technical ideas may be brought to bear on musical experience—modeling or shaping it—in ways that are at once concrete and immediate. For the specialist wishing for more mathematical development, I hope the basic ideas introduced

---

1. In addition to my comments here, readers may wish to consult John Clough's eloquent answer to this question in his review of David Lewin's *Generalized Musical Intervals and Transformations* (Clough 1989, 227).

here might provide preliminary material for exploration and extension in more specialized contexts.

I have introduced all formal ideas in prose, using plain English rather than formal definitions, theorems, or proofs. I have also included a Glossary that defines basic concepts from transformational theory and abstract algebra—again in plain English. Chapter 1 is an introduction to transformational thought for those new to it; readers well versed in the approach may wish to skip it and begin with Chapter 2.[2]

---

2. The book assumes a basic knowledge of tonal and post-tonal theories, including Schenkerian analysis. For readers new to Schenkerian thought, Cadwallader and Gagné 2010 is a fine introduction. Straus 2005 offers an accessible overview of post-tonal theory.

A NOTE ON ORTHOGRAPHY

Transformational theorists often write the names of transformations in all caps and/or in italics.[3] I have not employed either orthographic convention here. I have come to find the all-caps approach visually obtrusive; the all-italics approach is hard to sustain in all cases (for example, when transformation names are words rather than single letters). Transformation names in this book are thus simply written in Roman type, using a combination of upper and lowercase letters, depending on what seems most readable in a given case. (For example, Chapter 1 introduces a transformation that resolves all elements to C; it is notated ResC.) There is only one exception to this orthographic rule: the identity element in a group of intervals or transformations is always written as a lowercase italicized *e*, in keeping with mathematical conventions.

Note names follow the Acoustical Society of America, with C4 as middle C. Curly brackets { } indicate unordered sets, while parentheses ( ) indicate ordered sets. Pitch classes are often indicated by integers, using the familiar C = 0 convention. The letters t and e sometimes substitute for the numbers 10 and 11 when indicating pitch classes. Note that Roman e means "pitch class 11," while italicized *e* means the identity element in a group of intervals or operations. In many contexts, major and minor triads are indicated using familiar neo-Riemannian notation: the note name of the root is followed by a plus sign (+) for major or a minus sign (−) for minor: C+ = a C-major triad; E− = an E-minor triad.

---

3. The all-caps approach derives from artificial intelligence and early computer programming languages, both influential when David Lewin first formulated his transformational ideas in the 1970s. The italic approach derives from mathematical orthography, in which variables are typically italicized.

Tonality and Transformation

Introduction

The research that gave rise to this book began as an effort to connect neo-Riemannian theory more fruitfully to traditional ideas about tonal music.[1] The volume that has resulted, as is so often the case, is something rather different: an exploration of the ways in which transformational and GIS technologies may be used to model diverse tonal effects and experiences.[2] Neo-Riemannian theory makes an appearance here and there, but the book is not primarily about harmonic transformations; nor is it limited in scope to chromatic music. Nor, for that matter, does it have much to say about efficient voice leading, a major focus of neo-Riemannian studies and a central preoccupation of geometrical music theory.[3] Instead, the book seeks to return to certain fundamental ideas from transformational and GIS theory, exploring their potential to illuminate familiar aspects of tonal phenomenology.

The advent of neo-Riemannian theory nevertheless paved the way for the project in a broader disciplinary sense. The transformational models of chromatic harmony introduced in influential studies by David Lewin, Brian Hyer, and Richard Cohn gave rise to one of the more striking discursive shifts in music theory in recent decades, as an algebraic technology once reserved for atonal musics was applied to the tonal repertory.[4] I suspect that this work captured the imagination of many theorists not only because it focused on ear-catching progressions, or because it provided persuasive models of analytically challenging music, but also because of the frisson it generated by applying a mathematical metalanguage to familiar chromatic passages in Wagner, Schubert, Brahms, and others—music traditionally modeled by Schenkerian or other tonal methodologies. This discursive shift nevertheless seems to have created some confusion, binding

---

1. For an accessible introduction to neo-Riemannian theory, see Cohn 1998. A brief definition is also provided in the Glossary.
2. On "transformational and GIS technologies," see Chapter 1.
3. The major contributions to geometrical music theory have come from Clifton Callender, Ian Quinn, and Dmitri Tymoczko. See especially Tymoczko 2006 and Callender, Quinn, and Tymoczko 2008.
4. The seminal works in neo-Riemannian theory include Lewin 1982 and 1987 (the latter is cited hereafter as *GMIT*; see pp. 175–80); Hyer 1989 and 1995; and Cohn 1996 and 1997.

the technology employed to (implicit or explicit) assumptions about tonality and atonality. The mathematical apparatus of transformational analysis is still most familiar to theorists from atonal theory; this can foster the impression that something in its underlying logic is fundamentally nontonal. Such an impression is heightened by the fact that neo-Riemannian approaches have typically sought to model chromatic progressions whose tonal status is somehow in doubt. This can lead to the view that any application of transformational methods is an (implicit or explicit) assertion that the passage in question is, in some sense, "not tonal," or perhaps "not as tonal as we once thought." Of course, the underdefinition of "tonality" (and its opposite) is a central issue here. We will return to that issue in a moment.

Neo-Riemannian analysis—with its focus on local, chromatically striking passages, framed by more traditionally diatonic music—also seems to have led to a view that some works are divvied up into some music that is tonal (for example, because it is well analyzed by Schenkerian methods) and some that is transformational (because it is well analyzed by neo-Riemannian methods).[5] But this is to misconstrue the word transformational, treating it as a predicate for a certain kind of music, rather than as a predicate for a certain style of analytical and theoretical thought. That style of thought is moreover extremely capacious: GIS and transformational theories simply provide generalized models of musical intervals and musical actions, respectively. Intervals and actions are as fundamental to tonal music as they are to any other kind of music. There is nothing about transformational theory that makes it atonal in principle.

Nevertheless, to assert that transformational theory may be used to illuminate certain specifically *tonal* aspects of tonal music—as I intend to do in this volume—is to go one step further. It raises the question of what is meant by the italicized adjective, and its nominative form, the first word in this book's title. "Tonality" is at once one of the most familiar and most elusive terms in music-theoretical discourse.[6] It is tied to a set of aural habits and experiences that are so deeply ingrained and seemingly immediate among Western listeners that the concept is easily naturalized, complicating attempts to pin it down discursively. When theorists *have* sought to pin it down, they have constructed the concept in a bewildering variety of ways, leading to a "veritable profusion of definitions," as Brian Hyer has put it.[7] Further, the term has acquired a considerable amount of ideological freight over its relatively short life, making it not merely a descriptive label for a musical repertory or a set of aural habits, but a concept that has served a variety of ideological interests.[8]

---

5. Such a view is evident, for example, in Samarotto 2003.
6. For the definitive history of the term and its French and German cognates, see Beiche 1992.
7. Hyer 2002, 726. Hibberd 1961; Thomson 1999; Krumhansl 2004, 253–54; and Vos 2000 also offer valuable accounts of the term's definitional tensions and its semantic "fuzziness" (Vos's term).
8. See Hyer 2002, 745–50. As Hyer notes (pp. 748–49), the term's ideological baggage dates back to its earliest popularization in the writings of Fétis, in which it participates in a conspicuously Orientalist narrative of race and musical competence. Perhaps the most potent material example of such ideological entanglements has been presented by Kofi Agawu, who argues that tonality has served as a "colonizing force" in Africa (2003, 8ff; 2010).

Given the word's ideological charge and its lack of semantic focus, it might be tempting to jettison it altogether, perhaps replacing it with a more neutral neologism. But to do so would be overly fastidious. Despite its many problems, the word tonality continues to evoke a vivid sound world for many Western listeners—it is that very sound world that I wish to engage theoretically and analytically in these pages. Thus, the best approach is perhaps to be clear about how I will use the term here. I will be interested in the concept of tonality insofar as it relates to a set of aural experiences familiar to listeners enculturated in Western musical traditions, experiences that arise from organizing one's aural sensations with respect to a single pitch class, the tonic. In other words, to borrow Nattiez's (1990) terminology, this study is focused on the esthesics of tonality—tonality as something experienced—not on tonality as an immanent property of musical works.[9] We will be concerned with what it is like to hear tonally, and with exploring various ways to engage and shape that aural experience through the mediation of GIS and transformational models.

I have stated that tonal hearing, as I will understand it here, arises from "organizing one's aural sensations with respect to a single pitch class, the tonic."[10] This statement places a strong accent on pitch centricity as a defining aspect of tonal experience, following William Thomson, who states that "centricity, in the focal sense, is the sine qua non of tonality" (1999, 242). Of course, centricity is usually only one aspect of traditional definitions of Western tonality. Such definitions typically also include (in no particular order): a harmonic vocabulary focused on tertian sonorities; a melodic basis in diatonic scales; specified relationships between consonance and dissonance; cadence as a crucial rhetorical, syntactic, and key-defining event; coordination between counterpoint, harmony, and meter; and so on.[11] We will engage with these familiar categories in various ways in the following chapters. Our interest, however, will always be in the *effect* of tonal phenomena for the listener—the manifold ways in which an awareness of a tonic can color the sounding elements in the musical texture, seeming to invest them with characteristic qualities and affects, kinetic energy, syntactic purpose, and so on.

9. As Hyer notes, a "recurrent tension" in definitions of tonality regards "whether the term refers to the objective properties of the music—its fixed, internal structure—or the cognitive experience of listeners" (2002, 727). The present study is concerned with the second understanding of the term. This is not to imply that there must be a hard and fast dichotomy between immanent and esthesic statements about tonality. Often, literally immanent statements such as "passage *x* is tonal" can be understood to mean "passage *x* sounds tonal to me," or "when I listen to passage *x*, my aural experience is one of tonal-ness." Further, immanent theories of tonality typically relate to listener perceptions of tonal-ness, in various ways. For example, Brown, Headlam, and Dempster (1997, 157) define tonality as a "property that delimits a broad stylistic category of Western music"—an immanent definition, treating tonality as a property of works within a stylistic class—but then go on in a footnote (n. 8) to state that their theory should agree with (and be confirmed by) the "aural intuitions" of qualified listeners.

10. This echoes the concise definition proposed by David Huron (2006, 143): "One simple definition of tonality is a system for interpreting pitches or chords through their relationship to a reference pitch, dubbed the *tonic.*"

11. Two especially clear examples of this kind of "enumerated" definition of tonality are Straus 2005, 130, and Tymoczko 2011.

But surely we already have plenty of satisfying accounts of tonal experience. Why add to them with this book? First, and most pragmatically, many questions have arisen in recent years regarding the relationship between transformational theories—most notably neo-Riemannian ones—and more traditional tonal ideas. As noted above, my original purpose in beginning this project was to clarify that relationship. Though the book has outgrown its initial neo-Riemannian focus, I hope it can nevertheless help to make clear the ways in which transformational ideas can be re-infused with familiar tonal concepts. To be sure, neo-Riemannian analysts have purposefully avoided tonal categories in the past, as they have sought to explain music in which such categories are understood as problematic or even inappropriate. But many tonal theorists of more traditional bent will likely feel that tonal concepts, however weakened or problematized, still have at least *some* relevance to the music typically studied in neo-Riemannian analyses. The technologies introduced in this book will allow both parties to explore the interaction between typical neo-Riemannian harmonic progressions and familiar tonal effects. And they will allow transformational analysts to integrate tonal concepts into their work if so desired, and, perhaps more important, to exclude them out of a conscious choice, not simply *faute de mieux*.[12]

Second, and more substantively, this book is driven by the conviction that no musical phenomenon, however familiar, can be exhausted by a single theoretical paradigm. As an entailment to this conviction, if we wish to illuminate a phenomenon as brightly as possible, we will do well to bring multiple theoretical searchlights to bear on it. This commitment to pluralism is very much in keeping with the project of transformational theory in general. The technology of the theory is designed to encourage pluralism: a given musical phenomenon admits of multiple GIS and transformational perspectives, none of which excludes any other a priori (which is not the same as saying that all of them are equally valuable). The approach simply asks the analyst to pursue and extend various musical apperceptions[13] within an algebraic formal context, with the full recognition that no single formal context can lay claim to comprehensiveness—thus making obligatory multiple perspectives on the same music. Given this commitment to pluralism, it is disappointing, but perhaps not surprising, that antagonisms have arisen between practitioners of transformational methods and those committed to other methodologies, such as Schenkerian analysis. In this book I hope to show that competition between such divergent modes of analytical engagement is misplaced, that their methodologies differ in crucial ways, and that they may in fact coexist in analytical praxis. These matters are addressed more thoroughly in section 1.4.

Tonal music, like any richly allusive cultural phenomenon, exceeds any single interpretive or analytical method. I do not adopt this view out of obeisance to fashionable philosophical positions—though such positions could likely be adduced in its support—but instead from a simple awareness that any analytical approach will, of necessity, tend to focus on some aspects of musical experience and neglect

12. Cf. Lewin 1982–83, 335.
13. Lewin prefers the word *intuitions*. On both terms, see section 1.2.3.

others.[14] Any analytical act will thus leave a surplus—a vast, unruly realm of musical experience that eludes the grasp of the single analytical model. Corners of that vast realm may nevertheless be illuminated via other analytical approaches, but those approaches will leave their own surpluses. And so on. In short, and in less grandiose terms, there will always be something new to notice in music we cherish—new sonic characteristics to attend to, new ways to focus our ears on familiar patterns, new ways to experience sounds as meaningful. This is no less true of tonal music, with its rich history of theoretical models. To borrow Alfred North Whitehead's memorable phrase, tonal music, like all music, is "patient of interpretation."[15]

The models I develop here thus offer new ways of thinking about some very familiar aural experiences. The hope is that those experiences may be defamiliarized in the process, making us acutely alive to them again, and allowing us to sense tonal effects with renewed intensity, and in new ways.[16] Surely one of the great values of music theory is its potential to refract, alter, and intensify musical experience, in ways both subtle and not so subtle, as new discursive concepts are brought to bear on the sonic stuff of music. Tonal music is no different from any other music in this regard: it admits of, and rewards, many modes of analytical engagement.

Part I of the book covers theoretical and methodological ground, while Part II contains four analytical essays. Chapter 1 is intended primarily for those new to transformational theory: it includes primers on GIS and transformational approaches as well as two model analyses in a traditional transformational style (of passages by Bach and Schubert). Section 1.4 discusses methodological differences between transformational analysis and Schenkerian analysis.

Chapters 2 and 3 present the main theoretical substance of the book. Chapter 2 introduces a GIS that models intervals between pitches imbued with special tonal characters, or *qualia*. In addition to surveying the formal resources of this GIS, the chapter includes several short analytical vignettes on music from Bach to Mahler. While Chapter 2 is GIS-based, Chapter 3 is transformational in focus, introducing a special kind of transformational network that can impose an orientation on a given transformational space, directing all of its elements toward one central element. Such networks model the ways in which a tonal center can act as a locus of attraction in a musical passage. The directing of the listener's attention toward a tonal center, which I call *tonal intention,* can be conceived as a special kind of transformational action.

The chapters of Part II present analyses of a Bach fugue, a Mozart aria, a Brahms intermezzo, and a Brahms quintet movement. The fact that there are two Brahms

---

14. This view in fact accords with the methodology of a rather *un*fashionable school of literary criticism: the Chicago School of R. S. Crane, Elder Olson, Richard McKeon, and others. For a good overview of this style of pluralism, see Booth 1979.

15. Whitehead 1967, 136.

16. Here I follow Hepokoski and Darcy (2006, 12), who express a similar desire for defamiliarization through novel modes of analytical reflection.

analyses is not meant to suggest that these ideas are more applicable to his music than to that of others. These four chapters aim to demonstrate applications of the technologies in Part I to diatonic music that might not be immediately obvious to the reader as apt for transformational study; it just so happened that two Brahms movements fit the bill nicely. The transformational literature abounds in studies of highly chromatic works, and I expect the reader will find it obvious how to apply the technologies of Part I to favorite chromatic passages in Schubert, Wagner, Wolf, Strauss, and others. I have indeed included analytical vignettes in Part I that point the way toward the application of these ideas to typical neo-Riemannian progressions.[17] Part II, by contrast, stresses the applicability of the present ideas to diatonic idioms that have been largely neglected in the recent transformational literature. The essays employ the concepts from Part I in various ways. While the Bach analysis draws primarily on the GIS from Chapter 2, the Mozart analysis makes considerable use of the oriented networks from Chapter 3; both technologies are in evidence in the Brahms analyses. The Mozart and Brahms analyses further include Schenkerian components, while the Bach draws on ideas from Fuxian fugal pedagogy.

17. See in particular the Liszt example in section 2.8; the analysis of the chromatic Grail motive in section 2.9.2; and the analysis of Brahms's op. 119, no. 2, in section 3.7. The reader is also referred to my analyses of works by Schubert in Rings 2006, 2007, and 2011a.

PART I

Theory and Methodology

One

Intervals, Transformations, and Tonal Analysis

Introduction

Though transformational theory is by now a familiar presence on the musicological landscape, ubiquitous in conference programs and theoretical journals, it remains a specialist subdiscipline within a specialist field, largely the province of initiates. Most music theorists have at least a casual acquaintance with transformational ideas, but only a handful actively pursue research in the area; for other music scholars (historians, for example), the theory is surely a closed book. As Ramon Satyendra has noted, this is due at least in part to the mathematical aspects of the approach, which he calls a "language barrier" that has inhibited "broad-based critique and commentary" (2004, 99). While that broad-based discussion has yet to emerge, the theory's reception among specialists has moved into a new critical phase, with certain of the method's foundational assumptions being held up to scrutiny on both technological and conceptual grounds—a sign of the theory's continuing vitality. But such revisions also raise a worry: as refinements to transformational methodologies become ever more recherché, the theory threatens to leave behind a host of scholars who never had a chance to come to terms with it in its most basic guise. This would be unfortunate, for transformational methods, even in their simplest applications, represent a style of music-theoretic thought of considerable power and richness, and one that is in principle accessible to a wide range of analytically minded musicians.

Thus, while this book is primarily about the application of transformational ideas to tonal phenomena, I hope it can also serve as an accessible general introduction to transformational theory. The present chapter presents an overview of the theory for the reader new to the approach (or for those who would like a refresher).[1] After a capsule summary in section 1.1, sections 1.2 and 1.3 serve as primers on the two main branches of transformational thought: generalized

---

1. The discussion here complements the fine introductions to the theory from Satyendra (2004) and Michael Cherlin (1993).

intervals and transformational networks. These sections introduce what we might call "classical" Lewinian intervals and transformations, as formulated in David Lewin's *Generalized Musical Intervals and Transformations* (hereafter *GMIT*), the foundational text in the field. They also survey recent criticisms of and revisions to Lewin's ideas. Each section includes a little model analysis of a tonal passage, the first by Bach, the second by Schubert. The analyses are meant to display the theory in action and to demonstrate its efficacy in illuminating aspects of tonal works, even before introducing the new technologies of this book. The analyses are again in a rather "classical" transformational idiom, adopting modes of interpretation common in the literature. This will allow us, in section 1.4, to contrast such transformational approaches with Schenkerian analysis.

1.1 Transformational Theory in Nuce

Transformational theory is a branch of systematic music theory that seeks to model relational and dynamic aspects of musical experience. The theory explores the manifold ways in which we as musical actants—listeners, performers, composers, interpreters—can experience and construe relationships among a wide range of musical entities (not only pitches). The formal apparatus of the theory allows the analyst to develop, pursue, and extend diverse relational hearings of musical phenomena. The theory articulates into two broad perspectives. One is intervallic, in which the subject "measures" the relationship between two musical objects, as a passive observer. The other is transformational, in which the subject actively seeks to recreate a given relationship in his or her hearing, traversing the space in question through an imaginative gesture.[2] The conceptual difference between intervals and transformations is subtle, and some recent theorists have sought to downplay it.[3] We will explore such matters in more detail later. For now we can simply note that the emphasis in both modalities is on the *relationships* between musical entities, not on the entities as isolated monads. Transformational theory thematizes such relationships and seeks to sensitize the analyst to them.

   In both the intervallic and transformational perspectives, musical entities are members of *sets,* while the intervals or transformations that join them are members of *groups* or *semigroups.* We will discuss the italicized terms in the following section (definitions may also be found in the Glossary); readers need not worry about their formal meaning for the moment. Intervallic structures are modeled via *Generalized Interval Systems,* or GISes, which comprise a set of elements, a group of intervals, and a function that maps the former into the latter. Transformational

---

2. As Henry Klumpenhouwer puts it, transformations model "moments of action carried out by and within the analyst" (2006, 278).

3. See, for example, Hook 2007b, 172–77. The distinction between the intervallic and transformational perspectives was of central importance to Lewin, forming part of a general critique of Cartesian views of musical experience, as discussed in section 1.2.2 (see also Klumpenhouwer 2006).

relationships are modeled by *transformational networks*: configurations of nodes and arrows, with arrows labeled by transformations (drawn from some semigroup) and nodes filled with musical entities (drawn from some set).[4] Any GIS statement may be converted into a transformational statement, a technological conversion that also implies (in Lewin's thought) a conceptual conversion from (passive) intervallic thinking to (active) transformational thinking.[5] The converse, however, is not true: there exist transformational statements that can*not* be rendered in GIS terms. The transformational perspective is thus broader than the GIS perspective. For this reason, the term *transformational theory* is often used, as here, to encompass both modes of thought.

1.2 Intervals

1.2.1 GISes

GIS statements take the form int(s, t) = i. This is a mathematical expression with formal content, which we will unpack in a moment. I would like first, however, simply to note that its arrangement on the page mimics a plain English sentence: it can be read from left to right as a formal rendering of the statement "The interval from s to t is i." We can understand GIS technology as an attempt to render explicit the conceptual structure underlying such everyday statements about musical intervals.[6]

Figure 1.1 will help us begin to explore that underlying conceptual structure. The figure shows our GIS formula again, now with its various components labeled. The italicized words indicate mathematical concepts. Here I will present informal definitions of these words, offering just enough information so that the reader understands their overall structure and can begin to appreciate their suggestiveness—both singly and in combination—as models for intervallic concepts. More detailed discussions of each term may be found in the Glossary.

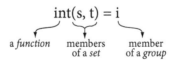

$$\text{int}(s, t) = i$$

a *function*   members of a *set*   member of a *group*

Figure 1.1 A GIS statement with components labeled.

4. Given the theory's emphasis on relationships over isolated musical elements, the technical emphasis in the discourse is typically on groups and semigroups, basic concepts from abstract algebra. Transformational theory is thus an algebraic music theory. Recent developments in geometrical music theory—see, for example, Callender, Quinn, and Tymoczko 2008—represent a departure from this algebraic foundation. Though such geometrical approaches are sometimes considered subsets of transformational theory writ large, I will limit the term *transformational* here to algebraic approaches.
5. Klumpenhouwer (2006) describes the conceptual transition from intervallic to transformational thinking as the general theme of *GMIT*.
6. Whether GISes succeed fully in this regard is a question to which we will return.

As the figure shows, the elements s and t are both members of a mathematical *set*. For present purposes, a set may simply be understood as a collection of distinct elements, finite or infinite. The elements are *distinct* in that none of them occurs more than once in the set.[7] Lewin calls the set that contains s and t the *space* of the GIS, which he labels S. The space S may consist of pitches, or pitch classes, or harmonies of a particular kind, or time points, or contrapuntal configurations, or timbral spectra—and so on. GISes thus extend the idea of interval to a whole host of musical phenomena, not just pitches; this is one of the senses in which they are "generalized."

Note that the elements s and t are given in parentheses in the formula, separated by a comma. This indicates that they form an *ordered pair*: (s, t) means "s then t." The ordered pair (s, t) is distinct from (t, s). GISes thus measure *directed* intervals—the interval *from* s to t, not simply the undirected interval *between* s and t. For example, measuring in diatonic steps, the interval from C4 to D4 is different from the interval from D4 to C4: int(C4, D4) = +1, while int(D4, C4) = –1. This differs from some everyday uses of the word interval, in which we might say, for example, "The interval between C4 and D4 is a diatonic step." GISes do not model such statements, but instead statements of the form "The interval from C4 to D4 is one diatonic step up (i.e., +1 in diatonic space)" or "The interval from D4 to C4 is one diatonic step down (i.e., –1 in diatonic space)."

The element i to the right of the equals sign is a member of a *group*. Lewin calls the group of intervals for a given GIS IVLS. A group is a *set* (that is, a collection of distinct elements, finite or infinite) plus an additional structuring feature: an inner law or rule of composition that states how any two elements in the set can be combined to yield another element in the set. Lewin calls this inner rule a "binary composition," and we will follow that usage here.[8] Groups underlie a great many familiar conceptual structures. For example, take the set of all integers, positive, negative, and zero. As a set, this is simply an infinite collection of distinct entities: {… , –3, –2, –1, 0, 1, 2, 3, …}. But once we introduce the concept of *addition* as our binary composition, the set of integers coheres into a group, which we call "the integers under addition." Addition, as a binary composition, offers one way in which we can combine any two integers to yield another integer: given any two integers x and y, $x + y$ will always yield another integer z. This is called the group property of *closure*: the composition of any two elements under the binary composition always yields another element in the same set.

Groups have three other properties. First, they contain an *identity element*, labeled *e* (for the German word *Einheit*). The composition of *e* with any other group element *g* yields *g* itself. In our group of integers under addition, the identity element is 0: 0 added to any integer *x* yields *x* itself. Further, for every element

---

7. A set in which elements appear more than once is called a *multiset*. Multisets have music-theoretical applications, but we will not explore them in this study.

8. Most mathematicians call Lewin's "binary composition" a *group operation* or *binary operation*. Lewin, however, somewhat idiosyncratically reserves the word *operation* for a different formal concept, as we will see, thus making *binary composition* preferable in this context.

g in a group there also exists an element g^{-1} in the group such that when g and g^{-1} are combined e is the result. The element g^{-1} is called the *inverse* of g (g^{-1} is read "g-inverse"). In the group of integers under addition, the inverse of any integer x is $-x$ (e.g., the inverse of 3 is -3, as the two of them added together yield 0, the identity element). Finally, composition within any group is *associative*. That is, given three group elements f, g, and h, then $(f \cdot g) \cdot h = f \cdot (g \cdot h)$.[9] To return once again to our example, addition of integers is clearly associative: for any three integers x, y, and z, $(x + y) + z = x + (y + z)$.

Mathematicians study groups primarily for their abstract structure, a structure that is suggested in its most basic terms by the four conditions outlined above (closure, existence of an identity, existence of inverses, associativity). The GIS formulation rests on the idea that intervals, at a very general level, have this same abstract structure—they are group-like. That is, the combination of any two intervals will yield another interval (closure). Any musical element lies the identity interval from itself (existence of identities). Given an interval i from s to t, there exists an interval from t to s that is the "reverse" of i—that is, i^{-1} (existence of inverses). Finally, we recognize that intervals combine associatively: given intervals i, j, and k, $(i \cdot j) \cdot k = i \cdot (j \cdot k)$.[10]

Note that these abstract, group-like characteristics do not encompass certain common ideas about intervals. For instance, there is nothing in the four group conditions that says anything about *direction* or *distance*—two attributes often attributed to intervals. This is one area in which the GIS concept has recently been criticized.[11] Though it is tempting to interpret the numbers that we use to label group elements—like the integers +1, −5, and so on in a diatonic or chromatic pitch space—as representative of distances and directions (treating +1 as "one step up," and −5 as "five steps down," for example), those interpretations are not inherent in the abstract structure of the group. That is, the group itself, qua abstract algebraic structure, knows nothing of "one step up" or "five steps down." Instead, it knows only about the ways in which its elements combine with one another according to the properties of closure, existence of an identity and inverses, and associativity. We can conclude two things from this: (1) GISes are formally quite abstract, and may not capture everything we might mean by *interval* in a given context; and (2) not all of the intervals modeled by GISes need to be bound up with the metaphor of distance.[12] While the distance metaphor will likely be quite comfortable for most readers in discussions of pitch intervals, it nevertheless will feel inappropriate in other GIS contexts—for example, when one is measuring intervals between timbral spectra, or between contrapuntal configurations in triple counterpoint (à la Harrison 1988).[13] Indeed, the metaphor of distance will not

---

9. The symbol • here is a generic symbol for the binary composition in any group. When the idea of group composition is understood, such symbols are sometimes eliminated. In that case, our associativity notation would look like this: $(fg)h = f(gh)$.
10. See *GMIT*, 25–26.
11. Tymoczko 2008 and 2009.
12. As Rachel Hall puts it, "GISes *can* express notions about distance, but are not forced to do so" (2009, 209).
13. Cf. Hall 2009, 208–9.

always feel apt in the primary GIS in this book, introduced in Chapter 2.[14] The GIS concept thus abstracts away from notions of distance, generalizing the idea of interval to relational phenomena in which the distance metaphor might not be appropriate.

We are nevertheless free to add notions of distance and direction to our interpretations of GIS statements, if so desired. Dmitri Tymoczko (2009), Lewin's main critic on this front, has indicated how distance may be reintroduced into a GIS by adding a metric that formally ranks the distances between all pairs of elements in the space of the GIS. In practice, this usually amounts to reading numeric GIS intervals—like +1, –5, and so on—as indicators of distance and direction, in the usual arithmetic sense (with –5 larger than +1, and proceeding in the opposite direction). We will not employ Tymoczko's distance metric explicitly in our formal work in this study, but we will often rely on the idea implicitly, whenever we wish to interpret intervals as representing various distances.[15]

Groups, for all of their abstraction, nevertheless remain suggestive as a model for generalized intervals. This is because each group has an underlying abstract structure—or, we might say figuratively, a certain "shape." This shape is determined by the number of elements in the group and the various ways they combine with one another (and with themselves). A group, for example, may be finite or infinite. It may contain certain patterns of smaller groups (called *subgroups*) that articulate its structure in various ways. A group may be commutative or noncommutative: two group elements f and g commute if $f \bullet g = g \bullet f$; in a noncommutative group this property does not always hold.[16] If two groups are *isomorphic* they have the same abstract structure. A GIS inherits the particular structural characteristics of its group IVLS. One way to think of this is that a given intervallic statement in Lewin's model inhabits a certain conceptual topography—a sort of landscape of intervallic relationships given shape by the structure of the group IVLS. Different types of interval may thus inhabit considerably different conceptual topographies, based on the structure of their respective groups (e.g., whether the groups are finite or infinite, commutative or noncommutative, articulated into subgroups, and so forth). This suggests that the intervallic experiences corresponding to such intervals have

---

14. That GIS, which calculates intervals between qualitative tonal scale degrees, involves a group of intervals that might better be understood as comprising familiar intervallic *qualities* rather than distances, such as the quality of a minor third, as opposed to that of an augmented second. The distance metaphor is especially inapt in connection with certain exotic interval types that we will explore in sections 2.5 and 2.6.

15. Edward Gollin (2000) explores another model for distances in a GIS, measuring *word lengths* in the elements of the intervallic group. In the group of neo-Riemannian operations, for example, the word PLP, of length 3, is longer than the word RL, of length 2. A given group admits of multiple distance-based interpretations, based on which group elements are chosen as *unitary* (words of length 1) via the formalism of group presentation, as Gollin demonstrates.

16. Two familiar noncommutative groups in music theory are the group of transpositions and inversions from atonal theory, and the group of neo-Riemannian operations. In the former group, it is not generally true that T_m followed by I_n is the same as I_n followed by T_m. For example, T_3-then-I_2 equals I_{11}, while I_2-then-T_3 equals I_5. In the neo-Riemannian group, given operations X and Y, it is not generally true that XY = YX. For example, PL ≠ LP, RL ≠ LR, PR ≠ RP, and so on.

certain crucial differences in structure, differences embodied in the structures of their respective groups. Such differences are often interpretively productive—the formalism encourages us to attend to them carefully, as we pursue and extend any given intervallic statement within a particular analytical context.

Thus far in our survey of GIS structure, we have two separate collections that are as yet entirely independent: the space S of musical elements and the group IVLS of intervals. We have not yet shown how various intervals in IVLS can be understood to span pairs of elements in S. The leftmost element in the GIS formula, int, provides that connection. As indicated in Figure 1.1, int is a *function* or *mapping* (the two words are synonymous for our purposes). A function from a set X to a set Y sends each element x in X to some element y in Y. Drawing on familiar schoolbook notation, we write $f(x) = y$ to refer to the action of function f sending element x to element y. Note how the schoolbook orthography exactly matches the layout of our GIS statement: compare $f(x) = y$ and int(s, t) = i. The element x in the statement $f(x) = y$ is called the *argument* of the function, and the element y is the *image* or *value* of the argument x under f. The set X of all arguments is called the *domain* of the function, while the set of all images in Y is called the *range*.

The domain for our function int in a GIS is not simply the space of musical elements S itself, but the set of all *ordered pairs* of elements from S. Our arguments are thus not single elements from S, but ordered pairs of the form (s, t). We can see this by comparing again our two statements $f(x) = y$ and int(s, t) = i; the ordered pair (s, t) is "in the role of x" in our GIS statement, not simply some single element from S. The set of all ordered pairs (s, t) is labeled S × S and is called "S cross S" or the *Cartesian product* of S with itself. The function int sends each ordered pair to an element in IVLS. So, formally speaking, int maps S × S into IVLS.

As an example of how all of this works, let us take the two GIS statements suggested above, measuring the interval from C4 to D4 (and the reverse) in diatonic steps:

$$\text{int}(C4, D4) = +1$$
$$\text{int}(D4, C4) = -1$$

In both GIS statements, the space S consists of the conceptually infinite collection of diatonic "white-note" pitches (NB, not pitch classes). The group IVLS is the integers under addition, our familiar group discussed above. The mapping int sends every ordered pair of diatonic pitches to some element in the group of integers. It sends the ordered pair (C4, D4) to the group element +1 in IVLS, modeling the statement "The interval from C4 to D4 is one diatonic step up." It then sends the ordered pair (D4, C4) to a different element in IVLS, –1, modeling the statement "The interval from D4 to C4 is one diatonic step down."[17] The two intervals, +1 and –1, are inversionally related, indicating that int(C4, D4) followed by int(D4, C4) will leave us back where we started, with an overall interval of 0, as intuition dictates. This relates to a general condition for a GIS, Condition (A): given any three musical elements r, s, and t in S, int(r, s)int(s, t) = int(r, t). That is, the interval from

---

17. The locutions "one diatonic step up" and "one diatonic step down" evoke ideas of distance and direction, suggesting the pertinence of Tymoczko's distance metric to this particular GIS.

r to s, plus the interval from s to t, must equal the interval from r to t. Thus, in our example int(C4, D4)int(D4, C4) = int(C4, C4) = 0. Or int(C4, D4)int(D4, E4) = int(C4, E4) = +2. A second condition, Condition (B), states that, for every musical element s in S and every interval i in IVLS, there exists exactly one element t in S such that int(s, t) = i.[18] Again, a musical context makes the condition clear: let the element s be the note C4 and the interval i be "one diatonic step up." Within the set of all diatonic "white-note" pitches, there is of course only one pitch that lies "one diatonic step up" from C4, that is, D4. These two conditions lend a certain logical tightness to GIS structure, providing only one interval between any two musical elements within a GIS.[19] This property is called *simple transitivity*. As a result of the two conditions, in any GIS there will always be exactly as many elements in S as there are intervals in IVLS. For example, in the GIS corresponding to pitch classes in 12-tone equal temperament, there are 12 elements in S (the 12 pitch classes) and 12 intervals in IVLS (the integers mod 12).

We now turn to some philosophical and methodological matters raised by GISes.

1.2.2 GISes and Cartesian Dualism

The cumbersome structure of GIS statements enacts aspects of Lewin's critique of Cartesian dualism. Note that the main action modeled in a GIS is the action carried out by the mapping int. It is int that carries us "across the equals sign" from the left-hand side to the right-hand side of the formula int(s, t) = i. The active nature of int is especially evident if we use an arrow notation to rewrite the function. The schoolbook function $f(x) = y$ may also be written $x \xrightarrow{f} y$, showing that the function f takes x to y. Similarly, we can rewrite the GIS function int(s, t) = i as $(s, t) \xrightarrow{\text{int}} i$, showing that int takes (s, t) to i. This notation makes visually vivid the fact that int is the primary action involved in a GIS statement, capturing the act of pairing two musical elements with an interval. The relevant thought process might be verbalized thus: "I just heard a C4 and now I hear a D4; the interval from the former to the latter is one diatonic step up."

Lewin characterizes this attitude as Cartesian because it is the attitude of someone passively calculating relationships between entities as points in some external space. The action of passively measuring is embodied by the mapping int itself. One might think of int as analogous to pulling out some calculating device and applying it to two musical entities "out there" to discern their intervallic relationship. The action in question is *not* one of imaginatively traversing the space from C4 to D4 in time, construing and experiencing a musical relationship along

---

18. Conditions (A) and (B) appear in the formal definition of a GIS in *GMIT*, 26.
19. To be clear, there is only one interval between two musical entities *within a single GIS*. As discussed in section 1.2.5, GIS methodology rests on the idea that there is in fact an indeterminate *multiplicity* of possible intervals between two musical entities. That multiplicity arises not within a single GIS, but via the multiple potential GIS structures that may embed the two elements in question.

the way. The GIS formula is further like the Cartesian mindset in that it exhibits a certain fracturing of experience, a conceptual split between musical elements (the space S), musical intervals (the group IVLS), and the conceptual action (int) that relates the two. The cumbersome nature of the GIS formalism—with its three components (S, IVLS, int), all of which need to be coordinated, and with the action int placing the musical "perceiver" in an explicit subject-object relationship vis-à-vis the music being "perceived"—thus encodes aspects of the Cartesian split between *res cogitans* and *res extensa*, a familiar trope in Lewin's writings.[20]

We should not conclude from this that GISes are "bad" and that we should not use them in our analytical and theoretical work. Lewin himself continued to find intervallic thinking fascinating and productive long after *GMIT*, as a historical phenomenon, a theoretical/formal problem, and a mode of generating insights into musical works.[21] In *GMIT* itself he also observes certain ways in which transformational thinking is "impoverished" in comparison to intervallic thinking (*GMIT*, 245–46). In short, despite the fact that the GIS formalism enacts the Cartesian problematic that Lewin so eloquently criticized, it is still a productive and suggestive technology in many theoretical and analytical contexts.[22] GIS models will play an important role in this book.

1.2.3 Intervallic Apperceptions

Lewin often refers to *intuitions* in his writings about intervals and transformations, but he never says exactly what he means by the word. It will be valuable for us to spend a little time here thinking about the matter, as the questions that it raises bear directly on the relationship between transformational technology and musical experience.

Though Lewin gives us no clear definition of what he means by intuitions, we can infer two crucial characteristics of the term as he uses it in his writings:

(1) His intuitions are culturally conditioned.
(2) They may be sharpened, extended, or altered through analytical reflection.

Lewin states (1) explicitly: "Personally, I am convinced that our intuitions are highly conditioned by cultural factors" (*GMIT*, 17). By "cultural factors," Lewin

---

20. The relevant philosophical matters are penetratingly treated in Klumpenhouwer 2006. On the problematics of the subject-object relationship in passive musical *perception*, see Lewin's well-known phenomenology essay (Lewin 2006, Chapter 4).
21. Lewin published three extensive articles specifically on GISes, not transformational systems, after *GMIT*: Lewin 1995, 1997, and 2000–2001.
22. My ideas on these matters were clarified through conversation with Henry Klumpenhouwer. My view differs slightly from Klumpenhouwer's published comments, in which he states that Lewin wants us to "replace intervallic thinking with transformational thinking" (2006, 277). I feel that Lewin's ethical directive in *GMIT* is not quite this strong—that he wants us not to *replace* intervallic thinking but to become more aware of its Cartesian bias, and to be self-conscious about that bias whenever "thinking intervallically" in some analytical context.

seems to mean not only differences between various world cultures—though he certainly does mean that—but also historical cultural differences within the history of European art music. For example, a sixteenth-century musician conditioned by ideas about modes, hexachordal mutation, *mi-contra-fa* prohibitions, and so forth would have different *intuitions* about a given musical passage—say in a motet by Palestrina—than would a modern musician conditioned by ideas about keys, diatonic scales, tonal modulation, and so forth.[23] The modern listener can of course seek to develop hexachordal hearings of the music in question, but to that extent—and this leads to characteristic (2)—the listener will be modifying her or his intuitions (à la Lewin) by analytical intervention. The general pertinence of characteristic (2) to Lewin's thought is manifest throughout his writings, as theoretical structures of various kinds are brought to bear on various musical experiences, sharpening, extending, or altering those experiences in diverse ways. Indeed, Lewin's entire analytical project can be understood as a process of digging into musical experience and building it up through analytical reflection. Stanley Cavell, paraphrasing Emerson, provides a very suggestive wording that we can borrow for the idea: such work involves a reciprocal "play of intuition and tuition," or, even more suggestively, it is a project of "providing the tuition for intuition."[24]

Lewin's intuitions are special in the degree to which they reflect the influence not only of broad cultural and historical conditioning, but also of theoretical concepts and other discursive constructions.[25] I thus prefer to think of such "intuitions" as *apperceptions*: perceptions that are influenced by past experience and may involve present reflection.[26] The second clause makes clear that such experiences are responsive to current analytical contemplation: a GIS or transformational statement need not be a report on some prereflective experience, but might instead help to shape a new experience (an apperception), or alter an old one, through analytical mediation. The word intuition, by contrast, runs the risk of naturalizing GIS and transformational statements, treating them as unmediated reports on prereflective (or at least minimally reflective) experience. This risk is especially

---

23. Cf. the discussions of hexachordal versus tonal perceptions in Lewin 1993, 48n13 and Lewin 1998b.
24. Cavell 1999, 236 ("a play of intuition and tuition") and Cavell 2002, section 4 ("providing the tuition for intuition"). For Emerson's original quote see Emerson 1993, 27.
25. As Henry Klumpenhouwer notes, "In distinction to other uses of the term, Lewin's intuitions have some conceptual content" (2006, 278n3).
26. In this book I will understand apperceptions loosely in William James's sense, as experiences colored by "the previous contents of the mind" (1939, 158). Such apperceptions may involve conscious reflection, or they may not. For example, one's past experiences with a certain musical idiom will strongly color one's current and future musical experiences with music in that idiom, whether one has consciously reflected on the idiom or not. Apperceptions, thus conceived, are simply current experiences under the influence of past experience, and open to present reflection. This departs from certain philosophical understandings, in which conscious reflection is a necessary component of all apperceptions.

evident when a given statement is made seemingly universal by locutions such as "when hearing music x, we [NB] have intuition y"—a rhetorical device that occurs with disconcerting frequency in Lewin's writings. By hewing to the word apperception, I instead hope to make clear that the sorts of experiences explored in this book are by no means universal, and will be strongly shaped not only by one's cultural background and historical context, but also by the concrete particulars of present analytical engagement.

1.2.4 GISes: Formal Limitations

As noted above, the abstract nature of GISes allows them to model a wide array of intervallic phenomena via algebraic groups. Yet, despite this abstraction, GISes are not as general as they might at first appear, nor are they applicable to all musical situations. GISes, for example, cannot model intervals in musical spaces that have a boundary or limit. Consider an example that Lewin himself raises: S is the space of all musical durations measured by some uniform unit. This space has a natural limit: the shortest duration lasts no time at all—there is no duration shorter than it. Now imagine that we choose to measure the interval from duration s to duration t in this space by subtracting s from t (IVLS would then be the integers under addition). For example, if s is 6 units long and t is 4 units long, the interval from s to t is 4–6 = –2. Formally, int(s, t) = int(6, 4) = –2. Now recall the Condition (B) for a GIS: given any element s in S and any i in IVLS, there must exist some t in S such that int(s, t) = i. Let us now set s = 0 and i = –2. There exists no t in S such that int(0, t) = –2. Such a t would be 2 units shorter than no time at all. As Lewin himself notes, this is an absurdity (*GMIT,* 29–30). Thus, the given musical space of durations under addition, though it is musically straightforward, can*not* be modeled by a GIS. Similar problems arise with any musical space that has a boundary beyond which no interval can be measured.

This relates to a more general limitation. Given Lewin's definition, any interval in a GIS must be applicable at all points in the space: if one can proceed the interval i from s, one must also be able to proceed the interval i from t, no matter what i, s, and t one selects. This limits GISes to only those spaces whose elements all have uniform intervallic environments. The vast majority of familiar musical spaces *do* have this property. For example, in the space of chromatic pitches, one can move up or down from any pitch by +1 semitone or –1 semitone. By extension, one can theoretically move up or down from any pitch by +n semitones or –n semitones, for any integer n. This is so even when the result would be too high or too low to hear—the space is still in principle unbounded.[27] Similarly, in modular spaces, such as the space of 12 pitch classes, or the space of seven scale degrees, every element inhabits an identical intervallic environment. Neo-Riemannian spaces are also

27. To bound it, one would need to assert a specific high pitch beyond which one cannot progress up by one semitone, and/or a specific low pitch beyond which one cannot progress downward by one semitone. On theoretically unbounded spaces that can be perceived only in part, see *GMIT,* 27.

uniform in this sense: one can apply any neo-Riemannian transformation to any major or minor triad. Nevertheless, there do exist spaces that do not have this uniform quality, such as the durational space outlined above, or any number of voice-leading spaces that are better modeled geometrically (as discussed in Tymoczko 2009). Thus, despite their generalized qualities, GISes are not as broad in scope as they might initially appear to be: they only apply to uniform intervallic spaces.[28]

Tymoczko (2009) raises another important criticism of GISes: they do not admit of multiple, path-like intervals between two entities. We will return to this important criticism in section 2.3, in which I will integrate Tymoczko's path-like conception into the GIS introduced in that chapter. Tymoczko also objects that GISes do not model entities such as "the interval G4→E♭4" at the opening of Beethoven's Fifth Symphony. Instead, a given GIS would model the interval from G4 to E♭4 as an instance of a more general intervallic type that applies throughout the space: for example, as a manifestation of the interval "a major third down." Such an interval could obtain between any other pair of major-third-related elements in the space, say F4→D♭4, or B6→G6. More generally, unlike Tymoczko's "interval G4→E♭4," intervals in a GIS are not defined by their endpoints, but by the relationship the listener or analyst construes between those endpoints, a relationship that is generalizable apart from the endpoints in question. The construing of that relationship is modeled by the statement int(s, t) = i, which produces generalized interval i as output. Tymoczko's formulation provides a different and useful perspective, focusing more attention on the concrete endpoints of a specific interval (s and t), and less on the ways in which a listener or analyst might construe the relationship between those endpoints as some general interval-type i. But an attractive aspect of GIS theory is lost in the process, to which we now turn.

1.2.5 GIS Apperceptions and Intervallic Multiplicity

GIS technology is responsive to the fact that one will be inclined to experience an interval from G4 to E♭4 in diverse ways based on the musical context within which one encounters those pitches. There is thus no single "interval from G4 to E♭4." Imagine the succession G4→E♭4 in: (1) the opening of Beethoven's Fifth; (2) a serial work by Schoenberg; (3) an octatonic passage by Bartók; (4) a pentatonic passage by Debussy (or, for that matter, in a Javanese gamelan performance in slendro tuning). These diverse contexts suggest the pertinence of various GIS apperceptions for the G4→E♭4 succession. In the Beethoven, the pitch topography is diatonic, and the GIS might be any one of a number of diatonic GISes (pitch-based or pitch-class-based).[29] The interval in Schoenberg would likely suggest a chromatic GIS,

---

28. What I have been calling *uniform*, Tymoczko (2009) calls *homogenous* and *parallelized*. The latter term means that one can move a given interval from point to point, applying it anywhere in the space.

29. The GIS introduced in Chapter 2 would be especially well suited to modeling the interval in question. It would further distinguish the G4→E♭4 at the outset of the Fifth from the same pitch succession in E♭ major (say, in the primary theme area of the *Eroica*), or from an enharmonically equivalent succession in E minor (say, in the "new theme" in the *Eroica* development [e.g., cello, downbeat of m. 285 to that of m. 286]).

while in Bartók it would evoke an octatonic GIS, and in Debussy (or the gamelan performance) a pentatonic GIS; any one of these GISes could be pc- or pitch-based. The various GISes capture the ways in which one's apperceptions of the G4→E♭4 succession might vary in response to its diverse musical/stylistic contexts.

This is a rather obvious instance of what we might call "apperceptive multiplicity" in intervallic experience. Less obvious, perhaps, is GIS theory's insistence on apperceptive multiplicity when confronting a *single* interval in a *single* musical passage. This suggests that the interval in question can inhabit multiple musical spaces at once. Lewin puts it somewhat more strongly than I would: "we do not really have one intuition of something called 'musical space.' Instead, we intuit several or many musical spaces at once" (*GMIT*, 250). Per the discussion in section 1.2.3 above, I would rephrase this as "we can conceive of a given interval in several different conceptual spaces when we are in the act of analytical contemplation. Those different conceptions can subtly change our experience of the interval, leading to new musical apperceptions."[30]

1.2.6 Vignette: Bach, Cello Suite in G, BWV 1007, Prelude, mm. 1–4

Figure 1.2(a) shows the first two beats of the Prelude from Bach's Cello Suite in G major, BWV 1007. An arrow labeled i extends from the cello's opening G2 to the B3 at the apex of its initial arpeggio. Figures 1.2(b)–(d) model three intervallic conceptions of i, situating it in different musical spaces.

Figure 1.2(b) models i as an *ascending tenth*. This suggests the context shown on the staff: B3 is nine steps up the G-major diatonic scale from G2. The figure shows this by placing in parentheses the elements that i "skips over" in the space S of the relevant GIS. S in this example comprises the elements of the (conceptually infinite) G-major diatonic pitch gamut, and IVLS is our familiar group of integers under addition, hereafter notated $(\mathbb{Z}, +)$.[31] Given two diatonic pitches s and t in G major, int(s, t) in this GIS tells us how many steps up the diatonic G-major gamut t is from s. The figure thus models the GIS-statement int(G2, B3) = +9.[32]

---

30. While my rewording focuses on listening experiences stimulated by analytical reflection, it is not clear from his comment what sorts of listening contexts Lewin has in mind. He may indeed have meant that multiplicity is a fact of everyday musical experience: when we hear music in any context, we "intuit" multiple musical spaces at once and thus hear intervallic relationships in manifold ways—even when we are not in an analytically reflective mode. This may be true, but I am not sure how one could test the idea, nor do I know what exactly is meant by "intuit" and "intuition" in Lewin's passage. Is the listener consciously aware of these manifold "intuitions"? Or are they perhaps instead a congeries of more or less inchoate sensations that one has when listening, which can be brought into focus through analytical reflection? I am more comfortable with the latter position, which moves toward my rewording.
31. $\mathbb{Z}$ is a common label for the set of integers, taken from the German *Zahlen* (numerals).
32. Lewin (*GMIT*, 16–17) discusses the discrepancy between the familiar ordinal intervallic names of tonal theory (tenths, fifths, thirds, etc.), which indicate number of scale steps *spanned* between two pitches, and the intervals in a scalar diatonic GIS, which indicate the number of scale steps *up* from one pitch to another (negative steps up are steps down). The GIS introduced in Chapter 2 employs the familiar ordinal names for intervals between scale degrees.

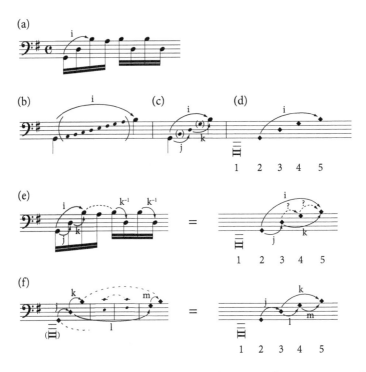

Figure 1.2 Bach, Prelude from the first suite for solo cello, BWV 1007: (a) the music for beats one and two, with one interval labeled; (b)–(f) various GIS perspectives on that interval.

The GIS of 1.2(b) does not do full justice to the harmonic character of i. If we say that i is a *tenth*, we are likely not thinking primarily about a number of steps up a scale, but about a privileged *harmonic* interval. Figure 1.2(c) provides one harmonic context for i, depicting it as spanning elements in a *G-major arpeggio*. Our space S no longer consists of all of the elements of the G-major diatonic gamut, but just those pitches belonging to the (conceptually infinite) G-major triad, that is: {...G1, B1, D2, G2, B2, D3, G3, B3, D4, G4,...}. G2 is *adjacent* to B2 in this space, as is B2 to D3, and so on.[33] In this space, B3 is "four triadic steps up" from G2: that is, int(G2, B3) = +4.[34] Note that the D3 in the opening gesture divides i into two smaller intervals, labeled j and k on the figure; both are "skips" of +2 in the GIS.

33. Adjacent pitches here correspond to the "steps" in Fred Lerdahl's "triadic space" (2001), or to "steps" in the "chordal scale" of William Rothstein's imaginary continuo (1991, 296).
34. IVLS is once again (ℤ, +). Note, however, that the integers now represent acoustically larger intervals than did the same group elements in the GIS of Figure 1.2(b). For example, in the GIS of 1.2(b) int(G2, B2) = +2, while in the GIS of 1.2(c), int(G2, B2) = +1. Hook 2007a offers relevant comments on relating two GISes that have the same abstract group of intervals (like (ℤ, +) here), though the group elements in the two different GISes may represent intervals of different acoustic size. See also Tymoczko 2008 and 2009.

This arpeggio space is highly relevant to the historical and stylistic context of the prelude, which imitates the French lutenists' *style brisé*. The intervals available to the *style brisé* lutenist within any given harmony are exactly those of the present GIS.

Figure 1.2(d) invokes a different harmonic space, one of *just* intervals in which i is the ratio 5:2. This model is suggestive, given the spacing of Bach's opening arpeggio: the G2–D3–B3 succession corresponds to partials 2, 3, and 5 in the overtone series of G1. (In a more historical-theoretic vein, we might say that the notes project elements 2, 3, and 5 of a Zarlinian *senario*.) The group IVLS here differs in algebraic structure from those in Figures 1.2(b) and (c): it is the positive rational numbers under multiplication, not the integers under addition. This suggests that the harmonic interval of 5:2 inhabits a considerably different "conceptual topography" than do our stepwise (and additive) intervals of +9 and +4 in 1.2(b) and (c). We can sense that difference in topography when we recognize that, in the arpeggio GIS of 1.2(c), the interval from G2 to D3 is the same as the interval from D3 to B3: that is, both represent an interval of +2. In the just ratio GIS of 1.2(d), however, the intervals are different: int(G2, D3) = 3:2 while int(D3, B3) = 5:3. The difference registers the acoustic distinction between a just perfect fifth and a just major sixth. The resonant, partial-rich open strings of G2 and D3 with which the arpeggio begins strengthen the relevance of the just-ratio GIS here.[35]

Figure 1.2(e) shows the articulation of i into its two subintervals, again labeled j and k, as in 1.2(c). While both j and k were "skips" in 1.2(c), in 1.2(d) only k represents a "skip" in the overtone series above G1; j connects two adjacent elements in the series.[36] Bach emphasizes the "gapped" interval k, repeating it twice, as k⁻¹, in the second half of the bar. This calls attention to the "missing" G3, partial 4 in the overtone series (note the question-marked dotted arrows on the example's right side). As Figure 1.2(f) shows, this G3 does eventually arrive in m. 4, at the close of the movement's opening harmonic progression. The G3 bears a considerable tonal accent as a pitch that completes several processes set in motion in the work's opening measures. Note that the interval from D3 to G3—labeled l in the example—is filled in by step. This stepwise motion is the

---

35. The cellist can emphasize the partial series by placing a slight agogic accent on the opening G2, a gesture that makes good musical sense anyway, given the work's upcoming stream of constant sixteenth notes. The partials activated by the G2 are an octave higher than those in Figure 1.2(d), but they nevertheless still suggest the pertinence of the just-ratio GIS in this resonant opening.

36. I have worded this carefully: interval k in 1.2(d) is a skip in the overtone series above G1. It is not, however, a "skip" *in the GIS*, in the same sense that j and k are "skips" in the GIS of 1.2(c)—further evidence of a shift in conceptual space. In 1.2(c) the space S of the GIS consists of the pitches of the G-major arpeggio, which are spanned by "steps" (modeled by additive integers). In the GIS underlying 1.2(d), the space S in fact consists of an infinitely dense set of pitches, which are spanned by frequency ratios (modeled by multiplicative rational numbers). The group IVLS in this GIS consists of *all* of the positive rational numbers—not just the low-integer ratios explored in the figure (3:2, 5:3, and so on), but also higher integer ratios like 16:15 (a "major semitone" in Pythagorean theory), and even enormous integer ratios such as 531,441:524,288 (the acoustically tiny Pythagorean comma). In conformance with GIS Condition (B), the space S of the GIS thus includes infinitely many pitches in the gap between, say, G2 and D3. (For example, it includes the pitch residing a Pythagorean comma above G2.) This makes clear that the GIS structuring Figure 1.2(d) is not a linearly plotted space of "steps" and "skips" as in 1.2(b) and (c)—it is a space of frequency ratios, which has a considerably different shape.

first concrete manifestation of the scalar GIS-space from Figure 1.2(b), now explicitly coordinating that scalar space with an interval from the harmonic spaces of 1.2(c)–(e). In fact, by the end of m. 3, G3 is the only note that has not been heard in the diatonic G-major gamut from D3 to C4—it has thus been "missing" in both the scalar and harmonic conceptual spaces; its arrival fills a notable gap.

One could invoke other GIS contexts for i as well. One could model i as spanning the interval from $\hat{1}$ to $\hat{3}$ in an abstract scale-degree space, or joining root and third of the tonic harmony (the ideas are related, but not identical). Many other intervallic contexts for i are possible as well, but not all of them are relevant to the opening bar of Bach's prelude. For example, one could conceive i to extend up 16 semitones in a chromatic pitch gamut. This is a somewhat strained understanding within the context of m. 1, which as yet explicitly invokes no such chromatic division of pitch space. Such a space *is* invoked, however, at the work's climax in mm. 37–39, via the cello's chromatic ascent to G4, the work's apex. Here it is very easy to hear the interval spanned from D3 in m. 37 to G4 in m. 39 in terms of steps in a chromatic gamut, and to coordinate the steps in this chromatic GIS with those in other diatonic and harmonic GISes relevant to the music in these bars.

Such an analysis could continue, modeling other notable intervallic phenomena in the prelude and exploring their interactions. For present purposes, it is important merely to note the style of the analysis, particularly its focus on multiple intervallic interpretations of single musical gesture.

1.3 Transformations

1.3.1 *The "Transformational Attitude"*

As already noted, the transformational model represents a shift in perspective from the GIS view of the passive, outside observer "measuring intervals" to that of an active participant in the musical process. As Lewin puts it in one of his most frequently quoted passages,

> instead of regarding the i-arrow on figure 0.1 [an arrow labeled i extending from a point s to a point t] as a measurement of extension between points s and t observed passively "out there" in a Cartesian *res extensa,* one can regard the situation actively, like a singer, player, or composer, thinking: "I am at s; what characteristic transformation do I perform to arrive at t?" (*GMIT,* xxxi)

Lewin elsewhere dubs this the "transformational attitude," and it has become a familiar part of the interpretive tradition of transformational theory. It is a subtle and somewhat elusive concept; I will offer my own gloss on the idea and its relevance to certain acts of tonal hearing in section 3.2.1. For now, the reader may simply conceive of transformational arrows as goads to a first-person experience of various gestural "actions" in a musical passage, actions that move musical entities or configurations along, or that transform them into other, related entities or configurations.

While formal statements in GIS theory take the form of int(s, t) = i, formal statements in transformational theory are expressed using *transformational graphs and networks*. A transformational network is a configuration of nodes and arrows whose nodes contain elements from some set S of musical elements (analogous to the set S of elements in a GIS) and whose arrows are labeled with various transformations on S. A transformational graph resembles a transformational network in all respects but one: its nodes are empty.

1.3.2 Transformations and Operations

A transformation on S is a *function* from S to S itself: that is, a mapping that sends each element in S to some element in S itself. We have already encountered functions in the GIS discussion above, with the function int. The transformations and operations in a transformational graph or network are also functions, but rather than mapping pairs of elements to intervals (as int does in a GIS), they act directly on single musical entities, transforming them into each other. Before exploring how this works in practice, it will be valuable to distinguish between a *transformation* and an *operation*.

Let us define S as the seven diatonic pitch classes in C major, that is, S = {C, D, E, F, G, A, B}. We now define a transformation on s that we will call "resolve to C," abbreviated ResC. This transformation sends every element in S to the element C. ResC is indeed a function from S to S itself: it takes as input each element of S, and returns as output an element of S. We can represent it by a mapping table, like that shown in Figure 1.3(a).[37] Figure 1.3(b) shows the mapping table for another transformation on S, which we will call Step: it moves each element in S up one diatonic step.

Both of these transformations can be conceived as idealized musical actions. But it is only when we consider the entire mapping table that we get a full sense of just what these actions *are*. To see this, consider the fact that both transformations have the same effect on the note B: they both map it to C. At this local level, the transformations appear to be indistinguishable. But if we perform the same actions elsewhere in the space, their differences emerge. For example, Step maps D to E, but ResC maps D to C; and Step maps E to F, while ResC maps E to C; and so on. It is only in this broader context that we can see that Step raises pitches by one step, while ResC resolves notes to C. These two actions have the same *effect* when applied to B, but the specific kinetics they imply are different—ResC suggests a gravitational centering on C, or an action that yields to such gravitation, while Step suggests a more neutral, uniform motion of single-step ascent anywhere in the space.

Step also differs from ResC in a more formal way. Every element from S appears on the right-hand side of the table for Step (Fig. 1.3(b)), while only the element C

---

37. Note that we could also use the functional notation from the discussion of GISes above as a replacement for any one of the arrows in this table: for example, we could write ResC(D) = C.

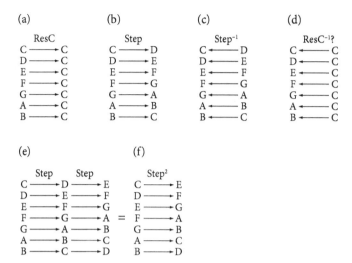

Figure 1.3 Mapping tables involving two transformations: ResC, a transformation that is not an operation (i.e., that is not one-to-one and onto), and Step, a transformation that *is* an operation.

appears on the right-hand side of the table for ResC (Fig. 1.3(a)). While both ResC and Step are transformations, Step is a special kind of transformation that we will call (after Lewin) an *operation:* an operation is a transformation that is *one-to-one* and *onto*.[38] If a transformation is one-to-one and onto, every element in the set appears once and only once as the "target" for an arrow in the relevant mapping table—in other words, on the right-hand side of Figure 1.3(b). Operations thus have inverses: one can "undo" any operation simply by reversing the arrows in its mapping table. Thus, we can define Step⁻¹, as shown in Figure 1.3(c); as the table indicates, Step⁻¹ moves each element in S one diatonic step down. We cannot, however, define an inverse function ResC⁻¹. As shown in Figure 1.3(d), if we reverse the arrows in the mapping table for ResC, only the note C appears "at the beginning of the arrows" in the table (now on the right-hand side). Functions must be defined on all elements of their domain, but ResC⁻¹ is not defined on all of the notes in S; for example, it is not defined on D, as D does not appear anywhere at the beginning of an arrow on the table for ResC⁻¹. Furthermore, ResC⁻¹ is not even well defined on C, as it seems to send that note to seven different places; a function must send each element it acts on to only *one* element. Thus, ResC has no inverse—it is a transformation, but not an operation.[39]

Transformations and operations can combine with one another through a process called *composition of mappings*. This process is illustrated in Figures 1.3(e)

38. Functions that are one-to-one and onto are also called *bijections*. For further discussion, see the entry for *Function* in the Glossary.
39. Most of the familiar transformations in transformational theory are operations (that is, they are one-to-one and onto, and thus have inverses). The neo-Riemannian transformations, for example, are all operations, as are the familiar T_n and I_n operations on pitch classes from atonal theory.

and (f), which show how Step followed by Step yields a new operation, Step². The new operation is defined by combining the mapping tables in 1.3(e); removing the middle column yields the table in 1.3(f), which shows the action of Step². Through processes like this, sets of transformations and operations can be combined to yield groups, or group-like entities called *semigroups,* in which composition of mappings serves as the inner law, or binary composition. Since operations have inverses, they can combine into groups. (We remember that each element in a group must have an inverse.) We speak in this case about a "group of operations." Transformations that are not operations, however, *cannot* combine into groups, as they do not have inverses. They can instead combine into a more general structure called a *semigroup.* A semigroup is a set of elements with a binary composition like a group, but one that needs only to satisfy two of the four group properties: closure and associativity. A semigroup need not contain an identity element, nor does each element in a semigroup need to have an inverse. We thus speak of a "semigroup of transformations."

The structure underlying transformational systems is thus what mathematicians would refer to as a "semigroup action on a set" (or a "group action on a set" if a group of operations is involved). The set in question is a set S of musical elements (notes, harmonies, rhythmic configurations, etc.), representatives of which occupy the nodes of a transformational network. The semigroup of transformations then "acts" on this set, modeling certain musical behaviors that are performed directly on entities in S, transforming them one into another along the arrows of the network. The action modeled by our formalism has thus changed in a subtle way from the GIS perspective. There, the action was one of calculating, modeled by the function int, which matched an ordered pair of elements with an intervallic distance. The action enshrined by a transformational arrow, by contrast, is the active performance of some characteristic musical gesture, which transforms one musical element into another. There is no equivalent to int here: semigroup (or group) elements act directly on the musical entities themselves.

1.3.3 Between GISes and Transformation Networks

There is nevertheless a "communication channel" between GISes and certain kinds of transformation networks. Specifically, any GIS statement can be refashioned into a transformational statement; such transformational statements can also be turned back into GISes. This process of translation, taking one from an intervallic perspective to a transformational perspective, is a central theme in *GMIT,* as Klumpenhouwer (2006) persuasively argues. A striking aspect of Lewin's project is the way in which the conceptual transition from intervallic to transformational thinking is mediated by the technology of his theory—the technological transformation from a GIS perspective to a transformational perspective enacts formally the conceptual transformation that Lewin wishes us to undergo as we switch from an intervallic (Cartesian, observational) mode of thought to a transformational (first-person, active) one. In the process, the action of measuring (int) disappears and is replaced by an imaginative musical gesture, which the analyst is urged to perform in his or her re-creative hearing.

While any GIS statement can become a transformational statement by the appropriate formal and conceptual translation, the reverse is not true: not just any transformational system can be refashioned back into a GIS. Only certain kinds of transformation statements are "GIS-able," or conceivable in intervallic terms. There are two requirements for such a conceptual shift from transformations back to intervals. First, the transformations in question must be operations. To see this, let us return to Figures 1.3(a) and (b). Note that we can conceive of the operation Step as "interval-like." First, there is an interval that we can associate with the distance traversed by Step, namely "up one step" in diatonic pc space. Second, Step is has an inverse, and is thus reversible, as we expect all intervals to be. We can thus reframe any transformational statement that we make using Step as a GIS statement, and vice versa. We cannot, however, develop an intervallic interpretation of ResC. First of all, it is very difficult to see how we could conceive of a *single* interval that would correspond to the action traced by all of the arrows in Figure 1.3(a). In such a case, the interval from some white note to C would be the same as the interval from any other white note to C! Even if we could wrap our heads around such a curious idea, this putative interval would lack an inverse, thus failing the basic requirement that all intervals should be reversible. In short, there are certain musical "actions" we can conceive of performing that cannot be interpreted intervallically; these are the actions modeled by transformations that are not operations.

Second, in addition to the requirement that a transformational graph or network must include only operations to be interpreted in GIS terms, that group of operations must act on the elements in the space S in a particular way, which is called *simply transitive* (an idea that already arose in our discussion of GISes). A group acts simply transitively on a set if, given any two elements a and b in the set, only one element g in the group takes a to b. Simple transitivity will not be a property of all transformation graphs or networks, even if they include only operations. Consider, for example, a transformation network with node contents drawn from the set of 12 chromatic pcs, and arrow labels bearing a mixture of atonal transpositions (T_n) and inversions (I_n). (Klumpenhouwer networks are familiar instances of this kind of network.) The T_n/I_n group does not act simply transitively on the 12 pcs: given any two pcs, there are always *two* operations in T_n/I_n that can take the first pc to the second: one transposition and one inversion. Ramon Satyendra clearly explains why such a non-simply-transitive situation conceptually resists translation into intervallic terms:

> When reckoning intervallic distances we intuitively expect unique answers. It is counterintuitive to describe the straight-line distance between the chair and the table as both two feet and three feet. By requiring that a musical system satisfy the simple transitivity condition we are assured that the interval formed between any two points in a musical space may be uniquely determined. If a system is not simply transitive, it becomes counterintuitive to shift between transformational and intervallic perspectives. For instance it is intuitive to say that both T_3 and I_3 transform C to E♭, but it is counterintuitive to think of the interval between C and E♭ as *both* T_3 and I_3. (2004, 103)

Thus, GISes may be understood as the conceptual "flip side" of a particular kind of transformational system: one whose transformations are all operations that act simply transitively on the space S of the network. The translation from such a transformational system into a GIS is formally rather involved, and I will not run through the details here. But the basic idea is simple. One merely keeps the space S the same from the transformational network to the GIS, reinterprets the group of operations in the transformational network as the group IVLS in the GIS, and applies int so that pairs of elements and intervals match up in agreement with the original transformational actions.[40]

1.3.4 Vignette: Schubert, Piano Sonata, D. 664, mvt. ii, mm. 1–7

Figure 1.4(a) shows the first seven measures of the slow movement from Schubert's Piano Sonata in A, D. 664. Figure 1.4(b) isolates and labels some three-note gestures of interest. X is the piece's *Hauptmotiv*—a falling figure first heard in mm. 1–2; Y is a one-bar gesture closely related to X, first heard in m. 5. Altered forms of both X and Y appear in the passage: X′ changes the intervallic structure of X slightly, and T(Y) is a transposition of Y. At the right-hand side of the example, two cadential gestures are identified, one in the soprano (Cad) and one in the bass (BassCad). The phrase concludes in m. 7 with a quick recollection of X, marked x. We will be interested in the way these gestures are internally structured, as well as in the ways in which they are transformed into one another.

The network of Figure 1.5(a) models pitch relationships within and between X and X′. The space S from which the node contents are drawn is the set of diatonic pitches (NB) in D major; the transformations are steps up and down the diatonic pitch gamut, which we will represent by the integers: $+x$ is x steps up the diatonic gamut; $-x$ is x steps down.[41] X traverses three falling diatonic steps, from B4 to F♯4 (-3), while X′ traverses four falling steps, from B4 to E4 (-4). Both X and X′ begin with B4$\xrightarrow{-1}$A4. Schubert's articulation makes these gestures vivid. The slurred appoggiatura from B4 to A4 underlies the -1 motion, pulling B4 forward to A4, and the three gently rebounding eighth notes that follow on A4 (staccato, and slurred together) lead forward to the motives' concluding pitches.[42] Schubert's calm repetition of the many X-related figures in the movement encourages us to attend closely to their evolving progress as the piece unfolds. (The "calm repetition" comes to seem unhealthily obsessive by the time of the climax in m. 42.)

Note that, despite the evident alteration of X's internal structure in X′, the gestural motives of -1 and -3 are retained in the latter. Yet -3 now acts as an "internal"

40. Satyendra 2004 offers a lucid account of this process of translation, which Lewin defines formally at the beginning of Chapter 7 in *GMIT*.
41. We are thus dealing with a group of operations—the integers under addition. The operations act simply transitively on the infinite set of diatonic pitches, from which our node contents are drawn. The networks in Figure 1.5 can thus be translated into GIS terms if we so desire.
42. Peter Smith (2000, 6) makes suggestive observations along these lines, especially involving the way A4's evident structural status is undercut by the articulation, which causes it to "lead ahead to F♯."

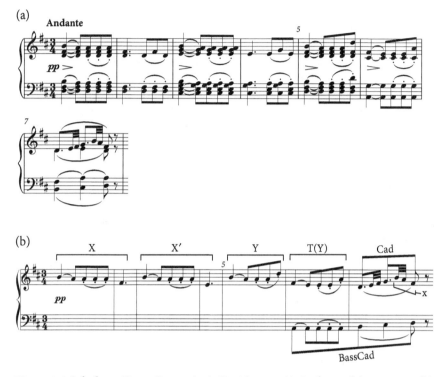

Figure 1.4 Schubert, Piano Sonata in A, D. 664, mvt. ii, Andante: (a) mm. 1–7; (b) some gestures of interest in these bars.

transformation, rather than the transformation that spans the entire gesture, as in X. For its part, –1 remains in its original initiating position, linking the B–A appoggiatura that plays such a prominent role in the movement. Indeed, –1 is the most persistent melodic figure in the piece, initiating nearly every one of its thematic and motivic units. The dashed arrow in 1.5(a) shows the influence of this "step descent" on a slightly larger scale, as the agent that transforms X into X′: the bottom pitch F♯4 of X is bumped down via –1 to produce the E4 that concludes X′.[43]

Figure 1.5(b) shows transformational relationships within and between the two Y-forms. The initiating –1 from X and X′ remains. In Y it joins B4 and A4, as in the X-forms. In T(Y), however, it joins F♯4 and E4, the pitches connected by the dashed –1 arrow in 1.5(a), making explicit the connection between the –1 arrow linking X and X′ and the appoggiatura incipits of X and Y. The other two gestural arrows in the Y-forms reverse the remaining two gestures in X: while the latter contains –2 and –3, the Y-forms contain +2 and +3. The sense of a change of direction in the Y-forms is reflected in other parameters as well, as we will see presently.

---

43. Other transformations could take X to X′, such as Jonathan Bernard's "unfolding" (1987, 74–75), or Lewin's related FLIPSTART (*GMIT,* 189). The resulting configuration would then need to be transposed by –1 to produce X′, once again demonstrating the thematic role of –1 in the music.

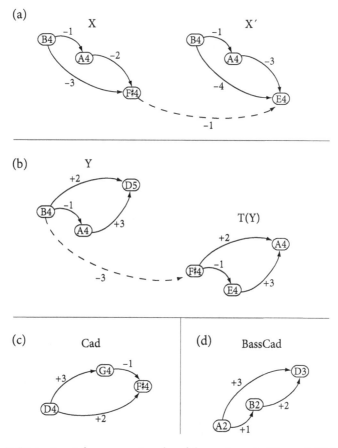

Figure 1.5 Diatonic pitch-space networks of the gestures in Figure 1.4(b).

As shown by the dashed arrow in 1.5(b), –3 is the transformational agent that takes Y to T(Y). Like –1, which took X to X′, –3 is also present locally in both X and X′. The –3 arrow in X connects the same two elements connected by the dashed –3 arrow in 1.5(b): B4 and F♯4. The dashed arrow in 1.5(b) leads not from last-note to last-note, as in 1.5(a), but from first-note to first-note. Rather than merely affecting one note, it serves to transpose *all* of Y into T(Y). Thus, while –1 acts as an internal transformation in X and as a single-note transformation between X and X′, –3 acts as a spanning transformation in X and as an agent of wholesale transposition between Y and T(Y).

Figure 1.5(c) shows the gestural kinetics of Cad, which includes the same three transformations as Y and T(Y), –1, +2, and +3, though in a different order. For the first time, –1 does not initiate the gesture, but terminates it. The reversal is appropriate for a cadence. The sense of reversal is heightened by the presence of x (the mini form of X) at the end of the phrase, turning the movement's initiating gesture into an agent of closure. Cad also reverses previous material in a more formal sense: it is a retrograde inversion of Y and T(Y). The diatonic pitch-space operation that takes T(Y) to Cad is retrograde-inversion-about-F♯4. F♯4 is both the initiating pitch in T(Y) and the cadential pitch in m. 7; the inversional balance around F♯4 strengthens its role as a point of temporary cadential repose. Cad is the first gesture to begin with an ascent, as well as the first to depart from the articulative pattern of X: it is fully legato, covered by a single slur, and linked by ornamental connectives between its nodal points.

Of the three transformations in X, only –1 does not appear in *positive*—that is, ascending—form in the melodic gestures of Figures 1.5(b) and (c). It *does* appear in ascending form in the bass, however, as shown in 1.5(d).[44] Moreover, the motivic A–B dyad is reversed here. Until this point, B has always proceeded to A via –1. BassCad now retrogrades this crucial gesture, taking A to B via +1. The sense of cadential retrograde interacts nicely with the comments just made about Cad's various reversals.[45] While Cad exhibits an inversional relationship with the Y-forms, BassCad exhibits an inversional relationship with X. Minus signs in X are replaced by pluses in BassCad, as X's falling, initiating gesture is transformed into a rising, cadential bass figure.

These pitch and contour relationships interact compellingly with durational aspects of the music. Some of these interactions are shown in Figure 1.6. The contents of the nodes in Figures 1.6(a)–(d) and (f) are ordered pairs of the form (pitch, duration), where duration is the note value corresponding to the length of time the given pitch persists (either literally or implicitly) in the music.[46] The transformational labels are also ordered pairs in which the first element is a diatonic pitch interval (as in Figure 1.5) and the second is a durational transformation. In the examples in the left column (1.6(a), (c), and (e)), the durational transformations are rational numbers indicating proportions. For example, the proportional transformation 2 in 1.6(a) takes the opening quarter note to the following half note; the proportional transformation 1/2 in 1.6(c), on the uppermost arrow, takes the opening quarter note to the concluding eighth note; and so on. In the examples in the right column (1.6(b), (d), and (f)), the durational transformations are *additive,* adding or subtracting note values in the intuitive way (e.g., half – quarter = quarter).[47] The two different methods of transforming durations offer different perspectives on the gestures. In X, for example, the successive durations increase

---

44. Note that in Figure 1.5(d) I have drawn an arrow from B2 directly to D3, bypassing the C♯3 on beat two of m. 7, in agreement with Schubert's slurring. The reading corresponds Peter Smith's understanding of C♯ as a passing tone (2000, 9, Ex. 4b). See also the Schenkerian sketch in Figure 1.8.
45. On the role of reversals as "closural," see Narmour 1990.
46. For example, the F♯4 in m. 2 is understood to have a dotted-half duration, as it is the melodic pitch that implicitly controls the entire bar.
47. This is a transformational equivalent of the problematic GIS space discussed above (and in *GMIT,* 29–30). I employ it here to show its musical intuitiveness, and to show that it *can* work as a transformational system, though it is formally awkward: one must posit an element α in the space S of durations that corresponds to a "duration-less instant." Any duration x is transformed to α if it is acted on by a negative duration whose absolute value is greater than x's. An elegant way around this problem is to treat the system in question not as a transformational system at all, but as a system based on a "tangent space," as explored in Tymoczko 2009. Such spaces admit of bounded "dead ends" beyond which no transformations or intervals may be conceived. Our duration-less instant is one such dead end.

by different sized proportions (2 and 1-1/2) as shown in 1.6(a), while the additive increases, shown in 1.6(b) are by the same amount (an added quarter in each case). The conceptual and experiential differences between the two species of rhythmic transformation are also reflected in their differing group structures: the integers under addition (in the additive rhythmic transformations) vs. the nonzero rational numbers under multiplication (in the proportional rhythmic transformations).

These dual transformation systems reveal interesting correspondences between pitch and rhythm in the passage. Note first that for all descending pitch motions, durations increase; for all ascending pitch motions, durations decrease. The connection is suggestive of a metaphorical correspondence between durations and weight, with the longer, "heavier" durations at the bottoms of the gestures. The aptness of the metaphor is especially evident in the Y-forms: the gesture flicks

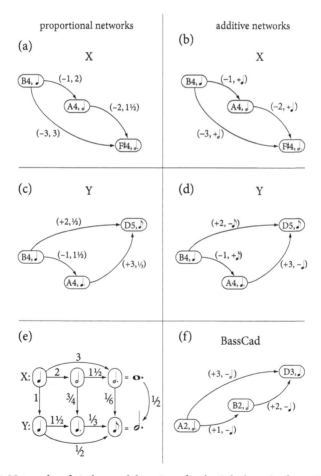

Figure 1.6 Networks of pitches and durations for the Schubert Andante. Durational transformations in (a), (c), and (e) are proportional, while those in (b), (d), and (f) are additive.

upward at the last moment to catch the eighth note, which floats up like a helium balloon. X, by contrast, constantly sinks, as note values gradually increase in length and heft.[48] Figure 1.6(e) compares the X- and Y-forms in this regard, showing the proportional relationships between their respective elements. The vertical arrows show the alteration of each successive element in the three-note gestures. Pitch one is not altered at all; it remains a quarter in both X and Y (durational proportion 1). Pitch two is then slightly shortened by the proportion 3/4—a proportion made evident by the repeated eighth notes (four in X, three in Y)—while the third pitch is shortened drastically, by 1/6. The rightmost events in each gesture are thus at the durational extremes of the network. The result is a net decrease in duration across the span of Y, reflected by the arched 1/2 arrow along the bottom of the example, as opposed to a net increase in X, the 3 in the upper arched arrow. Figure 1.6(e) provides a rich sense of the ways in which Y "pulls up short" in comparison to X. The proportional relationship of X to Y is palpable to both performer and listener; it corresponds to the increase in harmonic rhythm in mm. 5–6 and, ultimately, to the early arrival of the cadence on beat three of m. 7.[49]

There are other compelling correspondences in the examples. For example, the –3 gesture that links B4 and F♯4 in X is not only inverted in pitch space in Y's A4–D5; it is also inverted in durational-proportion space. That is (+3, 1/3) in 1.6(c) is the formal inverse of (–3, 3) in 1.6(a).[50] Note also that, just as BassCad is an inversion of X in pitch space, it is also an *exact inversion of X in additive duration space*. The arrow labels in 1.6(b) are replaced with their formal inverses in 1.6(f): to turn the transformations in 1.6(b) into those of 1.6(f), one needs merely to reverse the pluses and minuses for both pitches and durations. BassCad thus inverts X as a complete pitch/time gesture. This observation interacts suggestively with BassCad's role as a *textural inverse* of X (bass rather than melody) as well as a *syntactic inverse* (a cadential rather than initiating gesture).

1.3.5 Comment

The analyses of sections 1.2.6 (Bach) and 1.3.4 (Schubert) have demonstrated that GIS and transformational methodologies, even in their current state, make available suggestive insights into tonal music—insights that differ from those generated in other analytical approaches. Further, those insights in no way call into doubt

---

48. Such pitch/time transformational perspectives offer fruitful ways to think about Schubert's vividly somatic gestural language. For a compelling discussion of the thematic role of gesture in Schubert, see Hatten 2004.

49. Mm. 1–7 are a sentence in William Caplin's (1998) sense. X and X′ correspond to the basic idea (b.i.) and its repetition (b.i. ′). The increase in harmonic rhythm and surface activity in mm. 5ff. is typical of a sentence's continuation phrase. This increase in activity is visibly evident in the "piling up of gestures" shown on the right-hand side of Figure 1.4(b).

50. Formally, $(+3, \frac{1}{2})^{-1} = (-3, 3)$. In making this statement, we rely on the fact that the group of transformations in question is a *direct product group*, as discussed in the Glossary. Notice that the inversional relationship between these pitch/duration pairs does *not* hold in the additive networks of 1.6(b) and 1.6(d).

the tonal status of the music. Yet, while tonal aspects of the two works were discussed in informal ways in the analyses (through references to things like tonics, dominants, and cadences), the formal apparatus of the analyses did not model those ideas in any direct way. This was especially evident in the Schubert analysis, which made no attempt to explore the subtle interpenetration of D major and B minor that characterizes the movement's harmony. As Peter Smith (2000) has noted, the relationship between the pitches B and A is especially striking in this regard—their status relative to one another, as either stable or decorative pitches, depends heavily on tonal concepts. Consider the opening six-three sonority {D, F♯, B}. In the context of the opening bar, it functions as a tonic D chord subjected to a contrapuntal 5–6 displacement. But, as Smith notes, it also carries hints of B-minor in first inversion—hints that connect both to the concluding moments of the previous movement, and to later events in the Andante (such as the root position B-minor chord in mm. 10–11). The subtle shift of hearing that Smith notes in regard to the opening six-three is a characteristically tonal effect, but one that our transformational methodology, in its current state, cannot capture. The development of the apparatus's tonal sensitivity is the work of Chapters 2 and 3.

1.4 Comparisons with Schenkerian Theory

All new approaches to tonal analysis must at some point situate themselves with respect to the Schenkerian tradition, the *lingua franca* of tonal theory in the Anglo-American academy. The need to do this with transformational approaches is perhaps more pressing than usual, as developments in neo-Riemannian theory have generated a degree of antagonism between adherents of the two methods. In this section I will briefly compare the methodological characteristics of transformational and Schenkerian approaches with the aim of demonstrating that they differ in important ways in terms of analytical technique, theoretical content, and methodological goals. I will ultimately propose that any tension or competition between the two methodologies is misplaced and unnecessary. Such a tension suggests that Schenkerian and transformational theories represent two versions of the same kind of music theory—that their claims are equivalent and competing. I will instead argue that they are *not* competing forms of the same kind of music theory, but represent distinctly different styles of music-analytical thought.

Figure 1.7 presents a Schenkerian sketch of the first four measures of the Prelude to Bach's G-major Cello Suite, useful for comparison with the GIS analysis in section 1.2.6. The sketch shows a three-voice contrapuntal structure underlying mm. 1–4: a composing-out of the tonic *Stufe* in G. The Kopfton $\hat{3}$ (B3) is decorated with a complete neighbor C4, while the inner voice horizontalizes the fourth between D3 and G3 through stepwise motion. There are some evident visual parallels here with Figure 1.2, in particular with 1.2(f). But the two analyses diverge notably in their content and in the nature of their analytical claims. Figure 1.7 proposes an interpretation of the *structure* of the opening of the prelude, suggesting, for

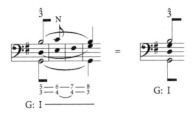

Figure 1.7 A Schenkerian sketch of the Bach Prelude (BWV 1007), mm. 1–4.

example, that it elaborates a three-voice contrapuntal setting, that it prolongs a tonic *Stufe*, that $\hat{3}$ is the *Kopfton*, and so on. Figure 1.2, by contrast, proposes no such structural interpretation of the music. Instead, it sketches multiple intervallic contexts in which the opening G2–B3 interval may be experienced. Its various analytical representations do not concern the immanent stuff of the piece per se, but rather model a handful of intervallic apperceptions that one might have when hearing the prelude's opening. One may even argue that Figure 1.2 does not make traditional analytical *claims* at all. It instead proposes diverse ways in which one might conceive of the G2–B3 interval, and, in so conceiving, potentially reconfigure one's experience of the suite's opening.

John Rahn has drawn a useful heuristic distinction between two kinds of theories: on the one hand is the "theory of experience," on the other, the "theory of piece" (2001, 51, 64–65). Rahn's categories recall two of the three levels of the tripartition of Jean Molino and Jean-Jacques Nattiez (Nattiez 1990): Rahn's "theory of experience" concerns the esthesic level, while his "theory of piece" concerns the neutral or immanent level (however problematic the latter is from a philosophical standpoint).[51] In a rather crude sense, we can say that the Bach GIS analysis of section 1.2.6 is of the "theory of experience," or esthesic, variety, while the Schenkerian sketch of Figure 1.7 is of the "theory of piece," or immanent, variety. The distinction is crude because it oversimplifies: the GIS analysis still takes a piece of music as the object for its apperceptual musings, while the Schenkerian sketch of 1.7 engages hearing in many satisfying ways. Yet, in addition to its esthesic aspects, the Schenkerian analysis of Figure 1.7 has an immanent component that is absent from the GIS analysis. The sketch purports to reveal work-immanent relationships, in which the work is conceived as a structural entity composed of interacting harmonic and linear components, hierarchical levels, and so on. Such an immanent perspective is evident in familiar locutions in Schenkerian discourse, such as "The work is a $\hat{3}$-line."[52] By contrast, the GIS formalism was used in section

---

51. For critiques of Nattiez's immanent level, or *niveau neutre*, see Kofi Agawu 1992, 318, and Nicholas Cook 2001, 181. The third level of the tripartition is the poietic, which is composer-focused.

52. In practice, this statement may of course mean "The work may be heard as a $\hat{3}$-line" or "I experience the work as a $\hat{3}$-line." It is nevertheless often hard to tell the extent to which the familiar immanent wording is meant in these esthesic terms, or is instead intended as a propositional statement about the piece as an entity separable from the observer. Most important for our purposes is the fact that, as a *discursive formation*, such a statement is framed in immanent terms. The conflicts discussed in this section arise as a result of such discursive formations. Nattiez (1990, 142) provides a pertinent discussion of the admixture of work-immanent, esthesic, and poietic claims in Schenkerian discourse. (For a strongly poietic account of Schenkerian theory as a "model of expert monotonal composition," see Brown 2005.)

1.2.6 not as a tool for making such work-immanent statements, but as a tool for exploring (and generating) diverse intervallic experiences.

A look back at *GMIT* is helpful here. Lewin does not introduce his project by saying "Music is made up of intervals," or even "Music consists of a countless multiplicity of intervals." Instead, he frames the issue in decidedly esthesic terms:

> In conceptualizing a particular musical space, it often happens that we conceptualize along with it, as one of its characteristic textural features, a family of directed measurements, distances, or motions of some sort. Contemplating elements s and t of such a musical space, we are characteristically aware of the particular directed measurement, distance, or motion that proceeds "from s to t." (*GMIT*, 16)

Note what is being characterized: not the music as a *Ding an sich*, but our *encounter* with that music, and our concomitant "conceptualizing" or "contemplating" of it (as a *Ding an mich*, as it were). The statement introduces intervals and transformations not as things in the world, but as relationships actively construed and apperceived by an individual in contact with some musical phenomenon.[53] The analyses of Figure 1.2 sought to enact such a process of active construal. As one consequence of this fluid interpretive activity, the sounding entities of the music became definitionally mobile: the G2 and B3 in the Bach were variously construed as elements within a diatonic pitch space, elements of an infinite arpeggio, just overtones of a conceptual G1, $\hat{1}$ and $\hat{3}$ in an ideal scale degree space, and root and third in an ideal chord-member space. Other construals were possible as well (none of these GISes, for example, construed G and B as pitch classes, either diatonic or chromatic). To the extent that such analyses reveal "structures" at all, they are *esthesic structures* rather than immanent structures. If, by contrast, transformational statements are taken to have an immanent component—as proposing alternative accounts of "the structure of the piece"—a conflict with a Schenkerian approach is not far off, as both approaches seek to lay claim to "the" immanent structure in question.[54]

Transformational approaches, with their emphasis on a conscious construction of myriad apperceptual contexts, give rise to analytical strategies that differ notably from the strategies fostered by Schenkerian thought. If any given passage of music admits of an indeterminate number of intervallic or transformational apperceptions, it of course becomes impossible to execute anything approaching a complete

---

53. As the discussion in sections 1.2 and 1.3 has made clear, the nature of that "active construal" differs for Lewin depending on whether one is in a Cartesian-intervallic mindset or in a transformational-participatory mindset. In either case, however, the intervallic or transformational relationships come into being only through the activity of a musical interpreter (performer, listener, composer, analyst). This strongly esthesic stance is of a piece with Lewin's work as a whole; that stance is nowhere more in evidence than in his phenomenology essay (Lewin 2006, Chapter 4), one of the most strenuously esthesic of all music-theoretic writings in recent decades. The essay as a whole adopts a radical skepticism as regards any immanent statements about musical works.

54. Such conflicts can be almost comical in their pitting of theoretical apples against theoretical oranges. (If "the" structure of passage X is a composing out of an upper neighbor to the *Kopfton*, then "the" structure of passage X cannot be a progression between hexatonically related *Klänge*.) See Rings 2007, 43–45 and Lewin 2006, Ch. 19.

analysis of a given work. Instead, the apparatus encourages one to adopt an analytical technique that we might call *prismatic*, in which phenomenologically rich local passages are refracted and explored from multiple perspectives. Such a prismatic strategy is especially evident in the Bach analysis of Figure 1.2. A Schenkerian sketch, by contrast, joins its various structures into an integrated account of an entire work or passage. In this sense, we might characterize transformational methodology as genuinely *analytic*—refracting a passage into multiple esthesic streams— while Schenkerian analysis is *synthetic* in its integration of elements of harmony, counterpoint, and so forth into an overarching account of a piece or passage.[55] This is not to deny that a Schenkerian analyst might explore multiple alternative analyses of a passage, or tease out ambiguities revealed by a sketch. Rather, it is simply to observe that any *single* Schenker sketch proposes a richly synthesized picture of the music in question, while transformational or GIS accounts tend toward prismatic refraction into multiple (and sometimes incommensurate) esthesic perspectives.

In light of these considerable methodological differences, we should eye with caution any effort to unite these two styles of analytical thought into a grand *über*-method. Transformational and Schenkerian approaches thrive best when their divergent analytic and synthetic strategies are allowed free rein; to re-create either in the image of the other would result in a substantial loss. Transformational theory is at its most powerful in the pluralistic exploration of phenomenologically rich local passages. The focus on local detail in much transformational writing is not a product of analytical myopia, but instead grows directly out of the structure of the theory, which encourages (and rewards) sustained contemplation of local musical effects. If a transformational account is instead asked to produce a Schenker-like picture of an entire movement, it quickly loses its explanatory punch, as potentially rich local observations are lost amid a welter of information. By contrast, Schenkerian theory gains its strength precisely through its ability to coordinate a great number of linear and harmonic musical parameters and to synthesize them into a structural account that is at once integrated and abundantly detailed. If we instead deploy a Schenkerian approach to dig into the phenomenological multiplicity of, say, a single harmonic succession, the apparatus will hardly have the necessary musical space to exercise its synthetic power.

In any case, it should be clear that nothing in either of these methods excludes the other. On the contrary, their differences of scope and emphasis make possible their dialogic coexistence in analytical practice. By the word *dialogic*, I do not mean anything fancy or Bakhtinian; I simply mean an interaction in which each discourse registers the presence of the other. Dialogue, of course, involves two independent interlocutors, not two individuals speaking in unison. Thus, we should not expect nodding agreement at all times. The technologies in question afford distinct modes of analytical behavior and means of engaging with musical sound; it should come as no surprise that they will notice different things. If our goal is as much insight as

---

55. The frequency with which the word *Synthese* occurs in Schenker's writings attests to the importance of such ideas in his thought. On the Kantian resonances of the word for Schenker, see Korsyn 1988, 19–43. See also Snarrenberg 1997, 99–138, and Rothstein 2001, 208. Lewin, for his part, calls Schenker's theory a "triumphal synthesis" (*GMIT*, 247).

possible, such dialogic diversity should be welcomed. Moreover, a careful vigilance regarding distinctions between the discourses will help us avoid detecting (monological) contradiction where in fact there is none. Consider, for example, the networks in Figures 1.5 and 1.6. These networks explore gestures that would cut across the contrapuntal strata of a Schenkerian reading of the Schubert passage. For example, gesture X spans two Schenkerian linear strands: an upper voice involving the B–A neighbor motion, and an inner voice that contains the F♯.[56] Strictly speaking from the Schenkerian perspective, the A does not "go to F♯," but is instead implicitly retained in register; nor does the piece's *Hauptmotiv* trace some malformed B4–A4–F♯4 *Zug*. If we are in an especially Schenkerian mood, we might thus be tempted to say that the networks are wrong to assert such continuities. But this would be a methodological slip, mistakenly imputing Schenkerian claims to the networks, and bad Schenkerian claims at that. It would be to evaluate the formal statements from one theory using the highly ramified native concepts (and terms of art) from another. Only when we recognize that the networks of Figures 1.5 and 1.6 are instead esthesic perspectives on certain *gestures* in the phrase—perspectives that remain essentially agnostic as regards questions of linear/structural priority and organization—does the false conflict evaporate, freeing us to explore the dialogic relationship between the networks and a Schenkerian account.

To suggest some aspects of that dialogue, Figure 1.8 offers a Schenkerian interpretation of the phrase, along with annotations indicating the gestures explored in Figures 1.5 and 1.6. The main Schenkerian focus in the right hand is on the alto-register linear strand beginning with F♯4 in m. 2, which is analyzed with down-stems (A4 acts as a cover tone in this hearing).[57] What is most interesting is the way in which the sketch interacts with the idea of *closural reversals* explored in connection with the transformational analyses. Specifically, at the very moment when the alto-register line completes its beamed $\hat{3}$–$\hat{2}$–$\hat{1}$ descent, on the downbeat of m. 7, the bass moves from A to B, reversing the pervasive B-to-A motive of the upper voices, and seemingly causing the alto voice to change direction as well, as it retraces its third progression with a $\hat{1}$–$\hat{2}$–$\hat{3}$ *ascent* (slurred in the figure). This is a moment of harmonic complication as well, as the vi chord insinuates itself into the V–I cadence: what seems to be a deceptive cadence on the downbeat of m. 7 is "corrected" to an imperfect authentic cadence by the 10–10–10 linear intervallic pattern.[58] While the idea of a change of direction in the alto interacts nicely with the closural kinetics of reversal explored in the networks of Figures 1.5 and 1.6,

---

56. Depending on how one reads the phrase, the acoustic upper voice B–A may in fact be a superposition of a conceptual inner voice, or a cover tone, with the "true" upper voice initiated by the F♯. The methodological issues remain the same, regardless of which voice one assigns conceptual upper-voice status.

57. Peter Smith (2000, Ex. 4b) also reads the F♯4 as initiating the main structural voice here, though his analysis differs in some small details from Figure 1.8.

58. One can consider this 10–10–10 as an instance of a "leads/follows" configuration familiar from Schenkerian thought, in which one voice—in this case, the alto-register voice—traces a *Zug* that expresses the local harmony, while the other voice "follows" in parallel tenths or sixths, outlining a linear span that is seemingly in conflict with that harmony (here, the B–C♯–D 3rd progression in the bass). The *locus classicus* is the outer-voice pattern in Schenker's analysis of the C-major Prelude from *WTC I*. See Schenker 1979, 80 (along with Figure 95, e, 3 in the supplement) and Schenker 1969.

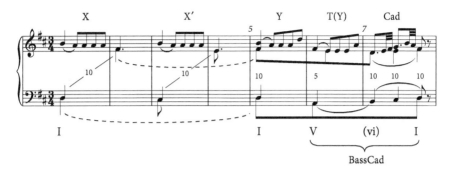

Figure 1.8 A sketch of the Schubert Andante, mm. 1–7, showing the gestures of Figure 1.4(b) along with Schenkerian annotations.

there is no clear transformational analogue for the harmonic complexity at the cadence. Thus the two discourses move in tandem in some respects, and diverge to pursue independent agendas in others.

In short, transformational statements and Schenkerian statements, though they may converse in analytical practice, remain methodologically orthogonal to one another. That orthogonal configuration need only trouble us if our goal is a unified theory of all tonal experience. If our aims are instead more pragmatic—a pluralistic exploration of the manifold effects and apperceptions that tonal music affords—then this methodological diversity becomes not something to bemoan, but something to embrace. I am fully aware that such a conciliatory conclusion will seem disappointingly bland to the dialectician, or to those who relish disciplinary conflict. It nevertheless has one signal virtue: it is interpretively productive. Such a position frees us to deploy various analytical methods as we see fit, to explore their interactions on a case-by-case basis, and—perhaps most important—to redirect intellectual energy from polemic back to the business of generating insights into musical experience.

CHAPTER Two

A Tonal GIS

2.1 Tonal Qualia

Let us begin by attending to some exceedingly familiar aural experiences. Imagine or play the music in Figure 2.1, and focus particular attention on the tone under the fermata. What does one experience when listening to that tone?

Figure 2.1

One naturally experiences a physical phenomenon, a fact of raw acoustics: in this case, a piano tone with a fundamental frequency of around 440 cycles per second. But one of course experiences a great deal more than that—a network of apperceptions underwritten by past musical experience, training, and enculturation. Among other apperceptions, listeners enculturated within Western musical traditions will hear a tone with a very familiar character or quality, what some philosophers of mind would call a *quale*. Those who have learned a bit of music theory will be able to attach a name to that quale, perhaps calling it "scale degree seven," or "the leading tone," or "ti in solfège."[1] But theoretically innocent listeners

---

1. For more on scale-degree qualia, including a stimulating account of the various poetic descriptions that experienced listeners give them, see Huron 2006, Ch. 9. Music theorists will be familiar with the concept of qualia from Boretz 1995, which takes Goodman 1951 as a point of departure. Boretz's pitch qualia are different from the qualia I explore here: he uses the term to discuss the experience

will still experience the quale in question, though perhaps to differing degrees.[2] Such listeners will, for example, sense a notably different quale at moment *y* in Figure 2.2.

Figure 2.2

Though the acoustic signal at *y* is identical to that at *x*, the pitch's scale-degree quale has changed to that of the tonic, or $\hat{1}$. The contrast clearly demonstrates the truism that scale-degree qualia are independent of the acoustic signals to which they may be momentarily attached. As David Huron puts it, "scale degrees are *cognitive* rather than *perceptual* phenomena. That is, 'scale degree' is how minds interpret physically sounding tones, not how tones are in the world" (2006, 143). Though this is intellectually obvious, it may not feel so obvious when one is in the moment of hearing. Some listeners may in fact experience tonal qualia so vividly that they seem to infuse the sounding medium itself. At *x*, for example, the raw acoustic signal may seem to be infused with "leading-tone-ness" or "$\hat{7}$-ness." But at *y*, the very same raw acoustic signal may now seem infused with "tonic-ness" or "$\hat{1}$-ness."

This is all so familiar that it rarely merits theoretical attention. But perhaps it should. The structure of the phenomenon is striking and worthy of theoretical consideration. Further, as Huron has suggested, a significant part of tonal experience for

of pitch or pitch class in the traditional sense, while I will reserve it for scale-degree sensations (as in Huron). This is not to imply that scale-degree sensations are somehow more qualitative than other musical phenomena (pitched and non-pitched); it is rather to limit the word for present purposes to avoid terminological confusion.

Qualia are controversial in philosophical circles: philosophers of mind disagree about what they are like and whether they even exist. I do not wish to enter into that controversy here—philosophically savvy readers who do not believe in qualia should feel free to substitute a different word for the phenomenon in question. (For strong arguments contra qualia, see Dennett 1990 and 1991; for a collection of recent essays in defense of the concept, see Wright 2008.)

I have tried to be careful to limit my comments above to listeners enculturated within Western musical traditions; that limitation applies for the remainder of this chapter. Even given such a limitation, I do not wish to gloss over important distinctions *among* such listeners. One such distinction is that between listeners with absolute pitch (AP) and those without it. The AP listener will have certain experiences when listening to Figures 2.1 and 2.2 that may differ not only in degree from those of non-AP listeners, but perhaps in kind. Those differences naturally involve the ability to assign letter names to the tones heard, an ability that might attenuate, or simply alter, other qualitative aspects of the AP listener's experience when compared to that of the non-AP listener.

2. Huron (2006, Ch. 9) proposes that scale-degree qualia arise from statistical learning and are not dependent on theoretical training. It nevertheless seems possible that musicians and theoretically informed listeners may have intensified experiences of scale-degree qualia as a result of extensive ear training, the ability to name such degrees and thus sharpen their categorical boundaries, and so on.

many listeners likely involves the experience of scale-degree qualia (2006, Ch. 9); Robert Gjerdingen (1988, 2007) also places scale degrees, not named pitches, at the center of his schematic theories of musical cognition. One might thus identify the experience of qualitative scale degrees as one of the defining characteristics of what it means to "hear tonally." The idea provides a suggestive new angle on perennial questions of tonal versus atonal experience. It is plausible that a listener new to atonal music might find such music disorienting not simply because of its preponderance of dissonance or its unfamiliar harmonic vocabulary, but also because those characteristics lead to the experience of pitches as *devoid* of tonal quality. Rather than hearing pitches as familiar tonal characters, the listener is struck by the pitches' tonal anonymity.[3]

As suggestive as these ideas might be for a general theory of tonal cognition, I am not proposing such a theory here. The transformational methods developed in these pages have an interpretive aim, not a scientific one. As such, this book's commitments are primarily (though not exclusively) to what David Temperley (1999) would call "suggestive" rather than "descriptive" music theory. Per Temperley, suggestive approaches seek to stimulate new (or perhaps more sharply focused) hearings of musical phenomena, while descriptive approaches seek to model prereflective hearings. The line between the two is not always crisp, however. The present study, for example, aims to pursue, develop, and extend certain familiar, prereflective tonal experiences via the mediation of GIS and transformational technologies. It thus takes basic descriptive hypotheses about listeners' prereflective experiences of tonal quale and intention[4] as points of departure for suggestive extension (or focusing) in diverse interpretive contexts.

Before proceeding in our study of qualia, it is worth stressing the novelty of the idea of scale degree under consideration in this chapter. In what follows, scale degrees are not invoked as part of the immanent stuff of music. Rather, they are treated as experiential qualities—familiar sensations of tonal character. Per the preceding comments, these qualities may be part of the reader's prereflective experience, or they may be stimulated (or sharpened) by analytical suggestion. In either case, the careted Arabic numbers in the GIS developed in this chapter are signifiers of what some philosophers of mind call "raw feels"—in this case, the raw feel of experiencing a sounding pitch as, say, scale degree three ($\hat{3}$) or scale degree five ($\hat{5}$). This leads to some fluidity and mobility in the analytical application of these labels, as sounding pitches are invested with new characters in shifting tonal contexts.[5] If some analytical statements in the coming pages at first appear surprising or counterintuitive, the reader should recall this special understanding of scale degree as sensed quale, not as immanent entity.

---

3. This is not to deny that the pitches in an atonal work may take on different, nontonal qualia as one becomes more familiar with a given atonal idiom; Christopher Hasty (1987, 195ff) offers suggestive observations about atonal intervallic qualities along these lines.
4. Tonal intention is the subject of Chapter 3.
5. Robert Gjerdingen argues that moveable-do styles of scale-degree labeling offer a good reflection of the "mobile cognition of pitch" (2007, 20–21). This locution fits well with the fluid model of scale-degree apperceptions to be developed in this chapter.

2.2 A GIS for Heard Scale Degrees

We first develop an ordered-pair notation for a heard scale degree. The left-hand slot in the ordered pair will include a careted scale degree, indicating a sensed scale-degree quale, while the right-hand slot will correspond to the acoustic signal. The notation $(\hat{7}, x)$ thus represents the apperception: "scale degree seven inheres in acoustic signal x." It is not initially obvious what kind of theoretical entity x should be. It could be a pitch class (like 3 or E♭) or a pitch (like E♭4 or MIDI-tone 63). If we use letter names for pitches or pcs, we might choose to invoke enharmonic equivalence (E♭ = D♯) or not (E♭ ≠ D♯). We should note, in any case, that x will have to be *some* kind of theoretical entity. Though it corresponds to a sounding event in the world, and thus might seem to be more "real" than the quale to its left, we need to *interpret* it in order to work it into our model. (The acoustic signal itself cannot be captured and put on the page.)[6]

As scale-degree qualia repeat at the octave, it is natural to invoke octave equivalence: if a given pitch C is heard as $\hat{1}$ in some tonal context, *all* Cs, in any hearable octave, will be heard as $\hat{1}$.[7] Though it is less immediately obvious, it also makes good sense to invoke enharmonic equivalence for x. Enharmonic distinctions are of course crucial in tonal music, but the effect of those distinctions on the listener innocent of the score is not a matter of spelling, or even a matter of subtle shifts in intonation—it is a matter of tonal context. And tonal context is modeled by the left-hand element in our ordered pair, not the right-hand one.[8] Given these observations, the most useful abstract entity for element x turns out to be the familiar chromatic pitch class, giving our ordered pairs the form (sd, pc). While the left-hand element in the pair denotes a scale-degree quale, the right-hand element denotes what psychologists call a *chroma:* the perceived "color" shared by all pitches related by octave. Pitch classes will sometimes be represented by integers mod 12 (using the familiar C = 0 convention),[9] and sometimes by note letter names, which are often easier to read. The letter names are always to be understood, however, as representatives of one of the 12 chromatic pitch classes (D♯, for example, means pitch class 3, as does E♭).

---

6. I should also stress that the acoustic signal is not simply a pitch. Rather, pitch is merely *one auditory attribute* of the acoustic signal. Our focus on this particular auditory attribute is guided by our interest in scale-degree apperceptions, which depend on our experience of pitch in a musical sound (as opposed, say, to our experience of the sound's loudness, timbre, or point of spatial origin).

7. One might quibble with this: our experiences of scale-degree qualia may be bent or distorted at the extremes of hearable pitch (very low and very high). This is a fascinating matter for investigation in music cognition and perception; such an investigation nevertheless falls outside of the scope of this book. For present purposes, we will rely on the "white lie" that scale-degree sensations are more or less uniform across the hearable pitch spectrum.

8. As we will see, the present GIS provides an elegant model of enharmonic effects without needing to distinguish between notated E♭ and D♯.

9. As already observed in the "Note on Orthography," I will sometimes use the shorthand t for pitch class 10 and e for pitch class 11. NB: Roman e means pitch class 11; italic e is the identity element in a group (of intervals or transformations).

Aside from some trivial orthographic differences, this ordered-pair model is formally identical to models of the diatonic system presented by Eytan Agmon (1986, 1989) and Alexander Brinkman (1986). The group of intervals to be developed in a moment is also identical to the mathematical structures underlying Agmon's and Brinkman's systems.[10] The interaction between diatonic and chromatic intervals that we will explore is further indebted to the pioneering work of Clough and Myerson (1985) and Clough and Douthett (1991). Nevertheless, the present focus on scale-degree qualia, as opposed to letter names or notated pitches, leads to notable conceptual differences from these earlier systems, as does the analytical implementation of these ideas within a GIS and transformational context. In fact, the present system is conceptually closer to a much older music-theoretic idea: the littera/vox pairing in Guidonian theory. The Guidonian note name *A la mi re*, for example, indicates that sung gamut pitch A can be experienced as hexachordal member la, mi, or re, depending on its context. One could translate each of these options into an ordered pair notation analogous to the present one, writing them as (la, A), (mi, A), and (re, A).[11]

The space S of the present GIS is the set of all 84 ordered pairs of the form (sd, pc).[12] We can visualize this space as a 12 × 7 grid, as shown in Figure 2.3. Each horizontal row corresponds to a pitch-class, or chroma; each vertical column corresponds to a scale-degree impression, or tonal quale. The horizontal and vertical dimensions wrap around, making Figure 2.3 a flat representation of a torus. Depending on the analytical context, the rows and columns of Figure 2.3 may sometimes be reoriented on the page; that is, we may choose to place some scale degree other than $\hat{1}$ in the leftmost column, and some pc other than 0 in the bottom

	$\hat{1}$	$\hat{2}$	$\hat{3}$	$\hat{4}$	$\hat{5}$	$\hat{6}$	$\hat{7}$
e							
t							
9	$(\hat{1}, 9)$						$(\hat{7}, 9)$
8							
7							
6							
5							
4							
3							
2							
1							
0							

Figure 2.3 A space of 84 pairs of the form (sd, pc), in which sd is a scale-degree quale and pc is a pitch class.

10. Brinkman, however, defines his space as an algebraic ring, adding a layer of structure beyond the group to be used here.
11. I am grateful to Kyle Adams for suggesting this historical connection.
12. As the elements and intervals of the GIS are ordered pairs, Lewin would call this a "direct-product GIS" (*GMIT*, 37–46).

row, so that the most relevant area of the torus appears contiguously in the figure. At other times we may wish to display only a portion of the space. These are merely cosmetic matters, representing no underlying change in the space S of the GIS.

Specific heard scale degrees reside at distinct addresses within this space. For example, the heard scale degree at *x* in Figure 2.2 is $(\hat{7}, 9)$, while that at *y* is $(\hat{1}, 9)$. The locations of both are shown on Figure 2.3. Note that $(\hat{1}, 9)$ resides in the same row as $(\hat{7}, 9)$, indicating that the two heard scale degrees share the same chroma; they nevertheless occupy different columns, indicating that they manifest different scale-degree qualia. The fact that these two apperceptions are represented by two distinct elements in the GIS—located at distinct addresses on Figure 2.3—makes clear that we can model an interval between them. We will explore this particular species of tonal interval in section 2.5.

Intervals between sd/pc elements in the GIS are ordered pairs of the form (sdint, pcint). The right element, pcint, is a familiar directed pitch-class interval from atonal theory. The left element, sdint, is an ordinal number—2nd, 3rd, 4th, and so on—indicating a generic interval between sensed scale degrees. Ordered pairs of scale degrees map to intervals in the intuitive way: the interval from $\hat{1}$ to $\hat{3}$ is a 3rd; that from $\hat{2}$ to $\hat{5}$ is a 4th; and so on. Formally, int$(\hat{1}, \hat{3})$ = 3rd, int$(\hat{2}, \hat{5})$ = 4th, etc. If there is no change in sensed scale degree, the identity symbol *e* will appear in the sdint slot. Though the ordinal interval labels appear familiar on paper, their application to qualitative scale degrees (as opposed to, say, note letter names) makes them somewhat novel, as we will see in the coming sections.

As Figure 2.4 shows, the seven elements of sdint are defined to be isomorphic to the cyclic group of order 7, or $\mathbb{Z}_7$, familiar to music theorists as the integers mod 7. This definition simply guarantees that the members of sdint will compose in an intuitive way, algebraically vouchsafing our ability to say things like 2nd + 2nd = 3rd.[13] As the ordered pc intervals (pcints) are isomorphic to $\mathbb{Z}_{12}$, IVLS as a whole

$\mathbb{Z}_7$	sdint	inverse labels
0	*e*	*e*
1	2nd	7th^{-1}
2	3rd	6th^{-1}
3	4th	5th^{-1}
4	5th	4th^{-1}
5	6th	3rd^{-1}
6	7th	2nd^{-1}

Figure 2.4 The ordinal scale-degree intervals, labeled sdint, are defined to be isomorphic to the elements of the cyclic group mod 7, or $\mathbb{Z}_7$.

13. Lewin points out the curious nature of diatonic interval names, which do not appear to "add up" in the usual way (*GMIT,* 17). For this reason, he prefers to use simple integers indicating the number of scale steps up in diatonic pitch or pitch class GISes (1 + 1 = 2, rather than 2nd + 2nd = 3rd). I have chosen to use the ordinal interval names because of their familiarity from tonal theory, and for the ways in which they abet an intuitive, "plain English" reading of certain formal expressions. The difference in notation has no effect on the underlying algebra.

is isomorphic to $\mathbb{Z}_7 \times \mathbb{Z}_{12}$ (that is, the *direct product group* of $\mathbb{Z}_7$ and $\mathbb{Z}_{12}$), which is itself isomorphic to $\mathbb{Z}_{84}$, the cyclic group of order 84.[14]

The intervallic ordered pairs (sdint, pcint) are designed to be intuitively readable in a familiar tonal-theoretic sense. For example, (2nd, 2) is a second spanning two semitones, or a major second; (3rd, 3) is a third spanning three semitones, or a minor third; (2nd, 3), by contrast, is a *second* spanning three semitones, or an augmented second. Figure 2.5 shows a 12 × 7 grid of all 84 intervals in IVLS.[15] The shading interprets the elements in IVLS based on the usual criteria for consonance and dissonance in traditional tonal theory: white cells are consonant, all shaded cells are dissonant.[16] I stress that this is an *interpretation* of the elements in IVLS, which in itself knows nothing of consonance and dissonance; it is merely an algebraic structure. But that algebraic structure is sufficiently textured to admit of suggestive interpretations along traditional tonal lines—indeed, the group structure allows us to model subtle but important distinctions from traditional tonal theory. For example, IVLS allows us to model the familiar tonal-theoretic idea that not all three-semitone intervals are consonant, nor are all thirds consonant, but a three-semitone interval experienced as a third *is* consonant. The relevant interval, (3rd, 3) is a white cell on

sdints

		e	2nd	3rd	4th	5th	6th	7th
	0	P1/P8						
	1	A1	m2					
	2		M2	d3				
	3		A2	m3				
	4			M3	d4			
pcints	5			A3	P4			
	6				A4	d5		
	7					P5	d6	
	8					A5	m6	
	9						M6	d7
	10						A6	m7
	11	d8						M7

Figure 2.5 A visual representation of the elements in the group IVLS for the sd/pc GIS, which contains 84 intervals of the form (sdint, pcint). Intervals that admit of traditional tonal interpretations are labeled. Clear cells indicate traditional consonances, shaded cells dissonances.

14. For more information on this algebraic structure, see the entry for *direct product group* in the Glossary.
15. Compare Brinkman 1986, 47, Table 4, and Agmon 1986, 163, Figure 4–5.
16. The perfect fourth is marked as a consonance in the figure, though it is of course a dissonance in traditional tonal theory if it sounds over the bass. The shading at the borders of the grid indicates some general patterns familiar from tonal theory: 2nds and 7ths are always dissonant (note the shading along the top border), while pc intervals 1, 2, 6, 10, and 11 are always dissonant (note the shading along the left border).

Figure 2.5, where it is given the familiar shorthand label m3. All other cells in the figure that admit of familiar tonal names are similarly labeled.[17] Unlabeled cells correspond to more exotic intervals, which nevertheless have suggestive meanings in the GIS. We will explore those intervals in sections 2.5 and 2.6.[18]

Figure 2.6 shows the GIS in action, using it to model two intervals from the first book of the *WTC*. The solid arrow in Figure 2.6(a) indicates an interval from pc 0 to pc 4 in the opening of the C-major Prelude; the dotted arrow in 2.6(b) indicates an interval between the same two pitch classes in the subject of the C♯-minor Fugue. Though the arrows traverse the same pc intervals, they traverse different *tonal* intervals. Pitch class 0, infused with the quale of $\hat{1}$ in the prelude, takes on the quale of $\hat{7}$ in the fugue; what was a major third thus becomes a diminished fourth. Formally, int(($\hat{1}$, 0), ($\hat{3}$, 4)) = (3rd, 4) in the prelude, while int(($\hat{7}$, 0), ($\hat{3}$, 4)) = (4th, 4) in the fugue. Figure 2.6(c) models those intervals in the sd/pc GIS space (the solid and dotted arrows correspond to Figures 2.6(a) and (b), respectively). Though the present GIS does not model enharmonic distinctions in pitch notation (notated C and B♯ are both represented by pc 0), it nevertheless

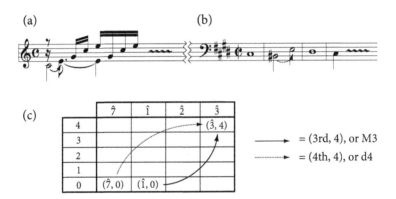

Figure 2.6 (a) Bach, Prelude in C major, *WTC I*, m. 1; (b) Bach, Fugue in C♯ minor, *WTC I*, mm. 1–4; (c) the intervals labeled in 2.6(a) and (b) plotted in the GIS space of Figure 2.3.

17. Such traditional labels are intuitively appropriate only when the interval in question remains within a single key (as formalized in section 2.7); intervals that span changes in key suggest other interpretations (see sections 2.5 and 2.6). The traditional labels in Figure 2.5 interpret the intervals in their simplest ascending manifestations within one octave. This leads to the somewhat awkward labels A1 and d8 in the leftmost column. More idiomatically, one could simply label these as "chromatic semitones." We can model the distinction between a descending chromatic semitone and a diminished octave by different paths in sd/pc space, as discussed in section 2.3.

18. Agmon (1986, 163, Figure 4-5) applies tonal interval labels to all cells in his analogous space, strewing *n*-tuply diminished and augmented intervals throughout the cells in his Figure 4-5 (equivalent to the present Figure 2.5). While such intervals are at least conceivable when the entities they link are notated pitches, it is a very different matter when one's entities are heard scale degrees. For now, we can simply note that the unlabeled cells in Figure 2.5 generally take on a much different meaning in the present GIS than in Agmon's system; see sections 2.5 and 2.6.

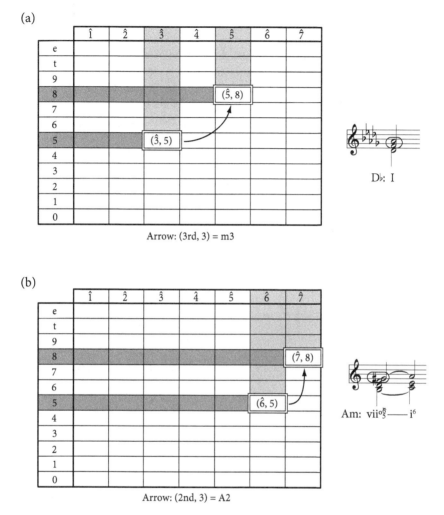

Figure 2.7 Two enharmonically equivalent intervals.

can model enharmonic distinctions between *heard intervals*. Specifically, enharmonically equivalent intervals in IVLS span the same number of semitones but a different number of sensed scale degrees. Such enharmonically equivalent intervals are located in the same rows in Figure 2.5. Figure 2.7 provides two further examples illustrating the same phenomenon. Note that the same two horizontal rows in the sd/pc grids are "lit up" in each case, indicating the same two sounding pitch classes; the vertical columns reflecting scale-degree qualia shift, however, modeling the change in apperceptual character from a consonant minor third in D♭ major (a) to a dissonant augmented second in A minor (b).

2.3 Excursus: Ascending and Descending Interval Labels

As the rightmost column in Figure 2.4 shows, it will sometimes be convenient to use inverse labels for scale-degree intervals. Such labels are useful when we wish to convey a sense of descent—for example, 2nd⁻¹ can be used to communicate the idea of "a second down," rather than "a seventh up." As is clear in Figure 2.4, 2nd⁻¹ and 7th are merely two labels for the same group element: our choice of label has no effect on the underlying group structure. Distinctions between labels like 2nd⁻¹ and 7th can nevertheless be modeled formally, creating a nonalgebraic overlay of interpretive structure above and beyond the more abstract contours of the GIS.

Some examples will provide a useful point of departure. Figure 2.8 shows two related descending gestures from *Eugene Onegin*: (a) is a climactic phrase from the letter scene, and (b) is the opening of Lensky's famous aria. Tatyana and Lensky both sing descending sixths; specifically, they sing sixths from $\hat{3}$ *down* to $\hat{5}$, not thirds from $\hat{3}$ *up* to $\hat{5}$.[19] By contrast, Tamino begins his familiar aria in Figure 2.9

(a)

(Are you my guardian angel?)

(b)

(What does the coming day hold for me?)

Figure 2.8 Two descending sixths in Tchaikovsky's *Eugene Onegin*. (a) A climactic phrase in Tatyana's letter scene (Act I, scene 2); (b) the opening of Lensky's aria (Act II, scene 2).

19. Russian musicians in fact refer to such sixths as "Lensky sixths" (Taruskin 1997, 242–43).

(This portrait is enchantingly beautiful, as no eye has ever seen!)

Figure 2.9 The opening of Tamino's aria "Dies Bildnis ist bezaubernd schön" from Mozart's *Magic Flute*.

with an ascending sixth from $\hat{5}$ *up* to $\hat{3}$ ("Dies Bild-").[20] Yet the phrase in its entirety traverses a descending third, from $\hat{5}$ *down* to $\hat{3}$.

The italicized words in the previous paragraph model familiar ideas about ascent and descent in these passages, ideas that the basic apparatus of our GIS cannot capture. The group of ordinal scale-degree intervals contains only a single element for the interval from $\hat{3}$ to $\hat{5}$ (and only one for its inverse, from $\hat{5}$ to $\hat{3}$). Yet Figures 2.8 and 2.9 make clear that such intervals may be traversed in a variety of ways, and that the distinctions between those traversals are musically important. Dmitri Tymoczko (2009) has offered a suggestive way to model such distinctions, observing that we can conceive of intervals in modular spaces (such as scale-degree space or pitch-class space) as *paths* within those spaces, rather than as *functions* on them, as in a Lewinian GIS.[21] We can use Tymoczko's idea to give formal substance to the distinctions between labels such as 3rd and 6th[-1]. Tymoczko's and Lewin's conceptions need not be considered mutually exclusive, however, as we will see.

Figure 2.10 shows the essence of Tymozcko's intervals-as-paths idea in scale-degree space (we will reintegrate pitch classes in a moment). Figure 2.10(a) illustrates the path traversed by the Tchaikovsky/Pushkin characters in their gestures from $\hat{3}$ to $\hat{5}$: both of them proceed *counterclockwise* around the scale-degree circle, tracing a path from $\hat{3}$ to $\hat{5}$ by passing through (or "over") scale degrees $\hat{2}$, $\hat{1}$, $\hat{7}$, and $\hat{6}$. Tymoczko's idea of traversing a path is especially apt here: both Tatyana and Lensky sing descending scales that explicitly pass through the scale degrees indicated. As

20. Pamina sings the same gesture—now in F major—in the Act II Finale, at "Ta-mi-[no mein!]" [mm. 277–78].
21. Recall that the basic structure of a GIS statement, int(s, t) = i, is that of a familiar function, f(x) = y, with int playing the role of f. As int is a function, it maps any ordered pair of elements from S to a *single* element i in IVLS.

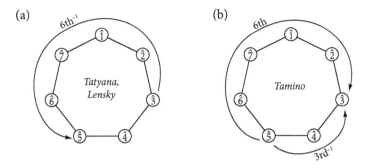

Figure 2.10 Paths in scale-degree space traced by the vocal gestures in Figures 2.8 and 2.9.

shown in Figure 2.10(b), Tamino traverses two different paths from $\hat{5}$ to $\hat{3}$. First he moves clockwise around the scale-degree circle, traversing a sixth up from $\hat{5}$ to $\hat{3}$ with "Dies Bild-," with his acoustic leap passing over scale degrees $\hat{6}$, $\hat{7}$, $\hat{1}$, and $\hat{2}$. Over the course of the phrase, however, he proceeds in the opposite direction, now passing explicitly through $\hat{4}$ as he sings a descending third from $\hat{5}$ to $\hat{3}$: "Dies ... schön, wie ... -seh'n." Note again the counterclockwise motion of the inverse interval, 3rd⁻¹.

This logic works just as well with pitch-class circles (Tymoczko's main focus). Just as we can say that Tatyana traverses a descending sixth in Figure 2.8(a), and a corresponding counterclockwise motion in Figure 2.10(a), we can also say that she traverses a path of nine descending semitones in pc space, or –9, and a corresponding counterclockwise path on a pc clock face. We can thus identify her interval as (6th⁻¹, –9), a label that clearly projects the idea of a descending major 6th. Lensky, by contrast, sings (6th⁻¹, –8), a descending minor 6th, while Tamino sings (6th, 9), an ascending major 6th, at "Dies Bild-."

In short, we can understand inverse interval labels in modular spaces to indicate *counterclockwise motion* around the relevant modular circle. Recto labels lacking inverse signs indicate *clockwise* motion around modular circles. Clockwise and counterclockwise correlate with ideas of *ascent* and *descent*, respectively, allowing us to model those ideas in modular spaces. Tymoczko's intervallic paths also admit of multiple "loops" around a modular space. Thus, one can model a motion of –13 (as distinct from –1) in pitch class space, or a motion of a 10th (as distinct from a 3rd) in scale-degree space. Such paths allow one to distinguish formally between simple and compound intervals in modular spaces.[22]

All of this might suggest that the underlying GIS is wrong for treating (6th⁻¹, –9) and (3rd, 3) as two labels for "the same interval." Indeed, Tymoczko intends his construction as a demonstration that the algebraic, function-based conception of interval enshrined in a GIS is wrong, and that geometric models are more adequate to intervallic experience. There are, however, many instances in tonal music in which

---

22. Formally, Tymoczko's multiple paths in modular spaces are *fiber bundles* on *tangent spaces*. See Tymoczko 2009.

the more abstract algebraic structure of the GIS is highly appropriate. Consider, for example, the bass voice in a V–I cadence. We regularly describe the bass in such a cadence as projecting a "descending fifth," even if the sounding bass line ascends by fourth. In this context, it makes good sense to say that (5th⁻¹, –7), a descending perfect fifth, and (4th, 5), an ascending perfect fourth, are two manifestations of "the same underlying interval." Similarly, the bass line in a descending-fifth sequence typically alternates between descending fifths and ascending fourths. There is nevertheless a sense in which the underlying diatonic intervals at each sequential stage are functionally the same—this is what we mean when we call such sequences "descending-fifth sequences." This is true even when the bass traces out *stepwise* ascending fourths in alternation with stepwise descending fifths. Despite the fact that such stepwise lines explicitly traverse different paths in scale-degree space, there is an underlying harmonic sense in which the sequence iterates a repeated harmonic interval at each stage. Such situations are not limited to root motion. The ascending sixths in the melody that opens Brahms's Fourth are at once obviously distinct from the descending thirds that surround them, and at the same time participants in a more abstract chain of repeated iterations of "the same underlying interval."

Intervals-as-group-elements are more abstract than intervals-as-paths. While Tymoczko's paths capture the alternation of fourths and fifths in a descending-fifth sequence, or sixths and thirds in the Brahms, the group elements abstract away from such paths, leaving more general intervals that may be realized in a variety of ways. It would be wrong to exclude either of these conceptual levels: to deny that fourths and fifths (or thirds and sixths) can play equivalent roles in some contexts or, conversely, to argue that distinctions between specific manifestations of those intervals are unimportant.

We can express the idea formally: each group element of IVLS represents *an equivalence class of intervallic paths*. Two paths are equivalent if they can connect the same two elements in the space S. Thus, (3rd, 3), (6th⁻¹, –9), and (10th, 15), to list only a few possibilities, are equivalent in that they can all span the same two elements in the space, say ($\hat{3}$, E) and ($\hat{5}$, G). A single group element in IVLS bundles these various intervallic paths together into a single equivalence class. In the present example, we could call that equivalence class "the ascending minor third, along with its inversions and compounds." To the extent that such an abstract class of intervals makes good musical sense, we are justified in retaining the algebraic generality of the GIS. Further, such equivalence classes allow us to make formally explicit the notion that intervallic paths like (5th, 7) and (4th⁻¹, –5) are closely related to one another— and in some contexts interchangeable—in a way that, say, (5th, 7) and (6th⁻¹, –9) are not. The path-based conception, taken alone, asserts no such equivalencies.

It is interesting to speculate on the phenomenological distinctions between equivalent sd/pc paths. Some such distinctions are obvious and aurally immediate, such as that between (3rd, 3), an ascending minor third, and (6th⁻¹, –9), a descending major sixth. The experiential distinction between (3rd, 3) and (10th, 15) is also clear, though one might wonder if the compound/simple contrast is as experientially crisp as that between ascending and descending intervals. Indeed, when tonal intervals become especially large, musicians may find their experience of them to be one not of multiply compounded intervals, as Tymoczko's looping-path conception seems to suggest, but instead of "acoustically expanded" simple intervals. Hearing, say, a very low C and a very high G, it seems unlikely that most musicians would experience a precisely defined compound interval—having an apperception of, say, a perfect thirty-third. Rather, most would likely have a sense of a perfect fifth in some very wide acoustic spacing. (The fact that one rarely encounters interval names larger than elevenths in traditional tonal theories attests to this.) To take a specific musical example, when I am faced with the vertiginous intervals in mm. 118–19 of the second movement of Beethoven's op. 111, I tend to experience massively expanded versions of simple ordinal intervals, in the manner just described, rather than massively *compounded* ordinal intervals. This is in part due to the variation process—the theme has already been heard several times in more compact form—but it also arises from the difficulty of "counting that many octaves," or better, of *experiencing* the number of octaves in question in any way more precise than "a lot."

The op. 111 passage also provides a fascinating instance in which an interval label with conflicting path directions might be appropriate. On the downbeat of m. 118, the left hand plays G1; the right hand plays E♭6; the local tonal context is a fleeting E♭ major. The E♭ is the local $\hat{1}$ and the root of a tonic harmony; the G is the local $\hat{3}$ and the third of the tonic harmony. One of the ways I tend to experience this interval is as a species of abstract major third from the soprano to the bass. This is a conceptually *ascending* hearing, even though it spans a yawning descending interval in acoustic space. We can capture the ascending-3rd aspect of the hearing in the scale-degree path, and its yawning acoustic descent in the pc path. Thus, hearing from root to third, I experience something like the interval (3rd, –56). I experience only "something like" that interval because I am not at all sure that I have any authentic experience of –56 as a path in pc space as opposed to, say, "–8 plus several octaves." The crucial formal point is that the group element in IVLS bundles together all of the relevant possibilities, allowing in this case for a certain indeterminacy when it comes to the precise acoustic size of the interval (and its corresponding path in pc space). Despite my uncertainty about paths in pc space, I do not have *any* uncertainty about the fact that I am experiencing a species of (abstractly ascending) major third. That apperception is exactly what the group element captures.

In summary, we may use ascending and descending interval labels in the present GIS when we wish to suggest ideas of ascent, descent, and compound intervals. Such labels imply a formal structure that goes above and beyond the abstract, function-based structure of the GIS, tracing precise paths among its elements in the manner of Tymoczko's paths in pc space.[23] When path direction is not a concern, I will simply employ ascending labels within one octave (such as those at the borders of Figure 2.3).

23. An important caveat: Tymoczko conceives of such paths as moving through a theoretically continuous space. GIS spaces, by contrast, are not continuous; they are instead made up of distinct elements (in the present case, the 84 ordered pairs of the form (sd, pc)). To fully formalize the notion of a path in any GIS, one would need to clarify that such paths move via discrete steps through the space by means of some privileged unit generator[s], in a manner analogous to the paths traversed in Gollin 2000. Gollin's dissertation would indeed provide a useful apparatus for further formalizing the idea of paths in the context of the present GIS, though I will not undertake such formal development here. I thank Dmitri Tymoczko for his clarifying comments along these lines.

2.4 Sets (I)

A *set* in any GIS is a finite subset of elements from the space S (*GMIT*, 88). We can construct many musically intuitive and analytically useful sets in the present sd/pc GIS. Figure 2.11 displays four such sets, each of them involving a C-major chord. As the figure makes clear, the GIS allows us to distinguish between C-major chords in various tonal contexts: C major as IV-in-G-major is a *distinct set in the GIS* from the same chord as I-in-C-major, or as III-in-A-minor, and so on.[24] In a similar manner, Figure 2.12 presents three sets involving A-minor chords. Figure 2.12(c) differs from 2.12(a) and (b) not only in tonal context; it also differs in interval structure, as we will see. It is not even an "A-minor chord" in the traditional sense, but a dissonant collection of pitch classes 9, 0, and 4 in a C♯-minor context. We will encounter this very chord in a Liszt example to be discussed in Figures 2.31 and 2.32.

(a)
$$\left\{\begin{array}{c}(\hat{5}, G)\\(\hat{3}, E)\\(\hat{1}, C)\end{array}\right\}$$
I in C major

(b)
$$\left\{\begin{array}{c}(\hat{1}, G)\\(\hat{6}, E)\\(\hat{4}, C)\end{array}\right\}$$
IV in G major

(c)
$$\left\{\begin{array}{c}(\hat{7}, G)\\(\hat{5}, E)\\(\hat{3}, C)\end{array}\right\}$$
III in A minor

(d)
$$\left\{\begin{array}{c}(\hat{3}, G)\\(\hat{1}, E)\\(\hat{6}, C)\end{array}\right\}$$
VI in E minor

Figure 2.11 Four distinct sets in the sd/pc GIS all involving a C-major triad.

(a)
$$\left\{\begin{array}{c}(\hat{5}, 4)\\(\hat{3}, 0)\\(\hat{1}, 9)\end{array}\right\}$$
i in A minor

(b)
$$\left\{\begin{array}{c}(\hat{3}, 4)\\(\hat{1}, 0)\\(\hat{6}, 9)\end{array}\right\}$$
vi in C major

(c)
$$\left\{\begin{array}{c}(\hat{3}, 4)\\(\hat{7}, 0)\\(\hat{6}, 9)\end{array}\right\}$$
a dissonant chord
in C♯ minor

Figure 2.12 Three distinct sets in the sd/pc GIS all involving the pitch classes 9, 0, and 4.

24. It should be stressed that this is a somewhat simplified notion of what it means for a collection of scale degrees to project a Roman numeral harmony. In sophisticated theories of tonal music, not all collections of scale degrees $\hat{1}$, $\hat{3}$, and $\hat{5}$ are "I chords"; nor are all collections of scale degrees $\hat{6}$, $\hat{1}$, and $\hat{3}$ "VI chords"; and so on. In Chapter 3, we will develop refinements that will allow us to distinguish between roots, subsidiary chord members, and nonchord tones.

We can calculate the interval content of any set in our GIS by using Lewin's IFUNC (*GMIT*, 88ff). IFUNC(X, Y)(i) counts the number of times interval i is spanned from set X to set Y; IFUNC(X, X)(i) counts the number of times interval i is spanned within set X itself. Using IFUNC(X, X)(i), and letting i range over all of the elements of IVLS, we can gain a picture of the complete interval content of set X in a manner loosely analogous to Forte's interval vector.[25] The easiest way to display such information for sets from the present GIS is by using the grid representation of IVLS from Figure 2.5. Figure 2.13(a) shows the results for IFUNC(triad, triad)(i), in which "triad" stands for any of the sets shown in 2.11(a)–(d), as well as those in 2.12(a) and (b). The grid displays IFUNC values when we let i range over all of the members of IVLS. If a cell is blank, IFUNC yields no instances of that interval; numbers within cells indicate the number of times each interval appears.[26] As the figure makes visually clear, all of the intervals contained in the triads in question reside in the white boxes of the grid, which we used above to label traditional harmonic consonances. Compare Figure 2.13(b), which shows the results for IFUNC(dissAm, dissAm)(i), in which "dissAm" is the set shown in Figure 2.12(c)—the "dissonant A-minor chord" in a C♯-minor context. Compared with 2.13(a), four of the intervals have shifted horizontally within the IVLS grid of 2.13(b), slipping out of their consonant cells into (enharmonically equivalent) dissonant cells.

One can construct sets corresponding to a vast array of tonal harmonies and scalar collections. All such sets include a defined tonal context; sets made up of the same pcs but different scale-degree qualia are distinct sets within the GIS. Thus, we can distinguish between

(1) V⁷ in F: {(5̂, 0), (7̂, 4), (2̂, 7), (4̂, t)};
(2) V⁷/IV in C: {(1̂, 0), (3̂, 4), (5̂, 7), (7̂, t)}; and
(3) Ger. 6 in E minor: {(6̂, 0), (1̂, 4), (3̂, 7), (4̂, t)}.[27]

Sets (1) and (2) have the same interval content; set (3) differs. (The interested reader can produce and compare the relevant IFUNC tables.) We can further define scalar sets like

(a) C major: {(1̂, 0), (2̂, 2), (3̂, 4), (4̂, 5), (5̂, 7), (6̂, 9), (7̂, e)};
(b) A natural minor: {(1̂, 9), (2̂, e), (3̂, 0), (4̂, 2), (5̂, 4), (6̂, 5), (7̂, 7)};
(c) F Lydian: {(1̂, 5), (2̂, 7), (3̂, 9), (4̂, e), (5̂, 0), (6̂, 2), (7̂, 4)};
(d) A melodic minor ↑: {(1̂, 9), (2̂, e), (3̂, 0), (4̂, 2), (5̂, 4), (6̂, 6), (7̂, 8)};
(e) D acoustic: {(1̂, 2), (2̂, 4), (3̂, 6), (4̂, 8), (5̂, 9), (6̂, e), (7̂, 0)};
(f) C "Gypsy minor":   {(1̂, 0), (2̂, 2), (3̂, 3), (4̂, 6), (5̂, 7), (6̂, 8), (7̂, e)}.

25. On the looseness of this analogy, see Lewin 1977 and *GMIT*, 104ff.
26. Note that IFUNC yields a tally of *directed* intervals (that is, GIS intervals), not interval classes in the Fortean sense. IFUNC thus counts intervals and their inversions separately, as is visually apparent in Figures 2.13(a) and (b).
27. Sets (2), (3), and the set in Figure 2.12(c) involve chromatically altered scale degrees. Section 2.7 presents a formalism (and notation) for modeling such chromatic alterations.

(a)

sdints

	e	2nd	3rd	4th	5th	6th	7th
0	3						
1							
2							
3			1				
4			1				
5				1			
6							
7					1		
8						1	
9						1	
10							
11							

pcints

(b)

sdints

	e	2nd	3rd	4th	5th	6th	7th
0	3						
1							
2							
3		1					
4				1			
5				1			
6							
7					1		
8					1		
9							1
10							
11							

pcints

Figure 2.13 The results for IFUNC(X, X)(i) as i ranges over all 84 elements of IVLS in the sd/pc GIS, with X defined as: (a) a major or minor triad (cf. the four sets in Figure 2.11 or the two sets in Figure 2.12(a) and (b)); (b) the "dissonant A-minor chord" in Figure 2.12(c).

Scales (a), (b), and (c) all have the same pc content and the same interval content, as do scales (d) and (e). They are all nevertheless distinct sets in the sd/pc GIS.

Though I have made observations above about interval content, the reader will note that I have not referred to any two sets as being "of the same type" or "of the same set class." This is because we have not yet defined a group of canonical operations that could lend formal meaning to the idea "of the same set type." To do so, we must first define basic transposition and inversion operators in our GIS. We can then explore some possible canonical groups and the set types to which they give rise. We will undertake that work in sections 2.9, 2.10, and 2.11.

2.5 Pivot Intervals

Figure 2.14 reproduces the sets from Figure 2.11(a) and 2.11(b). As the arrow shows, a special kind of interval links the two sets, which we will call a *pivot interval*. Pivot intervals are of the form $(n, 0)$, in which n is some scale-degree interval. Such intervals register a change in scale-degree quale, but no change in pitch-class chroma. Pivot intervals trace out horizontal motions on the sd/pc grid of Figure 2.3;[28] they are all located in the top row of the IVLS grid of Figure 2.5. As Figure 2.14 shows, the specific pivot interval that links C:I to G:IV is (4th, 0), which we will informally call a "pivot 4th."

Pivots such as that in Figure 2.14 are of course ubiquitous in tonal music, occurring in even the most prosaic contexts. We rarely attend to them closely, nor are we used to conceiving of their effect in intervallic terms. It will thus be helpful to explore some passages in which the pivot is highlighted or dramatized, allowing us to develop and intensify our sense of the intervallic experience in question. Opera is a good place to begin. Figure 2.15 sketches some key passages from the first 178 bars of Act III of *Götterdämmerung*. The act begins with Siegfried's horn call (he is on his ill-fated hunting trip with Hagen). At m. 51, a graceful 9/8 dance associated with the Rhine daughters begins; note the characteristic added-sixth sonorities, which are labeled T^{+6} in the figure.[29] After a grand pause in m. 176, the daughters, now sirens, sing the first syllable of Siegfried's name to an {A♭, C, F} chord. Given the big dominant of F heard in mm. 172–75, and all of the F-based music we have heard since the outset of the act, the chord at first sounds like i in F minor. Yet, over the second half of m. 177—as we hear the planing six-three chords of the daughters' beguiling dance rebegin—the chord morphs from a menacing tonic into a seductive added-sixth in A♭ major. It is an exquisite effect: the

Figure 2.14 A "pivot 4th" from I in C major to IV in G major.

---

28. A pivot interval in fact connects the two heard scale degrees indicated on Figure 2.3, which refer back to Figures 2.1 and 2.2: $(\hat{1}, 9)$ and $(\hat{7}, 9)$. Specifically, $int((\hat{1}, 9), (\hat{7}, 9)) = (7th, 0)$.
29. The emphasis on $\hat{6}$ derives from the "Rheingold!" motive, first heard in *Das Rheingold*, Scene 1. See section 3.8 for an exploration of that music (from a very different analytical angle).

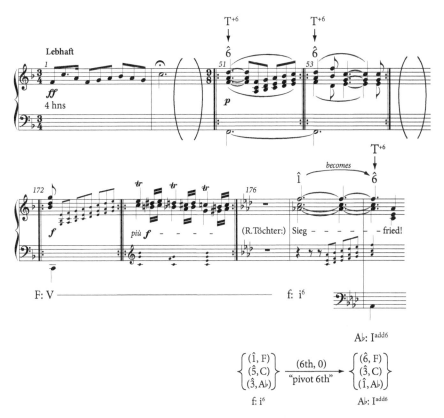

Figure 2.15 Wagner, *Götterdämmerung*, Act III, mm. 1–178.

listener pivots aurally at the very moment that Siegfried pivots on stage, on hearing his name—a classic Wagnerian "deed of music made visible." The specific pivot interval here is a "pivot 6th," or (6th, 0). The meaning of "6th" becomes evident if one attends to any single pitch in the chord. The highest pitch, F, for example, shifts "up a sixth" on an imaginary scale of qualia, morphing from $\hat{1}$ into a shimmering $\hat{6}$. The F-minor chord is thus audibly transformed over the course of mm. 177–78, though its sounding pitches do not change. The present technology offers an elegant model of such transformations.

Verdi offers us many opportunities to attend to pivot intervals. Figure 2.16 shows the end of the furtive duettino between Nannetta and Fenton in Act I of *Falstaff*. Fenton begins a couplet from Boccaccio's *Decameron*, which Nannetta completes from the other side of the stage as they quickly part. The sustained A♭ in the oboe acts locally as $\hat{5}$ in D♭ minor; the global key is A♭ major.[30] Nannetta

30. The D♭ tonicity of the "Bocca baciata" music is confirmed at the beginning of Act III, Scene 2 (mm. 42–48). There the couplet is expanded to a tercet that cadences in D♭ major, complete with five-flat key signature.

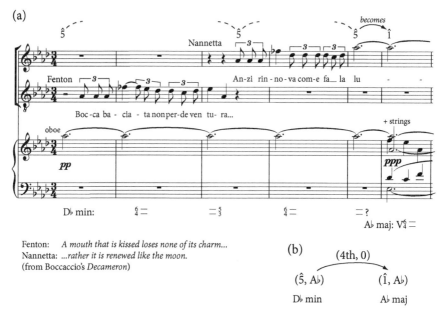

Figure 2.16 Verdi, *Falstaff,* Act I, part 2, beginning 2 bars after rehearsal 36.

comes to rest on that Ab on the first syllable of "luna," prodding the strings to enter. As they do, the tonal context shifts around her held pitch, from Db minor back to Ab major, transforming her hovering $\hat{5}$ into $\hat{1}$ via a pivot 4th. The pivot reinvests the sung pitch with tonic security, elegantly capturing the idea of renewal (*anzi rinnova*) in Boccaccio's sonnet.[31]

Figure 2.17(a) shows a passage from the Finale ultimo of *La traviata*. At the beginning of the excerpt (mm. 44–45), Germont cadences on V of A minor. Violetta enters in the orchestral pause with a conventional octave leap on the dominant pitch, E. Rather than continuing in A minor, however, she pivots to C♯ minor, her sustained E now taking on the quale of $\hat{3}$ in that key. The pivot is (3rd^{-1}, 0), a qualitative sinking of a third. (Here we rely on an inverse label—and its implied path in sd space—to capture the idea of descent.) The looseness of the resulting harmonic transition, a seemingly irrational slip between major-third-related minor keys, is suggestive of the tenuous thread of Violetta's consciousness. It also marks a shift in dramatic perspective from the agitated Germonts, *père et fils,* to the increasingly seraphic heroine. Figure 2.17(b) shows a similar effect in the seam between Philippe's scena and aria at the beginning of Act IV of *Don Carlos*;[32] now the effect is tied to the king's brooding nocturnal state. As in *La traviata,* the oboe plays a central role, and again the pivot interval spans two minor keys related by major

31. On the potentially bawdy connotations of *anzi rinnova,* see Hepokoski 1983, 29.
32. Act III in the later four-act Italian revisions.

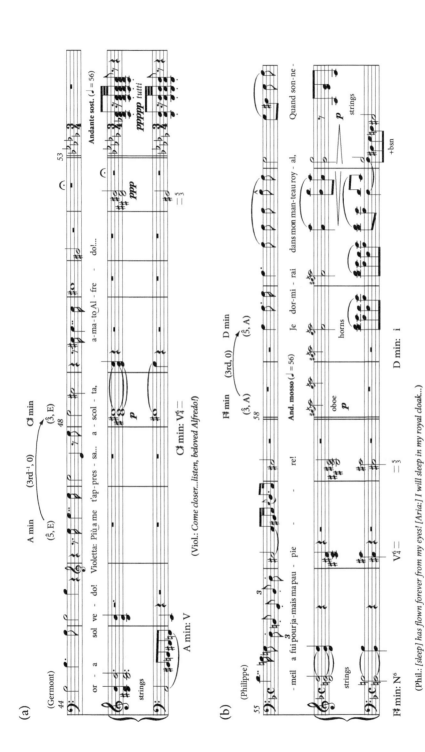

Figure 2.17 (a) Verdi, *La traviata*, Act III; (b) Verdi, *Don Carlos*, Act IV.

(Viol.: *Come closer...listen, beloved Alfredo!*)

(Phil.: *[sleep] has flown forever from my eyes! [Aria:] I will sleep in my royal cloak...*)

third. Moreover, the same two scale degrees are involved, $\hat{3}$ and $\hat{5}$, but now they sound in the reverse order, yielding the inverse of the pivot in *traviata:* (3rd, 0).

Such operatic examples—many more could be adduced[33]—allow us to focus on dramatically highlighted pivot intervals, developing our sense of their specific intervallic qualities. Having done so, we can now turn to some instrumental examples. Figure 2.18 shows the motivic link between Chopin's sixth and seventh preludes in op. 28. The curling three-note figure that crowns the melody of the B-minor Prelude is transformed by a pivot 2nd into the gesture that begins the waltz-like A-major Prelude.

Figure 2.19 explores pivot (and other) intervals within the first movement of Mozart's B♭-major Piano Sonata, K. 333. Figure 2.19(a) shows the final cadence of the exposition, which is followed first by the repeated exposition (above) and then by the development (below). Several motivic dyads are identified above the staves, with sd and pc elements aligned vertically in the interest of space. Figures 2.19(b) and (c) trace certain striking intervallic relationships between these dyads, showing ways in which the final cadential gesture of the exposition echoes into the following music. As shown in 2.19(b), the cadential appoggiatura (or implicit suspension) G–F that ends the exposition echoes immediately as the opening incipit dyad in the exposition repeat. In the cadence, the G–F dyad projects $\hat{2}$–$\hat{1}$, while in the incipit the dyad manifests the sonata's motivic $\hat{6}$–$\hat{5}$. The interval that links the two dyads is (5th, 0), a pivot 5th. The connection is underscored by the alto-register F–G motion in the left hand in m. 1, indicated in parentheses on Figure 2.19(a), which retrogrades the cadential

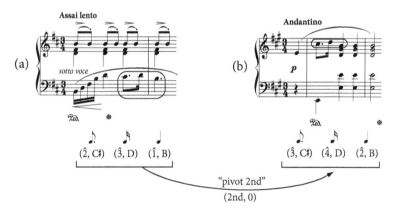

Figure 2.18 Chopin, Preludes, op. 28: (a) no. 6 in B minor; (b) no. 7 in A major.

33. The interested reader may wish to compare the Verdi passages in Figure 2.17 with *Tristan,* Act II, Scene 3, mm. 1807–9 (the seam between King Mark's phrases "Da ließ er's denn so sein" and "Dies wundervolle Weib"). The interval is once again (3rd^{-1}, 0), as in *La traviata,* the scale degrees are once again $\hat{3}$ and $\hat{5}$, and those degrees once again belong to minor keys related by major third (D minor and F♯ minor, as in *Don Carlos*). A sustained double reed is involved as well, now an English horn. Such dramatically highlighted pivots seem almost to attain the status of a topic in late Romantic opera, German and Italian; examples are legion not only in Wagner and Strauss but also in the works of the *giovane scuola*. For a wonderfully garish instance of the latter, see Alfano's completion of *Turandot,* Act III, Scene 2, five and six bars after rehearsal 53.

(a)

(b)

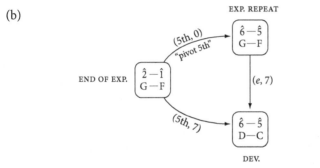

(c)

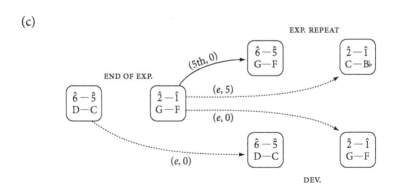

Figure 2.19 Mozart, Piano Sonata in B♭, K. 333.

G–F dyad in its original register. An additional prograde echo occurs in the higher octave, sounding across the bar line between mm. 1 and 2 (marked in 2.19(a)).

Figure 2.19(b) identifies two additional intervals. A perfect fifth (5th, 7) links the cadential dyad to the incipit dyad of the development. The development's incipit dyad itself resides an interval of $(e, 7)$ from the exposition's incipit. An interval of this form—(e, n), in which n is any pc interval—marks a change in pc chroma but no change in sd quale, the conceptual inverse of a pivot. These intervals correspond to *real transpositions,* discussed in section 2.9. Figure 2.19(c) shows more intervals linking the exposition's cadential gestures with events at the opening of the exposition and development. Among these are two instances of the identity element $(e, 0)$, indicating an especially strong echo between the cadential figure and the opening of the development. One could trace further motivic pivot transformations of the incipit dyad throughout the movement; especially suggestive would be an exploration of the secondary theme and its network of relationships with the primary theme, and with the movement's myriad cadential appoggiaturas.

Figure 2.20 explores some intervallic relationships in the initial subject–answer pair of the D♯-minor fugue from *WTC I.* The subject derives its quiet energy from its two leaps, bracketed below the staff of Figure 2.20(a). Leap one in the subject $(L1^S)$ is an ascending perfect fifth, while leap two $(L2^S)$ is an ascending perfect fourth. $L2^S$ at once echoes $L1^S$ and differs from it; it is a fourth, not a fifth, and it ebbs away toward the cadence, in contrast to the initiating surge of $L1^S$. The two leaps in the answer initially seem to resemble one another much more closely than do the leaps in the subject: due to the adjustment required by the tonal answer, $L1^A$ and $L2^A$ both span a perfect fourth between the same two pitches, A♯4 and D♯5. But Bach rather miraculously manages to maintain a sense of contrast between them due to the shifting tonal context: while $L1^A$ clearly sounds as $\hat{5}$–$\hat{1}$ in D♯ minor, confirming the key and the authentic division of the D♯4–D♯5 octave, $L2^A$ projects $\hat{1}$–$\hat{4}$ in A♯ minor, as the second half of the answer wends its way toward the cadence.[34] $L1^A$ and $L2^A$ thus relate via a pivot 4th, as shown in 2.20(b). This pivot 4th provides a subtle echo of the various acoustic fourths in the subject and answer. Figure 2.20(c) shows some additional intervals between the four leaps; ret means "retrograde." The network of 2.20(c) begins to convey a sense of the kaleidoscopic interrelations among Bach's leaps. Those interrelations become progressively denser and richer as the fugue passes through its various demonstrations of stretto, inversion, and augmentation.

A final pivot example: Figure 2.21(a) shows the link between the second and third movements of Beethoven's Third Piano Concerto, op. 37. The slow movement ends with a *tutti* E-major chord. As the piano begins the rondo theme that follows, it picks up the prominent {G♯5, B5} played by the first violins in that chord and recasts it as {A♭5, B5} in C minor. As shown in the network of

---

34. The listener's shift of commitment from D♯ minor to A♯ minor likely occurs somewhere within m. 4. As that bar lacks leading tones for *either* key, it exudes a mildly archaic, modal air. But one's ear easily settles on A♯ as tonic from beat three of the bar forward, the melodic C♯ (not C×) making a continued D♯-minor hearing untenable.

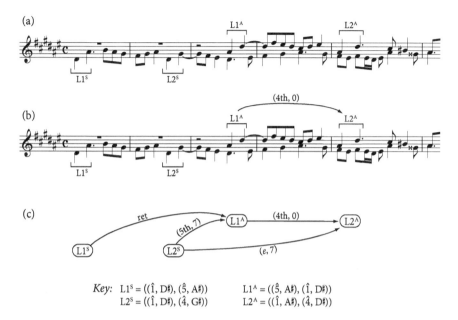

Key: $L1^S = ((\hat{1}, D\sharp), (\hat{5}, A\sharp))$ $L1^A = ((\hat{5}, A\sharp), (\hat{1}, D\sharp))$
       $L2^S = ((\hat{1}, D\sharp), (\hat{4}, G\sharp))$ $L2^A = ((\hat{1}, A\sharp), (\hat{4}, D\sharp))$

Figure 2.20 Bach, Fugue in D♯ minor, *WTC I*.

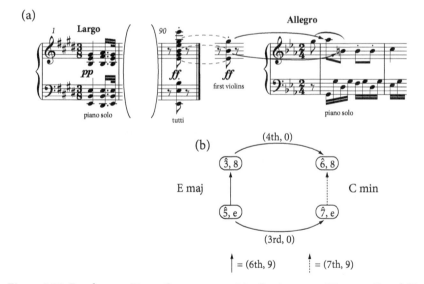

Figure 2.21 Beethoven, Piano Concerto no. 3 in C minor, op. 37, mvts. ii and iii.

Figure 2.21(b), the two common tones traverse different pivot intervals: G♯/A♭ traverses a pivot 4th, while B traverses a pivot 3rd. As a result, the harmonic interval between the two pitches changes: a consonant major sixth (6th, 9) in the slow movement becomes a dissonant diminished seventh (7th, 9) in the rondo.

2.6 Other Modulatory Intervals

Pivot intervals are one particular kind of *modulatory interval:* an sd/pc interval that spans a change in key. There are many more such modulatory intervals, and they can best be introduced by analogy to pivot intervals. Consider Figure 2.22(a), which shows the opening of the fandango theme in Schumann's First Piano Sonata, op. 11; Figure 2.22(b) sketches aspects of the passage's harmony. As the annotations below the staff of 2.22(b) show, Schumann's harmonically restless theme suggests three different fifth-related keys as it unfolds: F♯ minor, then C♯ minor, then G♯ minor.[35] Yet there is a striking element of continuity: the harmonies, when interpreted in Riemannian fashion, trace a *T–S–D–T* progression across those keys. More striking still, a *single* chord is gradually transformed so that it can serve each of those roles—the strummed, syncopated harmony around which the fandango theme weaves. The F♯-minor tonic triad, first sounded in m. 54, accrues a D♯ in m. 56, throwing its status as *T* in F♯ minor into doubt and seemingly transforming it into an added-sixth subdominant in C♯ minor. At m. 58, however, the chord is chromatically inflected to become a D♯ dominant seventh chord, strongly suggesting G♯ minor (which arrives later in m. 58, though over a dominant pedal, just like the F♯-minor tonic of m. 54). While the annotations below 2.22(b) capture this progression of keys and functions, they do not capture the ways in which a single harmony is minimally transformed to effect them, nor do they capture the ways in which the tonal qualia of the sustained pitches morph in the process. As Figure 2.22(c) demonstrates, the F♯-minor triad passes through a pivot 4th as a result of the added D♯ in m. 56, which momentarily invests the notes with scale-degree qualia in C♯ minor. The {C♯, D♯} dyad, the characteristic dissonance of the S^6 chord, is then transformed via another pivot 4th to become the characteristic dissonance of the dominant seventh of G♯. The bottom two voices of the S^6 chord, however, are inflected by a new kind of interval, labeled (4th, 1) on the figure. Given the context of pervasive pivot 4ths, we might consider this a sort of "skewed pivot 4th," one in which the chroma inches upward by 1 semitone as the quale changes by 4th.

Such skewed pivots are implicit in parsimonious transformations of diatonic scales. Figure 2.23 plots a shift from C major to G major on the sd/pc grid. Vertical

---

35. For suggestive comments on the tonal mobility of the theme, see Lester 1995, 201. In the present discussion, I explore a hearing that responds very credulously to the moment-to-moment tonal implications of each of Schumann's chords. Hearings that are more skeptical of fleeting tonal significers are naturally possible as well.

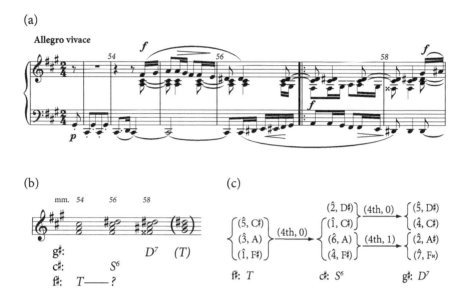

Figure 2.22 Schumann, Piano Sonata no. 1 in F♯ minor, op. 11, mvt. i.

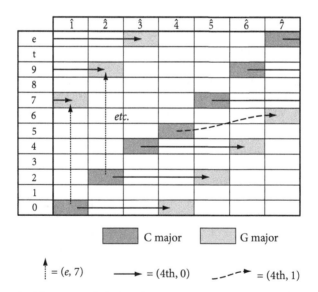

Figure 2.23 A "skew pivot" (4th, 1) in a parsimonious transformation from C major to G major.

dotted arrows show the real-transposition interval $(e, 7)$, which links every degree in C major to the corresponding degree in G major (linking $\hat{1}$ to $\hat{1}$, $\hat{2}$ to $\hat{2}$, etc.). The horizontal arrows, by contrast, show an efficient voice-leading perspective, in which all common tones are transformed by a pivot 4th. The element $(\hat{4}, 5)$ in C major, however, is inflected by semitone, resulting in the skewed pivot (4th, 1), which yields $(\hat{7}, 6)$ in G major. Skewed pivots thus interact in suggestive ways with much recent research on efficient voice leading, providing a phenomenological account of the sd/pc intervals traversed in such contexts. We will explore the interaction of sd/pc intervals and parsimonious transformations in greater analytical depth later in this chapter, in connection with a famous example (section 2.9.2).

Some reflection will make clear that we need not limit modulatory intervals to pivots and skew pivots. A great many sd/pc intervals arise across modulatory seams, many of which involve neither common tones nor semitonal shifts. By way of illustration, Figure 2.24 explores three stepwise dyads in the Aria from the *Goldberg Variations*. Dyad x in 2.24(a) is a simple ascending major second, which resides entirely in G major: $\mathrm{int}((\hat{1}, G), (\hat{2}, A)) = (\text{2nd}, 2)$. Dyad y in 2.24(b), by contrast, spans the first modulation in the piece, from G major to D major. The interval here is not (2nd, 2), but a "modulating whole-step," which actually spans a *fifth* in quale-space: $\mathrm{int}((\hat{3}, B), (\hat{7}, C\sharp)) = (\text{5th}, 2)$. After confirming D with a perfect authentic cadence in m. 16, Bach departs from that key with the bass interval marked z in 2.24(c). C$\sharp$ (the second pitch in interval z) signals the departure from D major, just as the C$\sharp$ in m. 9 (the second pitch of interval y) had signaled its arrival. Notably, interval z is the *formal inverse* of interval y: $\mathrm{int}((\hat{1}, D), (\hat{4}, C\sharp)) = (\text{5th}^{-1}, -2) = (\text{5th}, 2)^{-1} = y^{-1}$. Bach thus "undoes" his modulation with the inverse of the very sd/pc interval that had initiated it. The inverse relationship is made visually explicit on Figure 2.25(a), which plots the three intervals of Figure 2.24 on the sd/pc grid. The mirroring arrows for y and z render visible the inversional relationship of (5th, 2) and $(\text{5th}^{-1}, -2)$. The figure also provides a suggestive comparison between the major second of x and the qualitatively stretched whole steps of y and z, which reach across the horizontal dimension of the space: interval y stretches up to $\hat{7}$, while z relaxes down to $\hat{4}$.

Figure 2.25(b) locates intervals x, y, and z on the IVLS grid first presented as Figure 2.5. A bold border has been added to the grid, creating a diagonal seam

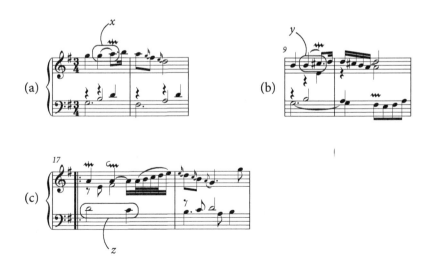

Figure 2.24 Three intervals in the Aria from Bach's *Goldberg Variations*.

(a)

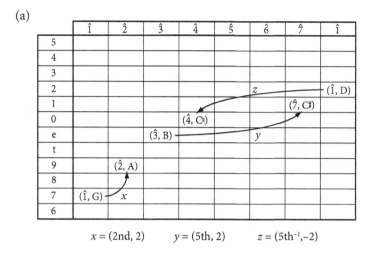

$$x = (2nd, 2) \qquad y = (5th, 2) \qquad z = (5th^{-1}, -2)$$

(b)

sdints

		e	2nd	3rd	4th	5th	6th	7th
	0							
	1							
	2		x			y		
	3							
	4							
pcints	5							
	6							
	7							
	8							
	9							
	10				z			
	11							

Figure 2.25 Intervals x, y, and z from Figure 2.24, plotted (a) in the space S of the sd/pc GIS; and (b) in the IVLS grid of Figure 2.5.

from NW to SE; this border encloses the cells that received traditional tonal labels in Figure 2.5. The intervals within the border arise most naturally within a single key; intervals outside of the border arise most naturally between keys—that is, as modulatory intervals.[36] Interval x resides inside the diagonal seam, while y and z reside outside of it. All of the intervals in IVLS thus have the potential to be

36. The locution "arise most naturally" has been chosen carefully. The intervals outside of the diagonal seam are not intrinsically modulatory, nor are those inside the seam intrinsically "intra-key." What distinguishes modulatory from intra-key intervals is not their absolute location on the grid of 2.25(b) or 2.26(b), but the presence or absence of a change of key (as defined formally in section 2.7) from the first note of the interval to the second. Modulatory and intra-key intervals, so defined,

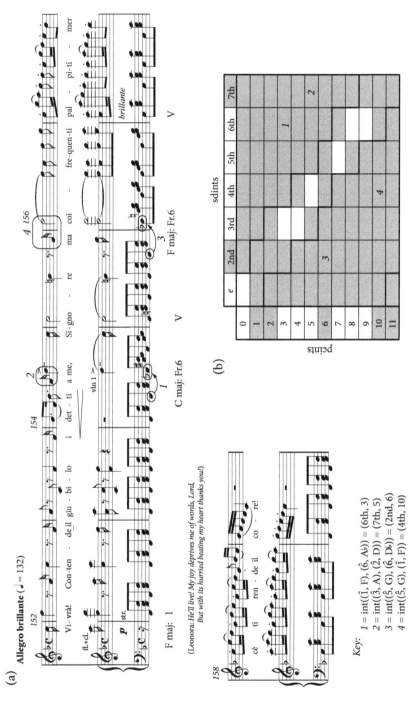

Figure 2.26 Verdi, *Il trovatore*, Act IV, scene 1.

(a) **Allegro brillante** (♩ = 132)

152 Vi-vrà! Con-ten - de il giu - bi - lo *154* i det - ti a me, Si-gno - re *4 156* ma coi - fre-quen-ti pal - pi-ti - mer

fl.+cl. *p* str.

F maj: I

vln 1 >

F maj: I   C maj: Fr.6   V   F maj: Fr.6   V

brillante

(Leonora: *He'll live! My joy deprives me of words, Lord,*
But with its hurried beating my heart thanks you!)

158 cè ti ren - de il co - re!

Key: 1 = int((1̂, F), (6̂, A♭)) = (6th, 3)
         2 = int((3̂, A), (2̂, D)) = (7th, 5)
         3 = int((5̂, G), (6̂, D♭)) = (2nd, 6)
         4 = int((5̂, G), (1̂, F)) = (4th, 10)

(b)

	e	2nd	3rd	4th	5th	6th	7th
0							
1							
2							
3			*1*				
4			*1*				
5				*1*			
6		*3*				*1*	
7							
8							
9						*1*	
10				*4*			
11							*2*

sdints

pcints

analytically meaningful, given the appropriate modulatory context. Rather than offering an exhaustive demonstration, one more example should make the point (and also motivate the following section). Figure 2.26(a) shows the opening of the cabaletta between Leonora and Di Luna from the final act of *Il trovatore*. The phrase is notable for its two French sixth chords, unusual in the typically diatonic world of the *cabaletta brillante*. The first French sixth sounds in the key of the dominant in m. 154, the second sounds back in the tonic in m. 156. The figure labels four intervals, two each in bass and soprano: intervals 1 and 2 span the shift to the dominant key (C major) at the first French sixth; intervals 3 and 4 span the shift back to the tonic (F major) at the second French sixth. The four resulting sd/pc intervals are identified in the key at the bottom of the example, and are shown on the IVLS grid in 2.26(b). Note that all four intervals reside outside of the NW–SE seam that contains the traditional intra-key intervals.

Figure 2.26 hears a genuine change of key in the cabaletta. But what if one hears the passage with *no* such change, instead experiencing all of its chromatic pitches as inflections of scale degrees in F? The question makes clear that the idea of "key" is thus far undertheorized in our model. We now address that deficiency.

2.7 Keys

To "hear in a key" is, among other things, to establish a momentarily fixed relationship between scale-degree quale and pitch-class chroma—to invest certain pitch classes with privileged status, as diatonic representatives of certain scale degrees. We can think of this as a sort of "fusing" between tonal quale and pc chroma: within a given key, each scale degree is fused to a particular pitch class as its diatonic representative. All "nonfused" pitch classes then become chromatic inflections of those fused sd/pc pairs—quite literally, deviations in chroma from the diatonic pcs.

We can formalize this idea elegantly in the context of the present GIS. We will define a *key* as an ordered septuple (diapc$_1$, diapc$_2$, diapc$_3$, diapc$_4$, diapc$_5$, diapc$_6$, diapc$_7$), in which diapc$_n$ is the diatonic pitch class corresponding to scale degree $\hat{n}$. Thus, the key of C major is the ordered septuple (0, 2, 4, 5, 7, 9, e); the key of F major is the septuple (5, 7, 9, t, 0, 2, 4). We will define minor keys using the natural minor collection; raised scale degrees $\hat{6}$ or $\hat{7}$ will be modeled as chromatic inflections. Thus, the key of A minor is the septuple (9, e, 0, 2, 4, 5, 7); F♯ minor is the septuple (6, 8, 9, e, 1, 2, 4); and so on. A formal key in the present context is thus an ordered set of seven referential pitch classes.[37]

"arise most naturally" in the quadrants indicated on 2.25(b) and 2.26(b), but not exclusively. In exceptional cases, certain intervals within the bold border can arise in modulatory contexts, just as certain intervals outside of that border can arise within a single key (as, for example, on the rare occasion when one experiences a doubly diminished or doubly augmented interval within a key; see section 2.8).

37. One could also define keys using modal collections or more exotic seven-element scales. The formalism is identical. We will not pursue such possibilities here, however.

We now define a function acc_n, which assigns accidentals to pcs by calculating a given pc's interval from its referential diatonic pc: $acc_n(pc) = int(diapc_n, pc)$.[38] In this formula, pc is any sounding pitch class; $diapc_n$ is the diatonic pitch class for scale degree $\hat{n}$ in some defined key septuple; int maps the pair into the group of ordered pc intervals (i.e., pcints). The function thus measures the chromatic interval from $diapc_n$ to any sounding pc.[39] NB: whenever we apply acc_n to some sounding pc we are assuming that the given pc is heard as an instance of scale degree $\hat{n}$. If it is heard as an instance of some *different* scale degree, say scale degree $\hat{m}$, we apply acc_m. An example will clarify. Let us assume the key of E♭ major—formally, the septuple (3, 5, 7, 8, t, 0, 2). We hear pc 4 and experience it in one context as a raised $\hat{1}$; formally, we apply acc_1. Thus $diapc_1 = 3$, pc = 4, and $acc_1(4) = int(3, 4) = 1$. The mod-12 integer 1 captures the idea that the sounding pc is "raised" by one semitone with respect to its diatonic point of reference. Now imagine that we once again hear pc 4 in E♭ major, but experience it this time (in a new context) as a lowered $\hat{2}$. We therefore apply acc_2. Thus: $acc_2(4) = int(5, 4) = 11$. The mod-12 integer 11 (or −1 mod 12) registers the idea that the sounding pc is "lowered" one semitone with respect to its diatonic point of reference.[40]

To make the idea of chromatic alterations notationally immediate, we will translate the integers mod 12 generated by acc_n into familiar accidental symbols: 0 = ♮, 1 = ♯, 2 = ×, 11 = ♭, 10 = ♭♭ and so on.[41] Note that these accidental symbols represent chromatic inflections of heard scale degrees, not notated sharps, flats, or naturals.

Having defined a key and the function acc_n, we can now define a *diatonically oriented heard scale degree* as the ordered triple (acc_n, sd_n, pc). The raised $\hat{1}$ in E♭ major discussed above is the triple (♯, $\hat{1}$, 4), while the lowered $\hat{2}$ in the same key is the triple (♭, $\hat{2}$, 4). As the ordered-triple notation is potentially unwieldy in networks and other graphic contexts, we will compress it by placing the accidental to the immediate left of the scale degree, if it is a sharp or flat, or removing it altogether if it is a natural. Thus, the triples above will be notated (♯$\hat{1}$, 4) and (♭$\hat{2}$, 4).[42]

Given these technologies, we can treat a key-as-pc-septuple as a sort of aligning field on the 84-element sd/pc grid. Once we have defined such a key, every element

---

38. We can clarify this somewhat unwieldy notation by comparison to the familiar $f(x) = y$: acc_n plays the role of f, and pc plays the role of x. acc_n maps pc to a directed pitch-class interval generated by the GIS formula $int(diapc_n, pc)$.

39. The function acc_n is analogous to Lewin's LABEL function (*GMIT*, 31) with the following difference: rather than assigning a single referential element ref to the set of pcs, the accidental function assigns *seven* such elements, one for each scale degree. These are the seven $diapc_n$, with $n = 1$–7.

40. There are complex phenomenological issues involved here regarding the hearing of pcs as chromatic alterations of one scale degree or another; we will address such matters in connection with the Tchaikovsky analysis in section 2.8.

41. In a somewhat different formal context, Hook (2007c, 101) also translates integers into *n*-tuples of accidentals (though he uses the infinite group of integers, positive, negative, and zero, as opposed to the integers mod 12, as here). The GIS presented in this chapter has interesting points of contact with, and points of divergence from, Hook's model of enharmonicism presented in the cited article, as well as his system of signature transformations (Hook 2008).

42. This notational simplification is analogous to the familiar condensation of the ordered-pair notation for triads: e.g., (C, +) is condensed to C+. The latter notation still implies an ordered pair, just as the condensed scale-degree notation above still implies an ordered triple.

in S—that is, every cell in the grid—is automatically assigned an accidental value by the function acc$_n$, registering its deviation from its column's diatonic pc. Figure 2.27(a) illustrates. The cells corresponding to the diapcs in E♭ major are shaded; accidentals corresponding to the values assigned by acc$_n$ fill every cell. The working of the function is visually evident on the figure (single flats reside one row below shaded cells; single sharps one row above, and so on). In practice, only those cells

(a)

	1̂	2̂	3̂	4̂	5̂	6̂	7̂
2	♭	3♯s	5♭s	6♯s/6♭s	4♯s	×	♮
1	♭♭	4♭s	6♯s/6♭s	5♯s	3♯s	♯	♭
0	3♭s	5♭s	5♯s	4♯s	×	♮	♭♭
e	4♭s	6♯s/6♭s	4♯s	3♯s	♯	♭	3♭s
t	5♭s	5♯s	3♯s	×	♮	♭♭	4♭s
9	6♯s/6♭s	4♯s	×	♯	♭	3♭s	5♭s
8	5♯s	3♯s	♯	♮	♭♭	4♭s	6♯s/6♭s
7	4♯s	×	♮	♭	3♭s	5♭s	5♯s
6	3♯s	♯	♭	♭♭	4♭s	6♯s/6♭s	4♯s
5	×	♮	♭♭	3♭s	5♭s	5♯s	3♯s
4	♯	♭	3♭s	4♭s	6♯s/6♭s	4♯s	×
3	♮	♭♭	4♭s	5♭s	5♯s	3♯s	♯

⬚ = diapcs in E♭ major

(b)

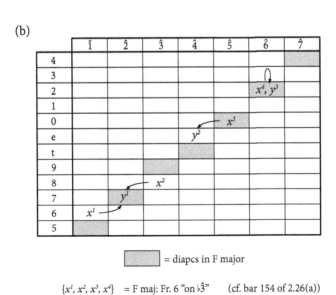

⬚ = diapcs in F major

{x¹, x², x³, x⁴} = F maj: Fr. 6 "on ♭3̂" (cf. bar 154 of 2.26(a))
{y¹, y², y³} = F maj: II♮ (cf. bar 155 of 2.26(a))

Figure 2.27 (a) Diatonic pcs and accidentals in E♭ major; (b) an F-major hearing of two chromatic harmonies from Figure 2.26.

with single sharps or flats will typically apply in analytical contexts. Though we can at least conceive of applying multiple sharps and flats to a *notated pitch*, it is not clear whether we can authentically experience a multiply altered scale degree, even one that is merely doubly raised or doubly lowered. We can thus conceive of diatonically oriented sd/pc spaces such as that in Figure 2.27(a) as shading off into apperceptual improbability the farther one moves from the gray cells of the diatonic pcs, into *n*-tuply raised or lowered scale degrees. We can in fact conceive of this realm of apperceptual improbability as exerting a certain pressure on our hearing, as it obliges us to reconcile sounding pitch classes with the current key septuple, situating heard scale degrees as close as possible to the gray, diatonic cells.

From now on in our analytical work, we will always assume the presence of a key as an aligning field on the space S of the GIS, in the manner of Figure 2.27(a). If the key is obvious, it may not be explicitly indicated on an example; when the key is not obvious, or when there is a change of key, simple annotations will be used to indicate it. For instance, the annotation "F maj" next to a network will indicate that the key orientation for F major, or (5, 7, 9, t, 0, 2, 4), is in effect, with accidentals assigned accordingly via acc$_n$. With this idea in mind, we can return to the cabaletta from *Il trovatore* shown in Figure 2.26(a). That analysis heard a genuine change of key in the passage, from F major to C major and back, a change signaled by the sequenced French sixth chords. The hearing thus assumed a change from the orienting key septuple of F major to that for C major, and back. If we instead choose to hear the entire passage in F major, we can now interpret the French sixth in m. 154 as an altered harmony in that key. Specifically, {A♭, C, D, F♯} becomes a French sixth "on ♭$\hat{3}$," which resolves to a II♯ chord in F, as shown in Figure 2.27(b). When looking at the figure, one can visually imagine the field of accidentals from 2.27(a). This makes clear that pitch x^1, the F♯ in m. 154 of the Verdi, is a raised $\hat{1}$ in this hearing, while x^2, the A♭ in the same chord, is a lowered $\hat{3}$.

We can now take stock of the current stage of formal development. Our GIS has acquired two new formal components: key septuples and the function acc$_n$. We can thus define the GIS, call it GIS$_{Tonal}$, as an ordered quintuple: (S, IVLS, int, keys, acc$_n$). The first three elements are standard to any GIS; we explored their workings in the present GIS in section 2.2. The fourth component, keys, is the set of 24 major and minor key septuples. The fifth component is the acc$_n$ function, which operates as defined above. Any formal statement made with this GIS thus assumes not only the familiar interrelationships among S, IVLS, and int, but also the presence of a key septuple and the activity of acc$_n$, which assigns every heard scale degree an accidental based on that key septuple. Intra-key and inter-key intervals are defined by change or maintenance of the key septuple: if the key remains the same from the first element of the interval to the second, the interval is intra-key; if the key changes, the interval is inter-key (or "modulating").

The formalization of key further makes our GIS more sensitive to modal distinctions. The issue can best be illustrated by referring back to Figure 2.6, the analyses of the intervals in the C-major Prelude and C♯-minor Fugue from *WTC I*. The upper heard scale degree in both cases is ($\hat{3}$, E). This seems to imply that pitch class E (or 4) has the same quality ($\hat{3}$) in both passages. Of course, the two $\hat{3}$s differ noticeably in one respect: the $\hat{3}$ in the C-major Prelude is *major*, while that in the C♯-minor Fugue is *minor*. The modal distinction is not captured in the ordered pair notation; nor is it captured in the ordered triple notation just developed, as the $\hat{3}$s in question are diatonic in each case (that is, $acc_3 = 0$ or ♮ in both excerpts).

The distinction *is* captured, however, when we take the entire *key septuple* of each passage into account. The intervallic relationships among the elements in each key situate a given heard scale degree in a modal context, yielding *specific* (rather than merely *generic*) intervallic relationships to a tonic, as well as to other scale degrees. Figure 2.28 illustrates, isolating a portion of the sd/pc space to show the first three scale degrees in C major and C♯ minor. Arrows from the keys' respective $\hat{1}$s demonstrate that the cell $(\hat{3}, E)$ resides a different interval from the tonic in each case: a minor third (3rd, 3) in C♯ minor, but a major third (3rd, 4) in C major. We can thus understand the formal key to provide a sort of "modal halo" that contextualizes a given heard scale degree. The modal halo idea is easily formalized: given some key septuple ($diapc_1$, $diapc_2$, …, $diapc_7$), $int((\hat{1}, diapc_1), (\hat{n}, diapc_n))$ determines the modal quality of any diatonic degree $(\hat{n}, diapc_n)$, indicating its *specific* intervallic distance from the tonic. Complete modal information is therefore provided when we take the key septuple into account: "$(\hat{3}, E)$ in C♯ min" versus "$(\hat{3}, E)$ in C maj." The formalism above has given the abbreviations "C♯ min" and "C maj" a concrete technical meaning in this regard. Specifically, it tells us that in a major key, $int(diapc_1, diapc_3) = 4$, while in a minor key, $int(diapc_1, diapc_3) = 3$. The subject of hearing with respect to a tonic is taken up in depth in Chapter 3. For now we can simply note that indications of key in this chapter's examples provide valuable information about the modal qualities of heard scale degrees.[43]

In certain highly chromatic contexts—in which major and minor can seem to interpenetrate, leading to a sense of a single modally mixed key[44]—another formal refinement is possible. We can define a *modally mixed key* as an ordered decuple that contains both modal variants for scale degrees $\hat{3}$, $\hat{6}$, and $\hat{7}$: ($diapc_1$, $diapc_2$, $diapc_3m$, $diapc_3M$, $diapc_4$, $diapc_5$, $diapc_6m$, $diapc_6M$, $diapc_7m$, $diapc_7M$). We further stipulate that $int(diapc_nm, diapc_nM) = 1$, guaranteeing that the major version of any of the "modally variable" scale degrees is one semitone above the minor version of that degree. I present this modally mixed possibility for those interested in

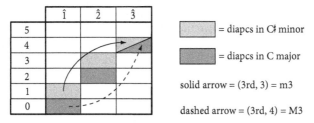

Figure 2.28 Modal qualities of scale degree $\hat{3}$ in the Bach analyses of Figure 2.6.

---

43. Note that such key indications have already been employed to this purpose in earlier figures. See especially Figures 2.17(a) and (b), in which the chromatically related minor keys provide crucial contextualizing information for the heard scale degrees in question.
44. Various theorists have suggested such a model of major/minor interpenetration, including Schenker (1954, 86–87), Schoenberg (1978, 389), Bailey (1985, 116), and Lerdahl (2001, 110ff).

pursuing it in their own analytical work. The remainder of this book will employ only the simple major or minor keys defined above.[45]

2.8 Two Chromatic Examples

Let us return to Tatyana's letter scene in *Eugene Onegin*. Figure 2.29(a) reproduces the passage first shown in Figure 2.8(a); we will focus particular attention on the chord marked x. Despite the chord's unusual spelling,[46] it likely strikes many listeners' ears as a familiar harmony: a characteristic—even cliché—modally darkened neighbor between two major tonics; theoretically trained listeners will likely hear a ♭VI chord in first inversion. In this hearing, the E♮ atop chord x (played by the first violins) takes on the quale of a lowered $\hat{3}$ (or ♭$\hat{3}$) in D♭ major, despite its spelling. The network in Figure 2.29(b) models such a hearing. Note that the linear intervals played by violin 1 are heard in this context as chromatic bendings of a single scale degree: $(e, -1)$ and $(e, 1)$. One might argue, however, that Tchaikovsky's spelling is meant to be *heard,* that the upper note of chord x should strike the ear as a raised $\hat{2}$, making x a dissonant harmony. The network in Figure 2.29(c) reflects *this* hearing. The linear intervals played by violin 1 are now minor seconds, ascending and descending: $(2nd^{-1}, -1)$ and $(2nd, 1)$, the same linear intervals projected (in reverse order) by the violas. The *vertical* interval between the violas' B♭♭ and violin 1's E♮, however, is now an extraordinary $(4th, 7)$—a seemingly genuine instance of a doubly augmented fourth.

Some readers may wonder whether the distinctions between the networks in 2.29(b) and (c) are phenomenologically meaningful. Is it possible for one to have an apperception that corresponds in some sense to Figure 2.29(b) and *not* to 2.29(c)—or vice versa? The question turns in part on whether there is any meaningful distinction between hearing the E♮ in violin 1 as an altered $\hat{2}$ or an altered $\hat{3}$. For readers who feel that there is no such distinction, I offer Figure 2.29(d). The figure adds two bars of dominant anacrusis (composed by the author) before Tatyana's phrase. The chord labeled y, just like chord x, has an E♮ in its upper voice. The reader is encouraged to play the example and compare the effect of E♮-atop-y with that of E♮-atop-x. The linear context of E♮-atop-y suggests a $\hat{2}$-pulled-sharp, while the linear context of E♮-atop-x suggests a $\hat{3}$-pulled-flat. The harmonic contexts reinforce these hearings. The modal brightness of the $\hat{2}$-pulled-sharp is intensified by its coincidence with the dominant leading tone, just as the modal darkness of $\hat{3}$-pulled-flat is intensified by its coincidence with ♭$\hat{6}$, the "subdominant leading tone."[47] The sonic effect is a striking shift in polarity from E♮-atop-y to E♮-atop-x. Readers who wish to develop a hearing that engages aspects of Figure 2.29(c) can first focus intently on the sensation of hearing

---

45. My reasons for doing so are similar to those offered by Daniel Harrison (1994, 19–22).
46. The spelling is present in the orchestral score, in which the first violins play the idiomatically notated neighbor figure F–E♮–F rather than F–F♭–F.
47. See Harrison 1994, 26–27. Harrison would describe both E♮s in 2.29(d)—E♮-atop-y and E♮-atop-x—as *specific accompaniments* to the functionally essential discharges in the inner voices of the two progressions ($\hat{7}$–$\hat{1}$ and ♭$\hat{6}$–$\hat{5}$, respectively). See Harrison 1994, 106–15.

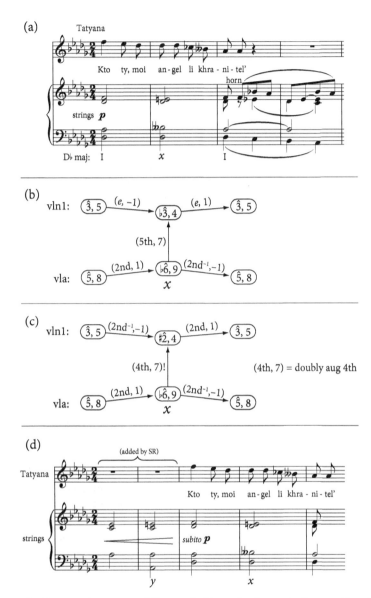

Figure 2.29 Harmonic aspects of Tatyana's climactic phrase in *Eugene Onegin*, Act I, scene 2.

E♮-atop-*y* as a $\hat{2}$-pulled-sharp, and then seek to import that apperception to E♮-atop-*x*. The difficulty (though not the impossibility) of doing so underscores the challenge of hearing a genuine doubly augmented fourth between viola and violin 1.[48]

48. Compare the apparent doubly diminished fifth in *Das Rheingold*, Scene 4, m. 3836 (the bar in which the Rhine daughters sing "wir nun klagen"). The chord in question is spelled {G, B♯, F♭} in A♭ major. In contrast to Tchaikovsky, Wagner "teaches" the listener to hear this as a genuine dissonance: the

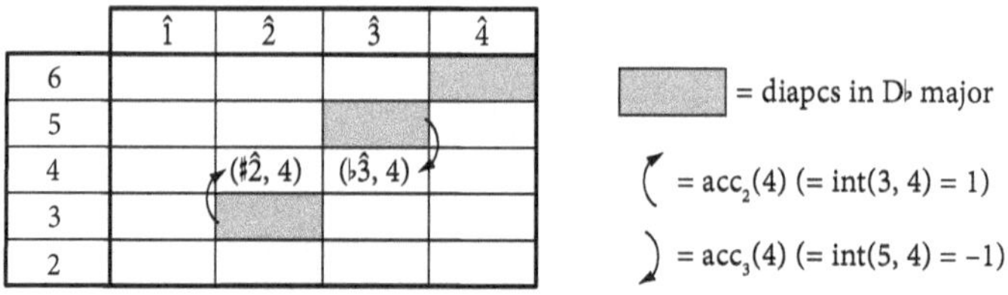

Figure 2.30 Chromatic inflections in D♭ major (cf. Figure 2.29).

Figure 2.30 graphs the distinction between ($\sharp\hat{2}$, 4) and ($\flat\hat{3}$, 4) in D♭ major. The figure offers a suggestive image of the interaction between quale and chroma. The arrows in the figure trace out the intervals associated with acc_2 and acc_3. The arrow for acc_2 pulls $\hat{2}$ up out of the gray box of $diapc_2$, bending its chroma sharpward from pc 3 to pc 4. The arrow for acc_3 pulls $\hat{3}$ down out of the gray box of $diapc_3$, bending its chroma flatward from pc 5 to pc 4. Such bending is possible only if there are diatonic pcs to act as reference points—fixed points of resistance, against which the inflections in chroma are felt to pull. Put another way, the difference in apperception discussed in the previous paragraph between E♮-atop-x and E♮-atop-y registers in the present technology not only in the different locations of the two cells in Figure 2.30, but also in the location of those cells with respect to their diatonic counterparts. The sense of "reversed polarity" between E♮-atop-y and E♮-atop-x is formally portrayed by the inverse relationship of acc_2 and acc_3.

Figure 2.31(a) shows the opening phrase of Liszt's *Il penseroso,* from the Italian year of the *Années de pèlerinage.* The simple Schenkerian reading of Figure 2.31(b) shows the passage's $\hat{3}$–$\hat{2}$–$\hat{1}$ melodic descent over an idiomatic bass line. The neo-Riemannian account of 2.31(c) focuses on the chromaticism in the upper three voices, which project C♯-minor and A-minor *Klänge* related by LP and PL transforms. Though both accounts capture crucial aspects of the passage, neither does full justice to the striking aural effect of the second chord, the A-minor triad of bar 2. The neo-Riemannian account merely notes its efficient voice leading, while the Schenkerian account treats the chromatic oddities as inner-voice filler within a diatonic outer-voice framework. But the harmonic interest in the passage resides precisely in the inner voices, centering specifically on the C♮; if we remove the natural sign before that note the music loses its effect. *With* the C♮, however, the harmony in bar 2 is invested with ear-tingling strangeness. The C♮ causes the alto line to traverse a fascinatingly Escher-like progression: C♯–C♮–B♯–C♯, indicated with diamond noteheads in 2.31(b). This is not merely a matter of notation: the

{G, B♮, F♭} in m. 3836 is a chromatic inflection of a {G, B♮, F♮} chord in the previous bar, both of them acting explicitly as dissonant neighbors to the A♭-major tonic. Despite this explicit ear training, the {G, B♮, F♭} can nevertheless seem to "snap" in one's hearing to a consonant minor triad once it sounds. The flickering effect of these competing hearings is dramatically apt: the "Rheingold!"-based call is distorted as it travels up from the deep of the valley (*aus der Tiefe des Thales*)—the sonic equivalent of heat ripples distorting a distant object (perhaps augmented by Doppler shifts as the daughters swim back and forth). The {G, B♮, F♭} chord is the hexatonic pole of the tonic in A♭ major. Richard Cohn (2004, 303–8 and *passim*) offers pertinent comments on the ways in which hexatonic-polar chords can seem consonant and dissonant from different perspectives (cf. section 2.9.2). See also Ernst Kurth's discussion of the "glorious color diffraction" created by the Rhine daughters' {G, B♮, F♭} chord (1991, 107).

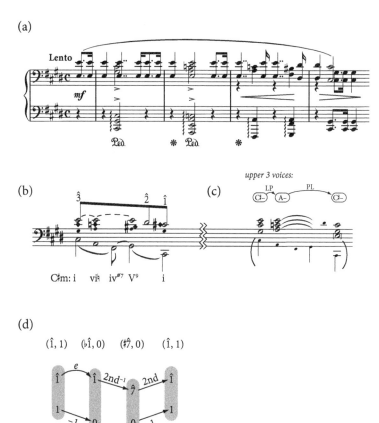

Figure 2.31 Liszt, "Il penseroso," mm. 1–4.

alto can in fact be heard to project a peculiarly staggered progression of quale and chroma. If the A-minor chord in bar 2 is heard as a consonance, then the alto's C♯ projects a highly unusual lowered tonic in C♯ minor—a chromatic bending of 1̂ from pc 1 to pc 0.[49] But when the bass moves to G♯ in m. 3, signaling the arrival of the dominant, the alto takes on the quale of the leading tone. This results in a *qualitative* bending of the sustained pc 0, from ♭1̂ to ♯7̂. This peculiar staggering in fact lends the entire alto line the rhythm of a suspension. See Figure 2.31(d), which vertically aligns the sd and pc elements, using gray ellipses to animate the pulling and resolving interaction of quale and chroma in the passage. The initial (1̂, 1) acts as the preparation of the sd/pc suspension, with both quale and chroma at rest, so

49. Were the alto heard as ♯7̂ here, it would create an augmented second (2nd, 3) with the bass's 6̂ and a diminished fourth (4th, 4) with the soprano's 3̂. If one hears the progression with generic norms in mind, the consonant A-minor hearing is preferred: Liszt's progression is clearly a variant of a diatonic i–VI–iv–V progression, with the VI chord inflected from major to minor.

to speak. The following stage is the suspension proper: the chroma shifts downward, but the quale remains suspended on $\hat{1}$. It is not until the third stage that the scale-degree quale succumbs to the downward pressure of the chroma, shifting to $\hat{7}$; this is the resolution of the sd/pc suspension. With quale and chroma now once again "in phase," the two progress back to $(\hat{1}, 1)$ in m. 4, moving together for the first time. This subtle sense of sd/pc resolution interacts with the harmonic resolution from dominant to tonic in mm. 3–4.

Figure 2.32 provides a more global perspective, integrating the alto line just analyzed into the entire progression. The network of 2.32(a) analyzes the three

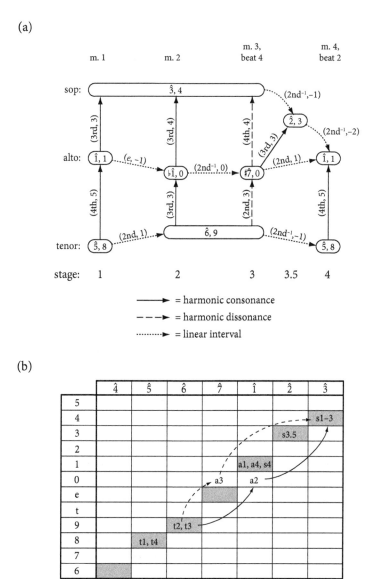

Figure 2.32 Harmonic aspects of "Il penseroso."

upper voices. Below the network the events of the progression are labeled as stages 1–4. The soprano, alto, and tenor voices are indicated to the left of the network; the alto voice just discussed can be read directly off of the middle horizontal stratum. Melodic intervals are shown with dotted arrows. Dashed vertical arrows show harmonic dissonances; solid arrows show harmonic consonances. The dashed vertical arrows make visually vivid the transformation of the A-minor *Klang* from a consonance in stage 2 to a dissonance in stage 3. That harmonic dissonance finally manages to dislodge the tolling, melodic $(\hat{3}, 4)$ in stage 3.5, thus initiating the $\hat{3}$–$\hat{2}$–$\hat{1}$ descent of the Schenkerian reading. The two (dashed) harmonic dissonances thereby resolve to (solid) harmonic consonances: the (4th, 4) between alto and soprano resolves to (3rd, 3); the (2nd, 3) between tenor and alto resolves to (4th, 5).

Figure 2.32(b) presents the same information from a different perspective, situating the elements of the network in 2.32(a) in the sd/pc GIS space. The labels in the cells indicate voice part and stage. Thus, a1 means "alto voice in stage 1"; t3 means "tenor voice in stage 3"; and so on. Solid and dashed arrows indicate the harmonic intervals within the A-minor *Klang* of stages 2 and 3. The shift from consonant to dissonant *Klang* is effected by the leftward shift of the alto voice as it progresses from a2 to a3. This shift has a paradoxical effect: it transforms the exotic ♭$\hat{1}$ into a familiar ♯$\hat{7}$—this is the resolution of the sd/pc "suspension"—but at the same time it transforms the familiar A-minor triad into an exotic, enharmonically equivalent dissonance: the "dissonant A-minor triad" discussed earlier in section 2.4, in connection with Figures 2.12(c) and 2.13(b).[50]

2.9 Transposition

2.9.1 Definitions

We can define various species of transposition and inversion in the present GIS.[51] We will first explore the transpositions, representatives of which are illustrated in Figure 2.33. Figure 2.33(a) shows a *diatonic transposition* within C major: T_{2nd} transposes C: I up a diatonic second to C: ii. Figure 2.33(b) shows a *chromatic transposition*: $T_{(2nd, 2)}$ transposes C: I by (2nd, 2) to yield the chromatically inflected C: II♯. Finally, Figure 2.33(c) shows a special type of chromatic transposition that we will call a *real transposition*: $T_{(e, 2)}$ chromatically transposes C: I by two semitones, leaving the scale degrees unchanged. It further transposes the underlying key septuple by 2, yielding a D-major key, and making the D-major triad the new tonic—thus, D: I.

---

50. A similar "dissonant minor triad"—indeed, one involving the same scale degrees—can be found in Brahms's Intermezzo in B♭ minor, op. 117, no. 2, m. 8.
51. On transposition and inversion in GISes generally, see *GMIT*, 46–59.

(a)   (b)

$$\begin{Bmatrix} (\hat{5}, G) \\ (\hat{3}, E) \\ (\hat{1}, C) \end{Bmatrix} \xrightarrow{\ T_{2nd}\ } \begin{Bmatrix} (\hat{6}, A) \\ (\hat{4}, F) \\ (\hat{2}, D) \end{Bmatrix} \qquad\qquad \begin{Bmatrix} (\hat{5}, G) \\ (\hat{3}, E) \\ (\hat{1}, C) \end{Bmatrix} \xrightarrow{\ T_{(2nd,\,2)}\ } \begin{Bmatrix} (\hat{6}, A) \\ (\sharp\hat{4}, F\sharp) \\ (\hat{2}, D) \end{Bmatrix}$$

  C: I   C: ii   C: I   C: II♯

(c)

$$\begin{Bmatrix} (\hat{5}, G) \\ (\hat{3}, E) \\ (\hat{1}, C) \end{Bmatrix} \xrightarrow{\ T_{(e,\,2)}\ } \begin{Bmatrix} (\hat{5}, A) \\ (\hat{3}, F\sharp) \\ (\hat{1}, D) \end{Bmatrix}$$

  C: I   D: I

Figure 2.33 Three species of transposition in the sd/pc GIS: (a) diatonic transposition; (b) chromatic transposition; (c) real transposition.

We can easily define these transpositions using the apparatus of GIS_{Tonal}. *Chromatic transposition*, notated $T_{(sdint,\,pcint)}$ and illustrated in 2.33(b), is formally the simplest of the three: it transposes any (sd, pc) pair by (sdint, pcint). This is the standard Lewinian transposition for the sd/pc GIS (as defined in *GMIT*, section 3.4.1). *Real transposition*, notated $T_{(e,\,pcint)}$ and illustrated in 2.33(c), transposes the pcs in each ordered pair by pcint, leaving the scale degrees fixed. The result is simply a standard pc transposition. We further stipulate that $T_{(e,\,pcint)}$ transposes every diapc in the orienting key septuple by pcint. Thus, in Figure 2.33(c), $T_{(e,\,2)}$ not only transposes the pcs in the right-hand slot of each ordered pair by 2; it also transposes the complete governing key septuple for C major (0, 2, 4, 5, 7, 9, e) by 2, yielding that for D major: (2, 4, 6, 7, 9, e, 1). *Diatonic transposition*, notated T_{sdint} and illustrated in 2.33(a), operates only on diatonic sd/pc pairs, that is, pairs of the form $(\hat{n}, diapc_n)$. T_{sdint} transposes $(\hat{m}, diapc_m)$ to $(\hat{n}, diapc_n)$, given scale degrees $\hat{m}$ and $\hat{n}$, such that $int(\hat{m}, \hat{n}) = sdint$, and given $diapc_m$ and $diapc_n$ belonging to the same key septuple.[52] In effect, diatonic transposition treats the seven diatonic sd/pc pairs in a given key as the space S of a seven-element diatonic GIS.

Note that chromatic transposition, in contrast to real transposition and diatonic transposition, is undefined with respect to key. Some chromatic transpositions will motivate a change of key, while others (such as that in 2.33(b)) will not. Though such matters can be formalized, the result is unwieldy; questions of key in connection with chromatic transpositions are thus left to the discretion of the analyst (such flexibility is welcome when one is confronting thorny chromatic

---

52. Compare Brinkman's diatonic operations (1986, 48), which act in essentially the same manner as the present diatonic transposition (and the diatonic inversion defined in section 2.10). Diatonic transposition and inversion as defined here and in section 2.10.1 depart from Lewin's formal definitions of GIS transposition and inversion, as they do not apply to all members of the sd/pc GIS but only to *diatonic* members of that GIS—that is, pairs of the form $(\hat{n}, diapc_n)$, given some defined key. The concept of key has no equivalent in *GMIT*.

passages).[53] We will address an additional formal issue raised by these three types of transposition in section 2.12. For now, let us turn to an example.

2.9.2 Vignette: Parsifal

These transpositions shed new light on a heavily analyzed passage: the chromatic Grail music from *Parsifal*. Figure 2.34(a) shows the diatonic Grail theme, as first heard in the Act I *Vorspiel;* a Roman numeral analysis below the staff analyzes the progression in A♭ major. Figure 2.34(b) shows a chromatic variant of the theme near the end of Act III, a passage that has received abundant neo-Riemannian attention;[54] symbols beneath the staff analyze the progression of triads via the neo-Riemannian symbols H (hexatonic pole) and L (leading-tone change). There

(a)

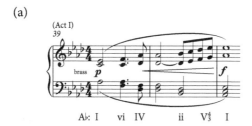

(b)

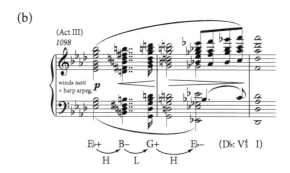

Figure 2.34 The Grail progression in *Parsifal* (a) in diatonic form in the Act I *Vorspiel;* and (b) in a chromatic form late in Act III.

53. Dmitri Tymoczko (in private communication) has suggested that the sd/pc transpositions defined here (along with the inversions defined in section 2.10.1) might profitably be understood to include an active component, which transposes or inverts pitch classes, and a passive component, which re-orients the listener's hearing by situating the newly transformed pcs in a given scalar context. To fully formalize transposition and inversion along these lines would require us to specify the exact behavior of the formal key septuples for each operation; as noted above, this would result in a considerably more elaborate apparatus in the case of the chromatic operations. In the interest of accessibility and ease of application, I have opted not to undertake such formal development here. This remains an area, however, for further formal exploration in a more specialized context.
54. Notable discussions include Clampitt 1998; Cohn 1996, 23, and 2006, 233–34; and Lewin 2006, 209–11.

is some grinding of conceptual gears at the end of the phrase, which is analyzed (in parentheses) not in neo-Riemannian terms, but as a traditional Roman-numeral progression in D♭ major.[55]

Figure 2.35(b) explores a different hearing of the passage, one that seeks to maintain contact with the tonal hearing of the diatonic Grail theme, which is analyzed in GIS terms in Figure 2.35(a). The readings in Figure 2.35 are resolutely harmonic, modeling root motions via sd/pc transpositions; we will reintegrate this harmonic perspective with the passage's efficient voice leading in a moment. Figure 2.35(a) analyzes the diatonic Grail theme as a series of descending third progressions in A♭ major, via the diatonic transposition $T_{3rd^{-1}}$; the final cadence breaks this pattern, resolving to the A♭ tonic via $T_{5th^{-1}}$. Roman numerals running along the top of the figure label the constituent harmonies; these Roman numeral columns apply to Figure 2.35(b) as well. The latter figure hears the chromatically altered theme as traversing the same harmonic stages as the diatonic theme. Such a strategy is hardly far-fetched: the listener has by now heard over four hours of the drama, including countless diatonic statements of the Grail music. When heard in this way, the chromatic Grail progression includes two downward lurches in key: the first between the E♭+ and B– chords (in the columns headed I and vi), the second between the G+ and E♭– chords (in the columns headed IV and ii). These are the very moments at which the hexatonic-polar progressions occur. The lurches are represented on Figure 2.35(b) by dotted arrows that trace out L-shaped jogs. The first leg of those jogs, represented by a rightward arrow, is a diatonic transposition of $T_{3rd^{-1}}$, modeling the harmonic progression a listener is led to expect by schematic recollection of the diatonic Grail. The anticipated harmony is shown in dashed brackets. Before it can sound, however, the second leg of the jog pulls the harmony downward by semitone via a real transposition of $T_{(e,-1)}$. By definition, $T_{(e,-1)}$ also forces a change of key—from E♭ major to D major at the first jog, and from D major to D♭ major at the second jog.[56] As a result of these downward lurches, the conclusion of the Dresden-amen cadence is two semitones too low with respect to the phrase's opening. This is modeled by the long dashed arrow on the right-hand side of the example, marked $T_{(e,-2)}$.[57]

The downward semitonal lurches in key interact suggestively with the hexatonic-polar voice leading at these moments. Figure 2.36(a) illustrates, plotting the voice leading of the first such progression, E♭+ → B–, in the space of the

55. Compare Lewin 2006, 209, Example 11.9c, which similarly analyzes the concluding cadence in Roman numerals (and in brackets). Lewin makes much interpretive hay out of the "conceptual grinding of gears" between Riemannian and Roman-numeral-based harmonic systems in his essay on Amfortas's prayer (Lewin 2006, ch. 10). For a suggestive attempt to integrate the final cadence into a fully neo-Riemannian account, see Clampitt 1998, 328–30, esp. Figure 5.

56. In an empirical study, Krumhansl and Lerdahl (2007, 350–53) have proposed that listeners prefer to hear the chromatic Grail passage in just this way—as traversing the diatonic keys of E♭ major, D major, and D♭ major.

57. Lewin proposes a hearing of the entire progression as tracing out a large-scale motion from E♭-as-V to D♭-as-IV within a global A♭ (2006, 195, esp. Example 10.3c and its accompanying text). Figure 2.35(b), by contrast, analyzes the progression based on its local tonics, and on the local tonicity of the Dresden-amen cadence; nevertheless, the long $T_{(e,-2)}$ arrow on the right-hand side of the figure interacts with Lewin's large-scale shift from E♭-as-tonicized-*Stufe* to D♭-as-tonicized-*Stufe*. The semitonal lurches along the way further interact with the various semitonal substitutions that Lewin hears in Amfortas's prayer.

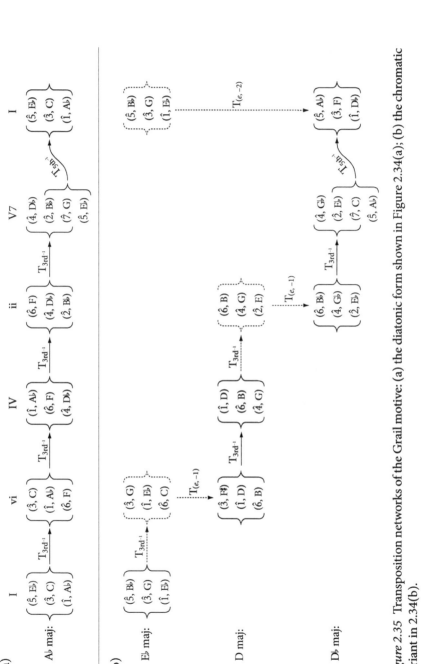

Figure 2.35 Transposition networks of the Grail motive: (a) the diatonic form shown in Figure 2.34(a); (b) the chromatic variant in 2.34(b).

sd/pc GIS. Along the left-hand border, next to the pc integers, curved arrows show the pc motion of the hexatonic-polar progression. Within the sd/pc space, cells are labeled in an attempt to hear the progression entirely within E♭ major, resist-ing, for the moment, any impulse to hear a change of key.[58] The E♭-major tonic is

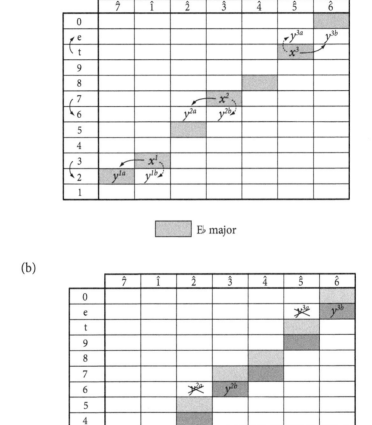

Figure 2.36 Tonal hearings of the E♭+ → B− progression at the outset of the chromatic Grail progression, plotted in the sd/pc GIS space.

---

58. This perspective is closely related to Daniel Harrison's technique of "prospective accumulative analysis" (1994, 153–66 and 2002, 123), which seeks to interpret the second chord in a two-chord progression with respect to the key of the first.

represented by the set $\{x^1, x^2, x^3\}$; cells labeled with superscripted ys interpret the B-minor chord. There are two y alternatives for each voice; the alternatives model the difficulty of interpreting the B-minor triad securely within E♭. Only one note in the chord admits of a diatonic interpretation in E♭: pc 2 (or D♮), which may be heard as $\hat{7}$, as shown by y^{1a}. The other two pcs, 6 and e, are chromatic in E♭ major: y^{2a} hears pc 6 as a raised $\hat{2}$, while y^{2b} hears it as a lowered $\hat{3}$; y^{3a} hears pc e as a raised $\hat{5}$, while y^{3b} hears it as a lowered $\hat{6}$. In keeping with the two possibilities presented in these voices, y^{1b} adds an additional interpretation of pc 2: a lowered $\hat{1}$ reminiscent of the Liszt analysis above.

Interpretation y^{1b} may initially seem unworthy of inclusion, especially as pc 2 admits of a diatonic hearing. Nevertheless, intervallic pressures from the other sd/pc apperceptions make it valuable to have around. For instance, imagine a listener who has the following two apperceptions:

(1) Pitch classes 6 and e are modally darkened (or lowered) instances of $\hat{3}$ and $\hat{6}$ in E♭ major.
(2) The B-minor chord is a consonant triad.

Apperception (1) hears y^{2b} and y^{3b}, rejecting the chromatically "brightened" y^{2a} and y^{3a}. But if apperception (1) is to coexist with apperception (2), we must also reject y^{1a}, as the set $\{y^{1a}, y^{2b}, y^{3b}\}$ is not a consonant triad. Most notably, int(y^{1a}, y^{2b}) = (4th, 4), a diminished fourth, while int(y^{1a}, y^{3b}) = (7th, 9), a diminished seventh. If we rebel against the grotesque lowered tonic of y^{1b}, we might then try to add apperception (3) to the mix:

(3) Pitch class 2 is a diatonic leading tone in E♭.

But apperceptions (1), (2), and (3) cannot coexist; only two of them may be entertained at a time. We can discard apperception (2) and retain (1) and (3), hearing the chord as the dissonant assemblage $\{y^{1a}, y^{2b}, y^{3b}\}$, that is, $\{\hat{7}, ♭\hat{3}, ♭\hat{6}\}$ in E♭ major. Or we can discard apperception (1), now hearing the consonant triad $\{y^{1a}, y^{2a}, y^{3a}\}$, that is, $\{\hat{7}, ♯\hat{2}, ♯\hat{5}\}$, a highly improbable raised minor dominant chord (♯v). Or we can discard apperception (3), returning to our initial hearing of $\{y^{1b}, y^{2b}, y^{3b}\}$, that is, $\{♭\hat{1}, ♭\hat{3}, ♭\hat{6}\}$, the minor lowered submediant (♭vi). Alfred Lorenz (1933, 89–90) takes yet a different approach, constructing his hearing of the chord by discarding our apperceptions (1) and (2) and adding a new apperception (4):

(4) All of the intervals traversed in the E♭+ → B– progression are minor seconds, i.e., GIS intervals (2nd, 1) or (2nd⁻¹, –1), not chromatic semitones, i.e., GIS intervals $(e, 1)$ or $(e, –1)$.

Solid arrows on Figure 2.36(a) indicate minor seconds; dashed arrows indicate chromatic semitones. Lorenz thus hears the B-minor chord (initially) as $\{y^{1a}, y^{2a}, y^{3b}\}$, or $\{\hat{7}, ♯\hat{2}, ♭\hat{6}\}$ in E♭, which he indicates by spelling it as {D, F♯, C♭} in his notated example (1933, 90).

A reader impatient with all of this tonal horse-trading may throw up his or her hands at this point and argue that the E♭+ → B– progression simply frustrates tonal hearing: it is an efficient motion in pitch-class space that so violates traditional diatonic norms that it causes us to abandon our tonal listening strategies altogether. On hearing the hexatonic-polar progression, we slip into a fully chromatic space untroubled by tonal qualia, tendencies, and the like. The formal elegance of such arguments has been a principal attraction of much work in neo-Riemannian theory. That elegance exacts a cost, however, turning the B-minor chord into a collection of inert pitch classes, indistinct from any other [037] chord. But whatever this chord may be, it is far from inert: it thrums with energy. The system of tonal norms becomes *more* conspicuous, not less, in its seeming violation—it loudly colors the sounding music. The progression's aural fascination—its "supernatural strangeness" (à la Kurth 1991, 124)—arises in large part from the ways in which it generates contradictory and competing tonal apperceptions, yielding a flickering play of energetic contradictions: between chromatic brightening and darkening, consonance and dissonance, competing vectors of upward and downward tendency, and so on.[59] The present GIS insists on these contradictions, forcing us to weigh different tonal interpretations of the sounding pitches and to explore their interactions. The result is a volatile admixture of apperceptions created by various combinations of the y cells in 2.36(a). One might even go so far as to consider one's initial impression of the B-minor chord to be the entropic six-element set of all y elements from 2.36(a): $\{y^{1a}, y^{1b}, y^{2a}, y^{2b}, y^{3a}, y^{3b}\}$, a set of conflicting tonal potentialities, each of them jostling for preeminence in one's hearing when the chord first sounds.[60] It is that jostling that lends the sonority its peculiar refractory energy.

The GIS also provides a suggestive model of one way in which that energy might dissipate as the B-minor chord settles into the ear.[61] As Figure 2.36(b) shows, a minimal shift of the governing key septuple downward by one semitone provides a diatonic home for all members of the chord. Specifically, it situates all of the "b-superscripted" y elements, $\{y^{1b}, y^{2b}, y^{3b}\}$ in the context of D major. This is the very context predicted by the harmonic reading in Figure 2.35(b): a hearing of the B-minor chord as vi—its expected syntactic role of the second stage in the Grail theme—but in a key transformed by $T_{(e,-1)}$. Thus, the schematic-expectation-and-lurch modeled by 2.35(b) provides a "solution" to the apperceptual tangle of Figure 2.36(a). Far from lessening the magic of the moment, this tonal adjustment increases it: though the B-minor chord now has a diatonic home, that home is a jarring $T_{(e,-1)}$ off center.[62]

---

59. Cohn (2004, 303–8) offers highly suggestive observations along these lines. The present discussion provides a GIS-based means of formalizing some of the tonal-theoretic contradictions he explores.
60. Though the apperceptions associated with the various ys are in some cases contradictory, there is no *formal* contradiction in assembling all six ys into a single set from our GIS. A GIS set is simply any finite subset of GIS elements (cf. *GMIT*, 88, and section 2.4 above).
61. As Lorenz (1933, 89) puts it, "When sustained, such dissonant configurations come to strike the ear as consonances.... Hardly are the neighbor tones reached than they are covered over with the appearance of consonance—the effect is like a ray of light" (my translation). Cohn (2006, 232) offers a penetrating hermeneutic gloss of this idea in the context of *Parsifal*.
62. The interested reader is encouraged to undertake a similar analysis of the second hexatonic-polar progression in the passage, G+ → E♭−, which reveals analogous patterns in the vicinity of the diatonic IV and ii chords.

2.10 Inversion

2.10.1 Definitions

We now define diatonic and chromatic inversions within $\text{GIS}_{\text{Tonal}}$. Before beginning, it will be useful to summarize the individual actions of pc inversion and sd inversion. All inversions are notated in the form I_u^v, which maps GIS elements u and v onto each other, and inverts all other elements with respect to u and v.[63] Readers will be familiar with pc inversion from atonal theory: in the "atonal GIS" of twelve pcs, $I_{\text{pc1}}^{\text{pc2}}$ is formally equivalent to I_n or T_nI, in which $n = \text{pc1} + \text{pc2}$. Scale-degree inversion is less familiar, but it is easily intuited. For example, in a scale-degree GIS, $I_{\hat{1}}^{\hat{5}}$ swaps scale degrees as follows:

$$\hat{6} \leftrightarrow \hat{7}$$
$$\hat{5} \leftrightarrow \hat{1}$$
$$\hat{4} \leftrightarrow \hat{2}$$
$$\hat{3} \leftrightarrow \hat{3}$$

$I_{\hat{1}}^{\hat{5}}$ can thus also be notated $I_{\hat{6}}^{\hat{7}}$, or $I_{\hat{2}}^{\hat{4}}$, or $I_{\hat{3}}^{\hat{3}}$ (just as pc inversion $I_{\text{pc1}}^{\text{pc2}}$ can be noted by any of its inversionally related pc pairs). Note that all scale-degree inversions have a single scale degree as inversional axis—such as $\hat{3}$ above—due to the odd cardinality of the seven-element set. There are thus seven unique scale-degree inversions.

Figure 2.37 illustrates three $\text{GIS}_{\text{Tonal}}$ inversions in a musical context. In 2.37(a), the incipit of the *Art of Fugue* subject is inverted *diatonically* via $I_{\hat{1}}^{\hat{5}}$, which maps diatonic scale degrees $\hat{5}$ and $\hat{1}$ onto each other, maintaining their diapc affiliations. In 2.37(b), the tail of the subject is inverted *chromatically* via $I_{(\hat{1},D)}^{(\hat{5},A)}$, which maps sd/pc pairs $(\hat{1}, D)$ and $(\hat{5}, A)$ onto each other. In 2.37(c), the entire fugue subject is inverted chromatically via $I_{(\hat{1},D)}^{(\hat{5},D)}$, resulting in an inverted subject in the key of G.

Like the transpositions, the inversions are easily defined using the apparatus of $\text{GIS}_{\text{Tonal}}$. *Chromatic inversion,* like chromatic transposition, is analogous to the traditional Lewinian GIS inversion: $I_{(\text{sd1,pc1})}^{(\text{sd2,pc2})}$ inverts any (sd, pc) pair componentwise—sd via the inversion that maps sd1 onto sd2, and pc via the inversion that maps pc1 onto pc2. As with chromatic transposition, such inversions are kept formally independent from changes of key: they may coincide with a key change in a given analytical context, as in Figure 2.37(c), or they may not, as in 2.37(b). *Diatonic inversion,* notated $I_{(\text{sd1})}^{(\text{sd2})}$, operates only on pairs of the form $(\hat{n}, \text{diapc}_n)$. Given scale degrees $\hat{m}$ and $\hat{n}$, the diatonic inversion $I_{(\text{sd1})}^{(\text{sd2})}$ maps $(\hat{m}, \text{diapc}_m)$ to $(\hat{n}, \text{diapc}_n)$, such that $\hat{n}$ and $\hat{m}$ map onto each other via the inversion that maps sd1 onto sd2, and diapc_m and diapc_n are members of the same key septuple.[64]

---

63. The locution "with respect to u and v" is defined formally in *GMIT*, 50–51.
64. Note that there is no inversional analogue for real transposition. As with the transpositions, a further formal issue is addressed in section 2.12.

(a)

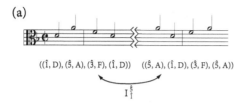

(b)

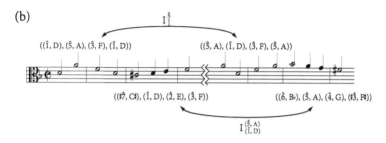

(c)

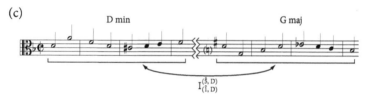

Figure 2.37 Diatonic and chromatic inversions in the sd/pc GIS, using the subject from the *Art of Fugue*: (a) diatonic inversion; (b) chromatic inversion (below staff) with no change of key; (c) chromatic inversion with change of key.

2.10.2 *Vignette: Mendelssohn's op. 19b, no. 1*

Figure 2.38(a) provides the opening of Mendelssohn's first Song without Words, op. 19b, no. 1;[65] 2.38(b) shows two operation graphs that are thematic in the piece. The right hand consistently plays the top graph; the left hand consistently plays the bottom graph. The graphs are inversionally related; that is, the operations in corresponding positions in the two graphs are formal inverses of one another.[66] The mirror-play of the piece depends much on this inversional relationship, which is somatically manifested in the inversional relationship of the player's hands on the keyboard, with outer-voice gestures converging toward the middle of the player's body.

---

65. Though the first published set of *Lieder ohne Worte* is often referred to as op. 19, Mendelssohn scholars now label it op. 19b to distinguish it from the *Sechs Gesänge*, op. 19a. I am grateful to Jay Hook for bringing this to my attention.

66. Formally, the graphs are *isomorphic* in the sense of *GMIT*, 199, Def. 9.4.2: they have the same node and arrow configurations, and a group isomorphism maps the labels on the arrows from one graph onto those for the other. The isomorphism in question is in fact an *auto*morphism: informally, it swaps inversionally related elements in IVLS.

(a)

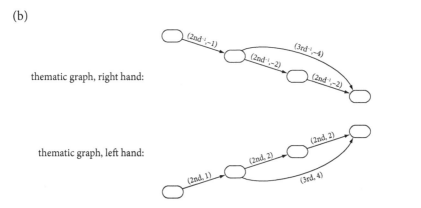

(b)

Figure 2.38 Mendelssohn *Lied ohne Worte*, op. 19b, no. 1, mm. 1–6.

Figure 2.39 presents two network analyses of the outer voices in the piece's main theme.[67] The networks align the thematic graphs of 2.38(b) vertically, illustrating the mirror-play just discussed, though arrow labels have been removed to reduce clutter; the labels from 2.38(b) should be understood. Inversional arrows link the initial nodes in each thematic wedge; the same inversional arrow implicitly connects the remaining three vertically aligned node pairs in each wedge. Figure 2.39(a) shows a hearing of the opening two gestures of the theme entirely in E major. The diatonic inversion I_i^3

67. The low D♯ shown in the bass in the networks does not sound on beat 4 of m. 2, in the theme's initial appearance. It does sound later, however, in the restatement that begins on beat 4 of m. 6.

(a)

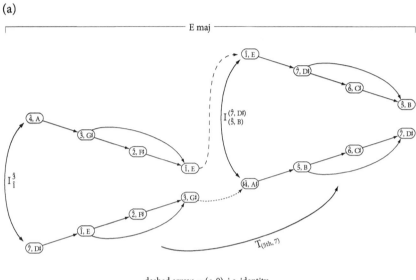

dashed arrow = (e, 0), i.e. identity
dotted arrow = (2nd, 2), i.e. major second

(b)

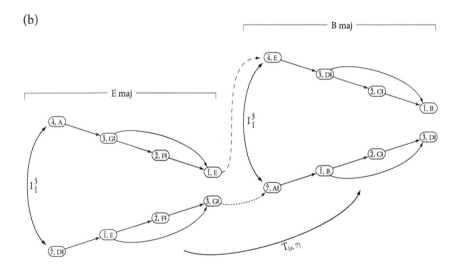

dashed arrow = (4th, 0), i.e. pivot 4th
dotted arrow = (5th, 2), i.e. "qualitatively stretched" whole step

Figure 2.39 Two networks modeling the outer-voice wedges in Mendelssohn's op. 19b, no. 1: (a) a hearing entirely in E major; (b) a hearing in E major and B major.

governs the initial thematic wedge.[68] The chromatic inversion $I_{(\hat{5},B)}^{(\hat{7},D\sharp)}$ governs the second thematic wedge, generating the chromatic element ($\sharp\hat{4}$, A$\sharp$) at the outset of the second left-hand gesture. Figure 2.39(b), by contrast, hears the second thematic wedge in B major. As a result, the *same* diatonic inversion governs both wedges: $I_i^{\hat{3}}$. This hearing captures the sense in which wedge two repeats the music of wedge one "in the key of the dominant." The hearing of 2.39(a), by contrast, captures the sense in which wedge two introduces a chromatic element into the governing E-major key.

Dashed and dotted arrows connect the concluding elements of wedge one to the initiating elements of wedge two in both analyses. In 2.39(a) the intervals traversed are the identity element (*e*, 0) in the soprano, and an ascending major second (2nd, 2) in the bass. In 2.39(b), the intervals traversed are more exotic, and more expressive: a pivot fourth (4th, 0) in the soprano, and a qualitatively stretched whole step (5th, 2) in the bass. The expressivity of the pivot fourth is heightened by the octave leap in pitch space; one could reflect this as a path in pc space (per the discussion in section 2.3) by employing the label (4th, 12): a pivot fourth with an implied "octave loop." The modulating hearing of 2.39(b) also reveals interesting sd/pc patterning in the upper voice: the initial right-hand element in the second wedge, ($\hat{4}$, E) fuses the sd from the initial right-hand gesture's first element with the pc from its final element. This fusing, along with the octave leap, the pivot fourth, and the qualitative stretching in the bass, account for much of the poetic effect of the transition from wedge one to wedge two, when heard along the lines of Figure 2.39(b).

2.11 Sets (II)

2.11.1 Set Types

Having defined transpositions and inversions, we can now return to the question of set types—that is, GIS set classes. A GIS set class is an equivalence class of all GIS sets that can be transformed into one another by some canonical group of operations, which Lewin calls CANON (*GMIT*, 104–5). We can define five such canonical groups using the sd/pc transpositions and inversions defined above:

(1) The group of diatonic transpositions
(2) The group of diatonic transpositions and diatonic inversions
(3) The group of chromatic transpositions
(4) The group of chromatic transpositions and chromatic inversions
(5) The group of real transpositions[69]

---

68. This inversion underlies the voice exchange of the passage, which explicitly swaps $\hat{3}$ and $\hat{1}$.

69. The algebraic structures of the five groups are as follows. The diatonic transpositions form a cyclic group of order 7, or $\mathbb{Z}_7$. The diatonic transpositions and diatonic inversions form a dihedral group of order 14, or $\mathbb{D}_{14}$. The chromatic transpositions form a cyclic group of order 84, or $\mathbb{Z}_{84}$. The chromatic transpositions and chromatic inversions form a dihedral group of order 168, or $\mathbb{D}_{168}$. The real transpositions form a cyclic group of order 12, or $\mathbb{Z}_{12}$.

Set classes in the sd/pc GIS will vary based on which of these five groups we choose as CANON. To demonstrate, let us begin with a V^7 chord in C major: $\{(\hat{5}, G), (\hat{7}, B), (\hat{2}, D), (\hat{4}, F)\}$, which we will abbreviate C: V^7. If we wish to answer the question "What set class does this chord belong to?" we must first give "set class" concrete meaning by defining CANON. Groups (3) and (4) yield relatively familiar results. If we define CANON as group (3), the chromatic transpositions, C: V^7 becomes a member of the set class "major-minor seventh chords built on any scale degree." Note that this set class excludes chords that are enharmonically equivalent to major-minor sevenths, such as German augmented sixths; the latter constitute a set class in their own right under the given canonical group. If we instead define CANON as group (4), the chromatic transpositions and inversions, C: V^7 becomes a member of the set class "major-minor and half-diminished seventh chords built on any scale degree." Once again, this class excludes enharmonic equivalents of those chord types, which, again, occupy their own set classes.

Groups (1) and (5) yield more novel set types. If we define CANON as group (5), the real transpositions, C: V^7 becomes a member of the set type "V^7 chords in major." That is, all members of this group-(5) set class are of the form $\{(\hat{5}, \text{diapc}_5),$ $(\hat{7}, \text{diapc}_7), (\hat{2}, \text{diapc}_2), (\hat{4}, \text{diapc}_4)\}$, in which the diapcs all belong to a single major key. Group-(5) set classes are of particular apperceptual interest, especially for listeners without absolute pitch. Non-AP listeners invoke such set types whenever they are aware that they are hearing, say, a "V^7 chord in major," or a "ii° chord in minor," or a "French sixth in major," but are unaware of the precise local key. Note that in all cases the set type specifies a governing major or minor key, as real transpositions can transpose formal keys, but cannot reverse mode. Thus, the group-(5) set class "V^7 chords in major" is distinct from the group-(5) set class "V^7 chords in minor."

If we define CANON as group (1), the diatonic transpositions, C: V^7 becomes a member of set class "diatonic seventh chords in C major." Note well: this set class bundles together all diatonic seventh chords *within C major*, not all diatonic seventh chords across keys; this is a novel result of the definition of diatonic transposition in the GIS. Under this canonical group, all of the chords in the sequence in mm. 2–5 of Brahms's B♭-minor Intermezzo, op. 117, no. 2 are members of the group-(1) set class "incomplete diatonic seventh chords in B♭ minor." By contrast, all of the chords in the chromatic sequence of mm. 11–13 of the same piece are members of the group-(3) set class "incomplete major-minor seventh chords on any scale degree."[70] In essence, Brahms turns the first progression into the second by changing the underlying canonical group that governs membership in the sequence.

Group (2), the canonical group of diatonic transpositions and inversions, results in the same set-class membership for C: V^7 as does group (1), as any diatonic seventh chord is inversionally symmetrical mod 7. The addition of the inversions *does*, however, change set-class membership for diatonically asymmetrical

---

70. The incomplete seventh chords in question all omit the chordal fifth. NB: this does not include the harmony on the downbeat of m. 14, which is an augmented sixth. This departure from the group-(3) set class effectively breaks the sequence.

chords, such as the incomplete dominant seventh: {($\hat{4}$, F), ($\hat{5}$, G), ($\hat{7}$, B)}. This set is grouped not only with its diatonic transpositions in C major under group (2), but also with inverted sets like {($\hat{2}$, D), ($\hat{4}$, F), ($\hat{5}$, G)} and {($\hat{1}$, C), ($\hat{3}$, E), ($\hat{4}$, F)}.

Note that groups (1) and (2) act only on diatonic sets. Thus, if either of these groups is taken as CANON, the resulting set types will encompass only diatonic sets—all nondiatonic sets will be excluded from the set classes.

2.11.2 Vignette: Das Lied von der Erde, "Der Einsame im Herbst"

Figure 2.40(a) sketches aspects of mm. 1–33 of "Der Einsame im Herbst," the second song in Mahler's *Das Lied von der Erde*. The three-note pentatonic motive from the opening song sounds in the oboe beginning in m. 3; it is labeled *X* on the figure.[71] The motive is draped over the local modal landscape via various diatonic transpositions in the first system of 2.40(a). Transposed motive-forms *Y* and *Z* alter *X*'s specific (but not generic) intervallic content; the four forms *W, X, Y,* and *Z* are all members of the same group-(1) set class of diatonic trichords in D minor. These four trichords all occupy the same row in the key shown in Figure 2.40(b). A vertical line in 2.40(b) separates the D-minor forms from two B♭-major forms that first sound in m. 33. Boxes enclose the tonic forms of the trichord in each key area— that is, the forms containing scale degrees $\hat{1}$, $\hat{7}$, and $\hat{5}$. Figure 2.40(b) also indicates the different intervallic species of the various trichords via T_n-type labels. These various intervallic species delineate group-(3) set classes. For example, sets *X, W,* and *Y′* are all members of the group-(3) set class containing the motivic trichords of the [035]-species. Sets *Y, Y″, X′,* and *X″* are all members of the group-(3) set class containing the motivic trichords of the [045]-species.

Motive-form *X* is the emblematic initial statement of the [035]-species; it sounds "on D" and is a tonic form. Motive-form *Y* is the emblematic initial statement of the [045]-species; it sounds "on B♭" and is a nontonic form. Over the course of the opening section (mm. 1–32), these relationships gradually shift, as the B♭-based/[045]/diatonic motive form gradually displaces the D-based /[035]/ pentatonic motive form, ultimately usurping the latter's tonic authority in m. 33. The two chromatic transpositions shown in the second system of Figure 2.40(a), formal inverses of one another, represent a preliminary stage in this process. The *X* motive is first transposed by $T_{(3rd^{-1}, -4)}$ in m. 28, yielding form *Y′*. This transposes the [035]-species trichord to B♭, the native pitch-level of [045]-form *Y*. It further yields a striking chromaticism, (♭$\hat{5}$, A♭), which sticks out painfully from the local modal landscape, defamiliarizing the pentatonic motive. The *Y* motive is then transposed by $T_{(3rd, 4)}$ in m. 31, yielding form *X′*. This transposes the [045]-species trichord to D, the native pitch-level of [035]-form *X*. This also yields a chromatic pitch: (♯$\hat{7}$, C♯). Though ♯$\hat{7}$ is a very common chromatic pitch in minor, in the present

---

71. Guido Adler called this the "fundamental motive" of the entire cycle in his 1914 essay on the composer (translated in Reilly 1982; see p. 66).

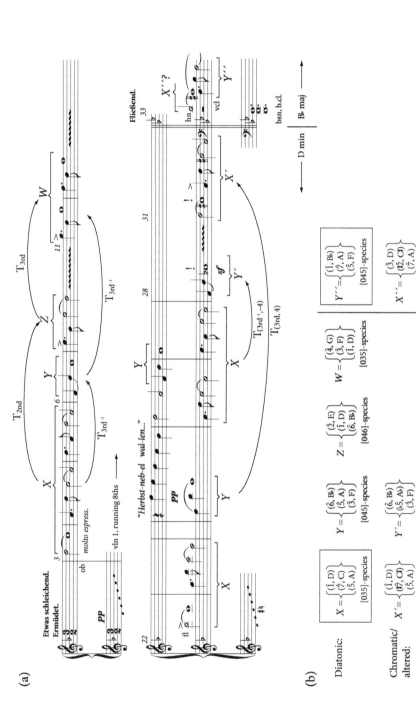

Figure 2.40 Motivic transformations in Mahler, *Das Lied von der Erde*, "Der Einsame im Herbst," mm. 1–33.

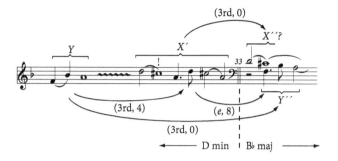

$$Y \quad\quad\quad\quad X'$$
$$\left\{\begin{matrix}(\hat{6}, B\flat)\\(\hat{5}, A)\\(\hat{3}, F)\end{matrix}\right\} \xrightarrow{(3rd, 4)} \left\{\begin{matrix}(\hat{1}, D)\\(\sharp\hat{7}, C\sharp)\\(\hat{5}, A)\end{matrix}\right\}$$

STAGE 2

$$Y \quad\quad\quad X' \quad\quad\quad Y''$$
$$\left\{\begin{matrix}(\hat{6}, B\flat)\\(\hat{5}, A)\\(\hat{3}, F)\end{matrix}\right\} \xrightarrow{(3rd, 4)} \left\{\begin{matrix}(\hat{1}, D)\\(\hat{7}, C\sharp)\\(\hat{5}, A)\end{matrix}\right\} \xrightarrow{(e, 8)} \left\{\begin{matrix}(\hat{1}, B\flat)\\(\hat{7}, A)\\(\hat{5}, F)\end{matrix}\right\}$$

$$(3rd, 0)$$

STAGE 3

$$X''$$
$$\left\{\begin{matrix}(\hat{3}, D)\\(\sharp\hat{2}, C\sharp)\\(\hat{7}, A)\end{matrix}\right\}$$

$$(3rd, 0)$$

$$Y \quad\quad\quad X' \quad\quad\quad Y''$$
$$\left\{\begin{matrix}(\hat{6}, B\flat)\\(\hat{5}, A)\\(\hat{3}, F)\end{matrix}\right\} \xrightarrow{(3rd, 4)} \left\{\begin{matrix}(\hat{1}, D)\\(\hat{7}, C\sharp)\\(\hat{5}, A)\end{matrix}\right\} \xrightarrow{(e, 8)} \left\{\begin{matrix}(\hat{1}, B\flat)\\(\hat{7}, A)\\(\hat{5}, F)\end{matrix}\right\}$$

$$(3rd, 0)$$

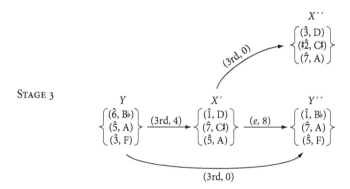

Figure 2.41 Mahler, "Der Einsame im Herbst," transformations across the formal seam at m. 33.

modal/pentatonic context—which has strongly emphasized (♮$\hat{7}$, C♮)—it sticks out nearly as painfully as the ♭$\hat{5}$ of m. 28.

Figure 2.41 traces the remaining stages in the ascendency of the B♭-based [045]-form as the music flows across the formal boundary into the B section at m. 33. Stage 1 shows the chromatic transformation of Y just discussed, which yields X′, the D-based [045]-form with the painful leading tone. This creates a "tonic version" of the [045]-species within D minor—the first stage in Y's gradual assumption of tonic authority. In stage 2, X′ is transformed via (*e*, 8) to become a tonic form in B♭ major. This brings the [045]-form back to Y's original pitch level, now with X's original scale-degree functions (i.e., {$\hat{1}$, $\hat{7}$, $\hat{5}$}). The net effect of this is a pivot third transformation (3rd, 0) of Y, yielding Y″. In stage 3, X′ is *itself* transformed by a pivot third, yielding the highly distorted X″ = {($\hat{3}$, D), (♯$\hat{2}$, C♯), ($\hat{7}$, A)}.[72] This completes the ascendancy of the B♭-based/[045]/diatonic attributes associated with Y over the D-based/[035]/pentatonic attributes associated with X, transforming the "fundamental motive" and its surrounding context from chilly D-based modality (*Herbst*) to warm, chromatically enriched, B♭-based tonality (premonitions of *Lenz?*).

2.12 Epilogue: A Formal Issue Regarding Transposition and Inversion

We conclude this chapter by surveying an area for further formal refinement regarding the transpositions and inversions introduced in sections 2.9 and 2.10. As the discussion of canonical groups in section 2.11.1 has made clear, the transpositions and inversions naturally combine into various groups. The diatonic transpositions alone may form a group, as may the diatonic transpositions and inversions together. Similarly, the chromatic transpositions alone may form a group, as may the chromatic transpositions and inversions together. Finally, the real transpositions may form a group. Note, however, that no group can be formed that *combines* diatonic and chromatic operations. This is because the groups act on different sets. The diatonic transpositions and inversions act on the set of seven diatonic scale degrees (which are fused to their representative diapcs in a given key). The chromatic transpositions and inversions, by contrast, act on the complete set of 84 sd/pc pairs. The real transpositions are a subgroup of the group of chromatic transpositions; this subgroup acts on the 12 pitch classes only, leaving scale degrees untouched.

This division into different groups was conceptually and analytically productive when it came to defining different kinds of GIS$_{Tonal}$ set classes. It raises a formal problem, however, with regard to graph and network construction. *GMIT* requires

---

72. Form X″ is, admittedly, only implicit: ($\hat{7}$, A) does not sound. The D–C♯ melodic gesture that begins the motive form in m. 33, however, is an unmistakable echo of the first two notes of X, encouraging the listener to complete the motive imaginatively.

CHAPTER Three

Oriented Networks

3.1 Tonic-Directed Transformations

In what is perhaps the most cited passage in *GMIT* (175–80), David Lewin defines several harmonic operations that act on major and minor triads. The passage has received considerable attention as the source of neo-Riemannian theory, but we will focus here on an aspect of it that has been largely ignored: the tonic-directedness of several of Lewin's operations.[1] Among these are DOM and SUBD, which take the dominant and subdominant chords, respectively, to their tonics.[2] Figure 3.1 sketches the operations in network format, substituting the labels D and S for DOM and SUBD, and employing a graphic convention—that of enclosing the tonic node in a double border—that we will make more formal later. Lewin says that the dominant and subdominant operations, so defined, "*drive* the network . . . in a natural musical way," modeling "our kinetic intuitions about the music under study" (*GMIT,* 176–77, emphasis original).

We can explore these "kinetic intuitions" by examining some networks created with S and D. Figure 3.2(a) models a half cadence, with a D arrow pointing from

---

1. One scholar who has not ignored this aspect of Lewin's harmonic transformations is Brian Hyer, who explores such tonic-directedness in engaging philosophical detail in his dissertation (Hyer 1989, esp. 99–109). The present discussion departs from Hyer in certain respects, both conceptual and technical—it does not adopt his semiotic framework, for example—but it is nevertheless indebted to his thought.

2. Lewin similarly defines mediant and submediant transformations (MED and SUBM) as tonic-directed. In earlier work (1982–83, 329–33), Lewin had defined the dominant and subdominant transformations in the opposite way: i.e., as operations that transform the tonic to the dominant or subdominant. Nevertheless, in the analyses in that article, Lewin used only the inverse forms of these transformations, so that all arrows point to the tonic, just as in *GMIT.* This suggests that the tonic-directedness in question is primarily a graph-theoretic matter (i.e., involving the ways in which one draws nodes and arrows) and not a group-theoretic one (i.e., involving the ways in which specific transformations are defined algebraically). We return to this issue in section 3.3.1.

(a)

(b)

Figure 3.1 The dominant (D) and subdominant (S) operations.

(a)   (b)

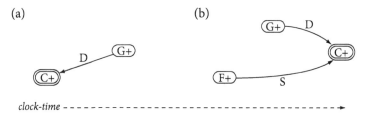

clock-time - →

Figure 3.2 Two networks using dominant and subdominant transformations, arranged in left-to-right chronological order.

right to left, from the dominant harmony G+ to the tonic harmony C+. The network follows Lewin's suggestion that temporal chronology may be reflected by left-to-right layout on the page; this is made explicit by the "clock-time" arrow along the bottom of the figure.[3] The D arrow thus points back in time from the half-cadential dominant to its preceding tonic, suggesting a "back-relating dominant." Figure 3.2(b) shows a forward-oriented example, with S and D arrows overlapping and pointing toward a C+ tonic node on the right-hand side of the network. Lewin uses networks of this form to model the openings of the "Waldstein" Sonata and "Dissonance" Quartet.[4]

Figure 3.3(a) reproduces a somewhat more complex network from *GMIT*, which interprets the harmonic progression that opens the slow movement of the "Appassionata," shown in 3.3(b). I have translated the network into the orthography of the present book. I have also made one subtle formal change: the network as it appears in *GMIT* includes three D♭+ tonic nodes, which are joined by arrows bearing the identity operation. I have removed those arrows and joined the three D♭+ nodes into a *single* formal node, as indicated by the incomplete branches extending between the double-bordered ovals. The formal and conceptual significance of this change will become clear as we proceed.

The G♭+ and E♭– nodes apply to the six-five chord on the final eighth of m. 2, interpreting it in the manner of Rameau's *double emploi*. The bracketed E♭+ *Klang* that follows is "not actually sounded but is theoretically understood" (*GMIT*, 213).

---

3. *GMIT*, 177–78. We will explore such matters of left-to-right chronology in graphs and networks in greater detail in section 3.9.

4. Lewin 1982–83, 329–31, Figs. 11–14. I have reinterpreted Lewin's subdominant and dominant transformations here to conform to his later practice in *GMIT*, replacing his S⁻¹ and D⁻¹ arrow labels with S and D. See note 2 above. I have also rearranged the network visually so that the subdominant is lower on the page than the dominant, and changed the node contents so that C+ is in the tonic node.

(a)

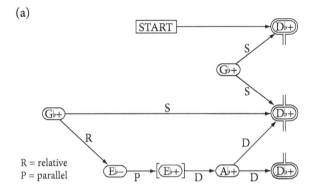

R = relative
P = parallel

(b)

Figure 3.3 (a) Lewin's network for the "Appassionata" slow movement, mm. 1–5 (*GMIT*, Figure 9.14b); (b) the music in question.

The node including the word START indicates where the passage begins; it also relates to a formal issue that need not concern us here.[5] That formal issue *does* relate, however, to the issue of arrows proceeding backward in time, which is relevant to the present discussion.

All of the arrows in the network point from left to right. Lewin uses this visual layout to explore interesting kinetic aspects of the theme. Specifically, he draws attention to those moments at which the graph shoots out to the left in the temporal progression of the music, calling such moments "carriage returns." The layout distinguishes between the intensity of the two carriage returns: the second G♭+ is farther leftward than is the first, to make room for the several nodes that must follow it before the return of the D♭+ tonic. As Lewin notes, this interacts nicely with the rhythm of the passage, with the sharp leftward jag of the second carriage return corresponding to the eighth-note anacrusis to m. 3, which provides the gentle push of momentum toward the cadence of m. 4.

These networks' arrows all flow in the direction of the tonic. They proceed sometimes forward in time, sometimes backward, and sometimes link noncontiguous harmonies in the music; contiguous harmonies may not be linked at all. The transformations take harmonies either directly to the tonic or to other harmonies "on the way" to the tonic (as in the string of arrows departing from the second G♭+ node in Figure 3.3). In this way, the networks differ from most networks in recent

5. The network appears in a discussion of the topic of "precedence ordering."

neo-Riemannian studies, in which transformational arrows typically proceed forward in time, linking one harmony to the next in the temporal flow of the music.

We can interpret the tonic-directed arrows in Figures 3.1–3.3 via familiar tonal metaphors: we might say, in a Kurthian vein, that they trace the flow of "tonal energy" in the music, or, in a more Rameauian vein, that they register the pull of "tonal gravity." Such metaphors sensitize us to the "kinetic intuitions" that Lewin alludes to—with them in mind, one senses strongly the difference between moving *away* from a tonic (proceeding against an arrow) and moving *toward* a tonic (proceeding with an arrow). An arrow that proceeds forward in time urges the music forward to an anticipated tonic, with the forces of tonal attraction, or the flow of tonal energy; arrows that proceed backward in time, in contrast, check forward momentum, suggesting the pull of an earlier tonic as a force to be overcome.

Such transformational networks explore an aspect of tonal experience not captured by the sd/pc GIS introduced in the previous chapter. While that GIS focused on intervals between heard scale degrees—pitches infused with tonal qualia—networks such as those in Figures 3.1–3.3 illuminate certain kinetic aspects of tonal experience, modeling the ways in which a tonic pitch or chord can act as an orienting presence: a locus of attraction for the music's various energetic vectors.

3.2 Intentions

3.2.1 Tonal Intention as Transformational Action

Can we reconcile these energeticist metaphors with the *transformational attitude*, the idea that transformations model first-person actions of some kind?[6] In what ways might we be understood to "perform" the tonic-directed transformations in Figures 3.1–3.3, as musical actants creating or hearing the music in question? These questions gain urgency from Lewin's own writing, in which he states that DOM and his other harmonic operations represent "something one *does* to a Klang to obtain another Klang" (*GMIT,* 177, emphasis original). The italics underscore the importance Lewin attached to the idea of transformation-as-first-person-action, even (perhaps especially?) in this tonal-harmonic context. But what is the nature

---

6. Though this attitude is a conspicuous element of the interpretive tradition of transformational theory, there is disagreement among current scholars—or at least some uncertainty—as to whether it is of the essence for the theory. After all, transformation is a mathematical concept that retains its formal meaning whether one adopts the transformational attitude, and its nexus of familiar metaphors, or not (as noted in Cherlin 1993, 21). While some theorists continue to explore the attitude as a central aspect of transformational methodology (Satyendra 2004, Klumpenhouwer 2006), others have begun to distance themselves from such language (Hook 2007b, 172–77). And indeed, much applied analytical work in the transformational literature makes no mention at all of first-person action (though the idea may be implicit). It is thus unclear what role the transformational attitude will play in the evolving interpretive practice of transformational theory. I would nevertheless like to take it seriously in the present context. (See Harrison 2011 for a perspicacious treatment of certain methodological issues raised by the transformational attitude.)

of this "doing"? How might we *perform* such tonic-directed arrows when we are in contact with the relevant music?

I will propose one answer to that question here, though I do not presume it was necessarily what Lewin had in mind.[7] Put simply, I suggest that we can understand such arrows to model one of the things one "does" to a sounding entity in the process of hearing it as tonal. To interpret a sounding entity as tonal is, among other things, to hear it as bearing some relationship to a tonic. The tonic-directed arrows in Figures 3.2 and 3.3 trace such acts of tonal interpretation, as the listener/performer/analyst relates sounding chords to the tonic in various ways, directing attention always *from* the sounding chords *to* the tonic in the process. Such a tonic may be anticipated, remembered, or simply felt as an orienting presence in the music, occupying no specific temporal location.[8] In this understanding, to hear a given harmony as a dominant is mentally to perform the dominant transformation, linking the sounding harmony to an understood tonic via D; it is our mental performance of D that invests the dominant with its special energetic charge, as we hear "through" the sounding chord, so to speak, toward the tonic via D. (This idea casts a considerable historical shadow, as we will see in section 3.2.2).

We can thus interpret the arrows in Figures 3.2–3.3 as records of particular acts of hearing carried out in the direction of the tonic. In Figure 3.2(a), on hearing the G+ chord of the half cadence, the listener/performer/analyst mentally performs D, relating the G+ chord back to the preceding C+ as its dominant. In Figure 3.2(b), the F+ and G+ sonorities are intentionally directed ahead to an anticipated cadential C+ tonic, via S and D, respectively. In Figure 3.3(a), the harmonies are intentionally directed toward D♭+ in a variety of syntactically mediated ways. Particularly interesting here is the G♭+ of the second "carriage return." The harmony is first experienced retrospectively as subdominant of the previous D♭+, which is intended (back in time) via the long rightward S arrow of 3.3(a). G♭+ is also experienced prospectively—via the *double emploi*—as a *pre*-dominant of the upcoming A♭+. This nicely captures the strong pull of forward momentum from the G♭+/E♭– six-five toward the A♭+ on the downbeat of m. 3, and from there toward the imminent tonic of m. 4. The change of intentional directions at the furthest point of the carriage return (the G♭+ node) marks the moment at which a listener begins to direct his or her attention toward the anticipated cadential tonic, via the chain of rightward arrows, as the "conveyor belt" of the conventional cadential progression engages.

As a general rubric for this species of transformational action, I propose the term *tonal intention*. Intention here is meant in the sense of "directing the mind or attention to[ward] something" (*OED*). The word is a basic term of art in phenomenology, the central tenet of which is that all consciousness is consciousness *of* something—that is, all consciousness is *intentional* in that it is directed toward objects. We can intend things that are physically present: for me at this moment,

---

7. Indeed, Lewin's writing on this topic seems intended to be suggestive and poetic rather than precise and propositional. As a result, the passage is open to multiple interpretations (perhaps by design). I offer one such interpretation here. For a semiotic interpretation, see Hyer 1989.

8. We will clarify the formal and conceptual distinctions between these temporal possibilities in section 3.9.

my laptop, my son playing with his cars on the rug (among other things); for you at this moment, this book (among other things). We can also intend things that are not physically present to our senses. An especially suggestive case is our intention of a cube.[9] We never see the entire cube at once, yet we are aware that it consists of more than the sides we can see at any given moment. We are conscious of a *complete cube,* not merely a congeries of visual facets. We thus intend the cube's hidden backside just as we intend its visually present front. Robert Sokolowski (2000) refers to our intention of the cube's hidden backside as an "empty intention." The idea is suggestive of our intention of a tonic in its acoustic absence.[10]

I suspect that we intend the tonic in manifold ways when we are in the moment of tonal hearing. If this is true, a given auditor's tonal intentions at any instant are multiple and perhaps partly inchoate, varying in degree of intensity and cognitive mediation. Thus, no single analytical representation can do full justice to our pre-reflective intentional activity. Analytical representations can, however, function suggestively, acting as goads to specific acts of intentional hearing, or as a means of focusing and refining prereflective hearings. Such analyses can encourage us to direct our ears to the tonic in specific ways, via the mediation of specific theoretical categories. (In Figures 3.1–3.3, for example, these categories are loosely Riemannian.) It should be clear, however, that the concept of tonal intention has implications beyond the realm of analytical pragmatics, opening suggestive routes of inquiry for studies in music cognition.

Figure 3.4 sketches the abstract structure of a tonal intention: a subjective pointing of the ears *from* some subordinate tonal element *to* the tonic. Such intentions may proceed directly to the tonic, as in 3.4(a), or they may pass first through intervening elements "on the way" to it, as in 3.4(b). The harmonic transformations of Figures 3.1–3.3 represent just one special case of tonal-intentional transformation. The objects in the nodes in Figure 3.4 need not be limited to harmonies (whether conceived as Riemannian *Klänge,* or as *Stufen,* or as thoroughbass

(a)

(b)

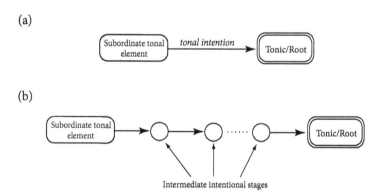

Figure 3.4 Networks modeling the basic idea of tonal intention.

---

9. This particular example is presented in Sokolowski 2000, 17–21. Sokolowski's book is a highly accessible introduction to (more or less Husserlian) phenomenology.
10. Hyer 1989 offers highly suggestive observations on the orienting power of absent tonics.

configurations, etc.); the nodes can contain pitches or pitch classes as well—including sd/pc ordered pairs from the GIS of Chapter 2—in a variety of melodic, harmonic, and contrapuntal contexts. Further, as the annotation "Tonic/Root" in the double-bordered nodes of Figure 3.4 suggests, we may sometimes wish to model intentional structures arranged around local centers of tonal attraction, like harmonic roots, which may not be global tonics (as discussed in section 3.5). When I wish to speak of tonal-intentional targets in a broad sense—encompassing both roots and tonics—I will use the locution *tonal center*.

3.2.2 Historical Resonances

Despite the bewildering range of semantic reference that the term tonality has taken on in its short life,[11] a near constant is the idea that to hear tonally is to organize one's aural sensations in relation to a central tonic. It is thus not surprising to find language suggestive of the concept of tonal intention running like a red thread throughout the history of tonal theory—that is, language in which the act of relating sounding entities to the tonic is thematized. Consider the following four excerpts from Rameau, Riemann, Zuckerkandl, and Schachter:

(a)   ...the chord called perfect, or natural [i.e., the tonic]... is the chord that we find most agreeable, the one to which all of our desires tend, and beyond which we desire nothing more.

Rameau 1737, 27–28[12]

(b)   If I imagine the C-major triad in its meaning in the key of C major, it is the tonic itself, the center, the closing chord. The image of it contains nothing that would contradict its consonance. It appears stable, pure, simple. If I imagine, on the other hand, the G-major chord in the sense of the key of C major, then I imagine it as the *Klang* of the upper fifth of the C major triad, i.e., the C-major triad itself is part of the imagination as that Klang by which the significance of the G-major triad is determined as something deviating from it—the center of its imagination lies, so to speak, outside of it. That is to say, a moment of instability emerges, a desire to progress to the C-major triad, dissonance. So it is with the F-major chord, and generally every chord of the key.

Riemann 1882, 188[13]

---

11. See Hyer 2002 and Beiche 1992.
12. "...l'Accord appellé Parfait, ou Naturel... c'est l'Accord qui nous affecte le plus agréablement, auquel tendent tous nos desirs, et après lequel nous ne souhaitons plus rien."
13. Translation by Alexander Rehding (2003, 71–72), slightly altered. "Denke ich mir den c-Durakkord im Sinne der c-Dur-Tonart, so ist er selbst Tonika, Centrum, schlußfähiger Akkord, seine Vorstellung enthält also nichts seiner Konsonanz Widersprechendes, erscheint ruhig, rein, einfach; denke ich mir dagegen den g-Durakkord im Sinne der c-Durtonart, so denke ich ihn mir als Klang der Oberquinte des c-Durakkordes, d.h. der c-Durakkord selbst geht mit in die Vorstellung ein als derjenige Klang, an welchem sich die Bedeutung des g-Durakkordes bestimmt als etwas von ihm Abweichendes – das Centrum der Vorstellung liegt also sozusagen außer ihr, d.h. es kommt ein Moment der Unruhe in dieselbe, das Verlangen der Fortschreitung zum c-Durakkord, die Dissonanz. Ebenso ist es mit dem f-Durakkord, überhaupt mit jedem Klange der Tonart."

that the labels on the arrows of any transformational graph or network all be drawn from a single (semi)group. As we have seen, the diatonic and chromatic operations cannot combine into a single group; nor, as it turns out, can they combine into a single semigroup, due to their action on different sets. The graph underlying the *Parsifal* analysis in Figure 2.35(b) thus runs afoul of *GMIT*'s formal requirements, as it combines diatonic transpositions and chromatic transpositions. The same can be said of the graphs underlying the Mendelssohn networks in Figure 2.39, as they combine diatonic and chromatic transpositions and inversions. These are all nevertheless fully *realizable* graphs, in a sense similar to Hook's (2007a) use of the italicized term: there exist elements from the space S that can fill their nodes in a way that agrees with the arrow labels.[73] Indeed, the networks of Figures 2.35(b) and 2.39 explicitly demonstrate the underlying graphs' realizability.

There is, however, a formal issue here that merits further study (in a more specialized context): if the diatonic and chromatic operations combine in ways that seem to make good musical sense in an analysis, but they nevertheless do not combine into a semigroup, what kind of mathematical structure might underwrite their interaction? Might such a mathematical structure open the door to new kinds of transformational networks (which may not be semigroup-based)? The questions bring to mind comments made by Julian Hook (regarding a transformational system similar in ambition to the GIS introduced in this chapter):

> For several reasons, the transformations of my system do not form a group, and I am unaware of a mathematical theory of whatever kind of structure it is that they *do* form. This situation has revived my long-standing suspicion that perhaps the reason why mathematical theories of music have not been more productive is that some of the appropriate mathematics has yet to be invented. (Hook 2006)

I am not certain that the "appropriate mathematics has yet to be invented" in the case of the GIS$_{\text{Tonal}}$ transpositions and inversions, but there certainly remains formal work to do. It is my hope that such work will not only satisfy our desire for formal completeness, but will also deepen our understanding of the musical experiences in question.

---

73. Hook introduces the term "realizability" in relation to the "path-consistency condition," which is not at issue here (that condition is discussed in section 3.3.4 of this book). The present discussion instead concerns the semigroup membership of arrow labels. The methodological issues are nevertheless similar. My borrowing of Hook's term in this context responds to a similar desire to recognize the analytical usefulness of certain structures that are technically disallowed by the rather stringent guidelines of *GMIT* (which Lewin himself did not even follow in all cases; see section 3.3.4).

Having said this, we can observe that the operation graphs underlying the *Parsifal* and Mendelssohn analyses may be broken up into subgraphs that are well formed by the criteria of *GMIT*. Such subgraphs consist of only diatonic operations, or only chromatic operations. One can create a diatonic subgraph simply by removing the arrows bearing chromatic labels; to create a chromatic subgraph, one simply removes the arrows bearing diatonic labels. Note that the *Parsifal* graph is arranged on the page to make this subgraph structure visible: all diatonic arrows point rightward, while all chromatic arrows (in this case, real transpositions) point downward.

(c) The [nontonic] <u>tone seems to point beyond itself</u> toward release from tension and restoration of equilibrium; <u>it seems to look in a definite direction</u> for the event that will bring about this change; it even seems to demand the event....What takes place here between the two tones is a sort of play of forces, comparable to that between magnetic needle and magnetic pole. The activity of the one is a placing itself in a direction, a pointing toward and striving after a goal; the activity of the other is a dictating of direction, a drawing to itself. The one wants to pass beyond itself, the other wants itself....

Zuckerkandl 1956, 19–20

(d) To hear something in a key, we have to be aware of <u>a tonic note, a pitch that functions as a center of orientation to which, directly or indirectly, we relate all the other pitches</u>....Tonal music's power to create a sense of future through the specificity of the expectations it can arouse has no parallel in any other kind of music of which I am aware....

Schachter 1999, 135

These quotes span a 250-year period and differ considerably in their historical contexts, theoretical aims (from the speculative to the pedagogical), and ideological commitments. I do not wish to gloss over these distinctions. Instead, I simply wish to point out the resonances between their language and the present idea of tonal intention.

In the underlined passages, Rameau, Riemann, and Schachter speak explicitly about intentional actions of auditors: we "desire" the tonic, "imagine" it, or "relate" all of the other pitches to it. In short, these writers are discussing something one *does* when one hears tonally (cf. Lewin). Zuckerkandl, by contrast, treats the directedness of tonal entities to the tonic as an immanent property of the tones themselves, not as a product of the listener's interpretive action. As we will see, his ideas are still highly suggestive in the present context. A few words on each quote will be helpful.

For Rameau in the *Génération* (quote (a)), the action modeled by the arrows of Figure 3.4 is one of desire: the tonic is the chord "to which all of our desires tend."[14] The fact that the quoted passage comes from the *Génération*—the first treatise in which Rameau's "Newtonian turn" is fully in evidence—recalls Rameau's familiar metaphor of "tonal gravitation," already mentioned in section 3.1.[15] Though much of Rameau's language in the treatise treats this gravitation as analogous to a natural law, at other places the text seems to contradict this: it is remarkable how often the words *désirer* and *souhaiter* occur. These highly subjective verbs seem to place the agency for "tonal gravitation" not out in the universe, but within the auditor.

Riemann in quote (b) also uses the word "desire" (*Verlangen*), as well as the more neutral verb "to imagine" (Rehding's translation of *denken*). Riemann's

14. Brian Hyer interprets Rameau's language here in sexual terms (2002, 731). That trope—figuring tonal intentions as erotic structures—has been a central theme in much of Susan McClary's writing (for example, McClary 1991, 53–79, and 2001, 63–108). The connection between tonal desire and other kinds of desire reappears in the Wagner analysis in section 3.8. Metaphors of musical force as desire (whether that of the auditor or of the tones themselves) have a long history that predates both tonal practice and Rameau. See Cohen 2001 and Rothfarb 2002, 931.

15. See Christensen 1993, 185–93.

language is highly suggestive: "the center of [the dominant chord's] imagination lies, so to speak, outside of it." The parallel here to Lewin's own definition of the dominant operation is striking, and suggests that his criticism of Riemann's harmonic theories as static and insensitive to our "kinetic intuitions" is at least partly inaccurate.[16] Passages similar to the one cited, which comes from Riemann's 1882 essay "Die Natur der Harmonik," can be found throughout his writings, especially in discussions of modern "tonality" (which he calls *Tonalität,* in contrast to the earlier, scale-based *Tonart*) as a system in which all sounding elements are mentally related back to a central *Klang.* Consider the following passage from the *Skizze einer neuen Methode der Harmonielehre* (1880):

> We find ourselves in C major whenever the C-major *Klang* forms the middle point of our harmonic imagination [*den Mittelpunkt unseres harmonischen Vorstellens bildet*], whenever it is the only chord that is appropriate as a closing chord, and all other chords receive their characteristic quality and significance through their relationship to this principal *Klang.* . . .[17]

A few years later, in 1893, Riemann would present a theory to model the ways in which a listener relates every harmony back to the tonic—the "middle point of our harmonic imagination"—via the system of harmonic functions. We will explore a transformational interpretation of this system in section 3.4.

In quote (c), Zuckerkandl speaks suggestively about a nontonic tone "pointing beyond itself" toward the tonic. Zuckerkandl is talking specifically about $\hat{2}$ in the excerpt quoted above, but he later makes clear that

> [t]he same is true of all other tones in the system. Each of them, exactly like the tone $\hat{2}$, points beyond itself, to $\hat{1}$; indeed, this pointing toward the same directional point, toward a common center, is precisely what makes them elements in one system. But each of them, again, points to the common center from a different locus, and so each does it in its particular, one might almost say personal, way, with a gesture that is its own, a tonal gesture. (Zuckerkandl 1956, 34–35)

Zuckerkandl's use of the word *gesture* is especially suggestive of the transformational attitude.[18] Carl Schachter's language in quote (d) is less figurative ("a tonic note . . . to

16. *GMIT,* 177. For additional critical responses to Lewin's characterization of Riemann see Alphonce 1988, 171; Klumpenhouwer 1994; Harrison 1994, 275n42; Gollin 2000, 216n10; Kopp 2002, 150; and Rehding 2003, 72.

17. Riemann 1880, 70 (my translation). "Wir befinden uns in *c*-Dur, so lange als der *c*+ Klang den Mittelpunkt unseres harmonischen Vorstellens bildet, so lange er als allein schlussfähiger Klang erscheint und alle anderen Klänge ihre eigenthümliche Wirkung und Bedeutung durch ihre Beziehung zu diesem Hauptklange erhalten . . . ."

18. What is not suggestive of that attitude is his insistence (hinted at in these two excerpts, stated more explicitly elsewhere) that these dynamic qualities inhere in the stuff of music itself, and are not products of interpretive (Zuckerkandl would say "psychic") activity on the part of the listener. This requires Zuckerkandl to posit a threefold division of the world into the physical world, the psychic world, and a "dynamic" world that is neither physical nor psychic—a precarious metaphsics.

which...we relate all other pitches"), but it is also perhaps the clearest expression of the meaning of the arrows in Figure 3.4. Schachter further stresses the idea that we relate pitches "directly or indirectly" to the tonic, a qualification that underscores the pertinence of Figure 3.4(b) in many contexts.

3.3 Oriented Networks

3.3.1 Oriented Digraphs

We will now develop a simple formal model for constructing networks that can model various kinds of tonal intentions. At the heart of this formalism is the *oriented digraph:* a configuration of nodes and arrows, all of whose arrows are directed toward a single node.[19] The centrality of the oriented digraph in the formal work to come indicates a shift in emphasis away from the semigroup structure of transformations—the central concern of much transformational theory—to the graph structure of nodes and arrows. Though configurations of nodes and arrows are often treated rather informally in the transformational literature—as ad hoc pictures meant to communicate transformational relationships in an intuitive or musically suggestive way—it is important to recognize that as mathematical digraphs, they are formal entities, just as groups and semigroups are. They thus admit of formal development, offering a simple yet rich mathematical context in which to explore many basic relationships.[20]

This shift in emphasis toward graphs grows out of the observation that the analyses in Figures 3.2–3.3 embody important constraints on graphs, rather than constraints on the underlying algebra of transformations. To see this, we simply need to observe that the analyses could all easily be "redrawn" with different node/arrow structures, while still employing the same underlying group of operations (the group containing S, D, and so on). Nothing prevents us, for example, from redrawing the networks so that their arrows all point forward in time, linking one event to the next as the music progresses. There exist operations in the group that would serve our purposes for every new forward-directed arrow. For example, we could replace the operations on the arrows that proceed backward in time on Figures 3.2(a) and 3.3(a) with their formal inverses on arrows that proceed in the

19. *Digraph* is short for "directed graph" in graph theory: a graph with arrows, rather than undirected lines (or "edges"), linking its nodes. Lewin calls digraphs "node/arrow systems" (*GMIT,* 193, Def. 9.1.1). The oriented digraphs defined here are related to (but more specific than) the oriented digraphs defined in Harary 1969, 10.
20. Trudeau 1993 is a highly accessible introduction to basic graph theory (though he does not discuss digraphs). Harary, Norman, and Cartwright 1965 is a fine study of digraphs as models for social phenomena; the interested reader will have little difficulty in extending their observations to a variety of suggestive musical contexts. One of the most sophisticated studies to explore the formal importance of graphs in transformational theory—specifically, Cayley graphs derived from group presentations—is Gollin 2000. Gollin's work reappears in our study of spatial networks in section 3.9.

opposite direction (e.g., replacing the leftward D arrow in 3.2(a) with a rightward S or D⁻¹ arrow). In short, the group of operations does not constrain the ways in which the nodes and arrows are drawn in the networks. It is the configuration of nodes and arrows itself that communicates important information about the "tonal kinetics" of the music in question, not the underlying algebra of the trans-formations. Specifically, the node/arrow configurations—that is, the digraphs—impose a particular *orientation* on the algebraic materials of the networks.

We can easily define a general species of digraph that guarantees such an ori-entation, directing all arrows toward a single node. We will call this an *oriented digraph*, which meets the following four conditions:

(A): All of the nodes in the system are connected to one another. That is, from any node, one can reach any other node in the network via some path of forward and/or backward arrows.
(B): The system has no "looped" arrows from any node to itself, nor does it have any "two-headed arrows" between any two distinct nodes.
(C): There is one node that has arrows pointing to it and no arrows issuing from it. We will call this the *root node*, and will set it off visually from the other nodes by a double border.
(D): There is at least one forward-oriented arrow path from every node to the root node.

The reader can develop an intuitive sense for the four conditions by examining Figure 3.5, which shows six digraphs, three that are oriented by the above criteria, (a)–(c), and three that are not, (d)–(f).

We now discuss the conceptual motivations for each of the conditions. Condition (A) stipulates that all of the nodes in the network must be connected to one another via some configuration of arrows. This eliminates the possibility of a single node floating free, or of a digraph that is made up of multiple, but unconnected, subdi-graphs. The motivation for the condition is simple: if a node is unconnected to the main graph it has no connection to the tonic node. In other words, the network stip-ulates no intentional path whereby the element can be interpreted with reference to the prevailing tonic. We will call this the condition of *intentional connectivity*.

Condition (B) requires that there are no "looped" arrows pointing from a node to itself, and that no pair of nodes is linked by a "double-headed" or "two-way" arrow.[21] We will call these the conditions of *irreflexievity* and *asymmetry*, respec-tively. The condition of asymmetry (no two-way arrows) states that given two directly connected nodes x and y, there will either be a transformational arrow from x to y, or one from y to x, but not both. The motivation for the idea should be clear if we substitute "dominant harmony" for x and "tonic harmony" for y. Our network would direct a one-way arrow from x to y, pointing from x-as-dominant to y-as-tonic (i.e., $x \xrightarrow{D} y$). The one-way arrow suggests that the situation is *intentionally asymmetrical*: x is intentionally directed toward y but y is not intentionally directed toward x. The idea

---

21. Formally, a "double-headed arrow" between nodes a and b is actually two arrows, known as a *symmetric pair* of arrows: one from a to b, the other from b to a.

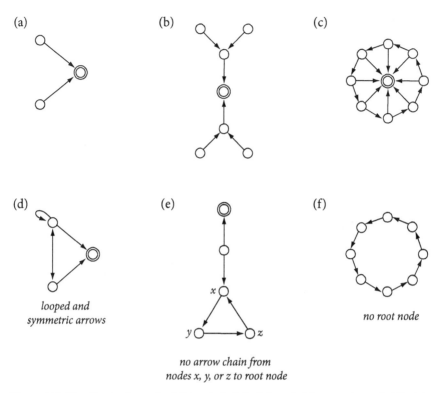

(a)

(b)

(c)

(d)

looped and symmetric arrows

(e)

x

y   z

no arrow chain from nodes x, y, or z to root node

(f)

no root node

Figure 3.5 Six directed graphs (digraphs): (a), (b), and (c) are oriented; (d), (e), and (f) are not.

recalls Zuckerkandl's wording: "The activity of the one [i.e., x] is a placing itself in a direction, a pointing toward and striving after a goal; the activity of the other [i.e., y] is a dictating of direction, a drawing to itself." It is this one-way kinetic/intentional structure that the asymmetry condition seeks to capture. The condition strews this intentional asymmetry throughout the network, making *every* pair of connected elements asymmetrical in the same fashion, even when the tonic is not directly involved.

The idea of intentional asymmetry complements the many other pitch-based asymmetries familiar from tonal discourse: the asymmetrical division of the chromatic scale into seven diatonic steps, the asymmetrical construction of the triad into major and minor thirds, the asymmetrical plagal and authentic divisions of the octave, and so on. The asymmetry under discussion here is nevertheless crucially different from these asymmetries in that it describes not a configuration of pitches, but an asymmetrical predisposition in one's hearing—a predisposition to turn one's ears in the direction of the tonic, so to speak, and to sense a strong distinction (that is, an asymmetry) between musical relationships directed toward that tonic and those directed away from it.[22]

22. For relevant comments on the "asymmetrical, unidirectional character of tonal music," see Morgan 1998.

The condition of irreflexivity (no looped arrows) simply arises because a looped arrow is difficult to square with the concepts of intention and asymmetry: such an arrow suggests an intentional act directed from a musical entity to itself. The idea may be suggestive in certain contexts involving the tonic node alone, but it would dilute our later formal development. We will thus exclude looped arrows from oriented digraphs.[23]

Condition (C) states that there must be one node in the digraph that has no arrows issuing from it (it has "outdegree zero"). This is the *root node,* a graph-theoretic term with felicitous musical resonances. The root node often corresponds to the tonic in an analysis; in such cases, we can speak of the "tonic node" without confusion. We will retain the term root node in general contexts, however, as we may sometimes wish to use this node to indicate a local center of tonal attraction, like a harmonic root, which may not be a global tonic (as mentioned above in section 3.2.1; see section 3.5). The graphic convention of indicating this node with a double border serves as a visual aid for locating it in a graph or network; it marks the one node that has arrows incident to it and none issuing from it.[24] The condition stipulates only *one* root node, capturing a sense of one tonal center governing a local set of musical relationships. We will later loosen this restriction, both to make it possible to model multiple instances of the same tonic at different temporal locations in some musical passage, and to accommodate the idea of modulation. To do so, however, we will need to think more carefully about how our networks can encode temporality, a subject we will take up in section 3.9.

Condition (D) specifies that for every node in the oriented digraph, there is at least one arrow path leading from it to the tonic. The condition guarantees that every node will point to the root node in at least one way, either via a single arrow, or via a chain of forward-directed arrows.

3.3.2 A Note on Graph and Network Interpretation

It should be stressed that the formal conditions for an oriented digraph simply guarantee that the energy in a transformational graph or network will flow in a certain way. Those formal conditions, in and of themselves, do not imply anything

---

23. Lewin (*GMIT,* 193) defines his node/arrow systems (i.e., digraphs) so that they contain reflexive (i.e., looped) arrows for every node; that is, the relation ARROW includes (N, N) for every node N. It is difficult to understand what formal desideratum this requirement satisfies. Hook (2007a, 36n30) speculates that it might relate to a formal matter that he calls the "path-consistency condition"; we return to that condition later. But Lewin's networks do not seem to require looped arrows in order to be well formed. Nor is the requirement common in digraph theories: many definitions of digraphs (e.g., Chartrand 1977, 16, and Harary, Norman, and Cartwright 1965, 9) in fact prohibit reflexive (looped) arrows.

24. Graph theorists often use a similar technique to identify the root node in a *rooted graph* or *rooted tree.* In digraph theory, our root nodes are also termed *sinks* (specifically, *global sinks*): arrows flow in, but not out.

about the *tonal interpretation* of the arrows in such networks. The transformational literature in fact abounds in oriented networks that have nothing to do with tonal kinetics, to say nothing of the specific ideas about tonal intention explored above. (Oriented networks are not uncommon in atonal analyses, for example.) Thus, the convention of enclosing the root node in a double border in the present study will serve a dual purpose: it will not only mark the location of the root node, it will also indicate that *the network in question is to be interpreted in tonal-intentional terms*. That is, the root node is to be interpreted as a tonal center, and the network's arrows are to be read as modeling (or suggesting) acts of hearing carried out in the direction of that tonal center. The double-bordered root node thus indicates not only a formal property of the network in question, but also signals the way in which the network is to be interpreted. This will allow us to distinguish between tonal-intentional networks and other networks whose digraphs may be formally oriented, but whose arrows nevertheless model different sorts of transformational actions and relationships.

3.3.3 Node Classes and Hierarchy

From our preceding work, it will be clear that there are three classes of node in an oriented digraph:

(1) *Root nodes:* nodes with no arrows issuing from them
(2) *Source nodes:* nodes with no arrows pointing to them
(3) *Intermediate nodes:* nodes with arrows both issuing from and pointing to them[25]

An oriented digraph may have no intermediate nodes, as in Figure 3.5(a), or no source nodes, as in Figure 3.5(c). If the digraph contains both source nodes and intermediate nodes, as in Figure 3.5(b), we will refer to it as *hierarchically robust*.

The three node types are suggestive of the basic "tonal attitudes" of the elements in the digraph.[26] We can interpret an arrow pointing to a node as granting that node a certain degree of hierarchical stability, while an arrow departing from a node destabilizes it, directing tonal energy elsewhere. The root node—from which no arrows depart—is the most hierarchically stable node in the system by these criteria. It is the only element that is not intentionally directed anywhere else, and is the ultimate goal of all other arrow paths in the graph. The kinetic stability

25. Harary, Norman, and Cartwright (1965) call our root, source, and intermediate nodes "receivers," "transmitters," and "carriers," respectively. Lewin calls root nodes "output nodes" and source nodes "input nodes," observing that "input/output formalities are suggestive in connection with tonal theory" (*GMIT*, 207–8). The three-level hierarchy of node classes can be expressed formally: the arrow relation in an oriented digraph induces an equivalence relation on the set of nodes; the nodes are sent, via a natural map, into the quotient set of equivalence classes {root, intermediate, source}. On equivalence classes, natural maps, and quotient sets, see *GMIT*, 7–10.
26. This use of the term "attitude" is borrowed from Harrison 1994, 37.

of the root node is nicely communicated by the double border, which gives the node some visual heft, anchoring it in place on the page.

3.3.4 Oriented Transformation (or Operation) Graphs

Having explored the formal and conceptual aspects of oriented digraphs, we can now define oriented transformation graphs and networks in relatively short order. An *oriented transformation graph* is simply an oriented network whose arrows have been labeled with transformations. If the transformations are all operations (that is, bijections: one-to-one and onto) the graph is an *oriented operation graph*. We will loosen one condition from Lewin's definition of transformation graphs, following the ideas of Julian Hook (2007a): our graphs need not be *path consistent,* but they must be *realizable.* A transformational graph is path consistent if the transformations on two arrow paths linking the same two nodes always "add up" to the same overall transformation—that is, they compose to produce the same (semi)group element. Path consistency is one of Lewin's requirements for all transformation graphs,[27] but even he does not successfully observe it at all times; the network in Figure 3.3(a), for example, fails the path-consistency test.[28] But the network is *realizable* in Hook's terminology. That is, it is possible to fill its nodes in a way that is consistent with the transformations that label its arrows. Specifically, the graph is realizable if one puts any major triad in the root node.[29]

This loosening of Lewin's path-consistency requirement is desirable in the present context in that it allows for flexibility when combining harmonic/functional transformations (such as D and S) with dualistic neo-Riemannian ones (P, L, R, and their compounds). It also frees one up considerably in combining transformations that are not operations with operations in a single graph. As this comment suggests, we will work in what follows with certain transformations that are not operations (i.e., that are not one-to-one and onto, or bijective; cf. section 1.3.2).

---

27. *GMIT,* 195, Def. 9.2.1, condition (D). Hook coined the term "path consistency" for this condition.
28. Lewin 2006, Ch. 11, offers a discussion of one of the violations of this condition in a *GMIT* analysis of Wagner; he never comments on the issue in connection with Beethoven network of Figure 3.3(a). The violation here obtains between the two arrow paths from the "second-carriage-return-G♭+" to the D♭+ node. One path is the long rightward S arrow. The other path is the lower edge of the trapezoid that extends beneath this arrow, passing through the nodes E♭–, [E♭+], and A♭+ on its bottom edge. If the network's underlying graph were path consistent, the product of all of the transformations on this lower path would yield the same transformation as the long rightward arrow—that is, S. But this is not the case. It is not generally true that R-then-P-then-D-then-D (or RPDD in right orthography) has the same effect as S. One can s ee this if one begins with a minor triad, say C minor (C–). C– is the subdominant of G–, that is, C– $\xrightarrow{S}$ G–. But C– $\xrightarrow{RPDD}$ D♭–, a tritone away from G– (C– $\xrightarrow{R}$ E♭+ $\xrightarrow{P}$ E♭– $\xrightarrow{D}$ A♭– $\xrightarrow{D}$ D♭–). Formally put, S ≠ RPDD in the group of operations underlying the network. The group-theoretic distinction is made explicit in Hook's (2002) system of Uniform Triadic Transformations (UTTs): S = ⟨+, 7, 7⟩, while RPDD = ⟨+, 7, 1⟩.
29. Hook would call this graph *universally realizable,* as *any* major triad will do the job. We will not require our oriented transformation graphs to be universally realizable, but simply realizable in the weaker sense (that there exists at least *one* way to fill the graph's nodes consistently).

Tonal contexts are of course replete with situations in which many-to-one transformations are desirable. (The basic logic of tonality is, after all, many-to-one.)
When such nonbijective transformations are present, the transformations in our
graphs will combine into a semigroup, not a group, resulting in transformation
graphs that are not operation graphs.[30]

3.3.5 Oriented Networks

An *oriented network* is an oriented transformation graph whose nodes contain elements from the space S of the transformational system. There are no conceptual or
formal complications here—this is simply a matter of "filling nodes" in a manner
consistent with the transformations on the arrows.

3.4 Riemannian Functions

Figure 3.6 employs oriented operation graphs (NB, not networks) to interpret the
intentional structure of some of Riemann's harmonic functions. This application
will at once give a concrete instantiation of the concepts defined above, clarify
certain formal issues, and demonstrate how oriented graphs and networks can
offer an intuitively appealing model of the tonal-intentional structure implied by
a given theory.

Riemann's functions deal not with progression—which is modeled by his root-
interval system of *Schritte* and *Wechsel*—but with the *identity* of individual chords
with respect to the tonic.[31] Recall Riemann's quote in section 3.2.2, in which he
states that our tonal imagination is drawn back toward the tonic whenever we
hear a dominant: the dominant's "center of imagination lies, so to speak, outside
of it." Though that statement predates the functional theory by about a decade, it
is clear that Riemann conceived of his function labels in the same terms: to apply

---

30. On the distinction between transformation and operation graphs, see *GMIT*, 195–96, Defs. 9.2.1
and 9.2.3.

31. We often think of Riemann's function theories syntactically, that is, as based on the model progression *T–S–D–T*. But, as Daniel Harrison (1994, 279–80), David Kopp (2002, 99), and Alex Rehding
(2003, 103–6) note, Riemann's functional labels are not strongly bound by syntax. Kopp observes
that function for Riemann "pertains to individual chords rather than progression"; functions sig-
nify the individual chord's "identity in relation to the tonic." Though neo-Riemannian theory has
adapted symbols and terms from Riemann's function theory, it has generally employed them in a
manner conceptually more consistent with the *Schritt/Wechsel* system, linking harmonies one after
another in progressions. Henry Klumpenhouwer (1994) was the first to observe the similarity of
neo-Riemannian analytical practice to Riemann's system of *Schritte* and *Wechsel*. The present section adopts a different approach, using transformational methods to model Riemann's function-as-
relationship-to-a-tonic. The graphs of Figure 3.6 thus model Riemann's functions not as labels for
chords, but as labels for particular intentional acts. On the distinction between "function as chord"
and "function as relation," see Mooney 1996, 102–108; Harrison, 1994, 266–76; and Rehding 2003,
61 and 78–79.

any functional label to a harmony is to specify just *how* we relate the chord in question back to the tonic, the *Centrum der Vorstellung*. In the sixth edition of the *Handbuch der Harmonielehre* (1917), Riemann makes the connection explicit:

> The concept of "tonality" [*Tonalität*], brought into theoretical terminology by Fétis, signifies nothing other than the relation of a melody, or harmonic progression, or even a complete piece, to a principal *Klang* as center [*Hauptklang als Centrum*], with respect to which all other harmonies receive their special quality, their significance for harmonic logic, cadence formation, etc. The theory of tonal functions is nothing but the development of the Fétisian notion of tonality. The sustained relation of all harmonies to one tonic [*Der festgehaltene Beziehung aller Harmonien auf eine Tonika*] has found its most concise expression in the denomination of all chords as a more or less modified appearance of the three primary pillars of the logical harmonic conception: the tonic itself and its two dominants [i.e., dominant and subdominant].[32]

Alexander Rehding provides a helpful gloss on the idea, relating it to the concept of *Tonvorstellung*, which Riemann developed around 1914:

> In the realm of mental representations of tones (*Tonvorstellungen*), a concept that Riemann did not fully develop until the final years of his life, the sounding of chords is always a mental act of comparing. A chord may in itself be nothing but a chord, but in the framework of tonality, Riemann explained, every chord is invariably compared with the harmonic centre....It is not necessary to sound the tonic itself to make this act of comparing possible. (Rehding 2003, 72)

Figure 3.6 models these acts of "mental comparison" transformationally, tracing the various ways in which Riemann's harmonic functions describe a particular intentional path from tonal subordinate to tonic.

Before examining the figure in detail, it is important to note that it consists of oriented operation *graphs*, not networks. That is, the arrows are labeled, but the nodes are not. This emphasizes the basic intentional structures of Riemann's harmonic functions, free from any realization in a specific key. This representation also calls attention to the fact that it is perfectly coherent to speak of a hearing "a subdominant" without being aware of the sounding chord's specific pitch identity. Indeed, for listeners without absolute pitch, this is the norm: such a listener's primary awareness is typically not of named pitches or pitch classes, but rather of characteristic tonal entities (scale degrees, harmonies, and the like) in characteristic

---

32. Riemann 1917, 214 (my translation). "Der von Fr J. Fétis in die theoretische Terminologie gebrachte Begriff der *Tonalität* bezeichnet nichts anderes als die Beziehung einer Melodie, einer Harmoniefolge, ja eines ganzen Tonstückes auf einen Hauptklang als das Centrum, durch die Stellung, zu welchem alle übrigen Harmonien ihren speciellen Sinn, ihre Bedeutung für die harmonische Logik, die Kadenzbildung u.s.w. erhalten. Unsere Lehre von den tonalen Funktionen die Harmonie ist nichts anderes aus der Ausbau des...Begriffes der Tonalität. Die festgehaltene Beziehung aller Harmonien auf eine Tonika hat ihren denkbar prägnantsten Ausdruck gefunden in der Bezeichnung aller Accorde als mehr oder minder stark modifizierte Erscheinungsform der drei Hauptsäulen des harmonisch-logischen Aufbaues: der Tonika selbst und ihrer beiden Dominanten."

relationships. The graphs in Figure 3.6 model such characteristic relationships as they are structured by Riemann's harmonic theory.[33]

Figure 3.6(a) shows the three-node oriented transformation graph that lies at the heart of Riemann's function theory, with S and D arrows linking the three

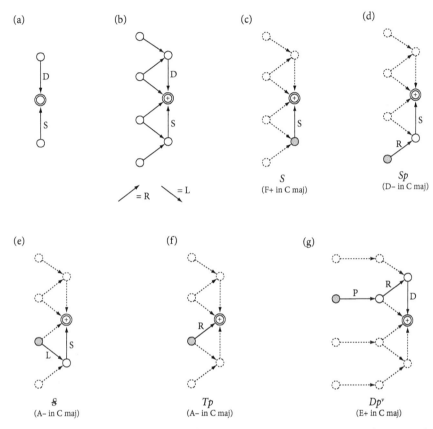

Figure 3.6 Oriented operation graphs modeling intentional aspects of Riemann's harmonic functions.

33. This raises an important general methodological point: transformation and operation graphs are to be understood not merely as "incomplete networks" that are missing the contents of their nodes. Rather, such graphs provide one means of modeling the relational character of musical experience. Our awareness of musical events can often be very specific in its relational content—as, for example, when we hear that a vocal gesture "leaps up by minor third," or that a pianist is "arpeggiating a triad"—even though we might be entirely unaware what actual notes are involved. Transformation and operation graphs model just such relational structures, free of specific node contents. It is interesting to note that this perspective agrees with Riemann's analytical practice. In his Beethoven sonata analyses, for example, function symbols appear beneath the reduced score, but not chord letter names. The implication is that, to hear a given entity as, say, T is more important than to hear it as, for example, "a C *Klang*." Cf. Lewin 2006, 194: "[t]he great virtue and power of Riemann function theory, which is also the source of its problems and difficulties, is precisely its ability to avoid assigning letter names ... to its objects."

primary *Klänge*. In 3.6(b), this graph is expanded with the addition of Riemann's apparent consonances, or *Scheinkonsonanzen*. These are derived from the three functional pillars by applying alterations equivalent to the neo-Riemannian oper-ations L and R.[34] The plus sign (+) in the middle of the tonic node in 3.6(b) indi-cates that the tonic here must be a major triad in order for the graph to be realized. This is because 3.6(b) is not path consistent: if a minor triad is placed in the tonic node, the other nodes cannot be filled consistently. This is a clear instance in which a non-path-consistent (but realizable) graph, per Hook, models a useful musical structure.

The oriented digraph underlying 3.6(b) is hierarchically robust: it contains one root node (the tonic), two intermediate nodes (the dominant and subdominant), and four source nodes (the various *Scheinkonsonanzen*). The hierarchical structure of the oriented system models the functional hierarchy implicit in Riemann's harmonic system, capturing the different functional attitudes and dependencies among its constituent elements. We can understand the graphs in 3.6 to model something of a tonal force field: each node is situated at a confluence of multiple intentional vectors, the directions of which indicate its relative stability, and its possible relations to the governing tonic, any of which may be activated within an appropriate context.

In Figures 3.6(c)–(g), filled nodes represent sounding harmonies; solid arrows model the intentional paths of the indicated Riemannian functions. Representative triadic names in C major are given in parentheses as an aid in imagining the harmony (as the above comments make clear, however, the graphs need not be understood in C major). Figure 3.6(c) models the intentional struc-ture of Riemann's subdominant. Figures 3.6(d) and (e) model two apparent consonances derived from the subdominant: the subdominant parallel (*Sp*)[35] and the subdominant leading-tone change (*Ş*). Figure 3.6(f) depicts the struc-ture of the tonic parallel (*Tp*). Note that the same node is shaded in 3.6(e) and (f); the same sounding entity in Riemann's theory can take different harmonic functions. The functions nevertheless represent different intentional structures. The subdominant leading-tone change (*Ş*) in 3.6(e) suggests the path LS back to the tonic, as the listener interprets the harmony as an L-variant of a sub-dominant. The tonic parallel (*Tp*) in 3.6(f), by contrast, suggests a direct link back to the tonic via R, as the listener interprets the sounding harmony as an R-variant of the tonic. The present model encourages us to think of Riemann's functions not simply as labels for sounding harmonies, but as cognitive tethers that draw the listener's ears back toward the tonic along familiar paths.

---

34. I have used the neo-Riemannian labels in this section for familiarity, even though neo-Riemannian R and P are at odds with Riemann's nomenclature. Neo-Riemannian R, for "relative," corresponds to Riemann's *parallel;* neo-Riemannian P, for "parallel" corresponds to Riemann's *variante,* intro-duced in Riemann 1917.

35. Riemannian functions are indicated here and throughout the book in italics.

(a)

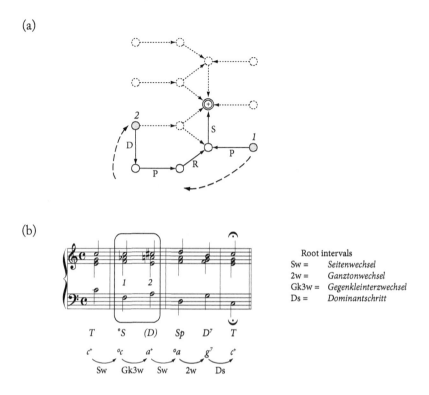

(b)

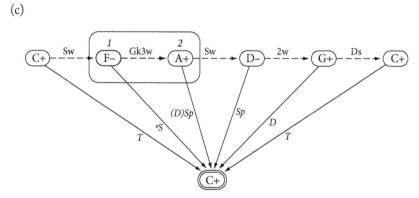

Root intervals

Sw =	*Seitenwechsel*
2w =	*Ganztonwechsel*
Gk3w =	*Gegenkleinterzwechsel*
Ds =	*Dominantschritt*

(c)

Figure 3.7 Progression between two *Klänge* related as hexatonic poles in Riemann's system. On the root-interval names in (b) and (c), see the entry on the *Schritt/ Wechsel system* in the Glossary.

Figure 3.6(g) expands the domain of the graph to the left by adding parallel modal variants of the *Scheinkonsonanzen* via P.[36] The example models Riemann's analysis of the second key area of the "Waldstein" Sonata as *Dp*ᵛ, the variant of the dominant parallel (1920, 3–4). Figure 3.7 maintains this expanded space, using it to model the interaction between harmonic progression (via *Schritte* and *Wechsel*) and harmonic function in Riemann's mature theory. The figure focuses on a chromatic progression that he discusses in the sixth edition of the *Handbuch der Harmonielehre* (1917, 128). There Riemann states that hexa-tonic-polar progressions (or *Gegenkleinterzwechsel* in his root-interval termi-nology) most often occur when one proceeds from the minor subdominant (F– in C major) to the dominant of the subdominant parallel in major (A+ as the dominant of D– in C major). In Riemann's notation, this is represented as °S — (D)Sp. The progression is modeled in Figure 3.7(a). The broken dashed arrow indicates the chronological progression from node *1* to node *2*, while the solid arrows, as in Figure 3.6, indicate intentional interpretations of the two harmonies. Figure 3.7(b) shows how the progression modeled in 3.7(a) might arise in a complete phrase in C major. The hexatonic progression from °S to (D)Sp is surrounded in a box. Functional labels are provided under the score, above the (dualistic) letter names for each chord in Riemann's system.[37] Curved arrows bearing abbreviations for Riemann's root-interval progressions link the dualistic roots. The technical details of the specific *Schritte* and *Wechsel* are not central to the discussion; the reader interested in understanding them better may consult the entry for the *Schritt/Wechsel system* in the Glossary.

In 3.7(c) the progression is represented transformationally. The chords from 3.7(b) are now given their familiar monistic names (°c becomes F– and °a becomes D–). Root-interval transformations link the chords via dashed arrows pointing left to right, while solid arrows link them, via their functional identities, to the central tonic. The functional labels on the solid arrows are shorthand for the various intentional paths the functions would trace in the space of 3.7(a).[38] Note that the root-interval progressions here are used in the same way transformations are in much neo-Riemannian theory: they carry the music forward in time, linking one chord to the next in a manner analogous to a performer realizing the passage. The functional transformations, by contrast, model the actions of the listener making tonal sense of the harmonies in Riemannian fashion, directing each to the tonic via Riemann's functional categories.

36. If the graph were extended further in the horizontal dimension and then wrapped into a 24-node torus, it would resemble the "chicken-wire torus" of Douthett and Steinbach (1998), and Michael Siciliano's "LRP Map" (2002), both of which are graph-theoretic duals of the neo-Riemannian *Tonnetz*.
37. Thus, c+ is a C-major chord (a "C over-triad") while °c is an F-minor chord (a "C under-triad").
38. The label *T* on the outer solid arrows in 3.7(c) represents no intentional path at all on Example 3.7(a). One can imagine it simply as the tonic node, with no intentional arrows directed toward it.

3.5 Tonal Intentions among Heard Scale Degrees

We now explore the efficacy of oriented networks in a different theoretical context—that of the sd/pc GIS introduced in Chapter 2. While that GIS modeled intervallic relationships among heard scale degrees as qualitative entities, oriented networks of sd/pc pairs allow us to animate various intentional relationships among such entities. For example, we can use oriented networks to model harmonic centers—that is, roots or Riemannian primes—within various sd/pc sets. To explore this, let us define two sd/pc sets in the key of C major: $X = \{(\hat{1}, C), (\hat{3}, E), (\hat{5}, G)\}$ and $Y = \{(\hat{4}, F), (\hat{6}, A), (\hat{1}, C)\}$. Now consider the finale of Mozart's Sonata K. 309, the opening of which is shown in Figure 3.8. Two instances of set X are indicated beneath the score, labeled X^1 and X^2; one instance of set Y is indicated. While it initially seems intuitive to call X a "I chord in C major," many theorists would argue that its manifestation as X^2 in the Mozart is in fact not a I chord at all, but a cadential six-four—an incidental (*zufällig*) verticality that embellishes V. There are good syntactical and contrapuntal arguments for this interpretation. I will nevertheless be most interested here in a phenomenological argument: the striking sonic difference between X^1 and X^2. We can sense that difference most vividly by focusing our ears on middle C (C4) in both chords. C4 in X^1 calmly resounds as the first and lowest pitch in each left-hand arpeggio, its privileged metrical and registral position underscoring its centrality as the chord's stable focal point. C4 in X^2, by contrast, leans precariously to one side. No longer the target of the listener's intentional activity, C4 in X^2 is intentionally directed elsewhere.

Figure 3.9(a) presents networks for chords X^1 and X^2: the X^1 network centers intentionally on $(\hat{1}, C)$, while the X^2 network centers on $(\hat{5}, G)$. The networks are arranged vertically on the page so that the root node is the lowest element, reflecting familiar monist conceptions that the harmonic center is conceptually, even if not acoustically, the lowest element in the harmony. In such a conception,

Figure 3.8 Mozart, Piano Sonata in C major, K. 309, mvt. iii, mm. 1–8, with three harmonic sets labeled.

(a)   (b)

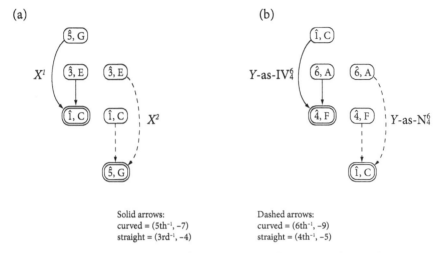

Solid arrows: Dashed arrows:
curved = (5th⁻¹, –7)   curved = (6th⁻¹, –9)
straight = (3rd⁻¹, –4)   straight = (4th⁻¹, –5)

Figure 3.9 Oriented networks modeling intentional hearings within the harmonies in Figure 3.8.

the listener "hears down" from harmonic subordinates toward the root. $(\hat{1}, C)$ in the X^1 network is situated within the root node; in the X^2 network, by contrast, $(\hat{1}, C)$ is situated in an unstable source node, intentionally directed toward $(\hat{5}, G)$. This hearing does not yet capture the sense that C "leans precariously to one side"; instead it simply registers the listener's experience that the chord's harmonic center is now a perfect fourth below $(\hat{1}, C)$. (We will return to the "leaning" aspect of $(\hat{1}, C)$ in section 3.6.) The "I_4^6" label for a cadential six-four, in addition to its syntactical problems, misleadingly suggests that the left-hand network in 3.9(a) models the internal dynamics of *both X^1 and X^2*, treating $\hat{1}$ as the chord's intentional center in both cases.

Some theorists may choose to interpret chord Y in bars 3–4 of the Mozart as IV$_4^6$—a genuine second inversion of the IV chord, with F as root—while others may prefer to understand it as a neighboring six-four (N$_4^6$) participating in an embellishing motion over a prolonged tonic harmony, the C root remaining in effect throughout. The left-hand network in 3.9(b) reflects the intentional dynamics implied by the Y-as-IV$_4^6$ hearing, while the right-hand network models Y-as-N$_4^6$. It is possible to focus one's aural attention in ways that generate either intentional structure. To sense Y-as-IV$_4^6$, focus on the right hand in mm. 3–4, which transposes the melodic gesture of mm. 1–2 up by a fourth. Having heard the reiterated melodic C5s in mm. 1–2 as root representatives, one can easily transfer that hearing to mm. 3–4, now hearing the reiterated melodic F5s as root representatives. By contrast, if one wishes to experience Y-as-N$_4^6$, one can direct one's ears to the left-hand arpeggios, specifically to the strong-beat C4s, which continue to assert the primacy of C throughout mm. 3 and 4.

Note the ways in which $(\hat{1}, C)$ is intentionally mobile throughout the networks of Figure 3.9, residing in a root node in X^1 and Y-as-N$_4^6$, and in source nodes in

X^2 and Y-as-IV$^6_4$. Further, in X^2 it is directed toward the root node via (4th^{-1},–5), as a suspended fourth over ($\hat{5}$, G), while in Y-as-IV$^6_4$ it is directed to the root via (5th^{-1},–7), as the fifth of ($\hat{4}$, F). The technological separation, and subsequent interaction, between intention and quale in the present apparatus is suggestive: the heard scale degree in question clearly retains its qualitative status as ($\hat{1}$, C) in all of the networks, but it is situated within diverse intentional webs as the harmonic context shifts over the course of the phrase.

We can observe similar suggestive interactions between quale and intention in the opening of Brahms's D-minor Piano Concerto, op. 15, shown in Figure 3.10(a). Figures 3.10(b)–(d) show three intentional hearings of the famous six-three chord that enters in m. 2.[39] Network (b) differs from (c) and (d) in its intentional struc-

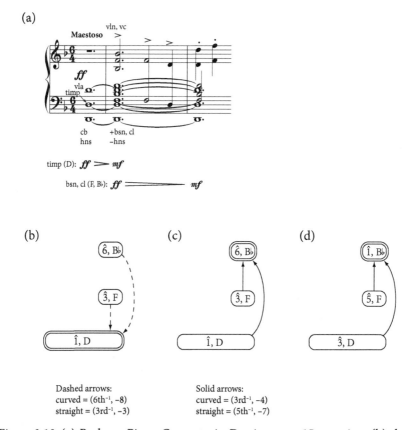

Figure 3.10 (a) Brahms, Piano Concerto in D minor, op. 15, opening; (b) three intentional hearings of the six-three chord in mm. 2–3.

---

39. For a pertinent discussion of Brahms's six-three chords, see Smith 1997. Dubiel 1994 offers highly compelling observations on the opening of the Brahms concerto and its ramifications later in the work.

ture, while (d) differs from (b) and (c) in its node contents. Network (b) hears D as root, while (c) and (d) are swayed by the entrance of B♭ and F in m. 2, directing attention to B♭ as root. Network (d) goes even further, hearing B♭ not only as root, but as tonic—a hearing that the tune in the strings does nothing to deny.[40] Brahms carefully calibrates his orchestration and dynamics to hold the various hearings of 3.10(b)–(d) in equipoise. The timpanist, who emphatically asserts D, decrescendos into bar 2, just as the {B♭, F} dyad sounds. The four horns, which had been playing D, also drop out in bar 2. But the {B♭, F} dyad in the woodwinds itself decrescendos into bar 3, while the violas and basses continue to assert D at *ff* throughout. Much of the electricity of the passage comes from the ways in which these waxing and waning forces vie for our attention, buffeting the credulous listener from one hearing to another as the chord persists in time. Again, the technological separation, and subsequent interaction, of sd qualia and intentional graphing makes possible a vivid account of the various apperceptual possibilities.

3.6 Resolving Transformations

Let us return to the "leaning $(\hat{1}, C)$" in chord X^2, the cadential six-four in the Mozart sonata. The $(\hat{1}, C)$ is of course a suspension, pulled downward to $(\hat{7}, B)$. A listener who senses this acutely will likely hear the $(\hat{1}, C)$ as bearing not (only) some subordinate relationship to the $(\hat{5}, G)$ bass note of chord X^2, but will also (and perhaps primarily) intend its anticipated resolution to $(\hat{7}, B)$. The $(\hat{3}, E)$ atop X^2 has a similar intentional character, as it leans into its resolution to $(\hat{2}, D)$.

We can define a transformation (NB, not operation) that models the pull of $(\hat{1}, C)$ and $(\hat{3}, E)$ to their intended resolutions. We will call this resV, which resolves heard scale degrees to the elements of the diatonic V chord, viz. $(\hat{5}, \text{diapc}_5)$, $(\hat{7}, \text{diapc}_7)$, and $(\hat{2}, \text{diapc}_2)$. The resV transformation in C major pulls $(\hat{1}, C)$ to $(\hat{7}, B)$; it likewise pulls $(\hat{3}, E)$ to $(\hat{2}, D)$. Figure 3.11(a) models the effect. The portion of the network in brackets indicates the resolution of X^2, which the resV arrows intend before it sounds. Figure 3.11(b) hears beyond the cadential six-four's resolving dominant to an intended tonic. The tonic is intended via resI, which resolves all heard scale degrees to the elements of the diatonic I chord, viz. $(\hat{1}, \text{diapc}_1)$, $(\hat{3}, \text{diapc}_3)$, and $(\hat{5}, \text{diapc}_5)$. Note that both networks in Figure 3.11 are hierarchically robust, containing source, intermediate, and root nodes. The "leaning $(\hat{1}, C)$" in X^2 is a source node in both networks; it is strongly distinguished thereby from the tonic-node $(\hat{1}, C)$ in 3.11(b).[41]

---

40. Until m. 4, that is, at which point an A♭ throws *both* D minor and B♭ major into doubt.

41. Figure 3.11 uses a graphic convention that I will sometimes employ in future networks involving a mixture of res transformations and sd/pc intervals: the res transformations are labeled, while sd/pc intervals are unlabeled to keep down clutter. As the sd/pc GIS, like all GISes, is simply transitive on its space (here the space of 84 sd/pc pairs), the intervals are uniquely determined in each case, and can be easily supplied by the reader. (Intervallic paths, in the sense of section 2.3, will not be uniquely determined, however. Unlabeled arrows will thus be used only when path-based distinctions are not consequential to the analysis. For a refinement, see the Brahms analysis in Chapter 6).

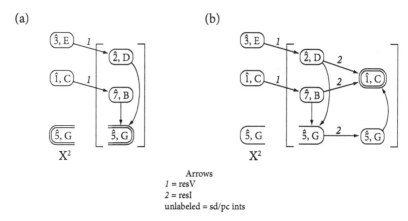

Figure 3.11 Networks modeling intentional hearings of the cadential six-four chord X^2 via res transformations.

Figures 3.12(a) and (b) show function tables for resI and resV. Both transformations take as their domains the entire space of the sd/pc GIS, as indicated in the ordered pairs of the left-hand columns; they are thus defined on chromatic as well as diatonic elements.[42] The range of resI is the set $\{(\hat{1}, \text{diapc}_1), (\hat{3}, \text{diapc}_3), (\hat{5}, \text{diapc}_5)\}$; the range of resV is $\{(\hat{5}, \text{diapc}_5), (\hat{7}, \text{diapc}_7), (\hat{2}, \text{diapc}_2)\}$. Note that both resI and resV are transformations, but not operations: they are not one-to-one and onto (bijective), but many-to-few: the elements in the range are targets of multiple elements in the domain. In resI, for example, $(\hat{1}, \text{diapc}_1)$ is the target of all sd/pc pairs of the form $(\hat{7}, \text{pc})$, $(\hat{1}, \text{pc})$, and $(\hat{2}, \text{pc})$. Figures 3.12(c) and (d) seek to render visible this many-to-few structure, showing the mapping patterns for the scale degrees in each res transformation (leaving aside, for the moment, their specific pc manifestations). A comparison of 3.12(c) and (d) reveals that the scale-degree mappings in resI and resV have a similar structure. This shared structure is diagrammed in 3.12(e), which labels the seven nodes with elements from the ordered set (*root, w, third, x, fifth, y, z*). We will call the elements of the subset {*w, x, y, z*} the *active* scale degrees under the res transformation; the elements of the subset {*root, third, fifth*} are the *target* scale degrees. As is evident from the figure, the active elements reside between the target elements: *w* is the scale degree between *root* and *third*, *x* is the degree between *third* and *fifth*, and *y* and *z* are the degrees between *fifth* and *root*. The res transformations map the active elements to *adjacent* targets only, constraining the resolutions of *y* and *z* to *fifth* and *root*, respectively; *w* and *x*, by contrast, may resolve in two possible ways, yielding different species of res transformations. One of these will be of particular interest: ires(triad), which resolves *w* "imperfectly" to the chordal third rather than the

---

42. Note that resI and resV are defined in 3.12(a) and (b) to act on *all* potential chromatic inflections of the seven scale degrees for formal completeness, though only a very small cluster of these chromatic elements will ever arise in a concrete analytical context, as discussed in section 2.7. Some inflections, furthermore, will resolve more naturally under some res transformations than others. ♯$\hat{2}$, for example, resolves more naturally via iresI (defined in a moment) than via resI.

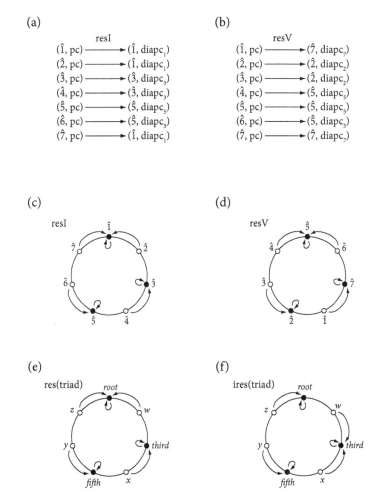

Figure 3.12 (a) and (b): Mapping tables for resI and resV. (c) and (d): Diagrams showing the behavior of scale degrees under resI and resV. (e) and (f): Schematic representations of the sd behavior of any res or ires transformation on some triad.

root; all other elements resolve as in res(triad). With the templates for res(triad) and ires(triad) shown in 3.12(e) and (f) we can define res transformations for any diatonic triad, yielding transformations like iresV, resII, iresIV, and so on.

Res transformations make possible an additional interpretation of the six-three chord in Brahms's D-minor concerto. Figure 3.13(a) shows a hearing of the chord as a 5–6 displacement of an underlying tonic triad in D minor. Like the network in 3.10(b), this hearing intends (Î, D) as root. Unlike that hearing, however, (6̂, B♭) is no longer heard in a direct relationship to (Î, D); instead it leans toward an intended but unsounded (5̂, A). Intentional energy flows from (6̂, B♭) to (Î, D) via (5̂, A). This hearing is an antipode of that graphed in 3.10(d), which heard B♭ not only as root but as tonic. Figure 3.13(b) presents a similar network, which analyzes the B-minor triad at the outset of the Andante from Schubert's D. 664, discussed

(a)   (b)

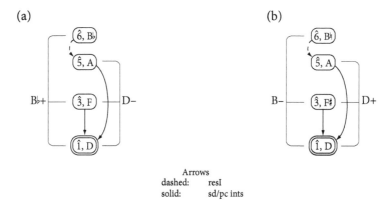

Arrows
dashed: resI
solid: sd/pc ints

Figure 3.13 (a) An intentional configuration involving the L-related triads B♭+ and D– (cf. Figure 3.10 and the *Schreckensfanfare* in Beethoven's Ninth); (b) an intentional configuration involving the R-related triads B– and D+ (cf. the Schubert analysis in section 1.3.4).

above in section 1.3.4. The triad is heard here as an elaboration of an underlying D-major tonic, to which it resolves, as resI pulls (6̂, B) to (5̂, A). The melody of mm. 1–2 gracefully traverses the entire network of 3.13(b).

Note the different ways in which the passages from Brahms and Schubert project the networks of 3.13(a) and (b). The Brahms concerto manifests 3.13(a) via a simultaneity, in which one of the nodes—that for (5̂, A)—does not sound. The Schubert manifests 3.13(b) not only in its first harmony, but also in its opening progression of B– to D+, as well as in the entire melody of mm. 1–2. The networks model an abstract configuration of kinetic tonal relationships that may be realized in a variety of concrete musical contexts. The point is underlined when we recognize that 3.13(a) also models the harmony of the *Schreckensfanfare* at the outset of the finale of Beethoven's Ninth, in which all *four* nodes sound simultaneously. More abstractly, 3.13(a) may be read as a model for the various interrelationships (both local and large-scale) between B♭ major and D minor throughout the Beethoven and Brahms works.[43]

More generally, networks such as those in Figure 3.13 may be used to model the intentional dynamics within and between two triads related by basic neo-Riemannian operations. Figure 3.14 provides a relevant example (more will follow in the analytical vignette of section 3.7). Figure 3.14(a) shows the opening of Strauss's song "Zueignung," op. 10, no. 1, which begins with an oscillation between E– and C+ triads via neo-Riemannian L. The network of 3.14(b) hears the E– triad as an embellishment of the tonic C+, as (7̂, B) pulls up to (1̂, C) via resI.[44] The network nicely captures the intentional asymmetry of the opening progression, with its systolic/diastolic undulation between harmonic instability and stability.

43. There can be little doubt that Brahms had the Ninth in mind when struggling with the concerto; the network of 3.13(a) thus serves, in one sense, as an abstract matrix for the intertextual relationship.
44. Daniel Harrison (1994, 62–64) offers a suggestive and relevant discussion of this passage.

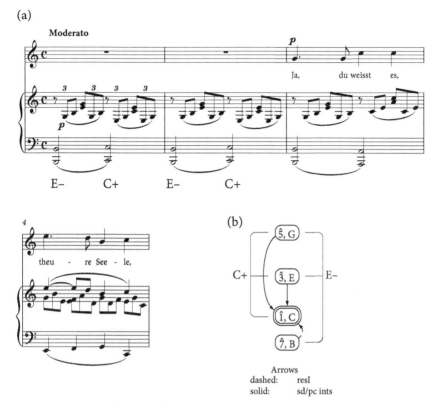

Figure 3.14 Richard Strauss, "Zueignung," op. 10, no. 1, mm. 1–4.

3.7 Vignette: Brahms, Intermezzo in E minor, op. 119, no. 2

Brahms's E-minor Intermezzo begins with the very triadic juxtaposition just encountered in the Strauss: E– and C+. Now, however, the tonal balance has shifted from the latter harmony to the former. Figure 3.15(a) shows the score of mm. 1–2; a box encloses the C+ simultaneity in m. 1, labeling it z.[45] Figure 3.15(b) presents a proto-Schenkerian reduction of the opening gesture, making explicit the neighboring role of the soprano C in chord z. Under the staff are three harmonic analyses, labeled "RN," "Riemann," and "NeoR." The Roman numeral (RN) analysis hears the progression as a 5–6 shift above a prolonged tonic *Stufe*. The Riemannian functional analysis hears a progression from tonic to tonic leading-tone change, or ^oT —$^o\mathcal{F}$. The neo-Riemannian reading hears an L transform from E– to C+.

The comparison of the paleo- and neo-Riemannian hearings is instructive. While the E– and C+ *Klänge* in the neo-Riemannian reading are, in principle, tonally neutral, in the Riemannian functional hearing they are freighted with tonal

---

45. Brahms's suppression of the E root on the upbeat creates a nice harmonic pun: {G, B} proceeds to {C, E, G}—a visual (but more or less inaudible) V–I in C.

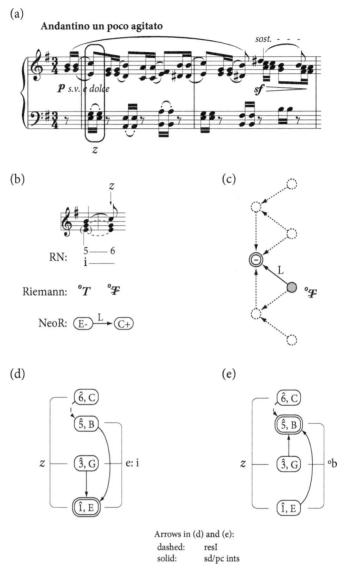

Figure 3.15 (a) Brahms, Intermezzo in E minor, op. 119, no. 2, mm. 1–2; (b)–(e) harmonic analyses of the first two chords.

meaning. Most notably, while E– is a genuine consonance for Riemann (the ulti-mate consonance, the tonic), C+'s consonance is only *apparent* (*scheinbar*): it is a conceptually dissonant alteration of (or stand-in for) the tonic. In this hearing, chord *z* is harmonically off balance, just as the intermezzo's rhythm and hock-et-like texture are off balance. The network of 3.15(c) renders this off-balance character visible, modeling Riemann's °𝔉 using the technology from Figure 3.6: chord *z* leans intentionally in the direction of the minor tonic node.

The Roman numeral hearing also has an off-balance quality, in which the C six-three chord is a displacement of an E-minor five-three. Figure 3.15(d) graphs the hearing's implicit intentional structure, using the network format from Figures 3.13 and 3.14. Riemann, too, would be highly sensitive to the kinetics between $(\hat{6}, C)$ and $(\hat{5}, B)$, but he would hear the internal dynamics of the E-minor triad differently: for him, the chord's root (i.e., prime) would be B, not E. 3.15(e) models this hearing, with $(\hat{1}, E)$ and $(\hat{3}, G)$ directed intentionally *upward* to the $(\hat{5}, B)$ prime of the B under triad (°b in Riemann's notation). Note the strong accent on $(\hat{5}, B)$ in 3.15(e): it is the intentional target of every pitch in chord z. Such a dualistic hearing may seem far-fetched to us now, but it has a certain appeal in this piece: just as the configuration of 3.15(e) focuses intently on B, so the upper voice of the Intermezzo as a whole centers on B, to the notable avoidance of E.[46] In mm. 1–2, the opening melody spreads outward from B4, extending down to F♯4 and up to D♯5, never reaching E4 or E5. This avoidance of a melodic E persists: E is not touched on in the melody until m. 8, in which it appears as a fleeting eighth note in a dominant context. It is not until mm. 13ff that the melody secures a hold on E, but here it is not the monistic root of E minor, but the dualistic prime of A minor.[47] Nor is there any PAC in E minor in the work—not even at the conclusion, in which the melody comes to rest on B4.[48]

Before proceeding, it will be helpful to review the tonal kinetics of Riemann's dual E minor. Figure 3.16 sketches the relevant relationships. Figure 3.16(a) shows

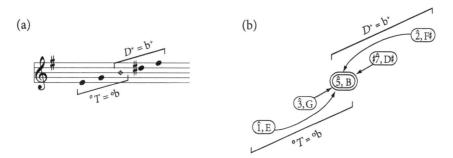

(a)   (b)

Figure 3.16 Riemann's dual conception of the tonic and dominant triads in E minor.

---

46. In his unpublished 1914 commentary on the work, Schenker emphasizes the melodic line's constant "circling around the tone B." This centering on B4 is also highlighted in Schenker's unpublished sketch from the 1920s. See Cadwallader and Pastille 1999.

47. This melodic centering on the dualistic root is closely related to the piece's almost obsessive focus on the opening tune, which recurs throughout the piece in continuous variations. Schenker calls the work "a series of variations" (Cadwallader and Pastille 1999, 43).

48. The B section in E major (mm. 36–71) contains the only clear PACs in the piece: in B major in mm. 50–51, and in E major in the first and second endings before the retransition (mm. 67a and b). The PACs in mm. 67a and b are the only clear arrivals on $\hat{1}$ in the piece; the fact that the passages are in major is significant. Note that the concluding tonic of the piece is also E major, but here the melody still clings to B. This complicates a traditional Riemannian dualist understanding of the harmony. In the present analytical context, we might consider the concluding harmony, following Lewin 1982 (see esp. pp. 40–43), as "dual E major": that is, a major triad conceived from the fifth downward.

the dual generation of Riemann's °*T* and *D*+ in E minor outward from B. Riemann's chord names for the key's two principal harmonies—°b and b+—capture B's centrality as a sort of functional axis or fulcrum in the key. Figure 3.16(b) translates 3.16(a) into an oriented network of sd/pc pairs, the elements of the dominant intentionally directed downward to (5̂, B), those of the tonic directed upward to it.

With these relationships in mind, let us return to the opening phrase of the intermezzo. Figure 3.17(a) sketches the upper voice of mm. 1–2 over a simplified bass line. The functional analysis below the staff interprets the tune as remaining under the broad influence of °*T* (inflected to °*F*) until beat 2 of m. 2, at which point it shifts decisively to *D*+. (Beats 2 and 3 of m. 1 project a hierarchically subordinate °*S* — *D*+ progression.) As observed in connection with Figure 3.15(c), °*F* is intentionally unstable, pulling back toward °*T* via L. This harmonic instability is prolonged over the course of the phrase, and is not released until the arrival of *D*+

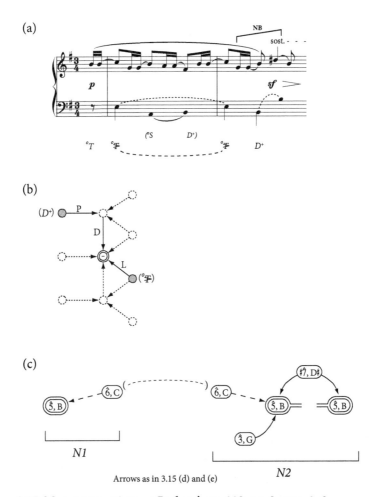

Figure 3.17 More perspectives on Brahms's op. 119, no. 2, mm. 1–2.

at the end of Brahms's long slur. The slur thus traces an arc of tension that is initiated by the opening B5–C5 gesture, held by the prolonged $^o\mathcal{F}$, and released with the arrival of D^+ and the melodic B5 on beat 2 of m. 2. We can trace the harmonic kinetics of this tension-and-release process on 3.17(b). The phrase begins by moving from the minor tonic node to $^o\mathcal{F}$. For the duration of the slur, we remain off balance at $^o\mathcal{F}$, intentionally leaning toward ^oT via L. At the end of the slur, this tension is released, and we swing, in compensatory fashion, past the tonic to D^+. The slur acts like the drawing and holding of a bow string, creating a tension that is released only on beat 2 of m. 2, sending us to D^+.

Figure 3.17(c) traces the *melodic* kinetics of this process. The example comprises two oriented networks, labeled *N1* and *N2*. *N1* corresponds to what we might call the "charging" gesture of the opening: the accumulation of $^o\mathcal{F}$'s charge via the displacement of $(\hat{5}, B)$ to $(\hat{6}, C)$. The melodic charge is manifested by the pull of $(\hat{6}, C)$ back to $(\hat{5}, B)$ via resI. The parenthesized dashed slur—a visual aid, not a formal part of the network—joins the "charged" $(\hat{6}, C)$ to its return in *N2*, suggesting the conceptual retention of the tone over the phrase. *N2* models the "release" of $(\hat{6}, C)$'s charge at the end of the slur, as it returns to $(\hat{5}, B)$. This return coincides with the harmonic swing from $^o\mathcal{F}$ to D^+ on 3.17(b). That is, just as $(\hat{6}, C)$ finally resolves to $(\hat{5}, B)$, the latter's harmonic polarity reverses: ^ob becomes b^+. This reversal of harmonic polarity is reflected directly in the melody: $(\hat{5}, B)$ is preceded by its tonic under-third and followed by its dominant over-third. These under- and over-thirds bring a semblance of balance to the B, stabilizing it for the conclusion of the phrase. Note that the D♯, rather than exhibiting directedness toward E as it would in a traditional monistic context, is pulled back to B at the end of the phrase. D♯ resolves not to E but to B, per the kinetics of Figure 3.16(b). As the NB bracket on 3.17(a) indicates, this relationship is manifested explicitly in pitch space: B4 is surrounded symmetrically by G4 and D♯5.

The tension of the phrase thus motivates a swing from the lower, tonic region of this space to the upper, dominant region, carrying the melody along with it. This shift is demonstrated most clearly by the fact that D♯5 opens up, for the first time, a space *above* B4. (Brahms marks the important moment with a *sf.*) With the exception of the two C5s—which are pulled emphatically downward—all of the melody under Brahms's long slur inhabits the space below B4. This is the tonic section of the phrase. Once we enter the dominant section, however, the melody swings to the dominant region above B4. B4 thus acts as functional axis or fulcrum in the melody, just as the root node $(\hat{5}, B)$ does in 3.16(b). Brahms repeats this pattern later, and with greater emphasis. In mm. 3–5, the first tonic leg of the phrase is repeated, now extended. Again, it is marked by a long slur, and again its pitches all reside below B4, with the exception of C5. Once again, at the end of the slur in m. 5, the tension is released and a dominant passage begins. As before, the melody for the dominant section swings entirely into the "dominant region" above B4. Now, however, it expands through D♯5 to F♯5 in mm. 6–7, tracing out the entire region of b^+.

This process reaches its apotheosis in the big dominant arrival in mm. 23–27. It is preceded by a grand expansion of the C→B resolution figure, now in the bass, persisting over mm. 18–21. The C and B provide dominant support for statements

Figure 3.18 An expression of Riemann's dual E minor in mm. 23–27 of Brahms's op. 119, no. 2 (cf. Figure 3.16).

of the tune in F minor and E minor. As in mm. 2 and 5, the final resolution of C to B unleashes a flurry of symmetrical, balancing activity around B4, but now this activity is commensurate with the size of the expanded C→B figure. The balancing gestures are presented in their most complete form in the piece, as sketched in Figure 3.18. B is indicated by diamond noteheads, as in 3.16(a). The first beamed gesture descends through all three members of °b (= °T), while its answer ascends through all three members of b⁺ (= D⁺). Though the passage has a large-scale dominant function, it exhibits a complex mixing of tonic and dominant in its harmonic and melodic details.[49] This mixing is suggested by the soprano in 3.18 and is also partially indicated by the bass line, which inverts B's role, treating it not as the pitch center, but as the upper and lower pitch-space boundaries, which surround the E2-based material in the middle. With its explicit melodic projections of °b and b⁺, its axial privileging of B in both melody and bass, and its curious sense of harmonic balance, the passage represents the fullest expression of Figure 3.16(b) in the piece.

3.8 Vignette: "Rheingold!"

Figure 3.19(a) provides a reduction of the Rhine daughters' famous panegyric to the gold, as first heard in Scene 1 of *Das Rheingold*. We will call this first statement of the "Rheingold!" motive RG1. This music corresponds to one of the first large-scale downbeats in the drama, and thus the tetralogy as a whole. A great amount of musical and dramatic energy is funneled into its first chord, which arrives with a considerable phenomenal impact, supporting the syllable "Rhein-." We will call the sd/pc set corresponding to this chord Rhein: {($\hat{7}$, B), ($\hat{2}$, D), ($\hat{4}$, F), ($\hat{6}$, A)}. The chord to which it resolves we will call Gold: {($\hat{1}$, C), ($\hat{3}$, E), ($\hat{5}$, G)}.

In traditional theoretical parlance, we would describe Rhein as a neighbor harmony—a vii half-diminished 7 over a tonic pedal. We would likely add that

49. Schenker comments on the harmonic mixing in the passage, which he calls "characteristically Brahmsian" (Cadwallader and Pastille 1999, 45).

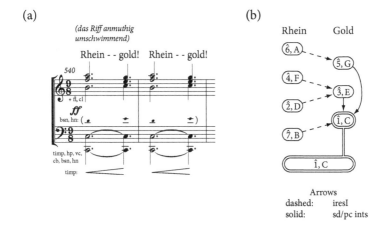

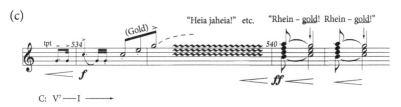

Figure 3.19 (a) Wagner, *Das Rheingold,* mm. 540–41, hereafter RG1; (b) an oriented network for RG1; (c) the context for RG1's emergence.

this chord "pulls toward" or "has an urge to resolve to" the tonic chord. Figure 3.19(b) renders that statement in an oriented network. Rhein contains precisely the active elements in C major under iresI; Gold comprises the target elements under that transformation. To say that Rhein "pulls toward" Gold is to suggest that, as listeners, we already perform the intentional arrows of 3.19(b) during the two beats of the Rhein chord. This intentional anticipation contributes to the Rhein chord's brilliance, which is already considerable given the acoustic spectacle of three Wagnerian sopranos singing in close position. The intentional situation also interacts with the vowels in the text: the high-formant diphthong rhEIn acts as a sort of phonetic dissonance, resolving to the low-formant monophthong of gOld.

All tonal energy in the gesture is directed toward the C major of Gold, just as all of the stage energy and action is now directed toward the Rheingold, which has just "awoken." Wagner has made it very clear that this particular C-major chord is the sonic embodiment the gold. Figure 3.19(c) sketches the context out of which RG1 emerges. The left-hand side of the example shows the C-major statement of the gold motive at the culmination of its "awakening." Open noteheads show the three pitches of Gold. In the dithyrambic outburst that follows ("Heia jaheia," etc.), the Rhine daughters reflect off of these pitches, vocally enacting the shimmering light now permeating the water. RG1 is the culmination of this extended anacrusis, but its metric arrival coincides with the momentary departure of the

Gold chord, which becomes even more an object of desire in its momentary sonic absence. Once again, Wagner dramatically reifies tonal energy here, both making such energy "visible" on stage and giving it physical, dramatically palpable shape. We enact in our hearing what the dramatis personae enact on stage, desiring the resolution of the Rhein chord just as they desire the gold.[50] Alberich, for one, is *angezogen und gefesselt* (attracted and enchained) by the sight of the gold. We are aurally *angezogen und gefesselt* by the pull of the massive downbeat of m. 540, which draws our ears irresistibly toward C and holds them there by the brilliance of all of the C-major activity now taking place. (Critics from Nietzsche to Kittler have made much of this coercive aspect of Wagner's music.)

The mapping between stage action and intentional structure here is more precise still, as Figure 3.20 indicates. As shown in 3.20(a), the Rhein chord surrounds the Gold chord in diatonic pitch space. Curved arrows show the action of iresI. This musical surrounding interacts compellingly with the stage directions: as they sing, the Rhine daughters swim around the gold (*das Riff anmuthig umschwimmend*). They surround it not only in pitch space but also harmonically. As 3.20(b) shows, Rhein contains two elements each from the subdominant and dominant chords in C major. Daniel Harrison (1994, 64–72) analyzes such leading-tone seventh chords as combinations of dominant and subdominant. This is loosely captured in the network of 3.20(c). The analysis is inexact as far as it goes—the complete F+ and G+ chords are not present—but it is nevertheless suggestive, demonstrating

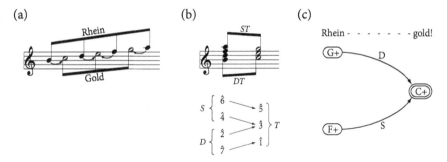

Figure 3.20 Further perspectives on RG1: (a) Rhein surrounds Gold in pitch space; (b) Rhein combines subdominant and dominant pitches, which harmonically surround the tonic pitches of Gold; (c) a *Klang* network (loosely) depicting aspects of (b).

50. The Rhine daughters' attraction to the gold is in stark contrast to their previous repulsion from Alberich. Cf. McGlathery 1998, 73: "the Rhinegold represents the object of love, desire, and affection for the Rhine Maidens; it is treasured by them the way that Alberich yearned to be (German *Schatz* 'treasure' is commonly used for 'beloved')." The scene is thus articulated by a shift, or transformation, in structures of desire, with Alberich's desire for the Rhine daughters (and their repulsion) transformed into the entire company's attraction to the gold. The funneling of all dramatic energy in one direction after the "awakening" of the gold is one of the reasons for the great the sense of focus that sets in at RG1 (concurrent with the emphatic tonal focus on C).

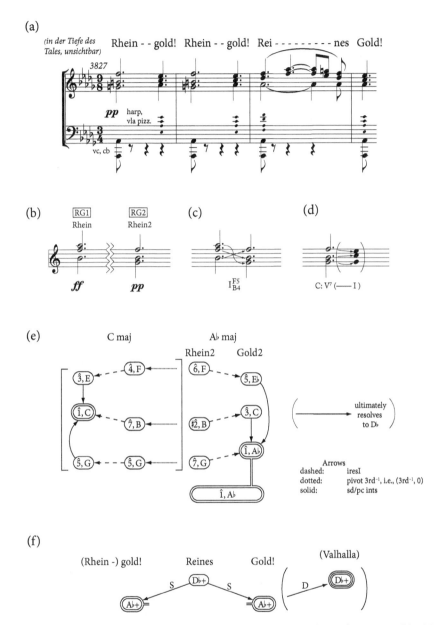

Figure 3.21 (a) Wagner, *Das Rheingold,* mm. 3827–30, hereafter RG2; (b)–(c) Rhein2 is an inversion of Rhein; (d) Rhein2 suggests V7 in C; (e) an oriented network for RG2, showing a retrospective intention back toward the (lost) C major of RG1; (f) the local tonic of RG2 is A♭, which acts globally as the dominant of D♭.

how the Rhine daughters (and we as auditors) focus in on the gold harmonically via a fusion of its dominant above and its dominant below.

After Scene 1, we next hear from the Rhine daughters at the end of the opera, when they restate the "Rheingold!" motive, as shown in Figure 3.21(a). We will call this statement RG2. The local key is A♭ major; the global key is D♭ major, as the key signature indicates. In contrast to the orgiastic outburst of RG1, RG2 is a distant entreaty, *pp* rather than *ff*. No longer at center stage gracefully swimming around the gold, the Rhine daughters are now out of sight, *in der Tiefe des Thales, unsichtbar*. Their location below the center of the action is reflected in their new Rhein chord, which we will call Rhein2 = {($\hat{7}$, G), ($\sharp\hat{2}$, B♮), ($\hat{6}$, F)}. As shown in 3.21(b), Rhein2 is an "upside-down" version of the sung notes in Rhein. In fact, as 3.21(c) shows, Rhein2 is an exact pitch-space inversion of the sung notes in Rhein, around the B4/F5 tritone. The major third now resides on the bottom of the chord and strains upward to its resolution. This sense of upward strain is intensified by the chromaticism in RG2, another new element: Wellgunde sings not diatonic ($\hat{2}$, B♭) in A♭ major, but chromatic ($\sharp\hat{2}$, B♮).

Wellgunde in fact sings a gesture proper to RG1, not RG2. That is, her B♮ is the leading tone in C major, and her B♮→C gesture can be heard to project a resolution in that key, not in A♭: that is, ($\hat{7}$, B)→ ($\hat{1}$, C). In fact, the pitches of Rhein2 in their entirety are proper to C major, not A♭, as shown in 3.21(d). The chord is fixated on the memory of the gold in its prelapsarian, C-major purity, in seeming denial of the present reality of A♭. This fixation is modeled in Figure 3.21(e) by a bracketed network that reinterprets Rhein2 via a pivot transformation, resolving it to an imagined (prior) C major. The unbracketed section of the network shows the chord's actual resolution to the local tonic of A♭. This local tonic ultimately acts as a global dominant, bent toward D♭ and Valhalla, the gravitational center of the opera's close.[51]

In addition to their "Rheingold!" cry, the Rhine daughters now add the *Stabreim* "Reines Gold!," their voices leaping upward over a D♭ harmony (see m. 3829 in 3.21(a)). The harmonic profile of the gesture is shown in 3.21(f). D♭+ is the subdominant of the local tonic A♭+, pulled forcibly back to it via S. Crucially, however, D♭+ is also the tonic of Valhalla, the object of the Rhine daughters' entreaty. This global tonic D♭+ is depicted in parentheses on the right side of the network, somewhat fancifully enclosed in a triple border (which looks appropriately fortress-like). The Rhine daughters thus strain upward toward Valhalla, but they remain *in der Tiefe*, their D♭+ pulled down under the local influence of A♭.

After Loge mockingly resolves the music of RG2 to D♭, the Rhine daughters take another tack, now stating the motive in G♭, the subdominant of D♭. This statement, RG3, is shown in Figure 3.22(a). The subdominant nature of RG3 is twofold:

---

51. Per Lorenz, D♭ is the center of tonal gravity of the entire tetralogy (1924, 51). *Götterdämmerung* ends with the destruction of Valhalla in D♭, just as *Das Rheingold* had ended with the triumphant entrance of the gods into Valhalla in the same key. Lorenz's key diagram on p. 48 contains a referential dashed line at the level of Des-dur that runs throughout the entire cycle. The same diagram also contains a secondary dashed line at the level of C-dur (the key of RG1).

not only is its key the large-scale subdominant of D♭, the new "Rhein-" chord, Rhein3 = {($\hat{4}$, C♭), ($\flat\hat{6}$, E♭♭), ($\hat{1}$, G♭)} decorates G♭ with its own minor subdominant. Figure 3.22(b) depicts this via a *Klang* network. As in RG2, the position of the subdominant, harmonically below the tonic, is contrasted with the vocal gesture, which reaches emphatically upward in pitch space. Figure 3.22(b) seeks to capture this by situating the C♭–/+ nodes above the G♭+ node. The Rhine daughters cast their complaint upward in pitch space, now resigned to their position in the (subdominant) deep: "Traulich und Treu ist's nur in der Tiefe." Figure 3.22(c) shows their doubly subdominant final cadence, as they hurl a final accusation upward toward the fortress.

The daughters' harmonic orientation toward the gold in Scene 1 is isographic to their orientation to Valhalla in Scene 4, as shown by the networks in Figure 3.23. In both, they harmonically flank their object of attention—the C of the Gold, the

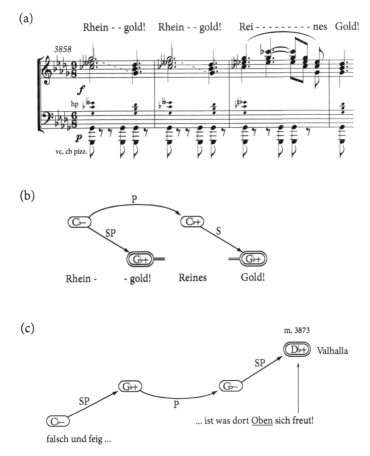

Figure 3.22 (a) Wagner, *Das Rheingold*, mm. 3858–61, hereafter RG3; (b) a *Klang* network of RG3; (c) the doubly subdominant structural cadence of *Das Rheingold* at m. 3873.

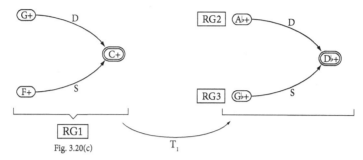

Fig. 3.20(c)

T_1

Figure 3.23 The harmonic configuration implicit in RG1 is isomorphic to the network created by the orientation of RG2 and RG3 toward Valhalla (D♭+).

D♭ of Valhalla—with dominants above and below. The T_1 transformation beneath the networks projects the semitonal lurch of the gold's theft from its pure, Edenic C major, to the accidental-filled worlds of corrupt divinity and corrupt humanity.[52]

3.9 Spatial and Event Networks

The networks explored in this chapter have been of two general types. On the one hand are networks like those in Figure 3.2, which are arrayed on the page in temporal order, from left to right. On the other hand are networks like those in Figure 3.6, which are arrayed in a spatial configuration that has no determinate relationship to the chronology of some musical passage. Lewin calls left-to-right temporal networks *figural networks* and spatial, temporally indeterminate networks *formal networks,* borrowing the terms "figural" and "formal" from Jeanne Bamberger.[53] I will here adopt John Roeder's (2009) more intuitive labels for these two network types, calling Lewin's figural networks *event networks* and his formal networks *spatial networks.* The two network types model different species of tonal-intentional behavior, as we will see. First it will be useful to discuss their differences more generally.

Nodes and arrows in event networks differ conceptually from nodes and arrows in spatial networks. The nodes in event networks occupy specific temporal locations within some musical passage: they occur before and after one another, or rep-

---

52. This effectively turns the C into a large-scale, synecdochic leading tone to D♭. C is the key not only of the Gold, but also of the Sword; Wotan intends to use both to secure the fortress, just as a leading tone secures a key. Wotan *sings* the C→D♭ gesture at a crucial moment: the first mention of the word Walhall in the tetralogy (*Rheingold,* mm. 3787–93 "Folge mir Frau! In Walhall wohne mit mir").

53. Lewin 1993, 45–53, citing Bamberger 1986. See also Bamberger 1991. For an additional discussion of Bamberger's research, focusing on its relevance to musical conceptualization, see Zbikowski 2002, 96–107.

resent entities that sound simultaneously. Each such node generally corresponds to a concrete, sounding event.[54] Arrows in an event network thus have a built-in temporal component: they proceed either forward or backward in time, or link two simultaneous events. In spatial networks, by contrast, the arrows have no a priori temporal status, nor do the nodes occupy any a priori temporal location in some musical passage. The arrangement of nodes and arrows in a spatial network rather models privileged *out-of-time* theoretical relationships, such as those in the Riemannian functional spaces of Figure 3.6. One can analytically traverse such a network in time in various ways, but the network itself remains fixed, its arrows always reflecting the space's privileged, atemporal theoretical relationships. Both network types are common in neo-Riemannian writings: some neo-Riemannian analyses array harmonic nodes from left to right on the page, in event-network fashion, while others trace harmonic trajectories on *Tonnetze,* in spatial-network fashion.

Edward Gollin (2000) has theorized the conceptual and formal bases of spatial networks in admirable detail. As Gollin observes, the arrows (or edges) in a spatial network are labeled with certain privileged transformations from the space's underlying group. A neo-Riemannian *Tonnetz,* for example, typically contains edges for the operations P, L, and R only. There are 21 other operations in the neo-Riemannian group (which is of order 24), but they are typically not given independent edges in neo-Riemannian *Tonnetze.* Edges are reserved for transformational "words" of length one—P, L, and R, rather than, say, PL (length two) or LPR (length three). One can of course execute transformational moves of PL or LPR in such spaces, but one must do so by traversing multiple edges. Such spatial networks thus amount to a particular *interpretation* of the underlying algebraic space via privileged elements in the group, an interpretation that Gollin formalizes through the concepts of group presentation and Cayley graphs.

We can define a *strict spatial network* as one in which every element from the space S of the transformational system is represented by exactly one node in the network. A toroidally conformed neo-Riemannian *Tonnetz* with 24 nodes is of this type. We can further define a *redundant spatial network* as one in which some or all of the elements of the space S appear more than once in the network. A neo-Riemannian *Tonnetz* that evokes enharmonic equivalence but is *not* toroidally conformed, instead stretching out infinitely in all directions, is of this kind. We can finally define an *incomplete spatial network,* in which only *some* elements from the space S are present in the nodes of the network. Figure 3.16(b) is a good example of such a network, as are all of the networks of Figure 3.6.[55]

Event networks have received much less theoretical attention than spatial networks in the literature. Lewin himself set the tone for this neglect, treating such networks merely as informal representations of the music's temporal succession,

---

54. The qualification "generally" allows for instances in which a node in an event network may be used for an implied or anticipated event that does not actually sound in the musical passage under consideration. Such implied or anticipated events nevertheless occupy a relative temporal location with respect to the other nodes in the network.

55. Lewin's networks in his Stockhausen essay—the essay in which he discusses the figural/formal distinction—are also incomplete spatial networks in the above sense. See Lewin 1993, esp. pp. 35–36.

arranged intuitively on the page. But we can be more precise about the ways in which event networks encode temporality. This formal precision pays dividends not only in an enriched understanding of the implicit conceptual structure of such networks, but also by allowing us to model certain intentional configurations central to Schenkerian theory.

Let us begin by considering the networks in Figures 3.24(a) and (b).[56] The networks are formally identical as far as *GMIT* is concerned: they both include identical digraphs (node/arrow systems), with identical node contents and arrow labels. The node contents are diatonic pitches in E major; the arrows label diatonic steps up or down, via positive and negative integers. The networks differ only in their arrangement on the page. But what a difference! While we can clearly recognize the subject of the E-major fugue from *WTC II* in (a), the subject is almost completely obliterated by the visual layout of (b). Clearly, the left-to-right layout of 3.24(a) is not merely incidental—it captures an aspect of temporal succession that is essential to the meaning of the network. That temporal structure is very easy to model; Figure 3.24(c) shows how. It divides the space of the network into a set of "event slots" labeled EV_0–EV_5, with the understanding that EV_{n+1} occurs immediately after EV_n (though the precise temporal interval in clock time is left unspecified). Figure 3.24(d) places a similar event grid over Lewin's well-known transformational graph for the opening of Webern's op. 5, no. 2 (1982–83, 324, Figure 8). With these event grids in place, the arrows in the networks of 3.24(c) and (d) exhibit clear distinctions in temporal direction and magnitude—what we might call temporal "vectors." All of the arrows in 3.24(c), for example, point forward in time, but via differing magnitudes. The +2 arrow linking the opening E3 to G♯3, for example, proceeds from EV_0 to EV_3, moving ahead three event stages, while all of the arrows bearing the label –1 proceed forward by only one event stage. And so on. The Webern network of 3.24(d), in addition to forward-oriented arrows, contains four arrows that begin and end in the same event slot, indicating relationships between simultaneous musical events. Neither network 3.24(c) nor 3.24(d) contains arrows that proceed backward in time, but we can easily see how an event grid would capture the chronological retrospection of such arrows, which would originate in some EV_n and end in some EV_m, with $n > m$.

The Webern network also includes "long nodes," which we have encountered already in several figures.[57] These are nodes that occupy multiple consecutive event slots, representing (conceptually or literally) sustained entities.[58] The event grid makes such a formal model simple: a long node is a node that has been assigned to two or more consecutive events: EV_n, $EV_{n+1}, \ldots, EV_{n+j}$. We can also define a "barbell node," one specimen of which we have already encountered

---

56. As the lack of a double-bordered node indicates, these networks are not to be interpreted intentionally (cf. section 3.3.2). Instead, 3.24(a) merely presents a melodic-gestural path that links both adjacent and nonadjacent pitches. (Figure 3.24(b) is a visually jumbled replication of 3.24(a).) On such "melodic" networks, see *GMIT*, 218–19.

57. Specifically, Figures 3.10(b)–(d), 3.11(a)–(b), 3.19(b), and 3.21(e).

58. Lewin himself comments on such nodes, but he offers no formal model for them (1982–83, 326, and 367n5).

(a)

(b)

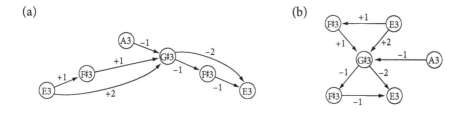

(c)

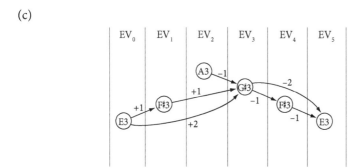

(d)

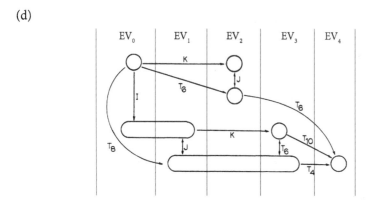

Figure 3.24 (a) and (b): two formally identical networks (per *GMIT*) arranged differently on the page; (c) the network of (a) superimposed over an event grid; (d) Lewin's (1982–83) operation graph for Webern's op. 5, no. 2 superimposed over an event grid.

in Figure 3.17(c).[59] Such a node is paired with two (or more) nonadjacent events. Barbell nodes make possible subtle and attractive distinctions involving repeated events, allowing us to model them as reactivations of a single, concep-

---

59. Figure 3.3(a) is an unusual case, in that it is not arrayed in temporal order from left to right on the page. It otherwise has all of the hallmarks of an event network. Were the figure arranged according to left-to-right chronology, its Db+ node would also be a barbell node.

tually retained musical entity (one suggestive application is to neighbor note configurations).

In short, we can define an *event network* as one whose nodes have been assigned to specific event slots within some pertinent event grid. Formally speaking, the set of nodes is placed in a *relation* with a set of events.[60] The network's nodes are thereby given relative chronological locations in some musical passage, and its arrows—which originate and end in specified events—are assigned chronological vectors (directions and magnitudes). As defined here, the event slots do not specify precise duration, much less metric relationships, but such refinements could easily be added.

When applied to the tonal concepts discussed in this chapter, the two network types enable us to model two distinct species of tonal-intentional activity. The intentions in an event network are strongly syntactical in nature: they are directed forward to a tonal center anticipated, backward to a tonal center remembered, or simultaneously to a tonal center currently sounding. The intentions in a spatial network, by contrast, proceed to a tonal center that occupies no determinate location in the music's temporal unfolding—a center that is sensed as an atemporal orienting presence.

This definition of event networks allows us to make one refinement to the definition of oriented networks in section 3.3. In 3.3.1(c), we specified that an oriented digraph can contain only one root node. We now remove that stipulation for oriented event networks *only*, stipulating that such a network may have more than one root node, but may have only one root node per formal event. This allows such networks to model both reiterations of a tonic at various points in a phrase, as well as fluctuations in tonal center (for example, in changes of key). The multiple root nodes in such event networks can thus model the shifting centers of tonal attraction over the course of a musical passage, as our intentional activity draws sounding events first into one tonal orbit and then another.

3.10 Schenkerian Intentions

Consider the *Zug*-like event networks shown in Figure 3.25. The network in 3.25(a) is obviously drawn to resemble an *Urlinie*, while 3.25(b) resembles an ascending linear progression to $\hat{1}$, perhaps a motion from an inner voice. But the relationship of the networks to such Schenkerian configurations is not merely cosmetic; their underlying formal content offers a simple but compelling model of certain intentional dynamics implicit in Schenker's theory.

We will call the curved arrow in such *Zug* networks the *spanning arrow*. When interpreted intentionally, the spanning arrow suggests a directedness of the listener's attention toward the goal at the end of the *Zug*. The concept of motion

---

60. The use of a relation rather than a function allows us to assign a single node to more than one event, thus allowing for long and barbell nodes. See the entry for *relation* in the Glossary.

(a)   (b)

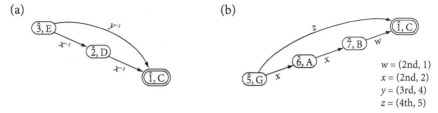

Figure 3.25 Two *Zug* networks: (a) a descending third; (b) an ascending fourth.

toward a goal is of course fundamental to Schenker's understanding of the *Zug* and the *Urlinie:* "the fundamental line signifies motion, striving toward a goal" (1979, 4). Or, more figuratively, "A person stretches forth his hand and indicates a direction with his finger. Immediately another person understands this sign. The same gesture-language exists in music: every linear progression is comparable to a pointing of the finger—its direction and goal are clearly indicated to the ear" (Schenker 1979, 5). One could hardly ask for a more explicit account of intentional hearing. The spanning arrow models Schenker's metaphorical "pointing finger," directing the listener's ear toward the *Zug*'s goal.

The idea of motion toward a goal also suggests a distinction between the events on the way to that goal and the goal itself. Indeed, to hear an event as passing at all implies an intentional structure—an awareness not only of a goal anticipated and held in consciousness, but also of intermediate events as not-yet-that-goal.[61] The middle nodes of the *Zug* networks in Figure 3.25 elegantly model this intentional structure: their status as "on the way but not yet there" is captured by the fact that they are passed over by the spanning arrow, which directs a large intentional vector beyond them. Formally, the passing node p occupies some event EV_j, while the spanning arrow originates in EV_i and ends in EV_k, such that $i < j < k$. The arrow that originates in EV_i and aims toward EV_k directs an intentional thread over EV_j, p's event slot, as though pulling p toward the progression's conclusion. The wording is apt: the term *Zug* derives from *ziehen*, "to pull, draw."[62]

Schenker's linear progressions have a complementary intentional element, often referred to as "mental retention." That is, not only do such structures suggest motion toward an intended goal, but they also suggest the retention in consciousness of the initial tone of the progression. Schenker used several terms for this phenomenon, including *Forttragen*, *Festhalten*, and *vorgestelltes Liegenbleiben*.[63] The word *Forttragen* is particularly suggestive in this regard, as it suggests the "carrying forward" of the primary tone.[64] This sense is captured in Schenker's

---

61. For two highly suggestive discussions of passing as the central "effect" in Schenker's thought, see Dubiel 1990 and Snarrenberg 1997.
62. On the additional resonances of *Zug* in German, see Snarrenberg 1997, 18–19.
63. See, for example, section 204 of *Der freie Satz* (Schenker 1956, 119), which contains the phrases "Das Forttragen des Kopftones" and "das Festhalten an dem Kopfton." The third locution, "vorgestelltes Liegenbleiben," occurs in section 93 (1956, 74). Oster translates all of these as "mental retention" (Schenker 1979, 73 and 38).
64. John Rothgeb translates *Forttragen* as "carrying forward" in Schenker 1996, 4; cf. Schenker 1926, 16.

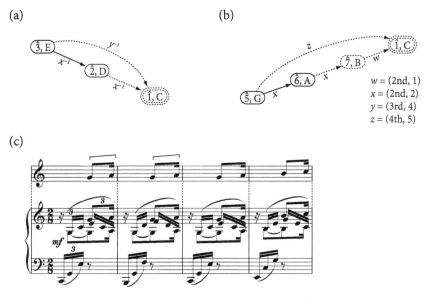

Figure 3.26 Interrupted *Zug* networks: (a) an interrupted descending third (cf. Figure 3.25(a)); (b) an interrupted ascending fourth (cf. Figure 3.25(b)); (c) Chopin, Prelude in C major, op. 28, no. 1 (cf. Samarotto 2005).

images of mental retention in the essay "Further Considerations of the Urlinie: II," in which he indicates the "carrying forward" of the primary tone with dotted slurs.[65] The spanning arrow interacts well with such ideas: we do not only anticipate a goal of motion, we direct the *initial tone* of the *Zug* to that goal, carrying it forward in consciousness as we hear the progression. These two forces—directedness toward a goal and the retention of the point of origin—create what Schenker (1996, 1) called a "conceptual tension" (*geistige Spannung*) that binds the linear progression into a unified entity.

Zug networks may also be used to depict interruption structures. Figure 3.26 shows interrupted versions of the two networks from Figure 3.25. Dotted nodes and arrows indicate pitches intended but not sounded. The networks are meant to capture Frank Samarotto's (2005) insight that an interruption, in Schenker's broadest sense of the term, is an "incomplete passing tone." Figure 3.26(a) thus shows a typical interrupted $\hat{3}$-line, while 3.26(b) models one of Samarotto's examples: the stuttering opening of Chopin's C-major Prelude, op. 28, no. 1, the score of which is shown in 3.26(c). As Samarotto persuasively argues, the oscillating G–A, G–A melodic motion, bracketed in mm. 1 and 2, is best heard not as a neighbor figure,

---

65. Schenker 1996, 4. Schenker's examples of ascending progressions show dotted slurs preceding the goal tone. William Rothstein has suggested interpreting such structures as "mental anticipations" (1981, 93). In addition to the *Meisterwerk* essay and familiar passages from *Free Composition*, Schenker provides a particularly vivid account of mental retention in Book II of *Counterpoint* (Schenker 1987, 56–59).

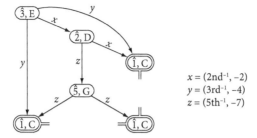

$x = (2\text{nd}^{-1}, -2)$
$y = (3\text{rd}^{-1}, -4)$
$z = (5\text{th}^{-1}, -7)$

Figure 3.27 An oriented network depicting intentional kinetics within a $\hat{3}$-line *Ursatz*.

but as an interrupted ascending fourth progression, which reaches completion only in m. 4. In such a hearing, ($\hat{5}$, G) and ($\hat{6}$, A)—the solid nodes in 3.26(b)—are intentionally directed upward toward ($\hat{7}$, B) and ($\hat{1}$, C) even in their first appearance in m. 1. ($\hat{6}$, A) is *not* intentionally directed back down to ($\hat{5}$, G), as an upper neighbor. In like fashion, the interrupted ($\hat{2}$, D) in 3.25(a) is not an incomplete lower neighbor to the *Kopfton* ($\hat{3}$, E); it is instead intentionally directed toward a goal tone ($\hat{1}$, C), which is sonically withheld.

These ideas are easily extendable to various contrapuntal configurations. Figure 3.27(a) presents the most obvious such extension: a network modeling intentional structures within a $\hat{3}$-line *Ursatz*. The network integrates the *Terzzug* from Figure 3.25(a) with a *Baßbrechung* from ($\hat{1}$, C) to ($\hat{5}$, G) and back. Transformational arrows indicate both linear and harmonic intentions: arrows labeled *y* are descending major thirds, those labeled *z* are descending perfect fifths, and those labeled *x* are descending whole steps. The *y* arrows comprise the spanning arrow of the *Urlinie* and the first verticality in the network. Formally, these two arrows are distinguished by their temporal vectors: the vertical arrow originates and ends in the same formal event slot, while the spanning arrow extends forward in time, to a later formal event slot. This creates an appealing picture of the interaction between potential and kinetic energy implicit in Schenkerian structures. We can understand the impetus for ($\hat{3}$, E)'s descent to ($\hat{1}$, C) as a product of its (vertical) intentional directedness to ($\hat{1}$, C) in the opening simultaneity. The vertical *y* arrow invests the *Kopfton* with a potential energy that is only released by the linear progression of the *Urlinie*. As Ernst Oster has stated, the "tensions" inherent in the opening harmonic interval "come to rest only when the $\hat{8}$, $\hat{5}$, or $\hat{3}$ have 'gone home'—when they have returned to where they came from, that is, to the fundamental which created them . . . the final $\hat{1}$ is an image of the fundamental bass tone and represents a return to it" (Schenker 1979, 13n5). The *y* arrows in Figure 3.27(a) animate this process, as the listener first intends a harmonic interval from *Kopfton* to tonic bass note, and then casts that intention forward in time, as the linear progression that will be required to realize the potential energy invested in opening configuration.

These observations relate to Schenker's comment that "[t]he first two vertical intervals . . . of the fundamental structure—the tenth (third) and the fifth—contain within themselves the possibility of composing out by means of a linear progression of a third and a fifth" (1979, 19). Schenker is speaking here of the composing-out

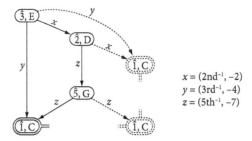

$x = (2\text{nd}^{-1}, -2)$
$y = (3\text{rd}^{-1}, -4)$
$z = (5\text{th}^{-1}, -7)$

Figure 3.28 An oriented network depicting intentional kinetics within an interrupted $\hat{3}$-line *Ursatz*.

of these intervals in the middleground, but Oster's comments suggest that the same horizontalizing relationship is operative between the *Urlinie* and the opening harmonic interval. In all such cases, the horizontalizing of a given vertical interval can be achieved simply by relocating the end point of its intentional arrow to a later formal event, causing the arrow to "spread out" on the x-axis of the network when laid out on the page. It is this operation that creates not only Schenker's *Spannung* but also his particular brand of musical content, and the *Tonraum* that such content occupies.

Figure 3.28 shows an interrupted version of Figure 3.27. Most noteworthy is the intentional environment of the middle stage of the network. $(\hat{2}, D)$ is intentionally directed ahead, toward the sonically withheld $(\hat{1}, C)$. The bass voice, on the other hand, projects both a back-relating dominant and an unrealized forward intention to the withheld tonic.

These little Schenkerian networks are at once more rudimentary and more cumbersome than Schenkerian sketching techniques; they clearly are no substitute for the latter.[66] Nor does it seem wise, or necessary, to develop even more elaborate transformational models that would accommodate the many other effects in Schenkerian theory (reachings over, couplings, voice exchanges, etc.), even if such development were technically feasible. Schenkerian analysis is a rich interpretive tradition, full of nuance and connotation that is all too easily lost in translation. In section 1.4, I argued against re-creating either Schenkerian or transformational theories in the image of the other. The networks introduced in this section, far from substituting for Schenkerian analyses, merely make explicit some basic intentional structures implicit in Schenkerian discourse. They also provide a means for modeling local instances of such structures within a broader transformational context, allowing the analyst to explore points of contact between Schenkerian styles of hearing and the various other modes of musical experience fostered by transformational thought. The Mozart and Brahms analyses in Chapters 5 and 6 offer further exploration of such networks, pursuing their interactions with other kinds of transformational structures.

---

66. For an entirely different transformational model of Schenkerian structures—one that places a greater emphasis on hierarchy—see *GMIT*, 216, Figure 9.16.

PART II

Analytical Essays

Bach, Fugue in E major, *Well-Tempered Clavier,* Book II, BWV 878

The subject of this antique-style fugue has a considerable pedigree, with numerous precedents in the polyphonic repertories of the sixteenth through eighteenth centuries and roots traceable to plainchant.[1] (Plate 4, at the end of this chapter, presents a lightly annotated score of the fugue.) Bach's most proximate source was the E-major fugue from Fischer's *Ariadne musica,* but the *WTC II* fugue also explicitly echoes passages from Froberger's fantasias and ricercares and Fux's *Gradus.*[2] The subject's prevalence in the polyphonic literature is due in part to its considerable potential to enter into stretti: it admits of them at the temporal interval of a half note, a whole note, a breve (double whole note), and a dotted breve. Bach, in his exhaustive fashion, surveys all of these in the E-major fugue, as indicated in the column "Stretto int." in the formal outline of Figure 4.1.[3] The exposition is itself a stretto of sorts, with each new entry stepping on the tail of the previous one at the interval of a dotted breve. Stretti 1, 2, and 3a expose the remaining stretto intervals; in 3b, the subject in diminution enters into a stretto with itself at the interval

---

1. The ascending cambiata figure that begins the subject is the incipit of many chants. Ledbetter (2002, 97) singles out the Mode 3 Magnificat as specifically relevant to the E-major fugue, while Wollenberg (1975, 783) adduces the hymn "Lucis creator." Both authors link keyboard works based on these chants to the organ verset tradition, with which the *WTC II* fugue may be in dialogue.

2. Specifically, Bach's countersubject, nowhere to be found in Fischer's fugue, appears literally in Froberger's Fantasia II and is hinted at in his Ricercare IV, both of which are based on the cambiata subject. Bach's countersubject is also present in three of Fux's fugues, though *not* those containing the cambiata incipit (see Mann 1958, Exx. 46, 63, and 70; for fugues based on the cambiata subject, see Exx. 48, 53, 65, 69, 71, and 83). Froberger's Fantasia II also exhibits two of the more striking techniques in Bach's fugue: the stepwise filling-in of the subject, and the eventual fusion of subject and countersubject into a single melodic gesture.

3. As a scan of the annotated score in Plate 4 confirms, the fugue is saturated with its subject; it is only absent at a few cadential approaches and in one brief passage (mm. 12–15) occupied with stretti of the countersubject. There are no episodes to speak of. I have thus followed Joseph Kerman (2005, 76) in labeling its sections Stretto 1, Stretto 2, and so on. I depart from Kerman in mm. 23–35, which I interpret as three short, interlinked stretto episodes (Stretti 3a, 3b, and 3c), rather than his two.

of a whole note, equivalent to a breve at the original tempo. Stretto intervals vary in the final two sections, due to the admixture of subject statements in diminution, diminuted inversion, and original form. Stretto 4 acts as a summative close, reprising aspects of Stretto 1 and bringing to culmination several developmental strands from the previous sections.

Bach's exhaustive survey of stretto intervals is matched by his (nearly) exhaustive survey of pitch levels for the subject. As the column labeled "Entries" in Figure 4.1 indicates, the fugue subject appears on six of the seven degrees of E major; only A is missing. In its place is a somewhat dubious entry on A♯ at the end of section 3c (mm. 33–34, tenor), indicated in parentheses on the figure and labeled with a question mark on Plate 4.[4] In addition, Bach presents a half-dozen inverted entries, labeled "i" on Figure 4.1. Though it is difficult to assign consistent pitch levels for the inverted entries—due to the variability of their initial intervals—it is plausible to assert two prominent inverted forms "on A♮," as we will see, thus completing the diatonic gamut. The many pitch levels of Bach's subject are in notable contrast to the antecedent works of Fischer, Froberger, and Fux, which present the subject at only two pitch levels throughout. Bach's fugue also departs from its predecessors in its tonal character: the prominent cadences and the variety of local keys that they define suggest a degree of local tonal focus and global tonal planning in sharp distinction to Froberger's and Fux's modality, and Fischer's rather diffuse E major. Bach's regular cadences—Kerman (2005, 76) likens them to the regular sounding of the *gong ageng* in a gamelan—offer a sense of rhetorical punctuation and tonal clarity that is in marked distinction to the *stile antico* sound world suggested by the subject. Nonetheless, Bach's local key areas are often evanescent things, especially when contrasted with the sharply delineated keys of Viennese classicism.

m.	Section	Commentary	Entries	Stretto int.	Cadence
1	Exposition		E, B, E, B	(𝅗𝅥·)	E: HC
9²	Stretto 1	CS stretto, mm. 12–15	B, E, B, E	o	c♯: PAC
16	Stretto 2	2 new CSs	E, B, B, F♯	𝅗𝅥	f♯: PAC
23	Stretto 3a	"filled" subject	F♯, C♯, G♯, D♯	𝅘𝅥	(c♯: evaded)
26⁴	Stretto 3b	diminution	G♯, D♯, B, F♯	o ≈ 𝅗𝅥	(E: deceptive)
30²	Stretto 3c	dim & inv	B, E, i×3, (A♯)	var.	g♯: PAC
35²	Stretto 4	cf. Stretto 1; inv/CS fusion	B, E, B, E, B i i i	var.	E: PAC

Figure 4.1 Bach, Fugue in E major, *WTC II*, BWV 878, formal overview.

4. The putative entry comes amid a pileup of figuration in the approach to a cadence; its rhythm matches that of no other statement of the theme. Players nevertheless sometimes bring it out as a genuine entry.

This is true in his fugues in general, in which local key sensations can be highly fluid, yielding a constant flux of scale-degree sensations. Fugue subject statements can often seem to morph tonally, pivoting seamlessly from one tonal location to another as they unfold. This is true even in fugues with short, *alla breve* themes such as the present work, or its more severe counterpart, the C♯-minor fugue in book one.

The subject in the E-major fugue spans a diatonic tetrachord. Figure 4.2 shows a chart of such tetrachords in the vicinity of E major, arranged into columns by species. The leftmost column shows tetrachords of the form X/TTS; such tetrachords begin on pitch X and proceed upward by tone–tone–semitone. The remaining columns present the remaining three diatonic species: TST, STT, and TTT.[5] Annotations and brackets along the left edge of the figure indicate the diatonic membership of the various tetrachords. For example, the bracket labeled E/c♯ indicates that the tetrachords in the middle two rows, along with A/TTT in the rightmost column, are all native to E major and C♯ minor. A box encloses the tetrachords projected by the subject in the present fugue (leaving aside the dubious A♯/STT entry, which is starred in the figure). All of the tetrachords in the box are native to E major; the only E-major tetrachord not traversed by the fugue subject is the tritone-spanning A/TTT.

Each perfect-fourth-spanning tetrachord may project a diatonic segment in four keys, two major and two minor, as the overlapping brackets on the left edge of Figure 4.2 suggest. For example, B/TTS may project $\hat{5}$–$\hat{8}$ in E major, $\hat{1}$–$\hat{4}$ in B major, $\hat{3}$–$\hat{6}$ in G♯ minor, or $\hat{7}$–$\hat{3}$ in C♯ minor. This last, with its unraised leading tone, might initially seem stylistically questionable, but such natural-minor possibilities are useful to retain, especially once we take ficta alterations into account. Figure 4.3 illustrates the potential key associations of each tetrachord by expanding the central section of Figure 4.2 into a spatial network. Each of the six large nodes in the network corresponds to one of the tetrachords in the box in Figure 4.2. The large nodes are arranged in accordance with the earlier figure; their vertical alignment also reflects their typical fifth-related disposition within stretto pairs: that is, E/TTS and B/TTS are typically paired in stretto, as are F♯/TST and C♯/TST, and G♯/

B/g♯	F♯/TTS	G♯/TST	A♯/STT*	E/TTT
E/c♯	B/TTS	C♯/TST	D♯/STT	A/TTT
A/f♯	E/TTS	F♯/TST	G♯/STT	D/TTT
	A/TTS	B/TST	C♯/STT	

Figure 4.2 Some diatonic tetrachords, arranged by species. The subject in the E-major fugue projects the tetrachords enclosed in the box. Brackets at the left edge of the example indicate diatonic membership of the tetrachords.

5. There are four species of diatonic tetrachord (TTS, TST, STT, and TTT), as predicted by the property "cardinality equals variety" in diatonic scale theory. Each of these species occurs twice in a given diatonic scale, with the exception of TTT, which occurs only once; this is predicted by the property "structure implies multiplicity." On these properties, see Clough and Myerson 1985. Johnson 2003 offers an accessible introduction to diatonic scale theory.

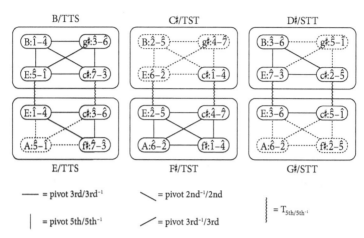

Figure 4.3 A spatial network displaying the possible tonal orientations of the boxed tetrachords from Figure 4.2. Solid nodes indicate tonal orientations taken on by the subject in the E-major fugue.

STT and D♯/STT. Within each large node, there are four smaller nodes indicating the given tetrachord's possible tonal affiliations. Lowercase note names indicate minor keys. Thus, c♯:$\hat{3}$–$\hat{6}$ indicates a diatonic span from scale degree $\hat{3}$ to $\hat{6}$ in C♯ minor. Interpreted via the apparatus of Chapter 2, these labels are shorthand for sd/pc sets: c♯:$\hat{3}$–$\hat{6}$ is shorthand for the set {($\hat{3}$, E), ($\hat{4}$, F♯), ($\hat{5}$, G♯), ($\hat{6}$, A)}. The tetrachordal sd/pc sets within each large node are related by pivot transformations, as the key at the bottom of the figure indicates. A given statement of the fugue subject may thus shift location via pivot transformation within one of the large nodes as it sounds, projecting first one local diatonic span, then another. Solid nodes in the network indicate the local keys touched on (sometimes fleetingly) by the various subject entries in the fugue. Dotted nodes and edges indicate tonal orientations not assayed in the piece. We will explore the ways in which the fugue navigates Figure 4.3 momentarily. For now, we can simply note some general patterns in the figure. First, observe that the B/TTS and F♯/TST tetrachords touch on all four of their possible key orientations at various points in the fugue; the remaining tetrachords survey only some of their tonal possibilities. The three tetrachords in the lower rank all touch on E major and C♯ minor, while the three tetrachords in the upper rank all touch on C♯ minor, and two of them touch on E major. The E-major and C♯-minor tetrachords, which run horizontally through the middle of the network, are connected by wavy vertical edges indicating diatonic transposition by T_{5th} or its inverse.

There are additional relationships of interest not explicitly indicated on Figure 4.3. Tetrachords occupying the same address in vertically aligned large nodes are related by real transposition. For example, B:$\hat{1}$–$\hat{4}$, in the upper-left corner of the B/TTS node, is a real transposition (via $T_{(e, 7)}$) of E:$\hat{1}$–$\hat{4}$, in the upper-left corner of the E/TTS node. Tetrachords occupying the same address in horizontally aligned large nodes are related by diatonic transposition. For example, E:$\hat{2}$–$\hat{5}$, in the upper-left corner of the F♯/TST node, is a diatonic transposition (via T_{2nd}) of E:$\hat{1}$–$\hat{4}$, in the upper-left corner of the E/TTS node.

Figure 4.3 does not tell the whole story regarding the fleeting key orientations of Bach's subject. Ficta alterations complicate the picture, momentarily altering tetrachordal species and aligning subjects with keys not suggested in the network. The explicit ficta alterations in the fugue are:

(1) The E♯ in the soprano in m. 12, which bends the tail of an E/TTS statement toward F♯ minor.
(2) The E♯ in the alto in m. 23, which likewise acts as a leading tone to F♯ minor, turning C♯/TST momentarily into C♯/TTS.
(3) The A♯ and B♯ in the bass in m. 25, which inflect G♯/STT to G♯/TTS, yielding raised $\hat{6}$ and $\hat{7}$ in C♯ minor.

Alterations (2) and (3) project ascending melodic minor segments; in each case, the "correct" tetrachordal form is stated in the descent. One additional exception should also be noted: in m. 20, an F♯/TST statement begins in the orbit of B major. We might consider the opening of this statement as an "implicit ficta" TTS alteration of the subject's underlying tetrachord, replacing the A♮ skipped over in the subject's minor-third leap with an understood A♯. (The A♯ in question sounds explicitly in the alto—in the correct register—in m. 20.) The key orientation shifts as the subject descends in m. 21, providing a diatonic home for A♮. Later we will explore an extension to Figure 4.3 that can accommodate these ficta alterations. For now, the network as it is offers a useful space within which we can trace most of the fluid key associations of Bach's subject.

Figure 4.4(a) shows the initial subject/answer pair, leaving aside the countersubject for the moment. In the limited context of 4.4(a), it is not clear whether one might hear the answer as E:$\hat{5}$–$\hat{1}$ or B:$\hat{1}$–$\hat{4}$. This choice is modeled in 4.4(b), which reproduces the pertinent section of Figure 4.3. A listener who hears E:$\hat{5}$–$\hat{1}$ will be

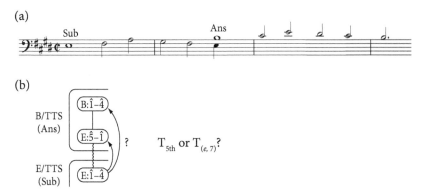

Figure 4.4 (a) Subject and answer at the outset of the fugue, minus countersubject; (b) two possible hearings of the relationship between subject and answer.

guided by a strong tendency to retain the key of the subject, mapping subject to answer via the diatonic transposition T_{5th}. Such a hearing would construe the first verticality in the piece—the E–B fifth at the overlap of subject and answer—as a perfect fifth (5th, 7) from local tonic to local dominant. By contrast, a listener who hears the answer as B:$\hat{1}$–$\hat{4}$ will be guided by a strong tendency to hear the answer's opening pitch as tonally analogous to the subject's opening pitch, mapping subject to answer via $T_{(e, 7)}$. Such a hearing would construe the first verticality in the piece as (e, 7), extending from the first local tonic to the second.

Of course, the suppression of the countersubject in 4.4(a) is artificial—its pitches provide valuable position finding information (à la Browne 1981). Figure 4.5(a) reproduces the answer, now including some crucial pitches from the countersubject. This leads to a more focused, and more complex, hearing of the answer: as beginning in E major under the influence of the quasi V–I gesture spanning the bar line, then pivoting briefly to B major under the influence of A♯, before returning to E major under the influence of A♮. The A♯ creates a tritone with the E at the answer's apex, bending the apex pitch back down to D♯, and thus providing a harmonic motivation for the change in direction after the answer's leap. The tritone dissonance is not obligatory: one could remove the A♯ in the countersubject without doing notable damage to Bach's local syntax—such a removal would simply tilt the piece's sound world closer to that of Froberger (or perhaps even Palestrina). Yet, throughout the fugue, Bach very often supplies a vertical tritone at exactly this moment, making the apex of the cambiata figure acoustically dissonant, and often causing it to take on a local quale of $\hat{4}$. In 4.5(a), this creates a

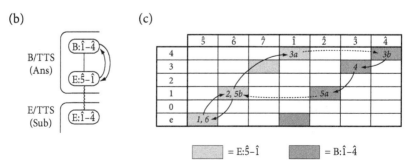

Figure 4.5 (a) The answer, with some pitches from the countersubject included; (b) and (c) qualitative path traversed by the answer in this hearing.

Figure 4.6 The *clausula formalis* suggested but evaded by the answer and counter-subject in mm. 3–4.

pivot 4th at the answer's apex: the music stretches upward qualitatively just as its pitches stretch upward acoustically. As the answer wends its way, stepwise, back to its point of origin, the pivot 4th also eventually relaxes, via its inverse. Figures 4.5(b) and (c) model the kinetics of the gesture respectively on the network space of Figure 4.3, and in the space of the sd/pc GIS. In 4.5(b), the qualitative stretch upward is captured by the arrow reaching up from E:$\hat{5}$–$\hat{1}$ to B:$\hat{1}$–$\hat{4}$. In 4.5(c) it is modeled by the pivot transformation stretching from cell *3a* to *3b*.[6]

The qualitative return to the realm of E major is motivated by the A♮ on the final quarter of m. 3; Fux would call the gesture an *inganno*.[7] One strongly senses the *inganno* after playing through Figure 4.6, which retains A♯ at the end of m. 3, revealing a highly conventional *clausula formalis:* tenor and bass converge on B3 via a standard 2–3 suspension figure. A contemporary listener would be highly attuned to this stock cadential rhetoric, likely sensing it already with the counter-subject's leap-decorated suspension. The gestural profile of Bach's countersubject thus strongly supports the hearing outlined above: the A♯ and cadential figuration signal an initial shift to B major (via a pivot 4th), while the *inganno* A♮ motivates the gentle easing back into E-major key sensations (via a pivot 4th⁻¹). All of this follows the physiognomy of the subject, with its ascending departure from, and descending return to, its starting pitch.

This hearing might seem overly fussy to modern ears, especially those conditioned by Schenkerian ideas of large-scale tonal unfolding. After all, we can easily hear the countersubject's A♯ as a ♯$\hat{4}$ in E major, allowing the answer to remain in the tonic key throughout; the sd/pc GIS indeed allows for such an option. But Bach's contemporaries may have been more prone than we are to hear local chromaticism, whenever possible, as evidence of a wholesale shift in diatonic collection. Indeed, famous pedagogical annotations for the C-minor fugue and D-minor prelude from *WTC I*, at one time erroneously attributed to Bach himself, suggest just such a manner of hearing.[8] These annotations label pitches using local scale degrees, showing shifts of diatonic collection at each applied leading tone (and shifts back with the leading tones' cancellations).[9] Thus, at the first F♯ in the C minor fugue, the scale-degree labels pivot immediately from C minor to

6. In this and subsequent sketches of the fugue subject in the sd/pc space, italicized numbers *1–6* indicate the six pitches of the subject.
7. Fux 1725, 155. See also Mann 1958, 91, and Renwick 1995, 123.
8. See Dürr 1986, Deppert 1987, and Lester 1992, 82–86. Spitta is the source for the erroneous attribution to Bach.
9. The scale-degree annotations label the lowest-sounding pitches in the texture; upper voices are analyzed by their intervals from the bass.

G minor. Such highly mobile scale-degree hearings have a certain kinship with earlier traditions of Guidonian solmization, in which each new semitone would motivate a hexachordal mutation. Indeed, if solmized, the B/TTS answer in Bach's fugue would require a hexachordal mutation in order to situate the E–D♯ at the answer's apex as *fa–mi* in a hexachord on B.[10] To be sure, there are important differences between scale-degree hearings and hexachordal hearings: $\hat{4}$ and *fa* are not the same thing.[11] All the same, both the Guidonian tradition and the *WTC I* annotations offer fluid models of local pitch perception that contrast with more recent theoretical approaches that place emphasis on long-range tonal audition.[12] If we listen closely to Bach's fugue in this way, we become attentive to the myriad ways in which its chameleon-like subject can take on the hues of its shifting tonal surroundings.

Consider, for example, the outset of Stretto 2. Stretto 1 cadences with a PAC in C♯ minor in m. 16, at which point Stretto 2 begins with another subject entry on E. This is, of course, the original pitch-level of the subject, but its coloring is notably changed: the initial E has become $\hat{3}$ in minor. The tonal reorientation prepares our ears for the coming stretto. As shown in Figure 4.7(a), the stretto interval of a breve pits the concluding E of the subject against C♯ in the answer. As the dashed arrows linking 4.7(a) and 4.7(b) indicate, Bach *begins* the passage with this very dyad, creating a sonic parallel between the first half of m. 16 and the second half of m. 17: these whole-note spans contain only the notes of the C♯-minor triad in all four voices. The {E4, C♯5} dyad thus bookends the E/TTS subject statement, situating its opening and concluding pitches in a C♯-minor sound world. The return of the C♯-minor chord at the end of the subject makes for an audible continuity with the earlier C♯-minor music in m. 16, but it is difficult to reconcile the intervening music with this hearing. The soprano's B♮ (not B♯) is especially problematic for the C♯-minor hearing; see the question mark in 4.7(b). Moreover, in the left-hand passage omitted from 4.7(b) the lower voices surge to an arrival on E major at the downbeat of m. 17. Figure 4.7(c) tracks this process in a new E-major stratum, which comes into greatest focus right around the bar line between mm. 16 and 17. But E major begins to lose focus with the arrival of the {E4, C♯5} stretto dyad. By the downbeat of m. 18, it seems to have dissolved altogether: the {F♯, A, D♯} chord on the downbeat, decorated by a 7–6 suspension in the alto, admits of no idiomatic hearing in E major—it certainly does not behave as a vii°⁶. It does, however, behave perfectly idiomatically in C♯ minor, as a ii°⁶ chord following the

---

10. Fux discusses the solmization of fugue subjects in Mann 1958, 82. See also Lewin 1998a for a suggestive discussion of hexachordal interpretations of fugue subjects, including relevant comments on the possible solmization practices of Bach and his contemporaries.

11. Guidonian *fa* designates the upper pitch of any semitone, not a fixed location in some diatonic scale. For a valuable discussion, see Gjerdingen 2007, 34–39, esp. 38. See also Gjerdingen's discussion of the importance of local key perceptions to eighteenth-century listeners on p. 21.

12. It should be noted that Schenker himself was highly sensitive to local (or foreground) keys in his analysis of the C-minor Fugue from *WTC I*. Like the eighteenth-century annotator, he hears a shift to G minor with the introduction of F♯ the answer (he calls the key a *Stufe als Tonart*). See Schenker 1996, 32, Fig. 1.

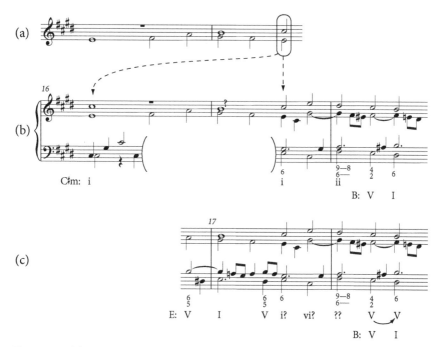

Figure 4.7 (a) Fugue statements on E4 and B4 at the stretto interval of a breve; (b) a C♯-minor hearing of portions of mm. 16–18; (c) an E-major hearing that coalesces around the bar line of m. 17, and then drifts out of focus. Both hearings settle into B major in m. 18.

tonic harmony of the previous half bar (complete with idiomatic $\hat{1}$–$\hat{4}$ bass motion across the bar line). Neither the C♯-minor stratum nor the E-major stratum is completely coherent in itself, yet they are difficult to join into a single analytical stream. As one plays the passage, the sensation can be of two key orientations moving independently in and out of focus, or perhaps shifting roles in a figure-ground configuration—an experience that persists until the music settles into B major in the second half of m. 18.

Through all of this, the E/B stretto pairing weaves, shuttling around Figure 4.8(a). The E/TTS subject tacks back and forth between c♯:$\hat{3}$–$\hat{6}$ and E:$\hat{1}$–$\hat{4}$, while the B/TTS answer tacks from E:$\hat{5}$–$\hat{1}$ to c♯:$\hat{7}$–$\hat{3}$, touching on B:$\hat{1}$–$\hat{4}$ at its conclusion. Figure 4.8(b) traces the path of the E/TTS subject in the sd/pc space. As in 4.5(c), there is a qualitative shift from cell *3a* to *3b* (again motivated by a position-finding tritone), investing the apex pitch with the quale of $\hat{4}$. The subject then descends in E major, but the reappearance of the C♯-minor chord at its conclusion—foreordained by the {E4, C♯5} stretto interval—motivates a qualitative drift back to C♯ minor, from *6a* to *6b*. Figure 4.8(c) traces the path of the B/TTS answer. Its first pivot—from *2a* to *2b*—occurs simultaneously with the pivot from *6a* to *6b* in 4.8(b). The B/TTS answer then rounds its upper portion in C♯ minor, for the first time coloring the apex as $\hat{3}$. This apex (cell *3*) is in fact the very cell that opened and closed the

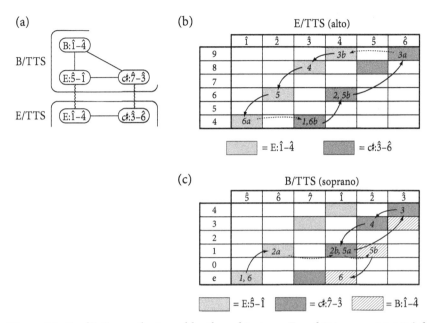

Figure 4.8 Qualitative paths traced by the subjects on E and B in mm. 16–18 (cf. Figure 4.7).

E/TTS subject (cell *1, 6b* in 4.8(c)). This is suggestive of a certain mirror-image relationship between the stretto voices. While the E/TTS subject pivots at its pitch extremes—its highest and lowest notes—the B/TTS answer pivots at its midpoint, on the crucial C♯. In fact, the C♯ takes on no fewer than three qualia in the B/TTS answer, as the key context flickers over the course of the phrase.

Figure 4.9 provides one additional perspective on the music of mm. 16–17. The lower staff of 4.9(a) shows one of the two new countersubjects added for Stretto 2: a *passus duriusculus* ascent from C♯3 to E3, with a return to C♯3 by leap. The upper staff shows the subject and answer in stretto. Figure 4.9(b) reduces these three voices to a first-species framework, revealing the clear motion in parallel tenths between the E/TTS subject and the new countersubject. Figures 4.9(c) and (d) present two hearings of the parallel-tenth progression, one in E major, the other in C♯ minor. The two networks are related by pivot 3rd: one can travel between any of the vertically aligned nodes in 4.9(c) and (d) via (3rd, 0) or (3rd⁻¹, 0). Indeed, when played, the first-species passage can seem to tonal ears to hover equivocally between the two keys, each tonal possibility allied to one of the three-note chords in the second bar. One can further focus one's ears to hear Î–2̂–3̂–Î in either of the two keys: in E major in the alto, or in C♯ minor in the bass. The abstract path of this gesture is graphed in 4.9(e). Figure 4.9(f) graphs its retrograde. While the lower two first-species voices traverse 4.9(e) in whole notes, the actual fugue subject traverses 4.9(f) in half notes with its middle four pitches; see, for example, the half-notes in the E/TTS subject in 4.9(a). When projected

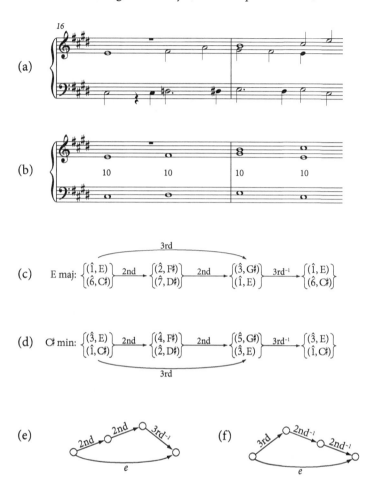

Figure 4.9 (a) The stretto-related subjects in mm. 16–17, accompanied by the *passus duriusculus* countersubject; (b) a first-species simplification of (a); (c) a hearing of (b) in E major; (d) a hearing of (b) in C♯ minor; (e) a gestural graph underlying (c) and (d); (f) a retrograde of the graph in (e).

by quarter notes, gestures 4.9(e) and (f) commonly arise in Fux's third species. By the time Bach's subject sounds in diminution, such third-species figures begin to proliferate in the fugue—they are marked with dashed brackets in Plate 4.

Stretto 2 ends with the first statement of the theme at a new pitch level: on F♯ in the tenor in mm. 20–21. This is the "implicit ficta" entry discussed above, which begins in the orbit of B major in m. 20, but then concludes firmly in F♯ minor, leading to the cadence in that key on the downbeat of m. 23. The implicit ficta pitch in the underlying tetrachord in m. 20 is A♯; as noted earlier, it sounds in the correct register in the alto. Figure 4.10(a) shows the location of the implied F♯/TTS tetrachord with respect to the network space of Figure 4.3. The F♯/TTS tetrachord resides in a large node directly above the B/TTS node in the upper left corner of the network. The remaining two ficta tetrachords in the piece reside yet higher in the same column, as shown on Figure 4.10(a). It is interesting to note that the subject entries on F♯, C♯, and G♯ all first sound (implicitly or explicitly) in TTS guise, imitating the species of the original tetrachord. From there, they migrate to their native locations on Figure 4.3 via the ficta "corrections" modeled in 4.10(b)–(d). These figures will serve as useful points of reference in the following discussion.

The stretto pair in mm. 19–21 traverses the bracketed region in Figure 4.10(a). The B/TTS statement in the bass tacks from E:$\hat{5}$–$\hat{1}$ to B:$\hat{1}$–$\hat{4}$, under the influence of A♮ and A♯. The F♯ statement in the tenor begins in m. 20 as the (implied) ficta tetrachord F♯/TTS in B, before pivoting to F♯ minor via the striking diminished seventh chord on the final half note of m. 20. Once again, a tritone against the apex pitch causes the music to pivot tonally. One can read the specific pivot off of Figure 4.10(b): the common pitches are transformed via pivot 4th, while the implicit ficta A♯ is transformed via the "skew pivot" (4th, –1). As though wishing to make the A♮ explicit on both ascent and descent, Bach begins Stretto 3a by presenting the F♯/TST subject in entirely stepwise form, filling in its characteristic third-leap. The F♯ statement is now paired with its "natural" stretto partner, on C♯, which sounds in

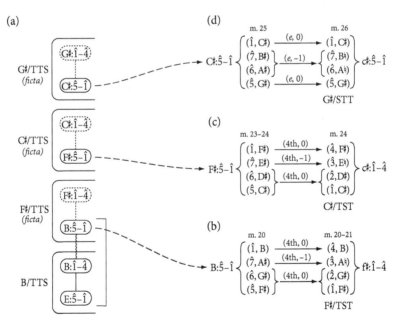

Figure 4.10 (a) An extension of the spatial network in Figure 4.3, showing the location of various ficta tetrachords above the B/TTS node in the upper left corner of that network. (b), (c), and (d): "corrections" of the ficta tetrachords to their diatonic versions.

the alto beginning in m. 23.[13] The C♯ statement begins in ficta form, before finding its uninflected form in the descent of m. 24. The ficta correction, modeled in
Figure 4.10(c), is identical to that in 4.10(b). The reader can trace the alto's filled C♯
statement on 4.10(c): the ascent moves stepwise up the left-hand (F♯:$\hat{5}$–$\hat{1}$) side of
the network, pivots at the top—again under the influence of a tritone—and returns
by descent down the right-hand (c♯:$\hat{1}$–$\hat{4}$) side.

Bach conceals this stretto beneath a welter of trichordal imitation. Figure 4.11
brackets the trichords in question, labeling them 1–6. The key at the bottom of the
figure identifies the trichords as diatonic sd/pc spans, indicating their trichordal
species in parentheses.[14] The listener is thrown off the scent of the stretto by the
imitation between trichords 1 and 2, which seems to place the alto in the role
of *dux* and the soprano in the role of *comes,* rather than the reverse, as in the
"true" stretto. Trichord 1 maps to trichord 2 via diatonic transposition T_{7th}, at the
temporal interval of a whole note. The temporal interval of trichordal imitation
then shrinks to a half note between trichords 2 and 3, and 4 and 5, in agreement
with the stretto interval of the fugue subjects.

One can trace a host of interesting connections on the figure. Trichords 1 and
6 are the only instances of species TT in the passage. They are also the only super-
fluous trichords, neither of them participating in the stretto. Trichord 1 maps to 6
via the real transposition $T_{(e, 7)}$. The same transposition takes trichord 4 to 5. The
1-to-6 transposition proceeds from alto to soprano, while the 4-to-5 transposition
proceeds from soprano to alto. Trichord 1 is to 4 as 6 is to 5: 1 and 6 proceed from
third to fifth of the tonic triad, while 4 and 5 proceed from third to root. Diatonic
inversion $I_{\hat{3}}^{\hat{3}}$ maps 1 and 4 onto each other; it also maps 6 and 5 onto each other.
Trichord 2 inverts into trichord 4 via diatonic inversion $I_{\hat{2}}^{\hat{3}}$. Trichord 3, however,

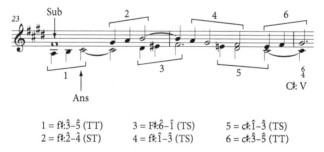

$1 = f\sharp{:}\hat{3}{-}\hat{5}$ (TT) $3 = F\sharp{:}\hat{6}{-}\hat{1}$ (TS) $5 = c\sharp{:}\hat{1}{-}\hat{3}$ (TS)
$2 = f\sharp{:}\hat{2}{-}\hat{4}$ (ST) $4 = f\sharp{:}\hat{1}{-}\hat{3}$ (TS) $6 = c\sharp{:}\hat{3}{-}\hat{5}$ (TT)

Figure 4.11 Trichordal imitations that obscure the stretto in mm. 23–25.

13. Note that the F♯ subject is the only one that occurs in two stretto configurations in the fugue, paired
     either with a stretto partner a fifth below, on B, or a fifth above, on C♯. The fifth-above pairing is the
     one modeled in the network of Figure 4.3. It is the "natural" pairing insofar as both tetrachords, F♯/
     TST and C♯/TST, are of the same diatonic species in the governing mode of the work, thus corre-
     lating with the other two stretto pairings: E/TTS + B/TTS, and G♯/STT + D♯/STT.
14. Trichords 4 and 5 span the modulation from F♯ minor to C♯ minor; in the interest of simplicity, the
     key reads them not as pivots, but as $\hat{3}$–$\hat{2}$–$\hat{1}$ descents in their tonal "homes" of F♯ minor and C♯
     minor, respectively.

does *not* invert into trichord 5, either diatonically or chromatically, due to the ficta E♯. Rather, 3 maps to 5 via chromatic transposition $T_{(3rd,-2)}$, followed by a retrograde. The presence of inversion and retrograde in the area of the subjects' change of direction interacts suggestively with the rhythmic transformation in trichords 4 and 5: their quarter–half–half rhythm is a retrograde inversion of the anapestic quarter–quarter–half rhythm of the other trichords, if we consider durational inversion here to mean "swap quarter notes and half notes."[15]

Figure 4.12(a) shows the next stretto pairing in Stretto 3a, followed by the first pairing in 3b. Both are based on G♯/STT and D♯/STT, but their tonal and rhetorical contexts differ markedly. The reader can trace the bass entry in mm. 25–26 from its initial ficta entry to its "correction" on Figure 4.10(d), again reading up the left side of the network and down the right side. The ficta-correcting transformation here differs from that in 4.10(b) and (c): both G♯ tetrachords reside in the same key, resulting in a combination of $(e, 0)$ identity intervals in the outer two voices, and semitonal inflections by $(e, -1)$ in the inner two. The D♯ entry in the tenor in

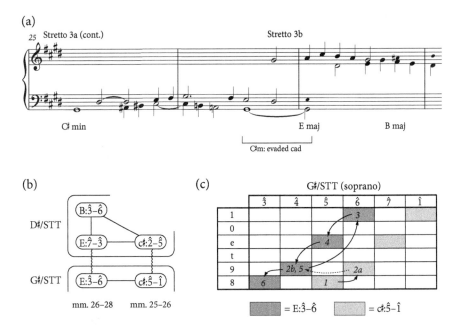

Figure 4.12 (a) Subject statements on G♯ and D♯ (two each) in mm. 25–28; (b) qualitative region surveyed by the subjects in mm. 25–28; (c) sd/pc path traversed by the first diminuted subject (beginning on G♯ in the soprano, m. 26).

---

15. Lewin explores such rhythmic inversions in his analytical discussion of a passage from Mozart's G-minor Symphony, K. 550 (*GMIT,* 220–25). The trichordal business in Figure 4.11 also has interesting points of contact with Lewin's discussion of the subject of the F♯-minor fugue from *WTC I* (Lewin 1998a).

mm. 25–26 is unique among the "filled" entries in two respects: (1) it involves no ficta alterations, and (2) it remains entirely in one key, C♯ minor. The tonal stability of this entry, the G♯ pedal, and the cadential rhetoric prepare the listener for a cadence in C♯ minor at the downbeat of m. 27. This is nevertheless evaded with the arrival of the first diminuted entry, which begins Stretto 3b. The music is diverted back to E major, marking a turning point in the fugue: the subject entries have ventured steadily rightward on Figure 4.3, reaching its right edge with the G♯/D♯ stretto pair in mm. 25–26. Now, with the first diminuted entries, the subjects reverse course on the network, turning back toward their point of origin. Figure 4.12(b) shows the rightmost portion of the network from Figure 4.3, in which this change of direction occurs; measure numbers beneath the network show the leftward turn of the G♯/D♯ entries. Figure 4.12(c) shows this turning point at a level of finer detail, tracing the progress of the first diminuted subject (on G♯) in the sd/pc space: the G♯–A motion that begins the subject originates as $\hat{5}$–$\hat{6}$ in C♯ minor (cells *1* and *2a*), but resolves as $\hat{4}$–$\hat{3}$ in E major (cells *5* and *6*).

With this turn back toward E major via the first diminuted subject, the fugue is nearly poised to perform its summative peroration in Stretto 4. To get a sense of where that summation is headed, consider Figure 4.13. Figure 4.13(a) graphs the fugue subject on a grid whose horizontal lines represent diatonic steps, and whose vertical lines represent the half-note tactus. The elements of the subject are numbered *1–6*, in accordance with earlier figures. The graph reveals some interesting kinetic properties in the subject. Note first that the (pitch, time point) interval from *1* to *2* is the same as that from *2* to *4*: both progress up by one diatonic step and forward by two half notes, or (+1, +2). The cambiata leap up to *3* introduces a

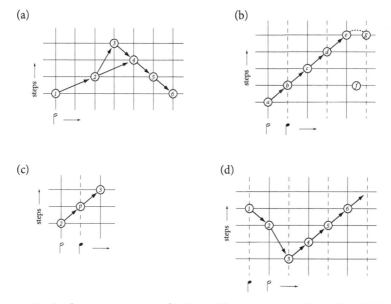

Figure 4.13 Grid representations of subject (a) and countersubject (b), which are eventually fused in the inverted subject (d).

kinetic surge into the subject. The interval from *2* to *3* progresses both twice as far and twice as fast as the *1*-to-*2* and *2*-to-*4* intervals: up by two diatonic steps and forward by one time point, or (+2, +1). The descending resolution then maintains the temporal energy of the *2*-to-*3* leap, via a string of (−1, +1) intervals. The subject thus shows a progression from linear gesture *1–2–4* to linear gesture *3–4–5–6*, with the latter moving twice as fast as the former, as a result of the infusion of energy from the cambiata leap.[16] The countersubject, graphed in 4.13(b), moves two times faster still. In this grid, solid vertical lines indicate the half-note tactus, while dashed vertical lines indicate sub-tactus quarter-note divisions. The project of Stretto 4 will be to map linear gesture *3–4–5–6* from the subject onto linear gesture *a–b–c–d* from the countersubject, fusing the two together into a single melodic figure.

Stretti 3a–3c prepare the way for this fusion. The filled subjects from Stretto 3a introduce quarter-note motion into the fugue. As graphed in Figure 4.13(c), the first quarter-note motion appears in the filled leap from *2* to *3*, the leap initially responsible for the infusion of energy into the subject. This filled-third rhythmic figure also pervades the trichordal activity analyzed in Figure 4.11 (see trichords 1, 2, 3, and 6). This pervasive quarter-note motion throughout Stretto 3a prepares the way for the diminuted entries of 3b; one can visualize the diminuted subject simply by imagining Figure 4.13(a) with alternating solid (half-note) and dashed (quarter-note) lines, as in 4.13(b)–(d). The final stage in this process is the inversion of the diminuted subject, graphed in Figure 4.13(d), whose ascending, double-time *3–4–5–6* is indistinguishable from the countersubject's *a–b–c–d*. The arrow departing from *6* in 4.13(d) suggests the inverted subject's potential to continue stepwise beyond its usual conclusion.

The inverted subject is prepared in m. 29, near the end of Stretto 3b: all four parts move in quarter notes, with soprano, tenor, and bass all stating the third-species figure graphed in 4.9(f); tenor and bass state it in recto form, while soprano states it in inversion, followed by an ascent to E5, which foreshadows the registral culmination of the piece in mm. 35–38. It also prepares the way for the complete inverted statements that appear in Stretto 3c, shown in Figure 4.14. Rather than a descending step, these inverted entries begin with a descending fifth. As Kerman notes, far from obscuring the inverted entries, these leaps have the effect of drawing attention to them: "it is exactly because of the hyperbolic expansion of the launch that we recognize the figure as an inversion … at all" (2005, 81). Nevertheless, the leaps require us to look at the subjects' conclusions, rather than their openings, to assign them a pitch level. Figure 4.14 does so, labeling the entries by their final notes: G♯, C♯, and A. Discounting the opening leap, the first two inverted entries are diatonic inversions of the earlier entries on G♯ and C♯, while the third is a diatonic inversion, via I_4^4, of the absent recto subject on A. Brackets on 4.14 label the

---

16. It is interesting to note that Fischer's fugue does not project this energetic profile: his subject descends from *4* to *5* and *5* to *6* via whole notes, not half notes, thus projecting intervals (−1, +2) on the grid of 4.13(a). Rather than Bach's (and Froberger's) implicit accelerando, Fischer presents a balanced arch in even note values: *1–2–4* ascending, and *4–5–6* descending.

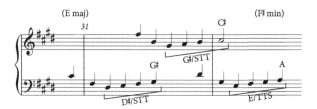

Figure 4.14 The first inverted entries, with initial descending fifth.

diatonic tetrachords traced out by the tails of the inverted subjects. Using the key indications shown above the staff (in parentheses), the reader can easily locate these entries on the network of Figure 4.3. Along with the inverted entries, a recto statement on E in the original rhythm tolls in the alto in mm. 30–32, like a cantus firmus; a diminuted recto statement also sounds on B in the bass in mm. 30–31. These E- and B-based statements, along with the E/TTS tetrachord in the inverted tenor statement of m. 32 (see 4.14), return us to the left-hand side of Figure 4.3, preparing the way for the peroration. Before that peroration arrives, Stretto 3c veers tonally, cadencing in G# minor and passing through the dubious A# statement along the way.

Stretto 4 begins in m. 35 with three closely packed entries, the recto statements representing the triumphant return to the left edge of Figure 4.3. The first of these is a B/TTS statement in the alto that begins under the qualitative shadow of G# minor, before pivoting quickly to E major. The second is a recto statement on E in the tenor. These entries recall the opening of Stretto 1, as does the entry on B in the bass in m. 36, giving Stretto 4 a recapitulatory character and enhancing the sense of a return to the fugue's opening concerns. Along with these recto statements, a summative inverted statement, shown in Figure 4.15, begins in m. 35. The opening leap is now a descending third, introducing what seems at first to be another inverted form ending on A. The inverted subject continues past A, however, to become a countersubject in E. The gesture is remarkable for its breaking open of the end of the subject, its resultant fusion of subject and countersubject, and its presentation of a complete ascending scale in E major. The effect is one of rhetorical achievement matched with tonal consolidation; the latter is especially striking given the almost constant tonal flux in the fugue thus far. As shown in Figure 4.15, the ascending scale traverses tetrachords E/TTS and B/TTS, surveying the E:$\hat{1}$–$\hat{4}$ and E:$\hat{5}$–$\hat{1}$ nodes of Figure 4.3 in the process, which are now arrayed as the disjunct tetrachords of a complete octave.

Figure 4.15 The inverted subject is fused to the countersubject.

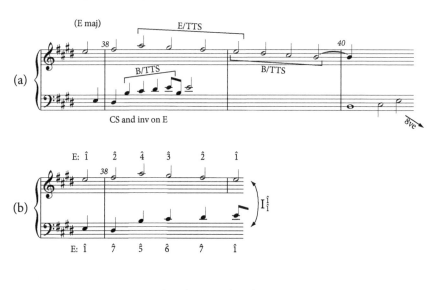

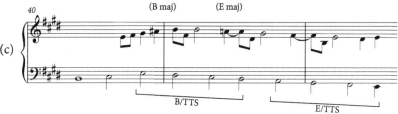

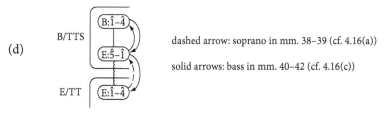

Figure 4.16 The summative peroration in Stretto 4: (a) a climactic subject statement in the soprano is paired with an inversion-*cum*-countersubject in the tenor, both of them on E; (b) the statements in (a) invert into one another around 1̂; (c) the final, extended subject on B, in the bass; (d) the climactic recto statements in (a) and (c) trace a complete circuit the through the region of Figure 4.3 assayed by the initial subject and answer (cf. Figure 4.5(b)).

Figure 4.16(a) shows the registral climax of the fugue: the soprano's A5 in m. 38.[17] This soprano statement occurs simultaneously with an inversion of the subject in the tenor, which once again morphs into the countersubject. This is the first inverted statement in which the initial interval is preserved intact, though it is now one octave too low (the alteration makes it playable by the left hand). It is also the first inverted statement "on E." As shown in Figure 4.16(b), it is a diatonic inversion around $\hat{1}$ of the E/TTS subject sounding simultaneously in the soprano. Recto subject, inverted subject, and the countersubject embedded in the latter all sound entirely in E major, heightening the effect of a rhetorical QED. Like the inverted statement in 4.15, the soprano in 4.16(a) extends past the subject's typical end point, tracing out a linear seventh from A5 to B4. This results once again in a scalar presentation of E/TTS and B/TTS, though now the tetrachords are arrayed in conjunct fashion, sharing the note E5, in contrast to the disjunct arrangement of Figure 4.15. That disjunct arrangement reappears in the culminating bass statement of mm. 40–42, shown in 4.16(c). The apex of the B/TTS subject is paired yet again with its tritone partner, A♯, in the alto at the end of m. 40, creating one last qualitative tilt toward B major. As shown in Figure 4.16(d), the descending scales of 4.16(a) and (c) trace out the very portion of Figure 4.3 explored in the initial statement of subject and answer (cf. Figure 4.5(b)). Having returned decisively to its point of origin, the fugue ends with a cadential flourish in a purely diatonic, valedictory E major.

17. Fischer's E-major fugue also climaxes on A5.

Plate 4: Bach, Fugue in E major, *Well-Tempered Clavier,* Book II, BWV 878

Plate 4 cont.

Plate 4 cont.

E: PAC

CHAPTER $\mathbb{F}$ ive

Mozart, "Un'aura amorosa"
from *Così fan tutte*

Ferrando's aria is the last number before the finale of Act I. Don Alfonso, who has just upbraided Guglielmo and Ferrando for laughing, instructs them to do as he says for the next day, causing Guglielmo to wonder whether they will even be able allowed to eat. Ferrando responds dreamily, in song, that they won't need food, as they will be nourished by the breath (*aura*, lit. "breeze") of their beloveds:

Un' aura amorosa	An amorous breath
Del nostro tesoro	From our treasures
Un dolce ristoro	Will afford our hearts
Al cor porgerà;	Sweet refreshment;
Al cor che, nudrito	A heart nourished
Da speme, d'amore	With hope and love
Di un'esca migliore	Has no need
Bisogno non ha.	Of greater enticement.

Mozart sets the aria in a characteristically amorous A major (the key of "Là ci darem la mano," "O wie ängstlich," the love duet between Ilia and Idamante, and that between Servilia and Annio; it is also the key of two other crucial numbers in *Così*, which we will discuss later). The aria is in a fittingly simple ternary (ABA) form, with A presenting the first quatrain, and B the second. The only key changes are in the B section: a brief tonicization of vi and a more substantive modulation to V. The A section, our focus in this chapter, remains entirely in the tonic.

For all of its ostensible simplicity, there is a great deal that one could explore transformationally in the aria, from the physiognomy of its local melodic gestures and their interaction with Da Ponte's prosody, to the subtle irregularities of the harmonic rhythm. Rather than presenting a lengthy analysis here, however, I would simply like to delve into two phenomenologically dense moments, and then radiate outward from them to broader interpretive considerations of the aria—and indeed the opera—as a whole.

171

Figure 5.1 The A section of Mozart's "Un'aura amorosa" from *Così fan tutte*, Act I (voice, bass line, and analytical annotations).

We begin with a general overview of the A section. Figure 5.1 shows the vocal and bass lines, accompanied by some analytical markings. Careted scale degrees above the staff mark the backbone of a $\hat{5}$-line descent; italicized numbers above the sung $\hat{5}$s label them for later discussion. The onsets of five vocal phrases are marked; Phrases 1–4 are four bars in length; Phrase 4bis is six bars. Mozart sets the entire quatrain two-and-a-half times through, as the layout of Figure 5.1 makes clear: each full setting of the quatrain occupies one system, while Phrase 4bis, which repeats the final two lines, occupies a partial third system. Each system ends with a cadence: HC in m. 9, IAC in m. 17, PAC in m. 23. The cadences mark exactly those moments where Da Ponte's quatrain "cadences" with an end-stopping *senario tronco* ("Al cor porgerà").[1]

The first two systems of Figure 5.1 are sentences in William Caplin's (1998) sense. In the presentation phrases (Phrases 1 and 3), Ferrando sings the opening two lines of the quatrain as a balanced pair, 2 bars + 2 bars. These presentation phrases both drift downward melodically, allowing the continuation phrases (2 and 4) to ascend in response—a fitting gesture for "dolce ristoro." Specifically, Ferrando descends from the *Kopfton* ($\hat{5}$, E) in Phrases 1 and 3, allowing it to be "sweetly restored" in Phrases 2 and 4. There are nevertheless notable differences between the sentences. Phrase 1 unfolds over a prolonged tonic, while Phrase 3 unfolds over a prolonged dominant. Phrase 1 presents its two lines of text in a melodic sequence, descending gradually through the space of the tonic triad, while Phrase 3 presents a literal 2 + 2 repetition, arpeggiating V^7. This literal repetition places the *Kopfton* ($\hat{5}$, E) on the downbeats of mm. 10 and 12; previously, Ferrando had sung the *Kopfton* off of the downbeat, after the brief ascending melismas characteristic of the aria.[2] The shift of the sung *Kopfton* to the downbeat, and its repetition at a two-bar interval in mm. 10 and 12, gathers and focuses the listener's attention, creating expectation for yet another sung *Kopfton* on the downbeat of m. 14. Ferrando obliges, celebrating the realized expectation with the most florid melisma in the aria, which attains the vocal line's highpoint, A5. After the IAC in m. 17, Ferrando begins Phrase 4bis by revisiting this ecstatic moment, singing the melisma again, and extending the phrase languorously; "un dolce ristoro" stretches from two bars to four. Ferrando's vocal effusion resonates into the first violins, which double the melisma and continue it sequentially.[3]

Figure 5.1 labels the moments when Ferrando sings the *Kopfton* E with italicized numerals *1–6*. The ecstatic sung *Kopftöne* in Phrases 4 and 4bis are *5* and *6* in this numbering. As Figure 5.2 illustrates, the six sung *Kopftöne* occupy a variety of harmonic, metric, and phonetic contexts. The arrows running along the top the figure make clear that the metric interval between the sung Es gradually decreases,

---

1. The first three lines of the quatrain are *senari piani,* that is, six-syllable lines (figuring in vowel elisions) with the accent falling on the penultimate syllable. A *senario tronco* is a truncated *senario piano:* a five-syllable line with the accent on the final syllable.

2. These downbeat melismas contribute to the sarabande-like character of the piece, causing each bar to glide toward beat two.

3. This is the only independent melodic material presented by the instruments in the A section. In the repeat of the A section, the winds also participate in this passage (mm. 57–62).

	+5 bars	+3 bars	+2 bars	+2 bars	+4 bars
sung *Kopfton:*	*1*	*2*	*3*	*4*	*5, 6*
bar in phrase:	bar 1	bar 2	bar 1	bar 3	bar 1
local beat:	beat 2–	beat 2–	beat 1	beat 1	beat 1
sung vowel(s):	AUrA	ristOrO	AUra	nOstro	dOlce
sd/pc int from bass:	(5th, 7)	(6th, 8)	(*e*, 0)	(*e*, 0)	(7th, 10)
local harmony:	I	V	V	V	IV? vi?
chord member:	fifth	root	root	root	seventh? sus?

Figure 5.2 Metric, phonetic, and harmonic contexts for sung *Kopftöne 1–6.*

from +5 bars (*1* to *2*), to +3 bars (*2* to *3*), to +2 bars (*3* to *4* and *4* to *5*). A large-scale accelerando thus leads to the first ecstatic *Kopfton;* the intervals further proceed from odd (+5, +3) to even (+2), creating a sense of gathering metric focus, which is then confirmed by the "stabilizing" interval of +4 bars from *5* to *6.* This sense of increasing metric focus is also underscored by the next two rows. The row labeled "bar in phrase" provides hypermetric information, indicating the location of the sung *Kopftöne* within their embedding phrases in Figure 5.1, while the third row indicates local beat.[4] Sung *Kopftöne 3–6* all occupy strong metric positions at both hypermetric and local metric levels.

The row labeled "sung vowel(s)" situates the above metric information with respect to the text, indicating which of the quatrain's sonorous back vowels project the *Kopfton* in each instance. This draws our attention to the remarkable *resonance* of Da Ponte's text: the aria offers a phonetic web to delight a Russian formalist. The composing-out of AuRA into AmoRosA only hints at the riot of phonemic echoes to follow: amOROsa / del nOsTRO TesORO / un dOlce risTORO / al cOR pORg-erà. Ferrando's sung (5̂, E) participates in this resonant web, projecting various of these vowels in shifting musical contexts. As it does so, it creates its own sort of resonance, a *musical* resonance that eventually seems to open up a space beneath the rococo conventionality of the aria's surface. That space opens up precisely at sung *Kopftöne 5* and *6,* as we will see.[5]

The bottom three rows in Figure 5.2 explore the harmonic context of each sung *Kopfton.* The row "sd/pc int from bass" displays the interval from the sounding or understood bass note at the moment the *Kopfton* is sung—a sort of transformational figured bass.[6] Figure 5.3 maps the progression of sd/pc intervals

---

4. The indication "beat 2–" means "just before beat 2."
5. It is worth noting here that the Italian word "aura" carries a secondary connotation of "ambience" or "atmosphere" (or indeed the English cognate "aura"). The resonant quality of the setting—especially the ways in which the sung E rings out in ever shifting contexts—reinforces the pertinence of those connotations, suggesting that the "aura" in question may not be so much a breath emanating from a carnal source as a sort of disembodied nimbus. Indeed, Scott Burnham refers to the aria as an exercise in "the otherworldly atmospherics of ideal love" (1994, 87).
6. The qualification "or understood" applies to sung *Kopftöne 3* and *4,* which sound over an acoustic rest in the continuo; bass note (5̂, E) is understood in both cases.

		sdints		
	5th	**6th**	**7th**	*e*
7	*1*			
8		*2*		
9				
10			*5, 6*	
11				
0				*3, 4*

Figure 5.3 The sd/pc intervals from bass to voice part for sung *Kopftöne 1–6*.

in a portion of the IVLS space of the sd/pc GIS, clearly showing the progression from the consonant *1–4* to the dissonant *5* and *6*. Though sung *Kopftöne 3–6* are all metrically stable, *harmonic* stability disappears with *5* and *6*. The "focusing" of the metric situation in the lead-up to *5* and *6* makes their harmonic dissonance all the more striking.

The bottom two rows of Figure 5.2 indicate the local harmony and the sung *Kopfton*'s role in that harmony. Again, the stability of *3* and *4* gives way to uncertainty in *5* and *6*—note the question marks. Is the harmony supporting the ecstatic *5* and *6* an essential seventh chord, that is vi⁷, or is it a IV⁶ with an incidental, suspended seventh? The issue was in the theoretical air at the time: Kirnberger's well-known distinction between essential (*wesentlich*) and incidental (*zufällig*) dissonances dates from the decade before *Così*.[7] As Kirnberger defined them, essential dissonances are chord members; they require a change of harmony in order to resolve. Incidental dissonances are not chord members; they require no change of harmony to resolve. A chordal seventh is an essential dissonance; a suspension is an incidental dissonance. Which species of dissonance are sung *Kopftöne 5* and *6*?

We should first note that Mozart spells the chord in question {F♯, A, E} with no C♯. This seven-three voicing strongly suggests a suspension of a six-three, *not* an incomplete seven-five-three (Kirnberger 1982, 97). The reader can confirm this aurally by adding a C♯ to the harmony in mm. 14 and 18 and noting the incongruous effect. Yet, as Figure 5.4(a) shows, Mozart complicates the situation by eliding the resolution of the seven-three. This elision is analyzed in 5.4(b), which presents the seven-three chord and its expected six-three resolution on the top staff, and the eliding progression on a second staff. Italicized letters above the staves label the chords for discussion: the seven-three chord is labeled *A*, while the F♯-minor chord that concludes the progression, on the second staff, is labeled *B*. The anticipated six-three resolution of chord *A* is labeled *X*, while the eliding vii-of-vi is labeled *Y*. The "dolce ristoro" progressions in Phrases 4 and 4bis both progress from *A* to *B*, with chords of type *X* and/or *Y* intervening.

---

7. See Kirnberger 1982, 78–98. Kirnberger's treatise was originally published in four parts from 1771 to 1779.

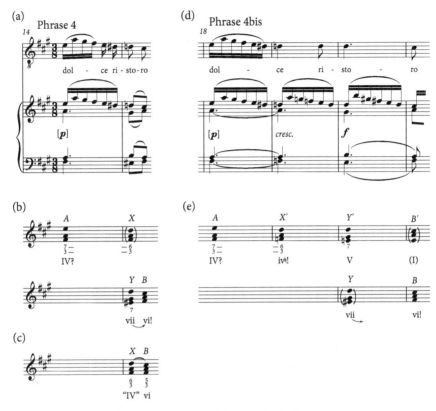

Figure 5.4 Aspects of harmony in mm. 14–15 and 18–21.

We now ask, are *A* and *B* two manifestations of "the same chord"? Both chords, after all, have F♯ as a bass note and A as an inner voice. Nevertheless, a hearing of *A* as a seven-three suspension chord suggests they are *not* the same. In this hearing, chord *A* is a decoration (or delay) of a IV⁶ chord (root: D), *not* a species of vi chord (root: F♯). Yet *B* is an explicit vi chord, its F♯ root strongly asserted by the applied leading-tone E♯ in chord *Y*. The "IV-or-vi?" question becomes more complex still when we consider Figure 5.4(c). This figure shows the underlying progression of *X*-to-*B* that emerges if we (1) reduce out chord *A* and its incidental, suspended E (that is, ecstatic *Kopfton* 5), leaving only its resolution, chord *X*; and (2) reduce out the tonicizing chord *Y*. The *X*-to-*B* progression is highly thematic for the opera, as we will see. We can note for now that such a progression raises its own questions of harmonic priority in traditional tonal theory. Specifically, do the two chords in such a progression have equal status, or is the "IV⁶" best understood as an embellishment of vi? Most American theorists would likely opt for the second interpretation, arguing that the IV⁶ is indeed only apparent, decorating the vi chord via a 6–5 motion.[8] This chain of reasoning suggests that perhaps the "dolce ristoro"

8. Aldwell and Schachter 2003, 299–302, offer a characteristic account of six-threes that "embellish or substitute for" five-threes.

passage of Phrase 4 has been under the control of vi all along. All of this invests the ecstatic sung *Kopfton 5* with considerable phenomenological complexity, its dissonance (incidental or essential? chord-tone or suspension?) opening up a space of musical and expressive complication not yet encountered in the aria.

Thus, when chord *A* reappears at the beginning of Phrase 4bis, shown in 5.4(d), our ears are highly sensitive to it. Now, rather than proceeding to the eliding *Y*-to-*B* progression, chord *A* explicitly resolves to a six-three chord, tilting the interpretive balance *back* in favor of the suspension-to-IV⁶ hearing. Chord *A* does not resolve to *X*, however, but to *X′*, a six-three over F♮, as shown in Figure 5.4(e). The F♮ in *X′* is enharmonically equivalent to the E♯ in *Y*, converting the latter's dissonant diminished seventh {E♯, D} into a consonant major sixth {F♮, D}. Chord *X′* thus acts as a substitute for both *X* and *Y*: it is a minor variant of the former and an enharmonic variant of the latter. The enharmonic substitution is a masterstroke, transforming an energetic applied dominant into a deeply affecting minor subdominant—the first and only bit of mixture in the aria. Unlike E♯-in-*Y*, which pulls quickly back up to F♯, yielding chord *B*, F♮-in-*X′* drifts down languorously toward E♮, yielding a V⁷ chord, labeled *Y′* in 5.4(e). *Y′* seems poised finally to resolve the tangle of these bars, pointing to an anticipated tonic chord. Yet chord *B* once again sounds. The displaced tonic is labeled *B′* in Figure 5.4(e) and enclosed in parentheses. The second stave in 5.4(e) reproduces the *Y*-to-*B* progression, making explicit the substitution of *Y′* for *Y* and *B* for *B′*.

The reader surely will have observed that the conclusion of Phrase 4bis is a deceptive cadence. The previous discussion and the arrangement of Figure 5.4 suggest that Phrases 4 and 4bis are in fact shot through with such deceptions, as the uncertainty of chord *A* gives way to a series of syntactical surprises.⁹ One notes that Ferrando's text here treats not deception but the putative renewal created by the encounter with the beloved. We will return to this later.

The oriented networks of Figure 5.5 seek to render visible some of these deceptions and to model their striking shifts in intentional context. The figure consists of a series of local networks, which unfold like a string of intentional snapshots, in loose coordination with the music's harmonic rhythm. The figure's arrangement into columns and rows is meant to evoke a paradigmatic analysis: each column represents a syntactic slot, while each row contains related paradigmatic networks.

Each intentional snapshot is oriented around the local harmonic root. As indicated by measure numbers along the top of the figure, the networks in 5.5(a) and (b) model the "dolce ristoro" progression in Phrase 4, while those in 5.5(c)–(g) model the progression in Phrase 4bis. The solid nodes in each network represent the sounding elements in a given bar. Dotted nodes and arrows indicate elements that are either prospectively intended (but not sounded) or that are retrospectively retained from previous bars. One can scan across Figure 5.5 from one solid chord to the next, tracing the progressions' sonic unfolding. One can also scan the vertically aligned portions of the networks at measures 15, 19, 20, and 21 to explore the substitutional interrelationships among chords *X, X′, Y, Y′, B,* and *B′*.

---

9. Chord *A* itself appears on the scene as a deception of sorts, following the prolonged V chord of mm. 10–13. We will discuss this deceptive progression later, including its thematic E–F♯ bass line.

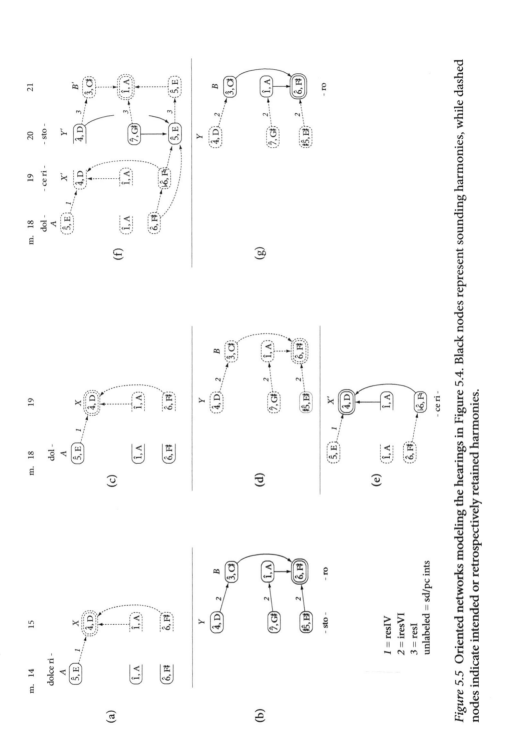

Figure 5.5 Oriented networks modeling the hearings in Figure 5.4. Black nodes represent sounding harmonies, while dashed nodes indicate intended or retrospectively retained harmonies.

Note that chords A and B never occupy the same network in Figure 5.5: they are always separated by some intentional disjunction, some shift in tonal focus. In Figure 5.5, chords A and B are emphatically *not* different instances of "the same chord"; they are instead unique moments in the kaleidoscopic unfolding of the "dolce ristoro" progressions. The "ristoro" of the text in each case motivates a deflection in harmonic focus, shunting the listener downward among the vertically aligned networks, ultimately toward chord B (which always sets the word's final syllable). These vertical journeys correspond to the deceptions discussed above.

Chord A has a strikingly open-ended, even unmoored appearance in the networks. In networks 5.5(a) and (c), its intentional focal point, $(\hat{4}, \text{D})$, is present only as a dotted node, intended but unsounded. This lack of a harmonic mooring for the chord seems to motivate the tumble downward into the lower networks, which occurs through the vertical channels of X/Y substitutions. In Figure 5.5(b), a toehold is gained on chord Y, which substitutes for the X of 5.5(a). In the process, $(\hat{4}, \text{D})$ is demoted from its role as root node in 5.5(a) to a source node in 5.5(b), strongly directed toward $(\hat{3}, \text{C♯})$. This demotion of chord A's intentional anchor motivates the "IV-or-vi?" question discussed above. In the middle column of the figure, the tumble proceeds all the way down to chord X' in Figure 5.5(e), which substitutes for both X in 5.5(c) and Y in 5.5(d). This *restores* $(\hat{4}, \text{D})$ to its role as local root, though the harmony has now picked up pitch class 5 (F♮), as though under the enharmonic influence of Y. In the rightmost column of the figure, it is the deceptive cadence of Y' to B that shunts us downward from network 5.5(f) to 5.5(g).

Though the vertical alignment of the networks in 5.5 offers a suggestive image for the various X/Y substitutions in the passages, the figure does not make explicit the ways in which we navigate those vertical channels—the ways in which X, Y, X', and Y' are transformed into one another. Figure 5.6 redresses this situation. Figure 5.6(a) shows the space of the sd/pc GIS, with the diatonic cells for A major shaded. Subscripted xs and ys identify the elements of the four chords. Chord $X = \{x_1, x_2, x_3\}$, while chord $X' = \{x'_1, x_2, x_3\}$; similarly, chord $Y = \{y_1, y_2, y_3\}$, while chord $Y' = \{y'_1, y_2, y_3\}$. One can easily transform the four chords into one another visually on 5.6(a) by tracing the motions between elements with the same numerical subscript. Arcs and arrows in the space point out some relationships of interest. The dashed arc indicates the (dissonant) diminished seventh from y_1 to y_3; that is, $\text{int}(y_1, y_3) = (\text{7th}, 9)$. The solid arc indicates the (consonant) major sixth from x'_1 to x_3; that is, $\text{int}(x'_1, x_3) = (\text{6th}, 9)$. The arrows departing from x'_1 and y_1 indicate their tendencies to resolve in inverse fashion: y_1 via ascending minor second, or $(\text{2nd}, 1)$, to x_1; and x'_1 via descending minor second, or $(\text{2nd}^{-1}, -1)$, to y'_1.

Figures 5.6(b) and (c) illustrate some notable proportions between the harmonies. As shown in 5.6(b), X is to X' as Y is to Y': in each case, the former harmony is transformed into the latter by lowering the subscript-1 pitch by $(e, -1)$, taking x_1 to x'_1 and y_1 to y'_1. This efficient motion transforms chord X in network 5.5(c) to chord X' in 5.5(e); it also transforms chord Y in 5.5(g) to chord Y' in 5.5(f). Figure 5.6(c) shows a related proportion: X is to Y as X' is to Y'. In each case, the former harmony is transformed into the latter by lowering the subscript-1 and subscript-2 pitches by $(\text{2nd}^{-1}, -1)$. This transformation takes X in

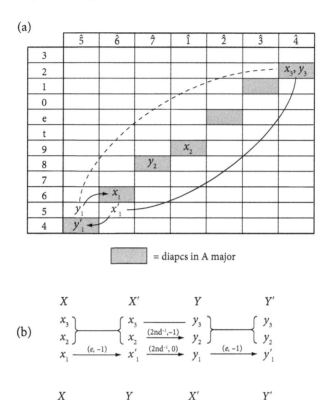

Figure 5.6 Transformations among chords *X*, *X′*, *Y*, and *Y′*.

network 5.5(a) to *Y* in network 5.5(b). It also takes *X′* to *Y′* in the acoustic time flow of the music in mm. 19–20.

The enharmonically related *X′* and *Y* form the fulcrum in both of these double proportions, in the middle of 5.6(b) and (c). They share pivot-related pitches x'_1 and y_1, the only two elements horizontally adjacent to one another on 5.6(a). These pitches reside in the chromatic seam between diatonic $\hat{5}$ and $\hat{6}$, the area of greatest activity in Figure 5.6(a). In the middle of this seam is pitch class 5, F♮/E♯, which takes on two radically different colorings in *Y* and *X′*: a raised $\hat{5}$ in the former (y_1), and a lowered $\hat{6}$ in the latter (x'_1). As Figure 5.7 shows, much motivic activity in the aria indeed centers on $\hat{5}$ and $\hat{6}$. Figure 5.7(a) shows the melodic highpoint of Phrase 2, as Ferrando surpasses the *Kopfton* ($\hat{5}$, E) to touch on its neighbor ($\hat{6}$, F♯). As shown in 5.7(b), this same motion recurs in the bass across the bar line into m. 14, now as an explicitly deceptive bass motion. The deceptive {$\hat{5}$, $\hat{6}$} dyad is then frozen into a ver-ticality for chord *A* at m. 14, as the long stem in 5.7(b) indicates. The $\hat{5}$ of this dyad is the first ecstatic sung *Kopfton*. Figure 5.7(c) shows the next ecstatic *Kopfton* and the extended "dolce ristoro" progression that follows, beaming the motivic motion between $\hat{5}$ and $\hat{6}$ in the bass. Annotations above the staff in 5.7(b) and (c) identify the harmonies that we've been discussing. Chord Y and its enharmonic substitute, chord X', are embedded within these motivic progressions, just as their bass notes are embedded in the chromatic seam between $\hat{5}$ and $\hat{6}$.

We noted above the dissonance between Ferrando's text, with its dreamy rhetoric of amorous renewal, and the music, with its string of deceptions. The dissonance is characteristic of the opera, as is the fact that the harmonic deceptions are themselves moments of surpassing beauty. Such moments have puzzled commentators since the work's premiere. That puzzlement has arisen in part from the fact that, as Scott Burnham puts it, "the music seems to become even more ravishing and heartfelt at those points in the opera where the basest sort of deception is practiced: where we might expect bald comedy, the music falls like a scrim of melancholy beauty over the often preposterous action" (1994, 77–78). Ferrando's rapturous melismas and harmonic adventures in "Un'aura amorosa" are indeed in exhilarating discord with the vapid artifice of the text—their phonetic charms aside, Da Ponte's empty-headed quatrains can hardly be taken seriously on paper.

Figure 5.7 Motivic activity involving $\hat{5}$ and $\hat{6}$.

Nor are we meant to take the aria seriously in its dramatic context. It represents Ferrando's idealized and credulously conventional view of love, before he is "Enlightened" by the bitter realizations of Act II.

So what are we to make of the excess of beauty in the aria, of the ways in which the ecstatic sung *Kopftöne* seem to prize open spaces of unexpected harmonic depth and emotion in Phrases 4 and 4bis? A conventional reading would have it that Mozart's setting humanizes Ferrando, creating a character of genuine three-dimensional depth and feeling where Da Ponte's libretto has only a two-dimensional puppet.[10] There is surely some truth to that view, but the matter becomes more complex when we listen closely to the ways in which the affecting passages in "Un'aura" resonate with other nodal points in the opera. They resonate first of all with the only two other numbers in A major: the sisters' duet "Ah guarda, sorella" in Act I (also Andante and in 3/8), and the seduction scene "Fra gli amplessi" between Ferrando and Fiordiligi in Act II, in whose opening some commentators hear an explicit echo of "Un'aura."[11] In addition to sharing the present aria's tempo and meter, "Ah guarda" also contains a striking instance of chord X', the D-minor six-three: Dorabella lands on the chord in m. 58, creating the first prominent turn to minor in the opera (aside from a couple flashes of mixture in the overture). But this is no moment of pathos. Dorabella is here offering a laughably hyperbolic account of Ferrando's sexual appeal and "threatening" masculinity,[12] her heart fluttering (in minor) as she looks at his picture. The horns, that reliable symbol of cuckoldry, enter simultaneously with chord X'—a telling commentary on the true depth of Dorabella's constancy.

"Fra gli amplessi" offers a more genuinely pathetic echo of "Un'aura," but the resonance is no less perplexing. As shown in Figure 5.8, the oboe in Fiordiligi's final capitulation to Ferrando—the dramatic turning point in the entire opera[13]—traverses the very tonal seam between $\hat{5}$ and $\hat{6}$ that Ferrando had assayed in "Un'aura," in the same key, navigating the lower-left-hand corner of Figure 5.6(a). This would seem like mere coincidence—passing motions from $\hat{5}$ to $\hat{6}$ are a dime a dozen, after all—were the two moments not so strikingly spotlighted in the drama: they are perhaps the most memorable moments in A-major in the entire opera, and their sonic pairing is deeply ironic. The space of Ferrando's fidelity to Dorabella in "Un'aura"—which the music asks us to take not as a naïve pose, but as something genuinely felt, genuinely human—becomes the space of Fiordiligi's infidelity, her equally human weakness. This infidelity is further committed *with* Ferrando; it is an infidelity that he vigorously encourages, in part to reassure himself of his virility—to salve the wound created by Guglielmo's all-too-easy wooing of Dorabella. A final, overarching irony, which has been much noted, is that it is *Fiordiligi*, not Dorabella, who is worthy of Ferrando's swooning in "Un'aura" in the first place:

---

10. On the puppet-like aspects of the characters, see Žižek and Dolar 2002, 62 and 98n63 and Burnham 1994, *passim*.
11. Kerman 1956, 115; Ford 1991, 204.
12. "Si vede una faccia / Che alletta e minaccia" (One sees a face / Both enticing and threatening).
13. For a highly sensitive discussion of this point see Rosen 1997, 316.

Fiordiligi: ...you've won...   ...do with me what you will.
Ferrando: ...my beloved...   ...don't delay any longer.

Figure 5.8 A dramatic nodal point in the opera: Fiordiligi's capitulation in "Fra gli amplessi" (Act II).

her musical idiom, especially in Act II's "Per pietá," reveals a moral complexity and depth of feeling entirely absent from Dorabella's *mezzo carattere* antics.

If we expand our survey to numbers in the opera not in A major, many more resonances emerge, typically involving melodic $\hat{5}$–#$\hat{5}$/♭$\hat{6}$–$\hat{6}$ motions and harmonic deceptions of various kinds. Dramatically prominent bass progressions of #$\hat{5}$–$\hat{6}$ supporting the harmonic progression V/vi→vi are exceedingly common, often occurring in moments of mock solemnity. One notable instance occurs repeatedly in the beautiful serenade "Secondate, aurette amiche," which shares a textual echo (*aura/aurette*) with the present aria. The serenade finds the disguised Guglielmo and Ferrando gamely attempting to woo each others' lovers, per the wager with Don Alfonso. The deceptions here are several. The women are deceived about the men's identities; they will also soon be deceived by their own inability to stay true in the face of such a beguiling charm offensive (from exotic "Albanians," no less!). The men, for their part, will soon be deceived by the unanticipated success of their wooing. Another striking resonance with "Un'aura" occurs in Dorabella's "È amore un ladroncello," her flippant celebration of her own infidelity after betraying Ferrando. In her arch repetition of "la pace" (m. 16 and parallel passages) she revels in the deceptive V/vi→vi progression, turning it into an illicit delight.

And then there is of course the *X*-to-*B* progression shown in Figure 5.4(c), the implicit presence lurking beneath Ferrando's first ecstatic "dolce ristoro." Those familiar with the opera will already have recognized this as nothing less than the harmonic progression that caps the opera's cynical motto, first stated at the outset of the overture, as shown in Figure 5.9, and later repeated by Don Alfonso and his disenchanted students. It is, moreover, the quintessential deceptive cadence in the work, a harmonic seal that hangs over the entire drama as a warning—both to Don Alfonso's students in the "Scuola degli amanti" and to us—against taking matters of the heart at face value.

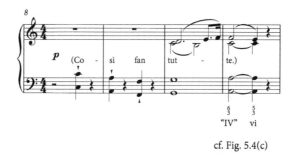

cf. Fig. 5.4(c)

Figure 5.9 The "Così fan tutte" motto, as initially stated in the Overture.

Do these resonances unmask Ferrando's emotion in "Un'aura" as somehow false, associating it with moments of superficiality, duplicity, and cynicism elsewhere in the work? Do they reveal an ultimate emptiness at the opera's core, a nihilism that led Žižek and Dolar, in a characteristically outrageous interpretive move, to call *Così* a work of "lethal despair"?[14] As titillating as such readings may be, they go too far in doubting the emotional core of Mozart's music, a core that is amply in evidence in the "dolce ristoro" passages we have studied in this chapter. As Joseph Kerman argues, Mozart takes emotion very seriously in the opera, even if Da Ponte does not: "Mozart's point is that emotions touch anyhow, even if they soon alter" (1956, 115). Ferrando's passions in "Un'aura" are real; his swooning is not feigned. But the attachment of those passions to their object is far more contingent than he realizes. The ecstatic *Kopftöne* of "Un'aura" make sonically palpable the intoxicating effect of deeply felt sentiment even (and perhaps especially) when it is deceived.

14. Žižek and Dolar 2002, viii.

CHAPTER Six

Brahms, Intermezzo in A major, op. 118, no. 2

Our focus will be the Intermezzo's A section, a score of which is provided in Plate 6. As boxed annotations above the score indicate, the section is in a lyric binary form (aaba')[1] with a brief codetta. There is a question about the onset of a'. Schenker places it at the modified thematic restatement that begins at m. 28[3], as does Allen Cadwallader.[2] I have marked this "a'?" in the score. A strong case can also be made for placing the onset of a' at m. 34[3]. I have labeled this "a'''" in the score; the lack of question mark indicates that I find it a more plausible reading. But the formal articulation is characteristically ambiguous: Brahms provides signals that support both hearings, as we will see.

Figure 6.1 reproduces the Intermezzo's opening measures, labeling its principal motives α and β. There is a subtle dialectical energy in these motives, resulting from the interaction between their *auftaktig* metrics and their melodic profiles: both leap up melodically across the bar line, gently contradicting the metric up-DOWN of beat 3-to-1 with a melodic down-UP. Both leap away from B4, which proves unable to descend to A4. Schenker hears the B4 in motive α as a passing tone in an implied *Terzzug*, a hearing that is reinforced by the realized *Terzzug* A–G♯–F♯ in the alto. As he notes, rather than proceeding to its expected goal, A4, the gesture "leaps off" of the *Zug* (*springt ab*) to the D5 on the downbeat of bar 1.[3]

---

1. On the term "lyric binary," see Hepokoski and Darcy 2006, 111.
2. Superscripts next to measure numbers indicate beats within the measure. For Cadwallader's analysis of op. 118, no. 2, see Cadwallader 1988, 64–74. Schenker's comments on the piece are contained in the "Brahms folder" (i.e., file 34) in the Oster Collection in the New York Public Library. (For a general discussion of the "Brahms folder," see Cadwallader and Pastille 1999; Kosovsky 1990 is the finding list for the collection.) Items 25–29 and 31 in the folder contain commentary and sketches related to op. 118, no. 2. Items 26–28 are a full prose commentary on the piece in Jeanette Schenker's hand, dated October 21, 1914; the other items include analytical sketch fragments related to the Intermezzo (those on item 29 are dated March 26, 1925). These will be referred to here following the "file/item" format in Cadwallader and Pastille 1999: "item 34/29," for example, refers to item 29 in file 34. Schenker's observations on the work's form are contained in the early 1914 commentary (item 34/26).
3. Oster item 34/26. This understanding is also reflected in the 1925 sketch fragment at the top of item 34/31, in which Schenker renotates the opening measures with an arrow leading from the upbeat B4 to a parenthesized A4 on the downbeat of m. 1.

Figure 6.1 Motives α and β (mm. 0³–2²).

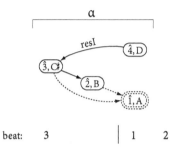

Figure 6.2 The intentional kinetics of motive α. (All unlabeled arrows in this and subsequent sd/pc networks in this chapter indicate the *shortest path* in sd/pc space.)

D-instead-of-A is a motivic substitution in the intermezzo: the music yearns for A but consistently gets D instead.

The event network of Figure 6.2 models aspects of Schenker's hearing of α. The arrows of the *Terzzug* flow forward in time, with the gesture's *auftaktig* impulse, funneling intentional energy toward an intended (1̂, A) on the downbeat. When that downbeat arrives, however, (4̂, D) sounds in (1̂, A)'s place. The usurping (4̂, D) funnels intentional energy *back* to the upbeat via resI, creating a sort of kinetic eddy around the bar line. One can sense that eddy by mentally hearing the motive in a repeating loop while following the solid nodes and arrows in the network. The eddy results from the fact that (4̂, D) and (1̂, A) occupy the same formal event slot in the network, while nevertheless residing at opposite ends of a chain of intentional arrows. This substitutional event slot is moreover the gesture's metric center of gravity—the downbeat. The α motive's intentional kinetics pull strongly to the downbeat, but the D-for-A substitution draws the ear back to the weak anacrusis (which then pulls back to the downbeat, and so on). Hence the eddy.

Before continuing, a formal note. As sd/pc *paths* will matter in this analysis,[4] the present chapter will adopt a notational convention for all sd/pc networks: unlabeled arrows [NB] will indicate the *shortest* path between two elements in sd/pc space. Thus, the spanning *Zug* arrow in Figure 6.2 traverses

4. On the formal and conceptual significance of sd/pc paths, see section 2.3

(a)

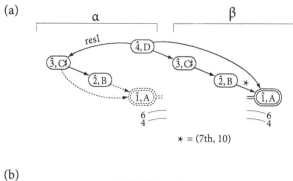

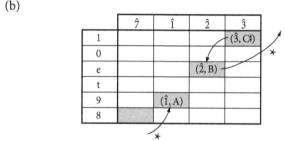

Figure 6.3 (a) The intentional kinetics of α+β; (b) the path traced by (7th, 10) loops around the sd/pc space in the opposite direction from the descending seconds, creating a cleft between (2̂, B) and (1̂, A).

the interval (3rd⁻¹, –4), a descending major third, which is the shortest path from (3̂, C♯) to (1̂, A). Likewise, the straight arrows in the *Zug* traverse the interval (2nd⁻¹, –2), a descending whole step, the shortest path between their respective sd/pc pairs.

The value of such path-based distinctions becomes clear in Figure 6.3(a), which models the intentional kinetics of motives α and β together. The latter motive provides the awaited (1̂, A) on the downbeat of m. 2, but multiple factors conspire to make it an unsatisfactory resolution to the subtle tensions created by α. Most notably, the upward leap over the bar line into m. 2 frustrates the desire for (2̂, B) to descend to (1̂, A) via (2nd⁻¹, –2). Instead, as the annotation on the figure indicates, the path traversed is (7th, 10), an ascending minor seventh. Figure 6.3(b) animates this path in the sd/pc GIS space, showing the change in direction after (2̂, B). The loop around the space in the opposite direction creates a visual cleft between (2̂, B) and (1̂, A), serving notice that the interval between these two elements will be a charged zone in the Intermezzo.

Note also that motive β participates in a *Quartzug* from D, not a *Terzzug* from C♯. As the accompanying arpeggios make clear, the six-four harmony that sets in on the downbeat of bar 1 remains in effect into bar 2; the C♯ that begins β is thus a passing tone (note the {D, A} dyad in the left hand on beat 3 of measure 1). Thus, while motive α lacks the endpoint of its *Zug*, motive β lacks its beginning, starting *in medias res,* as part of a *Zug* already under way. The head tone of β's *Quartzug* is ($\hat{4}$, D), which the spanning arrow binds intentionally to the concluding ($\hat{1}$, A). Both motives remain under the shadow of D, melodically and harmonically. These various factors combine to invest the ($\hat{1}$, A) on the downbeat of m. 2 with its own dialectical charge: it is a heard tonic pitch that forms an acoustic consonance with the bass, but it is registrally dissonant (with respect to the *Züge* of α and β) and embedded within a subdominant sound world.[5]

(a)

(b)

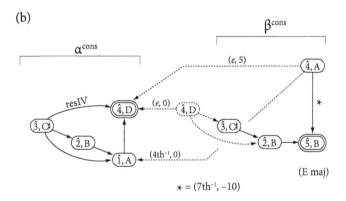

(c)

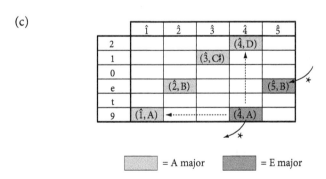

Figure 6.4 The intentional kinetics of α^cons+β^cons. Note the multiple connections of the climactic ($\hat{4}$, A): as pivot tone, real transposition, and harmonic seventh.

5. The B-to-A leap in motive β is an affective locus in the piece in ways that extend beyond the present discussion. Charles Rosen (2004, 9) notes that Brahms's arpeggiation on the downbeat of m. 2 gives the

Figure 6.4(a) shows the return of the two motives at the beginning of the consequent phrase (mm. 4³–8²), labeling them α^cons and β^cons. Figure 6.4(b) is an event
network of both motives, oriented around the local harmonic roots (4̂, D) and
(5̂, B). In place of the kinetic eddy of Figure 6.2, motive α^cons leads decisively to
its downbeat, but it does so to the greater glory of D. The applied dominant on
the upbeat to m. 5 directs (3̂, C♯) toward (4̂, D) as an applied leading tone. The
resulting res transformation, resIV, flows *with* the *Terzzug*. The alignment of all
intentional energy with the 3-to-1 upbeat creates a subtle shift in the harmonic
and metric center of gravity, tilting the motive now more conclusively toward the
downbeat and its D-based harmony. The transformation of motive β into β^cons is
more dramatic still. The registral dissonance created by the leap to A5 is now com-
plemented by an acoustic dissonance: the apex pitch participates in a B six-five
chord, creating a tritone over the bass D♯2 and investing the local pcs with qualia
in E major. The charged interval between A and B becomes a purposeful harmonic
seventh, rather than a displaced melodic second. Further, the apex of β^cons is now
invested with the quale of 4̂, just like the apexes of α and α^cons. Two dotted arrows
depart leftward from (4̂, A) in the upper right-hand corner of the network, modeling retrospective intentions to the (4̂, D) and (1̂, A) that concluded α^cons: the apex
note is a real transposition of the former, via (e, 5), and a pivot transformation of
the latter, via (4th⁻¹, 0). These two relationships are shown by the dotted arrows

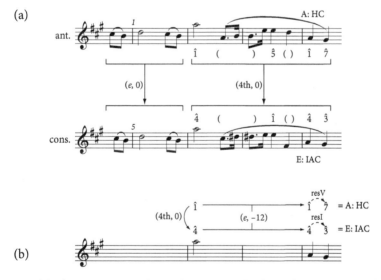

Figure 6.5 (a) The consequent phrase diverges tonally from the antecedent phrase
with the onset of the climactic (4̂, A) on the downbeat of m. 6; (b) the cadential
appoggiaturas in mm. 4 and 8 are resolutions-by-proxy for the high A5s.

leap a vocal intensity, delaying the arrival of the high A in the manner of a singer ascending to that
pitch. For more on such matters, and for a very different analytical and interpretive account of the present Intermezzo, see my essay "The Learned Self: Artifice in Brahms's Late Intermezzi" (Rings 2011b).

on Figure 6.4(c), which also indicates the "purposeful seventh" between $(\hat{4}, A)$ and $(\hat{5}, B)$ with a starred arrow. The expressive concentration of the $(\hat{4}, A)$ apex is reflected by its manifold connections in the space, which link it to the other sensitive pitches in the two motives: as harmonic seventh, real transposition, and pivot transformation.

The $(\hat{4}, A)$ apex in m. 6 marks the moment at which the consequent phrase diverges tonally from the antecedent, adjusting course to arrive at an authentic cadence in E rather than a half cadence in A. Figure 6.5(a) illustrates, aligning the melodic lines of the two phrases. As the brackets indicate, the tonal shift occurs in the middle of motive β^{cons}, right at the expressive leap to A5 in m. 6. The slurred phrases that conclude the antecedent and consequent correspond at crucial nodal points: the E5 peak at mm. 3^2 and 7^2 and the concluding A4–G♯4 appoggiatura in mm. 4 and 8. The pivot transformation of these nodal pitches is aurally striking, transforming a half-cadential phrase in the antecedent into an authentic-cadential one in the consequent, with minimal change in sounding pitch content. As shown in 6.5(b), the cadential appoggiaturas in mm. 4 and 8 restate the earlier apex pitches from mm. 2 and 6, transposed down an octave. The entire gesture mapped in 6.4(c) serves as a sort of resolution-by-proxy for the registral dissonances of the earlier leaps, easing the dialectically charged A down by octave, and then down by conventional dissonance resolution to a cadential G♯, first in the qualitative atmosphere of A major, then in that of E major.

Let us now flesh out the harmonic picture. Figure 6.6(a) presents the melody and bass line of the antecedent phrase, along with figured bass annotations. Two rows of note names below the figures indicate sounding thoroughbass pitches (TB) and theoretically understood fundamental bass pitches (FB). We will discuss the TB/FB annotations momentarily; for now, we will simply focus on the bass line and figures. Note first that the bass leaps across every bar line. The descending octave leaps from A2 to A1 mirror the ascending leaps in the melodic motives, projecting the up-DOWN *Auftaktigkeit* that is gently contradicted by the upper-voice leaps. The bass leaps reinforce the importance of bar-line-spanning gestures in the work: bass and melody consistently move across the bar line in carefully coordinated fashion, landing on expressive downbeat sonorities. Note that none of those downbeat sonorities in Figure 6.5(a) is a five-three chord. Instead, six-four chords sound on the downbeats of mm. 1, 2, and 4, while a four-two sounds on the downbeat of m. 3. The absence of metrically strong five-threes is characteristic of the Intermezzo—there are only four such chords on downbeats in the A section's 48 bars; each of these occurs at a crucial nodal point of harmonic, thematic, and formal arrival. The only downbeat five-three over an A bass in the piece is the one that concludes the A section in m. 48 (and the entire piece in m. 116).[6] This withholding of a

---

6. Cf. David Epstein (1979, 175): "the tonic—although evident and never unclear as far as the tonal orientation of the piece is concerned—is never heard as a point of rest until the closing measure of [the] outer sections. Its common role is that of anacrusis, passing chord, or as a bass that implies tonic harmony although chords heard above it are of other roots." The A section in this regard contrasts with the B section, which is grounded from the beginning by a downbeat tonic five-three chord in F♯ minor.

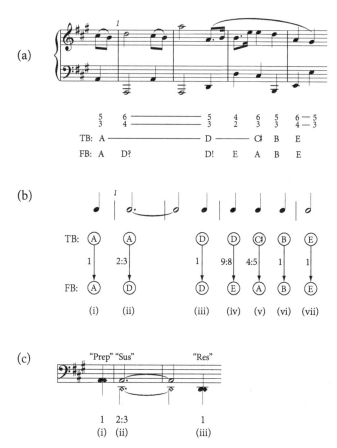

Figure 6.6 (a) Melody and bass line in the antecedent phrase (mm. 0³–4²), with figured-bass annotations: TB = sounding thoroughbass, FB = fundamental bass; (b) TB/FB networks; (c) a TB/FB "suspension."

downbeat root-position A chord is bound up with the melodic withholding of A discussed above, and the motivic D-instead-of-A idea. More generally, the prevalence of non-five-three sonorities in the piece creates a persistent tension between bass and root, which plays out in the music's many *auftaktig* gestures.

The TB and FB rows explore that tension, which emerges immediately with the six-four chord in m. 1. It is not immediately clear whether the fundamental bass shifts here to D or whether it remains on A, with the six-four chord acting as an embellishment to the five-three of the anacrusis. Roman numeral theorists would reflect this uncertainty by worrying over whether the chord in m. 1 is a genuine IV chord or a prolonged I. There is thus a haze of uncertainty in the relationship between TB and FB in mm. 1–2². That haze clears on beat 3 of m. 2, when the bass moves to D, decisively realigning TB and FB: a D five-three sonority emerges from the six-four uncertainty. TB and FB then again separate in the first two beats of m. 3, before joining again for the half cadence in mm. 3³–4.

We can model the relationship between TB and FB by creating simple networks in the spirit of Rameau. Such networks include a TB node aligned above an FB node, with an arrow bearing a just ratio linking the former to the latter. The just ratios suggest relationships between pitches in register, allowing us to model the distinction between conceptually descending TB-to-FB intervals, in which FB resides theoretically below TB, and the more unusual conceptually ascending TB-to-FB intervals, in which FB resides theoretically *above* the sounding bass (the *locus classicus* is supposition).[7] We will nevertheless use pitch-class letter names in the nodes, rather than pitch names with octave designations. This reflects the tension in Rameau's theory between fundamental bass as an entity with a specific pitch level, on the one hand, and as a register-independent pitch class on the other.[8]

Figure 6.6(b) shows such networks in action. The networks are labeled (i)–(vii) and are aligned to correspond with the relevant TB/FB pairs in 6.6(a). Arrow labels of 1 indicate complete agreement between TB and FB—a TB/FB unison, as it were. Ratios less than 1 indicate a conceptually descending hearing from TB to FB; ratios greater than 1 indicate a conceptually ascending hearing from TB to FB. The only such ascending ratio in 6.5(b) is the 9:8 of network (iv), which reflects the position of the sounding D a conceptual whole step below the fundamental E.

Network (ii) interprets the fundamental bass on the downbeat of m. 1 as D, under the influence of the later "clarification" of the harmonic situation on beat 3 of m. 2. This yields a staggered relationship between TB and FB in networks (i)–(iii): the thoroughbass progresses A–A–D, while the fundamental bass progresses A–D–D. Like the staggering between quale and chroma observed in the Liszt analysis of Figure 2.31(d), the staggered TB/FB relationship in the Brahms evokes the rhythm of a suspension. Figure 6.6(c) illustrates. Network (i), on the work's initiating upbeat, is the preparation of the TB/FB suspension. Network (ii), on the work's first downbeat, is the suspension proper, as the fundamental bass shifts to D but the thoroughbass remains on A. In network (iii), TB finally shifts to join FB on D, resolving the 2:3 suspension to 1 and dissipating the harmonic haze of mm. 1–2². The zone of the suspension proper is the zone in which α and β are "under the shadow of D," as discussed above.

Figure 6.7 links networks (i)–(vii) from 6.6(b) into a single oriented network, showing the kinetics of the progression to the half cadence in the antecedent phrase. Various arrows link the fundamental bass nodes to show progressions and

---

7. On supposition (sometimes translated "subposition"), see Christensen 1993, 124ff.

8. For a discussion of this tension in Rameau, see Keiler 1981. Formally, the present GIS takes as its group IVLS all rational numbers of the form $2^a 3^b 5^c$, in which a, b, and c are integers, and as the elements of its space S the set of justly tuned pitches. We can convert this into a pc-based GIS by asserting a congruence on IVLS, so that its elements are all of the form $3^a 5^b$ and the space consists of the set of just pitch classes. (On GIS congruences, see *GMIT*, 32–37; Lewin explores the just-pitch and just-pc GISes employed here on pp. 17–22.) The analytical networks in the figures of this chapter are poised in a sense between these two GISes, employing intervals of the form $2^a 3^b 5^c$ but using pitch-class names as node contents. As already noted, the formal tension models the conceptual tension in Rameau.

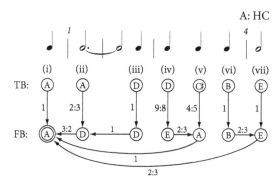

Figure 6.7 An oriented network of TB/FB kinetics in the antecedent (cf. Figure 6.6(b)).

large-scale intentional connections. The energy in the network flows generally leftward, indicating the retrospective nature of the half-cadential phrase; two important rightward jags by 2:3 (a descending fifth) provide the impetus toward that cadence. The second of these jags, from (vi) to (vii), connects two vertical 1-networks, which provide a strong close to the phrase. The straight leftward arrows from the D nodes in networks (ii) and (iii) indicate the retrospective character of the D bass in this passage, strongly oriented back toward the opening A, just as the melodic D in motive α is oriented leftward, toward the upbeat C♯ via resI (cf. Figure 6.2).

Figure 6.8 presents a similar analysis of the consequent phrase, forgoing the intermediate stage of presenting the individual TB/FB networks. Figure 6.8(b) clearly shows the strong infusion of rightward harmonic energy at m. 6, with the onset of the apex A5 in β^{cons}, and the concomitant shift in tonal orientation modeled in Figure 6.5. Notice the prominence of rightward 2:3 arrows in the network, indicating strong fundamental bass motions by descending fifth. Note also that only the rightmost vertical arrows are TB/FB unisons of 1; the rest of the phrase shows a constant flux in TB/FB values, as a result of the pervasive inverted harmonies.

This mode of harmonic analysis offers a suggestive window onto the b section as well, illuminating the relationship between metric dissonance and harmonic stability. Figure 6.9 shows the music for the first phrase of the b section, mm. 16³–20. Commentary above the staff describes the metric situation. The passage begins with a metric displacement dissonance of D3–1 in Harald Krebs's (1999) terminology. Such a dissonance displaces a three-beat pulse stream one beat leftward. In the Brahms, this represents a concession to the work's pervasive *Auftaktigkeit*, momentarily transforming its "3 | 2 1" groupings into implicit "1 2 3" groupings. This metric displacement coincides with a slide away from the harmonic security of the authentic cadence at the end of the consequent in m. 16. The thoroughbass remains on E, but the fundamental bass slips to the flat submediant C♮ on beat 3 of m. 16, yielding the vertical TB/FB interval 4:5. After chromatic passing motion in mm. 17³–18², TB and FB once again align on E with the upbeat

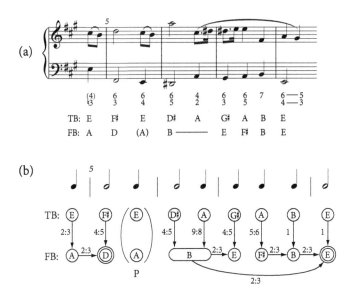

Figure 6.8 (a) Melody and bass line in the consequent phrase (mm. 4³–8²), with figured-bass and TB/FB annotations; (b) an oriented network of TB/FB kinetics in the consequent.

to m. 19. At this moment it also seems that the metric situation is about to resolve—harmony and meter seem ready to stabilize in tandem on the downbeat of m. 20. The thoroughbass shifts to A as expected, but the triple suspension in the arpeggios precariously delays harmonic resolution until beat 3, when it is too late—the metric dissonance reappears, and the fundamental bass once again slips away to a local flat submediant via 4:5. The network reads the fundamental bass on the downbeat of m. 20 as remaining on E, reflecting the strong sense that the harmony has not yet let go of its previous root, despite the shift in sounding bass. This is a very Rameauian hearing: the sounding bass A is supposed beneath the fundamental bass E; Rameau would interpret the D suspension as a seventh. Such a hearing is suggestive here: it animates the deferral of the A fundamental bass at the downbeat of m. 20. The hearing also interacts nicely with Brahms's slurring, treating all of the music under the long slur as under the control of E harmony, despite the shift in the sounding bass at its end. That shift nevertheless makes us pointedly aware of the deferred A fundamental bass, which hovers around the downbeat to m. 20 as an implicit presence. The network reflects this by including a dotted A node immediately beneath the solid nodes at the downbeat of m. 20—a sort of phantom fundamental bass. This is the fundamental bass that would have been, had meter and harmony resolved as expected.[9] Note that

9. One can easily experience that expected resolution by minimally recomposing m. 20: change the G♯ in the left hand on beat 2 to an A, and alter the right hand so that it projects a B4–A4 appoggiatura in quarter notes over tonic harmony.

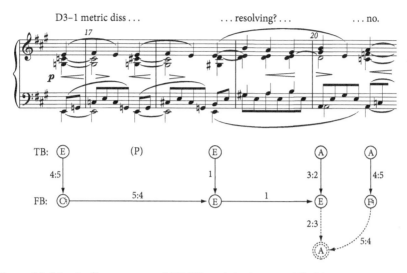

Figure 6.9 Metric dissonance and TB/FB activity in mm. 16³–20.

the transformational labels on the arrows leading from the TB nodes in m. 20 to the "phantom FB" sum to 1 (3:2 × 2:3 = 1; 4:5 × 5:4 = 1). The solid FB nodes thus occlude a potential TB/FB unison in this bar, as harmony and meter once again drift out of focus.

Figure 6.10 shows the next phrase in the b section. 6.10(a) analyzes mm. 20³–25¹. As the annotations above the staff indicate, the D3–1 metric dissonance reappears at 20³ and persists through m. 22.[10] At m. 23, however, the music seems to go into a sort of metric freefall, creating a wonderfully vertiginous sense of independence from any downbeat (dissonant or otherwise). The meter comes into focus again only with the downbeat of m. 25, which coincides with an emphatic TB/FB unison on E, resolving the unsettled TB/FB activity since the evaded cadence at m. 20. Indeed, it is not even entirely clear what the TB or FB might be in m. 24: the right hand seems to anticipate E major, while the left hand arpeggiates A minor, neither of which agrees with the diminished-seventh chord of the previous bar. (This sense of lost harmonic grounding is made acoustically vivid by the absence of a sounding bass note in mm. 23 and 24.) The metric freefall thus coincides with a harmonic freefall. We do not regain our metric and harmonic bearings until the dominant arrives in m. 25. It is the first downbeat five-three chord in the piece.

As shown in Figure 6.10(b), the music celebrates its newfound metric and harmonic stability in mm. 25–28 by emphatically stating E2 on every downbeat, generating expectation for an arrival on A—and perhaps a return of the main theme. In the event, the latter arrives, but not the former. The theme

---

10. The fundamental bass here traverses a highly dissonant 25:36 *fausse quinte* from F♯ to B. On the *fausse quinte*, see Rameau 1722, 24.

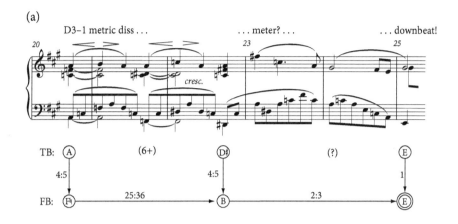

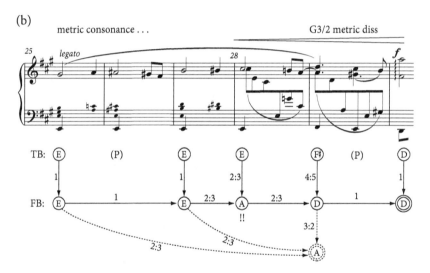

Figure 6.10 Metric dissonance and TB/FB activity in (a) mm. 20³–25¹, and (b) mm. 25–30¹.

returns with the pickup to m. 29, but at this point the harmony is deflected to D, in a grand apotheosis of the D-instead-of-A idea that has been at work since the opening of the piece. The deflection to D coincides with a return of metric dissonance: in this case, what Krebs would call a grouping disso-nance of G3/2—a three-against-two hemiola. The precipitating event for this is the shift of the fundamental bass to A in m. 28. While the fundamental bass foiled the metric and harmonic resolution in m. 20 (Figure 6.9) by moving too late, now it moves too early: the hypermeter creates an expectation for arrival on A in m. 29. But the arpeggios in m. 28 disastrously jump the gun, pro-jecting not only an A fundamental bass, but a dominant seventh on A, which points emphatically toward D at the hypermetric node. Once again, tonic A is

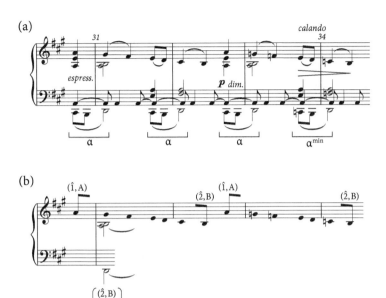

Figure 6.11 The cooldown of mm. 30³–34².

deferred, present only as an unrealized intention at the expected point of resolution. In its place is a celebratory D fundamental bass in mm. 29 and 30. The
climax of the D music in m. 30 (*forte*, the loudest dynamic thus far) coincides
with the second downbeat five-three chord in the piece.

Figure 6.11(a) shows the cooldown that follows this D-apotheosis. Motive
α rumbles in the bass, undergoing an inflection to minor in m. 33–34, which
we will call α^min. Above this, the right hand traces two *Septzüge* from A4 to
B3, isolated in the upper staff of 6.11(b). These *Septzüge* bring to mind the
sensitive sevenths between B4 and A5 in motive β. Recall that those seventh
leaps frustrated (2̂, B)'s attempt to progress to (1̂, A) via descending step. Now
the two elements are explicitly linked by descending stepwise motion, but they
reside at the *ends* of two lengthy seventh progressions, tracing an explicit sd/
pc path of (7th⁻¹, –10) from (2̂, B) down to (1̂, A). Note that the only diatonic
step *not* present in these progressions is the descending step from (2̂, B) to (1̂,
A). As the half notes in 6.11(b) show, the sensitive (2̂, B) and (1̂, A) are fused
together harmonically in this passage, joining the triumphant (4̂, D) in the
bass. These three sd/pc elements form a harmonic core that persists throughout
mm. 31–34². A fourth harmonic element—(6̂, F♯), then (♭6̂, F♮)—creates a ii6/5
chord, first in A major, then in A minor. We will explore these four-note chords
more in a moment. For now, we can note that the perturbing elements from
the work's opening are fused together harmonically here, in the wake of the
D-apotheosis: the melodically problematic (2̂, B) and (1̂, A), and the usurping
subdominant (4̂, D).

On beat 3 of m. 34, the dark trombone voicings of Figure 6.11(a) give way to a shimmering inverted statement of the work's principal motives.[11] We will call these inverted forms α⁻¹ and β⁻¹. Figures 6.12(a) and (b) reproduce the recto and inverted forms of the motive; the broken dashed slurs make clear that both forms have the same pitch boundaries: A5 and B4. These are, of course, the sensitive pitches from the seventh-leap in motive β; they now serve as the frame for the diatonic pitch inversion that takes α-and-β to α⁻¹-and-β⁻¹. In the context of the sd/pc GIS, motives α and β invert into α⁻¹ and β⁻¹ via diatonic inversion around 1̂ and 2̂, or I_1^2. As Figure 6.12(c) indicates, there is also a chromatic inversion afoot here. The minor statement of motive α in the bass, αᵐⁱⁿ, inverts chromatically into α⁻¹, both in pitch space and in sd/pc space. The center of chromatic pitch-space

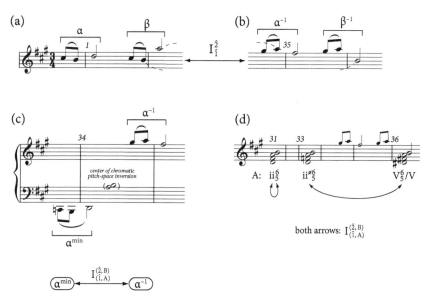

Figure 6.12 (a) and (b): Diatonic inversion of α and β into α⁻¹ and β⁻¹; (c) chromatic inversion of αᵐⁱⁿ into α⁻¹; (d) chromatic inversion of harmonies in the vicinity of the formal seam at m. 34³.

11. Given the explicit rhetorical set up for this formal return—as opposed to the rush of dynamic energy that flows past the thematic statement at m. 28³—I tend to hear m. 34³ as the onset of a′, contrary to Schenker and Cadwallader. Nevertheless, as the discussion above makes clear, Brahms creates a considerable expectation for a double return at 28³. Further, there is a sense in which the inverted thematic statements at m. 34³ take on characteristics of the *consequent* phrase; note especially in this context the bass D♯ in m. 36. This would make the thematic statement at m. 28³ the proper antecedent, strengthening Schenker's and Cadwallader's cases. This instance of Brahmsian ambiguity of course need not be adjudicated one way or the other. Indeed, the most persuasive hearing might be to consider mm. 28³–34² as a zone of formal indeterminacy, in which the b and a′ sections in a sense overlap—or better, in which processes appropriate to both b and a′ occur simultaneously. It is only at m. 34³ that this indeterminacy disappears and a′ emerges unclouded. This hearing suggests a formal analogue to the harmonic process in the opening bars, in which the harmonic uncertainty of the six-four chord in mm. 1–2² is resolved only with the arrival of the D five-three at m. 2³.

inversion is the dyad A3/B3, shown in open noteheads in the figure. This is the very dyad the pianist has been playing with the right-hand thumb since m. 31, during the A4-to-B3 *Septzüge* (cf. Figure 6.11). As the little network at the bottom of 6.12(c) indicates, the chromatic inversion that takes α^{min} to α^{-1} is $I_{(\hat{1},A)}^{(\hat{2},B)}$, which maps the sensitive heard scale degrees onto one another. This chromatic sd/pc inversion also interacts compellingly with the harmony here. As 6.12(d) indicates, $I_{(\hat{1},A)}^{(\hat{2},B)}$ maps the ii6/5 in A major in mm. 31–32 onto itself. This interacts nicely with the sense of harmonic stasis in these bars, as the music stalls out in the cooldown of mm. 31–32. The same inversion then points the way out of that stasis, mapping the inversionally asymmetrical, half-diminished ii6/5 in A minor in mm. 33–34² onto the V6/5-of-V in A major in m. 36. The inversion thus takes the unstable, modally darkened pre-dominant across the formal seam of m. 34³ to the luminous applied dominant after that seam—the chord that finally leads us out of this harmonic cul-de-sac, to the dominant and the cadence. In short, a welter of inversional activity occurs as we cross the threshold from the b section to the a′ section, much of it bound up with $I_{(\hat{1},A)}^{(\hat{2},B)}$, the inversion that maps the work's two sensitive heard degrees onto each other. These degrees act as a sort of inversional fulcrum, around which we swing as we travel from the chthonic rumble that concludes section b to the ethereal inversion that begins section a′.

Figure 6.13 provides a broader Schenkerian context for these details. Of special note here is the area of the sketch around the onset of section a′, in the vicinity of the bar line for m. 34. The Schenkerian account hears this area of the piece governed harmonically by D in the bass, treating the putative I chord at m. 34³ as a neighbor to the IV *Stufe* that follows. The sketch thus detects a figure-ground reversal of harmonic priorities between A and D in the area of the thematic inversion, a reading that interacts persuasively with our earlier observations: D has become the momentary center of harmonic gravity, pulling all other events into its orbit, and demoting the tonic six-three chord at the outset of α^{-1} to neighboring status.[12] As a melodic statement, α^{-1} is subsumed within the D-based prolongation: as shown in 6.13(a), it sounds in the midst of a *Terzzug* from A5 to F♯5. The reader can develop this hearing of α^{-1} by playing through Figure 6.14(a), paying careful attention to rhythm and dynamics. Figure 6.14(b) shows the resulting intentional structure of motive α^{-1}. These intentional dynamics bear an interesting inversional relationship to those in Figure 6.2, the network for motive α: while α traverses the first two elements of its descending *Terzzug*, α^{-1} traverses the last two elements of its *Terzzug*. Both motives further omit the $(\hat{1}, A)$ of their respective *Züge*.

Motive α^{-1} leads to the third downbeat five-three in the piece: the D-major chord at m. 35. This is the first time a five-three chord has appeared in an α motive-form since the work's opening antecedent statements (see mm. 0³ and 8³). Figure 6.15(a) collects TB/FB analyses of motives α, α^{cons}, and α^{-1} for comparison; 6.15(b) models these progressions with TB/FB networks. Every motive traverses

---

12. For two Schenkerian readings that differ from the present one in this regard, see Cadwallader 1988 and Wen 1999.

Figure 6.13 A Schenkerian hearing of the Intermezzo's A section, mm. 1–38.

a fundamental bass motion of A to D, but harmonic weight gradually shifts away from A toward D over the course of the motive statements. One can sense this by scanning visually from the upbeat five-three chord on A in motive α, at the left edge of the 6.15(a) and (b), to the downbeat five-three on D at the right edge. The motive's harmonic center thus gradually comes to be aligned with its metric center, as D assumes increasingly greater tonal authority. Note also the steady progression of vertical TB/FB intervals over the course of the three motives: 1 to 2:3 in motive α; 2:3 to 4:5 in α^{cons}; and 4:5 to 1 in α^{-1}. Motive α^{-1} thus inverts α in more

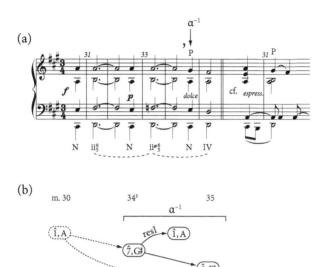

Figure 6.14 (a) A harmonic reduction of mm. 30³–35, useful for developing a hearing of motive α⁻¹ as embedded in a *Terzzug* from A5 to F♯5; (b) the intentional shape of α⁻¹ under this hearing.

than melodic direction—it is also an inversion of the previous motive's harmonic priorities and TB/FB intentional dynamics.

Paradoxically, this concession to D's force finally allows the music to cadence in A in m. 38, as though the usurping D is entirely spent. There remains unfinished motivic business, however: α and β have yet to descend persuasively from (2̂, B) to (1̂, A). The final cadence of the A section in mm. 46³–48 achieves this descent, linking the two motives together to project a complete descending third progression, as shown in Figure 6.16(a) and (b). Note, however, that Brahms

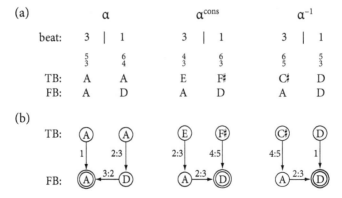

Figure 6.15 The shifting TB/FB kinetics in motives α, α^cons, and α⁻¹.

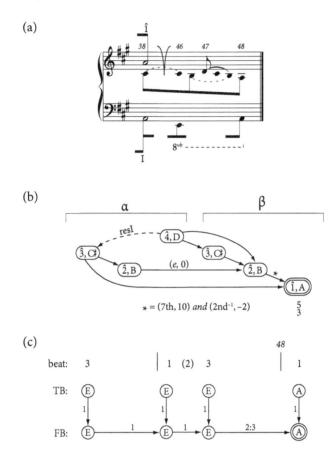

Figure 6.16 Linear and harmonic aspects of the A section's codetta. As shown in (b), $(\hat{2}, B)$ progresses to $(\hat{1}, A)$ at the final cadence by sd/pc paths $(2nd^{-1}, -2)$ *and* $(7th, 10)$, which both nevertheless manifest the same group element.

also maintains the ascending seventh in motive β's final statement, as a result of the arpeggiated final sonority in m. 48. The gesture both closes the motive and leaves it open. Formally, Brahms's conclusion elegantly demonstrates the algebraic identity of $(2nd^{-1}, -2)$ and $(7th, 10)$ within our GIS, as $(\hat{2}, B)$ proceeds to $(\hat{1}, A)$ via *both* paths. Figure 6.15(c) aligns this melodic analysis with a final harmonic reading, showing the emphatic root-position progression from E to A that yields the final downbeat five-three chord in the section—and the first such sonority on A—at m. 48.

Plate 6: Brahms, Intermezzo in A major, op. 118, no. 2 (A section)

CHAPTER $\mathbb{S}$even

Brahms, String Quintet in G major, op. 111, mvt. ii, Adagio

This slow movement is a set of free, rhapsodic variations. As Elaine Sisman notes, Brahms likely would have considered them "fantasy-variations."[1] Plate 7 provides a score of the movement, with annotations cued to the formal overview in Figure 7.1, which hears the variations as rotations of three modules: A, B, and C.[2] Module A is the work's two-bar motto. The motto's fiddle lament, dotted figures, pizzicato bass, and indirect but prominent augmented second {F4, G#4} immediately signal the *style hongrois*. Module B varies considerably across the piece; it presents hymn-like homophony over dotted figures, generating a certain tension between Western high styles (sacred/learned) and the work's exoticized Gypsy signifiers. The latter retake center stage in module C, complete with sobbing sigh figures and improvisational fiddle solos. As the formal chart indicates, module C gradually disappears over the course of the work, being replaced by a short but vigorous development section in Variation 3 and a massive dominant pedal in Variation 4. Module C is entirely absent in the coda-like Variation 5. I will touch on the interpretive implications of this formal process in a note toward the end of the chapter.

I have labeled the opening section (mm. 1–14) "Variation 1" rather than "Theme." The initial presentation of the material is already highly ornamented and acts little more like an originary theme than do any of the subsequent sections. This interpretation interacts suggestively with Brahms's evocation at several points of a slow, improvised style of Gypsy playing known as *hallgató*, in which the soloist—typically a fiddler—provides highly ornamented renditions of a preexisting

---

1. Sisman 1990, 152–53. There has been considerable disagreement over the form of the movement. Tovey called it a "cavatina" (1949, 265); Daverio analyzes it as a strophic form that both evokes and negates variation and sonata principles (1993, 145); Michael Musgrave hears a three-part song form (1985, 208). I follow Sisman in adopting the "fantasy-variations" understanding, as it is the most flexible label under which these various formal principles may be subsumed. As detailed in Sisman's article, Brahms discussed the idea of "fantasy-variations" in letters to Schubring (February 1869) and Herzogenberg (August 1876).

2. On rotations and modules, see Hepokoski and Darcy 2006.

m.	Variation	Modules			Local keys
1	Variation 1	A			d/A
3		B			C→A
9			C		d/A
15	Variation 2	A			d/A
17		B			C→d
25			C		d/g
33	Variation 3	A			g/D
35		B			F→D
48				mini-dev	B♭/g→D
52	Variation 4	A			D
54		B			D→d
62				dom (C?)	d
69	Variation 5 (coda)	A			d/A
71		B			D

Figure 7.1 A formal overview of the Adagio from Brahms's String Quintet, op. 111.

tune. Viola 1 plays the role of fiddle soloist in the first variation; the quintet's true fiddle, violin 1, takes the lead in all remaining variations but for one crucial cadenza at the end of Variation 4 (mm. 66–68), in which viola 1 once again steps to the fore. Bálint Sárosi describes the *hallgató* style: "On their instruments they can perform a *hallgató* melody—which normally has a text—much more loosely, like an instrumental fantasy, and working against the dictates of the text; with runs, touching languid pauses, and sustained snapped off notes, they virtually pull the original structure apart."[3] The sense of immediate fantasy and ornamentation at the Adagio's outset fits well with Sárosi's description, suggesting a string of variations on a tune never stated unadorned. We should also note that *hallgató* means "to be listened to" in Hungarian. This is, on the one hand, to distinguish such music from music for dancing, but it also suggests a certain close attention on the part of the auditor: "an active, involved kind of listening…is implied" (Bellman 1991, 221). This is fitting, as the harmonic and melodic complexities of Brahms's Adagio invite just such an active, close listening, as we try to make sense of not only the underlying tune but also its harmonic orientation.

As many commentators have noted, the motto may be heard in D minor or A major.[4] The column headed "Local keys" in Figure 7.1 indicates this with the entry d/A in the row for Module A in Variation 1.[5] Figure 7.2 explores these

---

3. Sárosi 1978, 245; quoted in Bellman 1991, 221. Bellman 1991 is a concise source for information on the *style hongrois*. He does not discuss the op. 111 Adagio or its *hallgató* aspects, but he does note the prevalence of the *hallgató* style in Brahms's music, citing a passage from the Clarinet Quintet, op. 115 (p. 222, Ex. 2). Notley (1999, 59) and Daverio (1993, 145–54) both discuss the Gypsy characteristics of op. 111/ii.
4. See, e.g., Keys 1974, 29; Daverio 1993, 150; and Smith 2006, 82–87.
5. In this column, slashes indicate ambiguity between two keys, while arrows indicate progression. For a critique of the idea of ambiguity in music analysis, see Agawu 1994. For a qualified defense of the concept in Brahms analysis, see Smith 2006, which includes a suggestive and relevant discussion of the present movement.

competing hearings of the motto. The harmonic analysis beneath 7.2(a) interprets the first bar as i–V in D minor, in conformance with the one-flat key signature and (if we look ahead in the score) with the final sonority of the movement
(D major in m. 80). Our eyes will likely tell us to prefer this hearing, as will our
knowledge of the piece as a whole. But aurally, especially in the context of mm.
1–2, the motto also projects a strong sense of iv–I in A major, as depicted in
7.2(b). In order to counteract the tendency to disbelieve this A-major hearing
when looking at the score, I have notated Examples 7.2(b) and (d) in a three-
sharp signature. The activity on the second eighth of beat 1 (about which more
below) is crucial to this hearing.

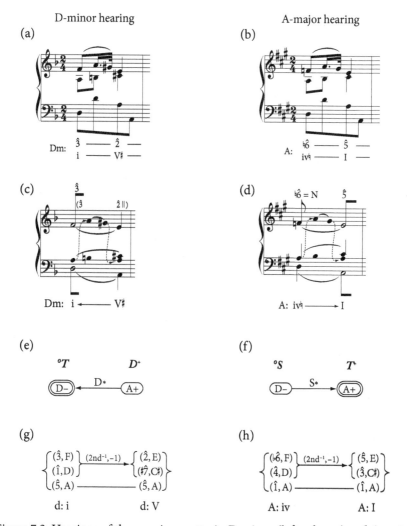

Figure 7.2 Hearings of the opening motto in D minor (left column) and A major
(right column).

The motto in 7.2(a) proceeds from minor tonic to major dominant. Viola 1's overall F4–E4 trajectory under this hearing moves from $\hat{3}$ to $\hat{2}$. This is an initiating gesture: a motion from stability to instability, with the A-major harmony oriented back toward the tonic. C♯ is a product of mixture in this hearing; it plays an important role as the (ascending, dominant) leading tone to D in the orientation of A+ toward D–. By contrast, in 7.2(b) the motto proceeds from minor subdominant to major tonic. Viola 1's overall F4–E4 trajectory under this hearing moves from ♭$\hat{6}$ to $\hat{5}$. This is a closing gesture: a motion from instability to stability, with the D-minor harmony oriented forward toward the tonic. F♮ is a product of mixture in this hearing; it plays an important role as the (descending, subdominant) leading tone to E in the orientation of D– toward A+.

The Schenkerian sketches of Figures 7.2(c) and (d) elaborate on these mirror-like relationships. Most evident is the role reversal between dependent and structural harmonies, made visually immediate by the relationship of black and white notes in the sketches. In 7.2(c), the A-major chord relates to the structural D-minor i/$\hat{3}$ as a prolongational suffix—a back-relating dominant (or dominant divider). In 7.2(d), by contrast, the D-minor chord relates to the structural A-major I/$\hat{5}$ as a prolongational prefix—a sort of plagal auxiliary cadence. Arrows linking the *Stufen* in the two analyses emphasize these back-relating and forward-relating kinetics.[6] The Schenkerian readings in fact assert more than this. They both hypothesize that their structural harmonies are *the* structural harmonies for the piece: they are, in each reading, the opening tonic *Stufen* that support the *Kopfton*.[7] The polarity between the two hearings of viola 1's F4–E4 gesture is thus intensified: one of the pitches becomes the work's principal structural tone, while the other arises at a relatively late stage of middleground prolongation.

Figures 7.2(e) and (f) present Riemannian accounts of the two hearings, via function symbols and oriented networks. The latter model the forward-relating and backward-relating kinetics just discussed. These networks employ mode-reversing subdominant and dominant transformations, notated S* and D*, which take a subdominant or dominant (respectively) to a tonic of the opposite mode.[8] In addition to their retrograde relationship, the Riemannian readings have an inversional component. In the D-minor interpretation of 7.2(e), the A-major chord is heard as D's upper, major dominant (D^+). In the A-major interpretation of 7.2(f), D-minor is heard as A's lower, minor dominant (i.e., subdominant, ^oS).[9]

---

6. On back-relating and forward-relating prolongations in general, see Brown 2005, 77.

7. It is, of course, exceedingly premature to make a hypothesis about what the *Kopfton* might be based on one measure alone. As the motto recurs throughout the piece, however, it soon becomes clear that these are the only viable *Kopfton* choices. Peter Smith presents a middle-ground sketch of most of the movement in A that takes E = $\hat{5}$ as *Kopfton* (2006, 85, Ex. 17).

8. S* and D* are algebraically equivalent to PS (or SP) and PD (or DP), in which P is the parallel transformation. In Hook's UTT terminology, S* = $\langle -, 7, 7 \rangle$ and D* = $\langle -, 5, 5 \rangle$.

9. Riemann would call the A-major hearing in Figure 7.2(f) an instance of "Molldurtonart," after Hauptmann. Riemann in fact discussed Brahms's use of such mixed key systems in his late works in a fascinating essay from 1889 (see Riemann 1967, section III, 109–23). I am grateful to Roger Moseley for bringing the article to my attention. Moseley (2010) discusses Brahms's use of various *molldur* configurations in the Double Concerto, op. 102.

The inversional balance of dominant and subdominant around a central tonic is, of course, a central aspect of Riemann's function theories. The inversional relationship is also captured in the algebra of the transformations: S* is the formal inverse of D* (i.e., D* = S*⁻¹ and S* = D*⁻¹).

Figures 7.2(g) and (h) provide a final perspective, analyzing the two hearings in terms of sd/pc sets. Hearing (g) maps to hearing (h) via pivot 4th, while (h) maps to (g) via the inverse, pivot 5th. Perhaps less immediately evident is their retrograde-inversional relationship. As Figure 7.3 illustrates, chromatic inversion $I_{(1,D)}^{(1,A)}$ maps the two tonic chords onto one another, and the two nontonic chords onto one another. The fulcrum of the inversion is pitch class A, which takes on the quale of $\hat{5}$ in the D-minor hearing, and that of $\hat{1}$ in the A-major hearing. A is the only pitch shared by both triads; it is also both chords' Riemannian dual root (or prime). The inversion also links the sensitive chromatic pitches in the two hearings, mapping F♮-as-♭$\hat{6}$-in-A and C♯-as-♯$\hat{7}$-in-D onto one another. There is thus a compelling (if abstract) retrograde-inversional relationship between the two hearings as energetic structures. We will note further instances of energetic inversion and retrogradation as the analysis proceeds.

The cello projects a somewhat less abstract inversional structure in the motto, as shown in Figure 7.4. Though one's initial tendency might be to group the cello's pitches into octave-related pairs, 7.4(a) presents a different hearing, as two overlapping three-note cadential gestures, labeled Plag and Auth. The cadential formula is most evident in the latter: the cello's A3–A2–D3 is an archetypal authentic cadential bass line, complete with descending octave leap and bar-line-spanning $\hat{5}$–$\hat{1}$. With this gesture in our ears, it is easy to hear an inverted plagal version of the cadential bass line in the cello's first three notes. The initial octave leap down is replaced by an octave leap up, which is then followed by a cadentially discharging descending fourth that provides a strong aural sense of $\hat{4}$–$\hat{1}$. The

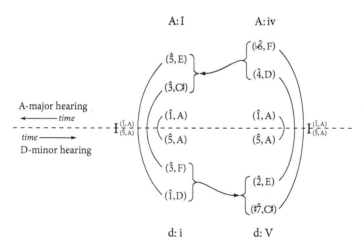

Figure 7.3 A retrograde inversion mapping the D-minor and A-major hearings onto each other.

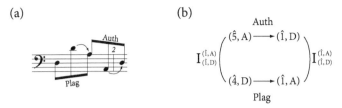

Figure 7.4 Plagal and authentic cadential bass lines projected by the cello in the motto.

plagal gesture asserts A as tonic, while the authentic asserts D. As shown in Figure 7.4(b), the two gestures map onto one another by a new chromatic inversion, $I_{(\hat{1},D)}^{(\hat{1},A)}$. While the harmonic inversion diagrammed in 7.3 mapped A-as-$\hat{1}$ onto A-as-$\hat{5}$, the bass-line inversion maps A-as-$\hat{1}$ onto D-as-$\hat{1}$.

Figure 7.5(a) detects a similar pattern in the motto's viola line, whose contour follows that of the cello exactly, though with compressed intervals. Trichords *x* and *y* map onto one another via the pitch-class inversion that maps A onto E. If

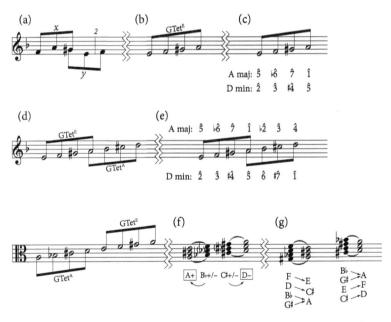

Figure 7.5 (a) Trichords *x* and *y* projected by the viola in the motto combine into (b) the "Gypsy tetrachord" on E (GTet^E), which may be heard in (c) A major or D minor. (d) GTet^E and GTet^A combine to form a "Gypsy scale," which may be heard in (e) A major or D minor. (f) This Gypsy scale contains six triads, only two of which—D– and A+—are not paired with their modal parallels. (g) These are also the only two triads of the six that are completely surrounded by semitonal neighbors in the scale.

we hear the gesture according to the tonal succession in Figure 7.4—a trichord "in A" followed by trichord "in D"—then x-in-A inverts to y-in-D via $I_{(\hat{5},A)}^{(\hat{5},E)}$, mapping the two keys' fifth scale degrees onto each other. This hearing feels more strained than the inversional hearing of the cello, due both to the rhythm and phrasing of the viola and to the tonal uncertainty created by the G♯—is it the leading tone in A or ♯$\hat{4}$ in D? More notable than the trichordal segmentation is the fact that the viola here outlines a so-called Gypsy tetrachord, with prominent augmented second, as shown in 7.5(b). We will label this particular form of the tetrachord GTet^E—the Gypsy tetrachord beginning on E. As 7.5(c) illustrates, in the tonal context of Brahms's motto, the tetrachord may be heard as the upper tetrachord of A major, with lowered $\hat{6}$, or as the $\hat{2}$–$\hat{5}$ tetrachord in D minor, with raised $\hat{4}$. Like the harmonic hearings in 7.2(g) and (h), these two hearings map onto each other either via pivot interval (pivot 4th/5th), or via inversion. The inversion, as noted above, is $I_{(\hat{5},A)}^{(\hat{5},E)}$. As in Figure 7.3, the inversion maps the two tetrachords' sensitive chromatic pitches onto each other: (♭$\hat{6}$, F) in A maps onto (♯$\hat{4}$, G♯) in D.

Any two fifth-related Gypsy tetrachords combine to produce what Liszt called the "Gypsy scale" (sometimes also called "Gypsy minor"). Brahms was undoubtedly aware of the scale from Liszt's music and writings as well as from his performances with Hungarian fiddle player Ede Reményi.[10] Figure 7.5(d) shows the scale that arises from combining GTet^E and GTet^A. As shown in 7.5(e), this scale admits of hearings as either an A-major scale with lowered $\hat{6}$ and $\hat{2}$, or as a D-minor scale with raised $\hat{4}$ and $\hat{7}$. Any Gypsy scale may be heard in two keys in this way—both tonal orientations occur in Liszt's music.[11] Bellman calls the result "a highly colored scale with an uncertain tonic," or a "bifocal tonic" (1991, 235). As he observes, the two notes in the scale that can take on tonic status are the top pitches of the two Gypsy tetrachords. Just like the two harmonic hearings in 7.2(g) and (h), the two hearings of the Gypsy scale in 7.5(e) map onto one another via pivot 4th/5th or via chromatic inversion $I_{(\hat{5},A)}^{(\hat{1},A)}$. Earlier we observed that A, the pc center of this inversion, is the fifth degree of D and the tonic of A. Here we observe that it is the sole pitch in the Gypsy scale that is surrounded by semitones above and below.

Figures 7.5(f) and (g) present two additional perspectives on the scale. As shown in 7.5(f), the collection contains six members of set class 3-11. Among these are D minor and A major, the two chords in Brahms's motto, and its two tonic candidates. These are paired with neighboring triads: B♭+/– a semitone above A+, and C♯+/– a semitone below D–. A+ and D– are the only two triads to occur in only one mode. They are further the only two of the six triads in the scale surrounded entirely by semitone neighbors, as illustrated in 7.5(g).

10. On Brahms's relationship with Reményi, including a lively account of their performances together, see Swafford 1998, 56–62. Liszt's book *The Gypsy in Music,* likely written with the help of Caroline Sayn-Wittgenstein and published in French in 1859, was widely read and well known. Liszt's Hungarian Rhapsodies, among his most famous compositions during his life, are rife with so-called Gypsy scales. Brahms certainly knew (though did not necessarily esteem) both Liszt's book and his rhapsodies.

11. See Bellman 1991, 234–35 and Huneker 1911, 162–63, whom Bellman cites. Though minor-key orientations are most common in Liszt, an emphatic major-key version sounds at the conclusion of the fifteenth Hungarian Rhapsody.

The Gypsy scale in 7.5(e) thus manifests several relationships of relevance to Brahms's motto. Nevertheless, the motto itself does not project the entire scale: the second viola plays B♮ instead of B♭. Only later in the movement does the complete scale involving GTet^E and GTet^A explicitly sound, at a crucial rhetorical and tonal juncture in which the music finally tilts in favor of D minor. For now, the tonal balance in the motto lists ever so slightly in the direction of A. The B♮ just discussed plays a crucial role in that listing, as we will see shortly. Though the motto proper does not project a complete Gypsy scale, the *viola* does so in the movement's opening bars, as shown in Figure 7.6(a). All of the viola's pitches up to the downbeat of m. 5 are drawn from the scale created by the union of GTet^E and GTet^B. Figure 7.6(b) beams together the four semitone pairs in the viola part, which project the four semitones in the scale. The up-stemmed semitone pairs all begin on members of the A-minor triad, A–G♯, C–B, E–D♯, arpeggiating upward through the chord in reaching-over fashion.

Figure 7.6(c) situates this Gypsy scale within a portion of a theoretical space of all Gypsy scales. Each column contains members of a single Gypsy tetrachord;

Figure 7.6 (a) The viola part in mm. 1–5, which projects (b) the Gypsy scale made up of GTet^E and GTet^B. (c) A portion of the space of all Gypsy tetrachords, arranged into columns by tetrachord and rows by Gypsy scale. The region in a dashed box is the "tonic region" for Brahms's Adagio; the viola in mm. 1–5 projects the scale in the solid box.

the tetrachords on B, E, A, and D are shown in the figure. Each row projects a single tonally oriented Gypsy scale. The annotation GS(x) indicates an "x-minor" Gypsy scale (i.e., minor with raised $\hat{4}$ and $\hat{7}$), while GS(X) indicates an "X-major" Gypsy scale (i.e., major with lowered $\hat{2}$ and $\hat{6}$). The viola in 7.6(a) projects GS(a), enclosed in a solid box in the figure. (The motivation for the hearing "in A" will be discussed shortly.) A dashed box encloses the two tonal forms of the Gypsy scale shown in Figure 7.5(e). One can navigate from any tetrachord in the map to any other by chromatic sd/pc transposition or chromatic sd/pc inversion. Vertically aligned tetrachords are all related by pivot transformation. Thus, any sensed shift in tonal orientation within a single sounding tetrachord may be conceived as a vertical motion within the space.

We return now to viola 2's B♮ in the motto. As shown Figure 7.7, this pitch leads us away from the exoticized modal vagaries of the Gypsy scale into a more Western mode of hearing, indeed an Enlightenment one. As shown in 7.7(b), the B♮ acts as a Rameauian characteristic dissonance over the initial D-minor harmony, destabilizing it and directing it toward the A chord. The A chord, by contrast, accrues no such characteristic dissonance; it remains a pure consonant triad. The characteristic dissonance appropriate to it would of course be a G♮, turning the chord into a *dominante-tonique* of D. Instead, Brahms emphasizes the absence of G♮ by including G♯ in the fiddle solo; as shown in 7.7(c), this directs the D chord even more energetically to A. The G♯ is of course the "exotic" pitch in the upper Gypsy tetrachord. B♮ rationalizes this G♯, tilting us tonally toward A and converting the pitch into a familiar leading tone.[12]

Module B seems to confirm A's local tonic status. Figure 7.8(a) shows a reduced score of the passage, aligned with a network of harmonic transformations in 7.8(b). Module B concludes in m. 8 with an imperfect authentic cadence in A, analyzed in 7.8(b) as a D transform from E+ to A+. The sequential music of mm. 3–7 prolongs C major through a series of subdominant moves. These notably include a prominent plagal cadence via S* in mm. 6–7, the very harmonic motion associated

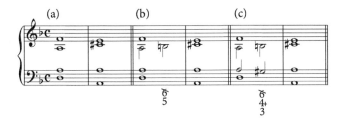

Figure 7.7 A Rameauian hearing of the motto. The D-minor chord acquires a characteristic added-sixth dissonance at (b), which gives it a subdominant tinge, tilting it toward A as tonic. The G♯ added in (c) reinforces this tonal orientation.

---

12. Note how the tensing and relaxing consonance and dissonance of Figure 7.7(c) interact with the contour profile of the motto: the one moment of harmonic dissonance—the "and" of beat 1—is also the registral highpoint of the viola 1 and cello gestures.

with the A-major hearing in Figure 7.2(f). When combined with the welter of right-ward subdominant motions in 7.8(b), this cadence from minor subdominant to major tonic can be heard as a retrospective confirmation of the A-based hearing of the motto (an interpretation further encouraged by the cadence in m. 8). Left out of the transformational analysis is the melodic D♯ in m. 4, which turns the F chord into an augmented sixth. The D♯ is the last chromatic vestige of the Gypsy scale shown in Figure 7.6. Every Gypsy scale contains a single, "signature" German sixth chord; the German sixth on F is the signature chord for the scale projected by the viola in Figure 7.6. The music that follows in mm. 5–8 leaves behind such Gypsy sounds in favor of purposeful sequential motion by ascending fifth. Driving that motion—in addition to the subdominant transformations already discussed—is canonic imitation between viola and cello, indicated on 7.8(a) by brackets labeled *1–4*. The canonic entries outline diatonic TTS tetrachords, in notable contrast to the earlier Gypsy tetrachords. The sd/pc interval between consecutive canonic entries may be construed either as (5th, 7), remaining within the key of C, as modeled in 7.8(c); or as (*e*, 7), with local changes of diatonic collection at each stage, as modeled in 7.8(d). The former hearing captures the sense of chromatic inflections generated by the sequence, while the second hearing models the fact that each leg can be heard to traverse 6̂–7̂–1̂–5̂ in a local major key. Whichever hearing we adopt, this sequential motion eventually subsides, as does the momentary key of C major, in favor of the tonal authority of the authentic cadence in A in m. 8.

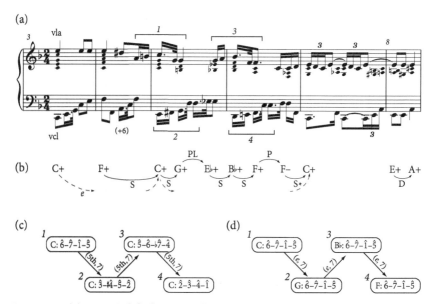

Figure 7.8 (a) A simplified score of mm. 3–8, accompanied by a harmonic-transformational analysis in (b). The latter shows a preponderance of forward-oriented subdominant motions, and only a single forward-oriented dominant, which creates an authentic cadence in A in m. 8. (c) and (d): two hearings of the imitative activity between the outer voices.

This authentic cadence is accompanied by a cimbalom shake in violin 2, viola 2, and cello, signaling the return of the *style hongrois* to the topical foreground. With it, the tonal certainty of the cadence is thrown into momentary doubt. As shown in Figure 7.9(a), the A harmony is transformed into V⁷-of-d in m. 9. The first sobbing figure in the upper voices includes a B♭, cancelling the B♮ so crucial to the tilt to A major, while the third sobbing figure projects an entire Gypsy tetrachord, GTet^A. Nevertheless, by m. 12 the music manages to reestablish A with a half cadence. In the wake of this cadence, the first *hallgató* episode occurs, shown in 7.9(b). The episode includes explicit fore-echoes of the motto, preparing its return in m. 15, at the onset of Variation 2. As Peter Smith (2006, 83) notes, these fore-echoes occur within an A-minor context—in the wake of the half-cadence in that key—priming the listener's ears to hear the motto in A when it returns in mm. 15–16. Indeed, the dominant of A returns at the end of m. 14, bracketing the entire *hallgató* passage, and preparing the return of the motto, now tilted vividly toward A.

The emphasis on A as tonal center in Modules B and C is prolongational as well. Figure 7.10 shows a Schenkerian sketch of mm. 1–12. As the sketch indicates, the music prolongs A via an ascending A–C♯–E arpeggiation in the bass and a coupling of E5 and E4 in the upper voice. The Roman numeral annotations beneath

Figure 7.9 (a) The V⁷-of-d in m. 9 seems to undercut the A tonicity of the previous cadence, but A-as-tonic is restored in the half cadence in m. 12. (b) The Gypsy tetrachord on E sounds within the prolonged dominant of A in mm. 12–14, preparing our ears to hear the coming motto firmly in A.

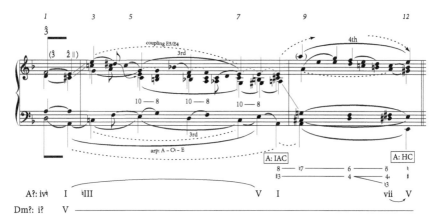

Figure 7.10 A Schenkerian sketch of mm. 1–12. A-as-*Stufe* dominates the prolongational structure, whether one analyzes the passage in A major or D minor.

the staff show a hearing of the sketch in A as well as a hearing in D. To convert the sketch entirely to the A-major hearing, one would need only to reverse the open and closed noteheads in the first two chords and relabel the careted scale degrees; the prolongation of the A *Stufe* would otherwise remain identical. The sketch does not reflect the vacillation in key sensations shown in 7.9(a), but it does present an effective picture of a synthetic, retrospective hearing of events up to the half cadence of m. 12, which reasserts A as local tonic.

When Module B recurs in Variation 2, the imitation modeled in Figure 7.8 is replaced by a greater emphasis on hymn-like homophony. While the earlier B module had ended with an authentic cadence in A, in Variation 2 it ends with a half cadence in D (m. 24). This prepares for an explicit "tonal correction" in the sobbing module C, modeled in Figure 7.11(a). The module begins as it did in m. 9 (with some added ornaments), but then shifts downward by fifth with the pickup to m. 26. In sd/pc terms, this is a transformation by $(e, -7)$, which leaves scale-degree qualia unchanged, but transposes the sounding pcs. As a result, the half cadence in m. 28—analogous to the earlier cadence in m. 12—now sounds in D, not in A. The *hallgató* episode that follows in 7.11(b) continues at this new pitch level, preparing for the return of the motto at the outset of Variation 3, one fifth below its pitch level in Variations 1 and 2. Brahms sets the stage for this moment by drawing the pitch content of bar 30, beat 2, to the downbeat of bar 33, from a single Gypsy scale—hearable as an inflection of D major or G minor—which resides in the lower right-hand corner of Figure 7.6(c), further underscoring a sense of "corrective shift," as the music swings subdominantward, balancing out the earlier statement of GS(a) in 7.6(a). The scale's signature German sixth sounds in m. 32.[13]

Figure 7.12 presents a spatial network of sd/pc motto hearings for Variations 1–3. Solid nodes and arrows show the hearings thus far emphasized by local tonal

---

13. If one disregards the E♮ in the motto in m. 33, the Gypsy scale may be continued through that bar, as the dashed bracket extension in Figure 7.11(b) indicates.

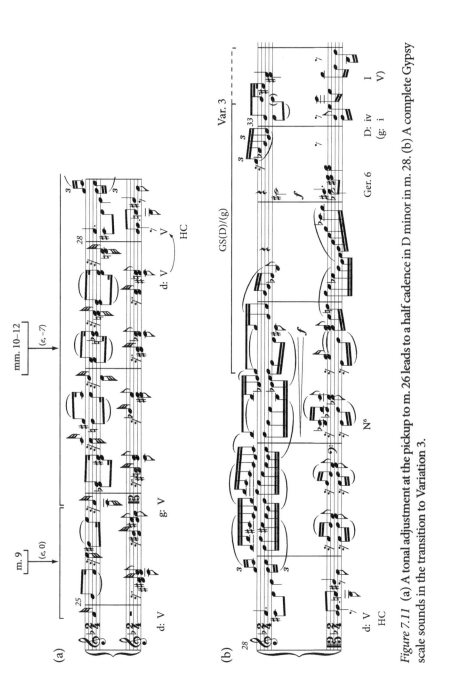

Figure 7.11 (a) A tonal adjustment at the pickup to m. 26 leads to a half cadence in D minor in m. 28. (b) A complete Gypsy scale sounds in the transition to Variation 3.

rhetoric: A:iv–I in Variations 1 and 2, and D:iv–I in Variation 3. Dotted nodes and arrows model the "shadowing" pivot hearings of these mottos. Horizontal arrows labeled (*e*, –7) reflect the shift in pitch level from Variations 1/2 to Variation 3, effected by the corrective lurch modeled in 7.11(a). An arrow labeled (5th, 7) leads diagonally from the northeast node to the southwest node, linking the two D-based hearings. The remaining work of the movement is to traverse this arrow, transforming the motto from D:iv–I to d:i–V.

This work is accomplished through the mini development, Variation 4, and the massive dominant that replaces Module C in the latter. The mini development begins by swinging away from D major to G minor, undercutting the cadence in the former in a manner that is by now becoming familiar. The vigorous imitative effort of the subsequent bars nevertheless manages to bring the music back to D for a half cadence in m. 51. As though wishing to guard against any further tonal slippage, Variation 4 begins with a statement of the motto that does not leave the D-major triad, eschewing the potential ambiguities of the earlier harmonic oscillations. Module B returns to the imitative material of Figure 7.8(a), now emphatically in D minor, setting up the massive dominant of that key, which arrives at the end of m. 61. The rhetoric of the imitative module and the dominant is strenuously *durchgearbeitet,* pushing aside all Gypsy rhetoric. The latter returns only once D minor has been assured, with the viola's *hallgató* cadenza shown in Figure 7.13, which now projects the Gypsy scale from Figure 7.5(e) in its entirety, safely domesticated in an explicit D-minor context.[14] Rather than engaging in clever tonal deception, the fiddle now takes on the character of a genuine lament.[15] This moves us finally into the central, dashed box of Figure 7.6(c). When the motto sounds at its original pitch level in m. 69, a D-minor hearing has been assured by the weight of events in that key stretching back to m. 55. The music thereby effectively traverses the diagonal arrow of Figure 7.14, transposing the motto of Variation 3 via (5th, 7) to d:i–V.

This is the first genuine reversal of energetic direction in the motto. All hearings thus far have ultimately tilted in favor of a local iv–I (or forward-oriented S*) hearing, directing tonic weight onto the second chord of the

---

14. The only pitches in the viola that fall outside GS(d) are the two G♯s in m. 65, enclosed in parentheses in the figure.

15. With the word "deception," I am thinking of the performance situations that Bellman describes, which are primarily commercial, and in which the "element of surprise" played a large role (1991, 233). The paying customer that Bellman discusses—likely a Westerner—evidently enjoyed such surprises. Exactly why *Brahms's quintet* does not seem to enjoy them—indeed reacts so violently to them—and further seeks to contain the Gypsy elements within the confines of Western tonal and contrapuntal control is a question I am not certain how to answer. I am not comfortable with the hermeneutics of suspicion that such a reading aims at Brahms. Nor am I prepared to address the question of voice or persona in the movement. As I have described it thus far, there seem to be two personae, or perhaps collections of personae, in the movement—Gypsy and Western-European, the latter engaged in characteristic Orientalist fantasizing. But the two are hard to tease apart. One would certainly not want to be overly literal about the reading (pointing to just which notes belong to which personae and so forth), nor would it be wise to attempt to map the personae somehow onto the players of the quintet (the ensemble changes stylistic registers largely as a group). The question calls for an essay in its own right, likely drawing on Cone 1974.

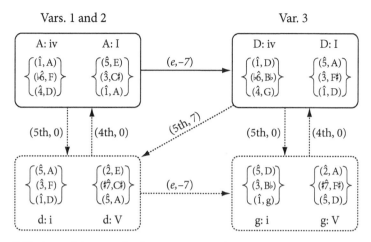

Figure 7.12 A spatial network of motto progressions.

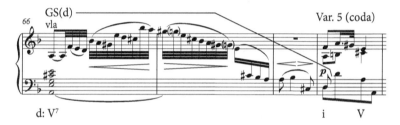

Figure 7.13 A complete Gypsy scale in D minor sounds in the transition to Variation 5 (coda).

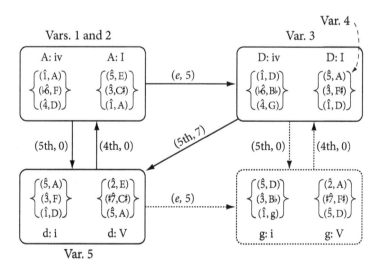

Figure 7.14 The spatial network from Figure 7.12, now showing the primary tonal orientations of the motto progression in all five variations.

gesture. Now, finally, the opening chord has accrued tonic authority, retrograding the intentional relationship between the two harmonies. Figure 7.15 renders this process visible via an oriented network of oriented networks. Each large node of the figure contains a smaller network resembling those of Figures 7.2(e) and (f). The nodes for Variations 1 and 2 contain forward-oriented S* networks, with the tonic node on the right. The node for Variation 5 contains a backward-oriented D* network, with the tonic node on the left. In between are the network for Variation 4, which contains only a D+ node, and the massive dominant of D minor. Note that the internal networks are oriented toward the massive dominant, pointing forward toward it in Variations 1–3, and backward toward it in Variation 5. The sonic weight of that dominant effects the energetic reversal of the motto.

As the arrows joining the network's large nodes indicate, this reversal can in fact be formalized as a pair of retrograde inversions, along the lines discussed in connection with Figure 7.3. An arrow labeled I_A^A(Ret) maps the node contents for Variations 1 and 2 to those for Variation 5. The I_A^A inversion maps the A+ and D– triads onto each other, while Ret retrogrades the resulting network. In similar fashion, I_A^D(Ret) maps the Variation 3 motto to that for Variation 5. I_A^D maps D+ onto D– and G– onto A+. We can conceive of the inversions here as effecting the modal reversal of the networks, as major tonic is replaced by minor tonic, and minor nontonic is replaced by major nontonic. Retrograde effects the reversal in intentional direction, from rightward (forward-relating) arrow to leftward (backward-relating) arrow.

Yet the motto retains its tonally ambiguous potential, as Brahms confirms with the piece's final gesture: in the final bars of the movement, he states the motto again in its S*, iv-to-I form, but now in D major, over a D pedal. Rather than presenting some sort of resolution—confirming a bland assertion, for example, that the piece "really was in D all along"—this conclusion instead *reinforces* the ambiguity of the motto. The piece offers a counterexample to Agawu's claim that "tonal structures, if they exhibit ambiguity, do so in an irreversible ambiguity-to-clarity order" (1994, 91). The relevant ambiguity here is, "Does the motto project a rightward S* or a leftward D*?" As the analytical narrative suggests, we are likely to lean toward the rightward-S* hearing before Variation 4 and the massive dominant arrive. The two choices do indeed seem to be in a hierarchical relationship up until Variation 4 (as Agawu says such choices always will be). After the massive dominant, however, we are led to a leftward-D* hearing. This might initially seem to reverse the hierarchy, perhaps causing us to exclaim, "Aha! The second chord really was a back-relating dominant all along!" But before we can comfortably settle into *that* new hierarchical understanding, one in which leftward-D* wins out over rightward-S*, Brahms revives rightward-S* in the movement's final bars, suggesting that the listener was correct to entertain such a hearing earlier. The two hearings are thus brought into equilibrium—Brahms makes it impossible for us to choose which intentional structure the motto "really" manifests. Conceived thus,

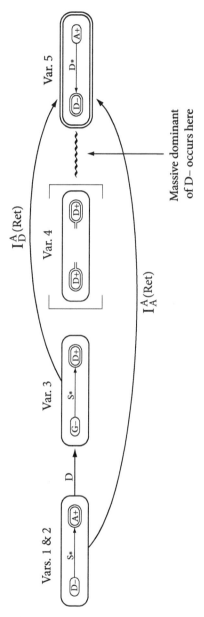

Figure 7.15 An oriented network of oriented networks, showing the gradual change in the motto's tonal orientation from rightward-S* to leftward-D* under the influence of the massive dominant.

the Adagio presents a reversal of Agawu's paradigm, one that proceeds in the direction of greater ambiguity, rather than greater clarity.[16]

If, on the other hand, one conceives of the question of ambiguity in terms of key—"Is the movement ultimately in D or A?"—Agawu's ambiguity-to-clarity paradigm may be upheld. But I hope the preceding discussion, indeed the preceding book, has cast at least a shadow of doubt on the value of such questions. Such language treats tonal orientations as immanent properties of pitch configurations—even of musical "works" tout court—rather than as emergent qualities sensed and nurtured by listeners in the act of hearing. Brahms's quintet movement in fact makes the point very vividly, staging a process whereby a listener is strongly encouraged to hear a single passage of music in two opposed ways. The music of the motto in Variation 1 (mm. 1–2) is all but identical to that at the beginning of Variation 5 (mm. 69)—the acoustic signals can hardly be distinguished.[17] Yet, while various factors at the work's opening encourage one to hear this music as A-oriented, the massive dominant of mm. 61–68 points the listener's ears so emphatically in the direction of D that it is all but impossible to avoid sensing the motto as D-oriented when it returns in m. 69. Brahms's movement teaches, more eloquently than any theoretical monograph could, that tonal qualities are not given in musical materials, but arise in the encounter between those materials and a listening subject.

---

16. This understanding is consonant with Smith's statement that "[t]he sum total of the process of hearing a motive that keeps switching meanings may indeed produce ambiguity" (2006, 59).
17. The only difference is one of instrumentation, with violins 1 and 2 in Variation 5 taking up the music of violas 1 and 2 in Variation 1, at the same pitch level.

Plate 7: Brahms, String Quintet in G major, op. 111, mvt. ii, Adagio

Plate 7 cont.

Plate 7 cont.

Plate 7 cont.

Plate 7 cont.

Var. 5 (coda)

Afterword

As stated in the Introduction, this book explores "ways in which transformational and GIS technologies may be used to model diverse tonal effects and experiences." The four analytical chapters of Part II have sought to demonstrate that diversity. In Chapter 4, the tonal GIS illuminated the fluid key sensations in Bach's fugue, as the subject took on the hues of its ever-shifting tonal surroundings. Chapter 5, by contrast, explored a passage that remained stoutly in a single key—the A section of Mozart's aria—using oriented networks to dig into the phenomenologically dense onsets of Ferrando's two ecstatic melismas. Chapter 6 pursued the interaction between metric and intentional kinetics in Brahms's Intermezzo, as the music worked through the consequences of its *Auftaktig* motives. Chapter 7, on the adagio from Brahms's Quintet, focused on the tonal orientations of a genuinely ambiguous motto, as the listener's ears were tilted first toward one hearing and then another by the tonal rhetoric of the surrounding music. These chapters do not exhaust the resources of the tonal GIS or of oriented networks; the vignettes in Part I suggest various avenues for further analytical exploration.

There is also room for further theoretical work. In seeking an elusive balance between formal substance and accessibility, I have inevitably left some formal loose ends. The most notable of these is discussed in section 2.12. Formal extension and clarification of this and other matters can proceed in tandem with analytical application—the latter need not wait for the former. While further theoretical work will enrich our sense of the conceptual landscape that these technologies inhabit, the GIS and transformational tools introduced here are ready for use, as pragmatic aids in the pleasurable business of focusing our ears on favorite tonal passages. Those interested in pursuing formal matters in greater depth will deepen our understanding of the "shape" of the resulting tonal apperceptions.

These technologies enter a field already crowded with methods for tonal analysis. They are intended not to displace those methods but to complement them, in a spirit consistent with the ideas on dialogical pluralism sketched in section 1.4. While I have previously argued for such pluralism on the premise that no single analytical method can lay claim to the entirety of a given musical experience, there is an additional ethical impulse behind this position when it comes to tonal music. As noted in the Introduction, tonal experience can feel powerfully unmediated to enculturated listeners—a set of aural sensations so familiar that it can seem to make an end run around the contingencies of history and culture. Adorno called this tonality's "second nature" (2002, 114). In any monological account of tonal experience there is a danger of mystifying this second nature as first nature—that is, nature pure and simple. A dialogically plural approach to tonal analysis, by contrast, resists absorption into a single unified representation, emphasizing both the unruly diversity of effects that tonal music affords, as well as the constitutive and mediating role that the technology itself can play in focusing or bringing out those effects. This mediation is not to be lamented as a stumbling block on the way to a pristine, transparent account of originary hearing; it is rather something to celebrate—an enabling construct that allows us to cultivate diverse and richly detailed experiences through conscious interpretive engagement. The technologies in this book are offered in such a spirit—as quickening agents for our manifold encounters with tonal music.

GLOSSARY

Argument: See *function.*

Automorphism: An *isomorphism* from a *group* to itself. Automorphisms are most familiar in music theory in the study of Klumpenhouwer networks (Lewin 1990; Klumpenhouwer 1998 is an accessible introduction to such networks). See also *group, homomorphism, isomorphism.*

Bijection: See *function.*

Binary composition: The "inner law" in a *group* or *semigroup* that dictates how any two elements in the group or semigroup combine to create a third element. Mathematicians typically call this a *binary operation,* or simply an *operation.* This volume follows Lewin in using the term binary composition, to avoid confusion with the word operation, which means something different in transformational theory. See also *group, semigroup, operation, transformation.*

Cardinality: The number of elements in a *set.*

Cartesian product: The Cartesian product of two *sets* A and B, notated $A \times B$, is the set of all *ordered pairs* of the form (a, b), such that a is a member of A and b is a member of B.

An example: with *Così fan tutte* in mind, let us define the sets U = {Ferr, Gug} and D = {Dor, Fior}. The Cartesian product $U \times D$ is the set {(Ferr, Dor), (Ferr, Fior), (Gug, Dor), (Gug, Fior)}, the set of all amorous pairings in the opera. Note that any Cartesian product is itself a set—a set of ordered pairs.

A set can enter into a Cartesian product with itself. Thus, we could define the set S as the set of 12 pitch classes. The Cartesian product $S \times S$ would then be the set of all pairs of pitch classes (pc_1, pc_2), in which pc_1 and pc_2 each run through all 12 pitch classes (pc_1 can equal pc_2). The set $S \times S$ contains 144 (12 times 12) ordered pairs. In general, the cardinality of any Cartesian product $A \times B$ equals the cardinality of A times the cardinality of B.

$A \times B$ is sometimes also called the "cross product" of A and B.

Commutativity: Two *group* elements f and g commute if $f \cdot g = g \cdot f$. To take a music-theoretical example, transpositions T_m and T_n in atonal theory always commute with one another: the result is the same whether one performs T_m-then-T_n or T_n-then-T_m. By contrast, transpositions and inversions in atonal theory do *not* generally commute with one another: T_m-then-I_n typically yields a different result than I_n-then-T_m (the result will only be the same if $T_m = T_6$ or T_0).

A group that consists entirely of elements that commute with one another is called a *commutative group* or an *Abelian group* (after Niels Abel). A group that contains elements that do not commute with one another is called a *noncommutative group* or a *non-Abelian group.*

Cyclic group ($\mathbb{Z}, \mathbb{Z}_n$)**:** A *commutative group* that can be generated by repeated iterations of a single group element. This element is called the *generator* of the group. Finite cyclic groups are very familiar in music theory. The group of twelve transpositions T_n is a cyclic group of order 12, notated $\mathbb{Z}_{12}$; it can be generated by twelve iterations of T_1, T_{11}, T_5, or T_7. The infinite cyclic group, notated $\mathbb{Z}$, is isomorphic to the integers under addition. See also *commutativity, group, isomorphism.*

Dihedral group ($\mathbb{D}_n$): A *noncommutative group* whose abstract structure is that of the group of flips and rotations on a regular polygon. The 24 transpositions and inversions from atonal theory form a dihedral group of order 24, as do the 24 neo-Riemannian operations. To develop an intuitive sense of this algebraic structure, one can imagine the transpositions and inversions as rotations and flips on a regular dodecagon: the transpositions rotate the dodecagon, while the inversions flip it. Similarly, the mode-preserving neo-Riemannian operations (similar in action to Riemann's *Schritte*) rotate the dodecagon, while the mode-reversing operations (similar to Riemann's *Wechsel*) flip it.

Smaller dihedral subgroups may be formed from the transpositions and inversions, or from the neo-Riemannian operations. For example, the neo-Riemannian subgroup consisting of the elements {e, P, L, PL, LP, PLP} is a dihedral group of order six that acts on a single hexatonic system. Dihedral groups of order six may also be formed using transpositions and inversions. One example is {T_0, T_4, T_8, I_1, I_5, I_9}, which can act on the Western hexatonic system {E♭+, E♭−, B+, B−, G+, G−}. Though this group has the same abstract structure as the neo-Riemannian subgroup above—they are isomorphic—the two behave in different ways when they act on the Western hexatonic system. The two groups in fact have an important relationship in Lewin's theory: they are *duals* of one another, in a rather special formal sense involving the idea of interval preservation. (For an accessible discussion, see Satyendra 2004; Lewin discusses the matter of interval preservation and dual groups more formally in *GMIT*, chapter 3; Clampitt 1998 offers a suggestive analytical exploration of the Grail progression in *Parsifal* using the two dual groups introduced in this paragraph.)

There are two notations for a dihedral group. Some label the dihedral group of order n $\mathbb{D}_n$, while others label it $\mathbb{D}_{n/2}$, as the group is isomorphic to the symmetries on a regular polygon with $n/2$ sides. We will adopt the former notation here, in which the subscript indicates the order of the group, in a manner consistent with the notation for a finite cyclic group. Thus, we label the dihedral group of order 24 $\mathbb{D}_{24}$, and the dihedral group of order 6 $\mathbb{D}_6$.

See also *cyclic group, group, hexatonic system, isomorphism, neo-Riemannian theory, Schritt/Wechsel system, subgroup.*

Directed graph (digraph): A *graph* whose set E of edges consists of *ordered pairs* of elements from the vertex set V. More formally, a directed graph is a *relation* on V. The ordered pairs in E are often called *directed edges* and are usually drawn with arrows. Directed graphs (which Lewin calls "node/arrow systems") are central to transformational graphs and networks.

Note that the only formal difference between a graph *simpliciter* and a digraph is that the elements of the edge set E in the former are (unordered) two-element subsets of V, while in the latter they are ordered pairs from V. An example: define the digraph $DG = (V_{DG}, E_{DG})$ such that $V_{DG} = \{1, 2, 3\}$ and $E_{DG} = \{(1, 2), (1, 3)\}$. We could depict this digraph visually with three dots or nodes, labeled 1, 2, and 3, and arrows pointing from 1 to 2, and 1 to 3. Compare this with the simple graph G discussed in the entry for *graph*: $G = (V_G, E_G)$ such that $V_G = \{1, 2, 3\}$ and $E_G = \{\{1, 2\}, \{1, 3\}\}$. The only difference between DG and G is in their edge sets: in DG, the edges are ordered pairs (in parentheses), while in G the edges are unordered pairs (in curly brackets). DG would thus be drawn with arrows connecting its nodes, while G would be drawn with undirected lines.

See also *graph, ordered pair, relation, transformational graphs and networks.*

Direct product group: A *group* generated by combining two pre-existing groups *G* and *H*. The set elements from *G* and *H* are combined via a Cartesian product and the binary composition is componentwise. Thus, the ordered pairs (g_1, h_1) and (g_2, h_2) generated by the Cartesian product compose in the direct product group thus:

$$(g_1, h_1) \times (g_2, h_2) = (g_1 \bullet g_2, h_1 * h_2)$$

in which $\times$ is the binary composition in the direct product group, $\bullet$ is the binary composition in *G*, and $*$ is the binary composition in *H*.

A comment on the group IVLS in the GIS of chapter 2: The group IVLS in the GIS introduced in Chapter 2 is a direct product of the cyclic groups $\mathbb{Z}_7$ and $\mathbb{Z}_{12}$. This group, notated $\mathbb{Z}_7 \times \mathbb{Z}_{12}$, is isomorphic to the cyclic group of order 84, or $\mathbb{Z}_{84}$. It is a basic finding of group theory that two cyclic groups $\mathbb{Z}_m$ and $\mathbb{Z}_n$ will combine into a direct product group that is isomorphic to the cyclic group $\mathbb{Z}_{m \bullet n}$ if *m* and *n* are coprime (1 is their only shared factor). 7 and 12 are coprime, thus $\mathbb{Z}_7 \times \mathbb{Z}_{12} = \mathbb{Z}_{7 \bullet 12} = \mathbb{Z}_{84}$. As $\mathbb{Z}_{84}$ is a cyclic group, it must contain at least one element of order 84—that is, an element that can combine iteratively with itself to produce the entire 84-element group. IVLS in fact contains 24 such generators, all of the form (sdint′, pcint′), in which sdint′ is any of the six nonidentity sdints, and pcint′ is 1, 5, 7, or 11 (the four generators in the mod 12 universe, all coprime with 12; these are sometimes known as the *units* mod 12). Two musically meaningful generators of IVLS are (5th, 7) and (4th, 5)—the perfect fifth and perfect fourth, respectively. One can generate a musically interesting ordering of the entire space S of the GIS if one begins with, say, $(\hat{4}, F)$ and repeatedly applies (5th, 7). This will produce all 84 members of S, arranged serially into major diatonic collections that are ordered internally by fifths, with the collections ascending by semitone (C major, C♯ major, D major,..., B♭ major, B major). Alternatively, one can begin on $(\hat{6}, F)$ and repeatedly apply (5th, 7) to produce all 84 members of S, now arranged into natural minor diatonic collections that are ordered internally by fifths, and that ascend by semitone (A minor, B♭ minor, B minor,..., G minor, G♯ minor). Other modal collections arise if one begins with different scale-degree qualia. One can also iteratively apply (4th, 5) to produce diatonic collections in *descending* semitonal order. The remaining generators of IVLS produce much more esoteric orderings of S.

See also *binary composition, cyclic group, Cartesian product, ordered pair.*

Domain: See *function.*

Function: A function f from set *X* to set *Y* sends every element *x* in *X* to some element *y* in *Y*. We can either write f(*x*) = *y* or $x \xrightarrow{f} y$ to indicate the action of function f sending *x* to *y*. A common metaphor for a function is a machine that takes as input members of the set *X* and returns as output members of the set *Y*. Set *X* is called the *domain* of the function, while the set of outputs that the function produces is called the *range*. The element *x* in the expression f(*x*) = *y* is called the *argument*, while *y* is called the *value* or *image*.

Note that f sends each element in *X* to only *one* element in *Y*. If f sends all of the elements in *X* to different elements in *Y*, we say that the function is *one-to-one*, or an *injection*. If every element in *Y* is the target of some element in *X* under f, we say that f is *onto*, or a *surjection*. If f is both *one-to-one* and *onto* we say that it is a *bijection*. For f to be a bijection from *X* to *Y* the cardinality of *X* must equal that of *Y*.

The mapping table in Figure 1.3(b) depicts the function Step, which is a bijection from the set of C-major pitch classes to itself (or an operation in Lewin's sense). As Figure 1.3(c) indicates, we can define an *inverse* function, Step⁻¹, that reverses the action of Step. All bijections have inverses, but functions that are not bijections do *not* have inverses.

See also *cardinality, set, relation, transformation.*

Generalized Interval System (GIS): A central construct in transformational theory, used to render intervallic statements and apperceptions formal. A Generalized Interval System, or GIS, is an *ordered triple* (S, IVLS, int), in which S is a *set*, IVLS is a *group*, and int is a *function* from the *Cartesian product* S × S into IVLS. A GIS must satisfy two conditions (as defined in *GMIT*, Def. 2.3.1):

(A): For all r, s, and t in S, int(r, s)int(s, t) = int(r, t).

(B): For every s in S and every i in IVLS, there must exist a unique t in S such that int(s, t) = i.

For a broader introduction to GISes, see section 1.2.

GIS set: See *set*.

Graph: A *set* V of vertices (or "nodes" or "dots") and a set E of edges (or "lines"), which are two-element subsets of V.

Note that this definition says nothing about pictures of nodes and lines. A graph is fully defined simply by enumerating the elements of its sets V and E. For example, we can define a graph G = (V_G, E_G) such that V_G = {1, 2, 3} and E_G = {{1, 2}, {1, 3}}. We could draw a picture to depict graph G containing three dots or nodes, labeled 1, 2, and 3, with lines connecting 1 and 2, and 1 and 3. But such a picture is not of the essence for the graph—it is fully defined by the enumeration of the elements of V_G and E_G above.

This is of relevance to the practice of drawing transformational networks. Such networks employ *directed graphs* (or digraphs) that are typically represented visually by configurations of nodes and arrows. These visual configurations are not formally constrained, however, nor are they of the essence for the formalities of the transformational network, whose underlying graph is fully defined simply by enumerating its nodes (vertices) and arrows (directed edges). Nevertheless, the arrangement of nodes and arrows on the page is an important part of the interpretive practice of transformational theory; it is simply not formally constrained by the theory as Lewin presents it (though see the discussion of spatial and event networks in section 3.9).

Not all of the elements of V need to have lines adjacent to them in a graph. One can in fact define a graph with no edges at all; it would simply consist of vertices—"dots" unattached to one another by "lines." In other words, the set E may be empty. The set V, by contrast, must be nonempty and finite.

See also *directed graph (digraph)*, *set*, *transformational graphs and networks*.

Group: A basic algebraic structure that consists of a *set* along with a *binary composition* that allows one to combine any two elements from the set to generate a third element in the set. The fact that the element so generated is a member of the set satisfies the property of *closure*. To qualify as a group, the structure must satisfy three more properties. *Existence of an identity:* There must be one element e in the group such that, when it is composed with any other element g in the group (via the binary composition), g is the result. (The label e comes from the German *Einheit*.) *Existence of inverses:* For every element g in the group there exists an element g^{-1} such that g composed with g^{-1} yields the identity element e. *Associativity:* Given three group elements f, g, and h, then f • (g • h) = (f • g) • h.

A familiar group is the integers (whole numbers—positive, negative, and zero) with addition as the binary composition. We call this group "the integers under addition." We can confirm that it is a group by seeing that it satisfies the four properties above. Any two integers added together yield another integer (closure). There exists one integer, namely 0, which, when added to any other integer x yields x itself (existence of an identity). Given any integer x, there exists an integer −x such that when x and −x are added, the identity, 0, is the result (existence of inverses). Finally, addition is associative (associativity).

Consider another structure: the integers under multiplication. Is this a group? As before, we need to see if it satisfies the four group properties of closure, existence of an identity, existence of inverses, and associativity. First, the requirement of closure is clearly satisfied: any two integers multiplied together yield another integer. We also know that multiplication is associative—that is, for any three integers x, y, and z, (x times y) times z is the same as x times (y times z). So associativity is satisfied. Is there an identity element? Yes: 1 is the identity; any number x multiplied by 1 yields x itself. Finally, does every element have an inverse? Here our putative "group" fails: given some integer x there generally does not exist an integer x^{-1} such that x-times-x^{-1} = 1. The only times when this idea holds are when x is either 1 itself or –1; both of those integers are their own inverses under multiplication (1 times 1 = 1; –1 times –1 = 1). Otherwise, no other integer has an integral inverse under multiplication. There is no integer, for example, that we can multiply 2 by in order to get 1 (we have to multiply 2 by 1/2 in order to get 1; but 1/2 is a *rational* number, not an integer—the noninteger rationals are not part of our underlying set). Thus, our structure, the integers under multiplication, passes three of the group conditions, but fails the fourth. It is thus not a group. It is a different kind of algebraic structure called a *monoid:* a group-like entity without inverses, but with an identity element.

Groups may be commutative or noncommutative. A common commutative group type in music theory is the *cyclic group*. A common noncommutative group type in music theory is the *dihedral group*.

A group whose set has n elements is said to be of "order n." Thus, the group of 12 transpositions in atonal theory is of order 12, while the group of 24 neo-Riemannian operations is of order 24.

See also *automorphism, cyclic group, dihedral group, homomorphism, involution, isomorphism, semigroup,* and *subgroup.*

Hexatonic system, hexatonic pole: As defined by Richard Cohn (1996), a hexatonic system is a cycle of triads related by alternating neo-Riemannian P and L transformations. There are four such cycles, of six triads each, which Cohn labels by the cardinal points of the compass. The "Northern" cycle, for instance, consists of the triads C+, C–, A♭+, A♭–, E+, and E–.

A triad and its hexatonic pole reside on opposite extremes of a hexatonic cycle; they share no common tones. In the Northern cycle, C major and A♭ minor are hexatonic poles, as are C minor and E major, and A♭ major and E minor. Triad X's hexatonic-polar counterpart is the only triad of the opposite mode in the 24-triad universe with which triad X (1) shares no common tones; and (2) is related by entirely semitonal voice leading. See Cohn 2004 for a sensitive discussion of the signifying potential of hexatonic poles.

See also *dihedral group, neo-Riemannian theory.*

Homomorphism: A *function* that maps the elements from one group to those in another so as to preserve the action of the *binary composition*. The homomorphism h from group G to group H sends the product of elements g_1 and g_2 in G to the product of $h(g_1)$ and $h(g_2)$ in H. If we notate the binary composition in group G as • and the binary composition in group H as *, then we write $h(g_1 • g_2) = h(g_1) * h(g_2)$. See also *binary composition, function, group, isomorphism.*

Injection: See *function.*

Inverse: See *function* and *group.*

Involution: A *group* element g is an involution if it is its own inverse—that is, if $g • g = e$.

Isomorphism: A *homomorphism* that is one-to-one and onto (i.e., a bijection). If two groups can be mapped onto one another via isomorphism, they have the same underlying algebraic structure and are said to be *isomorphic*. For example, the group of 24 transpositions and inversions from atonal theory is isomorphic to the group of 24 neo-Riemannian operations. One can define a bijective map from either one to the other that satisfies the conditions for a homomorphism. This means that the two groups have the same underlying algebraic structure. Specifically, they are both *dihedral groups* of order 24.

See also *dihedral group, function, homomorphism.*

Left (functional) orthography, right (functional) orthography: Two terms that refer to the way *functions* are written. The familiar schoolbook notation f(*x*) = *y* is an instance of left-functional orthography, as the function symbol f is written to the left of the argument *x*. In this orthography, the notation gf(*x*) means "perform f on *x* first, then perform g to the result." The atonal T$_n$ and I$_n$ operations are conventionally written following left orthography. T$_m$I$_n$(*x*) means "first invert *x* by I$_n$, then transpose the result by T$_m$."

Right functional orthography is notated (*x*)f = *y*. The notation (*x*)gf means "perform g first on *x*, then perform f to the result." Neo-Riemannian operations are typically written in right-functional orthography: PL means P-then-L.

Mapping: See *function.*

Neo-Riemannian theory: A branch of transformational theory that models relationships between consonant triads. There are three principal neo-Riemannian operations: the parallel operation, or P, transforms a triad into its parallel major or minor; the relative operation, or R, transforms a triad into its relative major or minor; and the leading-tone change, or L, transforms a triad by maintaining its minor third and moving the remaining element "outward" by semitone.

The three basic neo-Riemannian operations have several characteristic features (1) they all reverse mode; (2) they all preserve two common tones and move the remaining voice by step; (3) they are all involutions; (4) they all exhibit a dualistic logic. Point (4) means that the operations act in equal but opposite ways on major and minor triads. The leading-tone change, or L transform, for example, takes a major triad to the minor triad whose root lies a major third above, while it takes a minor triad to a major triad whose root lies a major third *below.* All neo Riemannian operations behave in the same dualistic fashion, transposing the roots of major and minor triads in equal but opposite directions. Julian Hook (2002) treats this dualistic behavior as the defining feature of Riemannian triadic transformations, which distinguishes them from all other uniform triadic transformations.

The neo-Riemannian operations do not all commute with one another. That is, given two neo-Riemannian operations *M* and *N*, *M*-then-*N* will not generally yield the same result as *N*-then-*M*. For example, PL applied to a C-major triad yields an A♭-major triad, while LP applied to the same C-major triad yields an E-major triad. The neo-Riemannian operations combine to form a *dihedral group* of order 24.

See also *commutativity, dihedral group, involution, operation, uniform triadic transformation.*

One-to-one (injection), onto (surjection), one-to-one and onto (bijection): See *function.*

Operation: A *transformation* that is one-to-one and onto (i.e., bijective). For more, see *transformation.*

Ordered pair, ordered *n*-tuple: A pair of elements notated in parentheses and separated by a comma for which order matters. (*a, b*) means "*a,* then *b.*" (*a, b*) is distinct from the ordered pair (*b, a*). One may also have ordered *n*-tuples of any length (ordered triples, quadruples, etc.). Such ordered *n*-tuples may occur in many contexts—they might indicate temporal order in some sequence of musical events, or they may simply serve as a means of keeping a set of independent formal components organized. A GIS, for example, is an ordered triple (S, IVLS, int).

Range: See *function.*

Relation: Any subset of a *Cartesian product.* In section 3.9 a relation is used to pair nodes with formal events in a spatial network. The two sets in question are the set of nodes, which we can call *N,* and the set of events, which we can call *EV.* As the relation in question is *any* subset of $N \times EV$, it can include, say, (n_1, EV$_1$), (n_1, EV$_2$), and (n_1, EV$_4$), which pair node n_1 with formal events 1, 2, and 4. By contrast, were we to define the relation between *N* and *EV* as a *function*, n_1 could be paired with only one formal event. A function is a special kind of relation: one in which every element in the first set is paired with only one element in the second set.

See also *Cartesian product, directed graph (digraph), function*.

Schritt/Wechsel system: Riemann's system of root-interval progressions between triads. The progressions divide into *Schritte* (steps), which link modally matched harmonies, and *Wechsel* (changes), which link modally opposite harmonies. The progressions are defined by the size and direction of motion between their Riemannian, dualistic roots. A *Gegen-* progression proceeds in a direction opposite of the generation of the triad. Recall that for Riemann, major triads are generated upward from the root, and minor triads are generated downward from the fifth. Thus, a *Quintschritt* takes c+ up to g+ (C major to G major), but °c down to °f (F minor to B♭ minor); a *Gegenquintschritt* takes c+ down to f+ (C major to F major) and °c up to °g (F minor to C minor). Riemann (1880, 7) also calls the *Gegenquintschritt* a *Dominantschritt*. (Note that this is *not* algebraically the same as Lewin's Dominant operation, which is not dualistic—it transposes *both* major and minor triads down by fifth.) The *Seitenwechsel* does not move the root, but merely alters its polarity, for example taking c+ to °c (i.e., C major to F minor). The *Gegenkleinterzwechsel*—Riemann's name for the hexatonic-polar progression—is slightly confusing, as Riemann considers minor-third progressions to proceed naturally in the direction *opposite* the triad's generation. Thus, a *Kleinterzwechsel* takes c+ down to °a (C major to D minor), while a *Gegenkleinterzwechsel* takes c+ up to °e♭ (C major to A♭ minor). For a more thorough overview of the root-interval system, see Kopp 2002, 68–74.

The 24 *Schritte* and *Wechsel* form a *dihedral group* of order 24 isomorphic to the group of neo-Riemannian operations.

Semigroup: A basic algebraic structure consisting of a *set* and a *binary composition* that allows any two elements of the set to combine to produce a third element of the set. Unlike a *group*, a semigroup only needs to satisfy two properties: closure and associativity. Put another way, a group is a special kind of semigroup, one with two additional structural properties: existence of an identity, and existence of inverses. See the *group* entry for a discussion of these four properties.

Set: A finite or infinite collection of distinct elements. The elements are distinct in that none of them occurs more than once in the set (a set that contains duplicates is called a *multiset*). If the elements of a set are considered unordered, they are enclosed in curly brackets { }. If they are ordered they are enclosed in parentheses ( ). Logicians sometimes specify that a set cannot contain itself as one of its elements, thus avoiding problems like Russell's paradox. Such logical refinements need not concern us here.

The set *B* is a *subset* of the set *A* if all of the elements of *B* are also members of *A*. Note that *B* could contain *all* of the members of *A*, and thus be indistinguishable from it. We say that *B* is a *proper subset* if it does not contain all of *A*. Given *B* as a subset of *A*, we can say conversely that *A* is a *superset* of *B*. *A* is a *proper superset* of *B* if *A* contains elements not in *B*.

In a Generalized Interval System or GIS, a set is any finite subset of elements from the space S of the GIS.

Simple transitivity: A *group* acts on a *set* in simply transitive fashion if, for any *s* and *t* in the set, there is only one element *g* in the group such that *g* takes *s* to *t*.

There are many simply transitive relationships in transformational theory. For example, the neo-Riemannian operations act on the 24 consonant triads in simply transitive fashion: given any two triads *A* and *B*, there is only one neo-Riemannian operation that will take *A* to *B*. There are nevertheless plenty of situations in transformational theory that are *not* simply transitive. A familiar one is the action of the 24 transpositions and inversions on the 12 pitch classes. Given any two pitch classes pc_1 and pc_2, there will always be both a transposition *and an inversion* that take pc_1 to pc_2.

Subgroup: A subset *H* of elements from a *group G* that satisfies all four of the conditions for a group under the initial binary composition (closure, existence of an identity, existence of inverses, associativity). The subgroup *H* will always contain the identity element of the group *G*.

Subset, superset: See *set*.

Surjection: See *function*.

Transformation: In transformational theory, a transformation is a *function* from a *set* to itself. An *operation* is a transformation that is a bijection—that is, one-to-one and onto.

  Most of the familiar transformations from atonal theory and transformational theory are in fact operations. For example, the transpositions and inversions of atonal theory are operations. T_n maps the set of twelve pcs one-to-one and onto itself, adding *n* to each pc integer. I_n also maps the set of twelve pcs one-to-one and onto itself, subtracting each pc from *n*. The neo-Riemannian transformations are operations as well, mapping the set of 24 consonant triads one-to-one and onto itself. The various resolving transformations introduced in this book are instances of transformations that are not operations—in other words, that are not one-to-one and onto.

  While all operations have inverses, transformations that are not operations do not. Operations can thus combine into *groups*, while transformations can combine only into *semigroups*.

Transformational graphs and networks: A central construction of transformational theory, meant to model dynamic relationships among musical entities. A transformational graph is a *digraph* whose arrows have been labeled with *transformations* from some *semigroup* (which may be a *group*). Lewin stipulates that the transformations on the arrows must "compose" in a certain way, so that the transformations on any two arrow paths between the same two nodes sum to the same semigroup element. Hook (2007a) has loosened this requirement (see section 3.3.4).

  A transformational network is a transformational graph whose nodes have been filled with elements from some set S, in accordance with the labels on the graph's arrows. For more on the methodology of transformational graphs and networks see section 1.3 and Chapter 3.

Transformational theory: A branch of systematic music theory that seeks to model dynamic and relational aspects of musical experience via Generalized Interval Systems (or GISes) and transformational graphs and networks. The foundational text of transformational theory is David Lewin's 1987 treatise *Generalized Musical Intervals and Transformations (GMIT)*.

Uniform Triadic Transformation: An *operation* that acts on all major triads in the same way and on all minor triads in the same way; abbreviated UTT and defined by Hook (2002). A UTT is an *ordered triple* of the form $\langle \sigma, t^+, t^- \rangle$. σ is either a plus (+), indicating preservation of mode, or a minus (–), indicating mode reversal; t^+ indicates the transposition level of an initial major triad, while t^- indicates the transposition level of an initial minor triad. For example, the UTT $\langle -, 8, 4 \rangle$ reverses the mode of a triad and transposes the result by eight semitones, if the initial triad was major, or by four semitones if the initial triad was minor. This is in fact the UTT for the hexatonic-pole transformation. There are $2 \times 12 \times 12 = 288$ UTTs. The UTT construct is eminently useful for clarifying the algebraic interactions among various species of triadic transformation (neo-Riemannian and otherwise).

WORKS CITED

All citations in the volume are in author/date format, with the sole exception of David Lewin's *Generalized Musical Intervals and Transformations*, revised ed. (New York: Oxford University Press 2007; original ed. New Haven: Yale University Press, 1987), which is cited throughout as *GMIT*.

Adorno, Theodor W. 2002. "Music, Language, and Composition." Trans. Susan Gillespie. In *Essays on Music*, ed. Richard D. Leppert, pp. 113–26. Berkeley: University of California Press.

Agawu, Victor Kofi. 1992. Review of *Music and Discourse: Toward a Semiology of Music*, by Jean-Jacques Nattiez, trans. Carolyn Abbate. *Music & Letters* 73: 317–19.

———. 1994. "Ambiguity in Tonal Music: A Preliminary Study." In *Theory, Analysis, and Meaning in Music*, ed. Anthony Pople, pp. 86–107. Cambridge: Cambridge University Press.

———. 2003. *Representing African Music: Postcolonial Notes, Queries, Positions*. New York: Routledge.

———. 2010. "Tonality as a Colonizing Force in Africa." Paper presented (in absentia) at the conference Music/Race/Empire, University of Chicago, April 21, 2010.

Agmon, Eytan. 1986. "Diatonicism, Chromaticism, and Enharmonicism: A Study in Cognition and Perception." Ph.D. diss., City University of New York.

———. 1989. "A Mathematical Model of the Diatonic System." *Journal of Music Theory* 33: 1–25.

Aldwell, Edward, and Carl Schachter. 2003. *Harmony and Voice Leading*, 3rd ed. Belmont, CA: Schirmer.

Alphonce, Bo. 1988. Review of *Generalized Musical Intervals and Transformations*, by David Lewin. *Intégral* 2: 161–77.

Bailey, Robert, ed. 1985. *Wagner: Prelude and Transfiguration from* Tristan and Isolde. New York: Norton.

Bamberger, Jeanne. 1986. "Cognitive Issues in the Development of Musically Gifted Children." In *Conceptions of Giftedness*, ed. Robert J. Sternberg and Janet E. Davidson, pp. 388–413. New York: Cambridge University Press.

———. 1991. *The Mind behind the Musical Ear: How Children Develop Musical Intelligence*. Cambridge, MA: Harvard University Press.

Beiche, Michael. 1992. "Tonalität." In *Handwörterbuch der musikalischen Terminologie*, ed. Hans Heinrich Eggebrecht. Stuttgart: Franz Steiner.

Bellman, Jonathan. 1991. "Toward a Lexicon for the *Style hongrois*." *Journal of Musicology* 9: 214–37.

Bernard, Jonathan. 1987. *The Music of Edgard Varèse*. New Haven: Yale University Press.

Booth, Wayne. 1979. *Critical Understanding: The Powers and Limits of Pluralism*. Chicago: University of Chicago Press.

Boretz, Benjamin. 1995. *Meta-Variations: Studies in the Foundations of Musical Thought.* Originally published serially in *Perspectives of New Music,* 1969–73. Red Hook, NY: Open Space.

Brinkman, Alexander R. 1986. "A Binomial Representation of Pitch for Computer Processing of Musical Data." *Music Theory Spectrum* 8: 44–57.

Brown, Matthew. 2005. *Explaining Tonality: Schenkerian Theory and Beyond.* Rochester, NY: University of Rochester Press.

Brown, Matthew, David Headlam, and Douglas Dempster. 1997. "The ♯IV(♭V) Hypothesis: Testing the Limits of Schenker's Theory of Tonality." *Music Theory Spectrum* 19: 155–83.

Browne, Richmond. 1981. "Tonal Implications of the Diatonic Set." *In Theory Only* 5, issue 6/7: 3–21.

Burnham, Scott. 1994. "Mozart's *felix culpa: Così fan tutte* and the Irony of Beauty." *Musical Quarterly* 78: 77–98.

Cadwallader, Allen. 1988. "Foreground Motivic Ambiguity: Its Clarification at Middleground Levels in Selected Late Piano Pieces of Johannes Brahms." *Music Analysis* 7: 59–91.

Cadwallader, Allen, and David Gagné. 2010. *Analysis of Tonal Music: A Schenkerian Approach.* 3rd ed. New York: Oxford University Press.

Cadwallader, Allen, and William Pastille. 1999. "Schenker's Unpublished Work with the Music of Johannes Brahms." In *Schenker Studies 2,* ed. Carl Schachter and Hedi Siegel, pp. 26–46. Cambridge: Cambridge University Press.

Callender, Clifton, Ian Quinn, and Dmitri Tymoczko. 2008. "Generalized Voice-Leading Spaces." *Science* 320: 346–48.

Caplin, William. 1998. *Classical Form: A Theory of Formal Functions for the Music of Haydn, Mozart, and Beethoven.* New York: Oxford University Press.

Cavell, Stanley. 1999. "Benjamin and Wittgenstein: Signals and Affinities." *Critical Inquiry* 25: 235–46.

———. 2002. "A Philosopher Goes to the Movies: Conversation with Stanley Cavell." http://globetrotter.berkeley.edu/people2/Cavell/cavell-con4.html. Accessed December 7, 2009.

Chartrand, Gary. 1977. *Introductory Graph Theory.* New York: Dover.

Cherlin, Michael. 1993. "On Adapting Theoretical Models from the Work of David Lewin." *Indiana Theory Review* 14: 19–43.

Christensen, Thomas. 1993. *Rameau and Musical Thought in the Enlightenment.* Cambridge: Cambridge University Press.

Clampitt, David. 1998. "Alternative Interpretations of Some Measures from *Parsifal.*" *Journal of Music Theory* 42: 321–34.

Clough, John. 1989. Review of *Generalized Musical Intervals and Transformations,* by David Lewin. *Music Theory Spectrum* 11: 226–31.

Clough, John, and Gerald Myerson. 1985. "Variety and Multiplicity in Diatonic Systems." *Journal of Music Theory* 29: 249–70.

Clough, John, and Jack Douthett. 1991. "Maximally Even Sets." *Journal of Music Theory* 35: 93–173.

Cohen, David. 2001. " 'The Imperfect Seeks Its Perfection': Harmonic Progression, Directed Motion, and Aristotelian Physics." *Music Theory Spectrum* 23: 139–69.

Cohn, Richard. 1996. "Maximally Smooth Cycles, Hexatonic Systems, and the Analysis of Late-Romantic Triadic Progressions." *Music Analysis* 15: 9–40.

———. 1997. "Neo-Riemannian Operations, Parsimonious Trichords, and Their *Tonnetz* Representations." *Journal of Music Theory* 41: 1–66.

———. 1998. "Introduction to Neo-Riemannian Theory: A Survey and a Historical Perspective." *Journal of Music Theory* 42: 167–80.

———. 2004. "Uncanny Resemblances: Tonal Signification in the Freudian Age." *Journal of the American Musicological Society* 57: 285–323.

———. 2006. "Hexatonic Poles and the Uncanny in *Parsifal*." *Opera Quarterly* 22: 230–48.

Cone, Edward T. 1974. *The Composer's Voice*. Berkeley: University of California Press.

Cook, Nicholas. 2001. "Theorizing Musical Meaning." *Music Theory Spectrum* 23: 170–95.

Daverio, John. 1993. *Nineteenth-Century Music and the German Romantic Ideology*. New York: Schirmer.

Dennett, Daniel. 1990. "Quining Qualia." In *Mind and Cognition*, ed. W. Lycan, pp. 519–48. Oxford: Blackwell.

———. 1991. *Consciousness Explained*. Boston: Little, Brown.

Deppert, Heinrich. 1987. "Anmerkungen zu Alfred Dürr." *Musiktheorie* 2: 107–8.

Douthett, Jack, and Peter Steinbach. 1998. "Parsimonious Graphs: A Study in Parsimony, Contextual Transformations, and Modes of Limited Transposition." *Journal of Music Theory* 42: 241–63.

Dubiel, Joseph. 1990. "'When You Are a Beethoven': Kinds of Rules in Schenker's *Counterpoint*." *Journal of Music Theory* 34: 291–340.

———. 1994. "Three Contradictory Criteria in a Work of Brahms." *Brahms Studies* 1: 81–110.

Dürr, Alfred. 1986. "Ein Dokument aus dem Unterricht Bachs?" *Musiktheorie* 1: 163–70.

Emerson, Ralph Waldo. 1993. *Self-Reliance and Other Essays*. New York: Dover.

Epstein, David. 1979. *Beyond Orpheus: Studies in Musical Structure*. Cambridge, MA: MIT Press.

Ford, Charles. 1991. *Così? Sexual Politics in Mozart's Operas*. Manchester: Manchester University Press.

Fux, Johann Joseph. 1725. *Gradus ad Parnassum*. Vienna. Facsimile. New York: Broude Brothers, 1966.

Gjerdingen, Robert O. 1988. *A Classic Turn of Phrase: Music and the Psychology of Convention*. Philadelphia: University of Pennsylvania Press.

———. 2007. *Music in the Galant Style*. New York: Oxford University Press.

Gollin, Edward. 2000. "Representations of Space and Conceptions of Distance in Transformational Music Theories." Ph.D. diss., Harvard University.

Goodman, Nelson. 1951. *The Structure of Appearance*. Cambridge, MA: Harvard University Press.

Hall, Rachel. 2009. Review of *Generalized Musical Intervals and Transformations* and *Musical Form and Transformation: Four Analytic Essays*, by David Lewin. *Journal of the American Musicological Society* 62: 206–22.

Harary, Frank. 1969. *Graph Theory*. Reading, MA: Addison-Wesley.

Harary, Frank, Robert Z. Norman, and Dorwin Cartwright. 1965. *Structural Models: An Introduction to the Theory of Directed Graphs*. New York: Wiley.

Harrison, Daniel. 1988. "Some Group Properties of Triple Counterpoint and Their Influence on Compositions by J. S. Bach." *Journal of Music Theory* 32: 23–49.

———. 1994. *Harmonic Function in Chromatic Music: A Renewed Dualist Theory and an Account of Its Precedents*. Chicago: University of Chicago Press.

———. 2002. "Nonconformist Notions of Nineteenth-Century Enharmonicism." *Music Analysis* 21: 115–60.

———. 2011. "Three Short Essays on Neo-Riemannian Theory." In *The Oxford Handbook of Neo-Riemannian Music Theories*, ed. Alexander Rehding and Edward Gollin. New York: Oxford University Press.

Hasty, Christopher. 1987. "An Intervallic Definition of Set Class." *Journal of Music Theory* 31: 183–204.

Hatten, Robert. 2004. *Interpreting Musical Gestures, Topics, and Tropes: Mozart, Beethoven, Schubert*. Bloomington: Indiana University Press.

Hepokoski, James. 1983. *Giuseppe Verdi: Falstaff*. Cambridge: Cambridge University Press.

Hepokoski, James, and Warren Darcy. 2006. *Elements of Sonata Theory: Norms, Types, and Deformations*. New York: Oxford University Press.

Hibberd, Lloyd. 1961. "'Tonality' and Related Problems in Terminology." *Music Review* 22: 13–20.

Hook, Julian. 2002. "Uniform Triadic Transformations." *Journal of Music Theory* 46: 57–126.

———. 2006. "An Integrated Transformational Theory of Diatonic and Chromatic Harmony." Paper presented at the annual meeting of the Society for Music Theory, Los Angeles, CA.

———. 2007a. "Cross-Type Transformations and the Path Consistency Condition." *Music Theory Spectrum* 29: 1–39.

———. 2007b. Review of *Generalized Musical Intervals and Transformations* and *Musical Form and Transformation: Four Analytic Essays*, by David Lewin. *Intégral* 21: 155–90.

———. 2007c. "Enharmonic Systems: A Theory of Key Signatures, Enharmonic Equivalence, and Diatonicism." *Journal of Mathematics and Music* 1: 99–120.

———. 2008. "Signature Transformations." In *Music Theory and Mathematics: Chords, Collections, and Transformations*, ed. Jack Douthett, Martha M. Hyde, and Charles J. Smith, pp. 137–60. Rochester, NY: University of Rochester Press.

Huneker, James. 1911. *Franz Liszt*. New York: C. Scribner's Sons.

Huron, David. 2006. *Sweet Anticipation: Music and the Psychology of Expectation*. Cambridge, MA: MIT Press.

Hyer, Brian. 1989. "Tonal Intuitions in *Tristan und Isolde*." Ph.D. diss., Yale University.

———. 1995. "Reimag(in)ing Riemann." *Journal of Music Theory* 39: 101–38.

———. 2002. "Tonality." In the *Cambridge History of Western Music Theory*, ed. Thomas Christensen, pp. 726–52. Cambridge: Cambridge University Press.

James, William. 1939. *Talks to Teachers on Psychology*. New York: Henry Holt.

Johnson, Timothy. 2003. *Foundations of Diatonic Theory: A Mathematically Based Approach to Music Fundamentals*. Emeryville, CA: Key College.

Keiler, Allan R. 1981. "Music as Metalanguage: Rameau's Fundamental Bass." In *Music Theory: Special Topics*, ed. Richmond Browne, pp. 83–100. New York: Academic Press.

Kerman, Joseph. 1956. *Opera as Drama*. New York: Knopf.

———. 2005. *The Art of Fugue: Bach Fugues for Keyboard, 1715–50*. Berkeley: University of California Press.

Keys, Ivor. 1974. *Brahms Chamber Music*. London: British Broadcasting.

Kirnberger, Johann Philipp. 1982. *The Art of Strict Musical Composition*. Trans. David Beach and Jürgen Thym. Original ed. 1771–79. New Haven: Yale University Press.

Klumpenhouwer, Henry. 1994. "Some Remarks on the Use of Riemann Transformations." *Music Theory Online* 0.9. http://mto.societymusictheory.org/issues/mto.94.0.9/mto.94.0.9.klumpenhouwer.art. Accessed December 7, 2009.

———. 1998. "Network Analysis and Webern's Opus 27/III." *Tijdschrift voor Muziektheorie* 3: 24–37.

———. 2006. "In Order to Stay Asleep as Observers: The Nature and Origins of Anti-Cartesianism in Lewin's *Generalized Musical Intervals and Transformations*." *Music Theory Spectrum* 28: 277–89.

Kopp, David. 2002. *Chromatic Transformations in Nineteenth-Century Music*. Cambridge: Cambridge University Press.

Korsyn, Kevin. 1988. "Schenker and Kantian Epistemology." *Theoria* 3: 1–58.

Kosovsky, Robert. 1990. *The Oster Collection: Papers of Heinrich Schenker.* New York: New York Public Library.

Krebs, Harald. 1999. *Fantasy Pieces: Metrical Dissonance in the Music of Robert Schumann.* New York: Oxford University Press.

Krumhansl, Carol. 2004. "The Cognition of Tonality—as We Know It Today." *Journal of New Music Research* 33: 253–68.

Krumhansl, Carol, and Fred Lerdahl. 2007. "Modeling Tonal Tension." *Music Perception* 24: 329–66.

Kurth, Ernst. 1991. *Selected Writings.* Ed. and trans. Lee A. Rothfarb. Cambridge: Cambridge University Press.

Ledbetter, David. 2002. *Bach's Well-Tempered Clavier: The 48 Preludes and Fugues.* New Haven: Yale University Press.

Lerdahl, Fred. 2001. *Tonal Pitch Space.* New York: Oxford University Press.

Lester, Joel. 1992. *Compositional Theory in the Eighteenth Century.* Cambridge, MA: Harvard University Press.

———. 1995. "Robert Schumann and Sonata Forms." *19th Century Music* 18: 189–210.

Lewin, David. 1977. "Forte's Interval Vector, My Interval Function, and Regener's Common-Note Function." *Journal of Music Theory* 21: 194–237.

———. 1982. "A Formal Theory of Generalized Tonal Functions." *Journal of Music Theory* 26: 23–60.

———. 1982–83. "Transformational Techniques in Atonal and Other Music Theories." *Perspectives of New Music* 21: 312–71.

———. 1987. *Generalized Musical Intervals and Transformations.* New Haven: Yale University Press. 2nd ed., New York: Oxford University Press, 2007. Cited throughout as *GMIT.*

———. 1990. "Klumpenhouwer Networks and Some Isographies that Involve Them." *Music Theory Spectrum* 12: 83–120.

———. 1993. *Musical Form and Transformation: Four Analytic Essays.* New Haven: Yale University Press. 2nd ed., New York: Oxford University Press, 2007.

———. 1995. "Generalized Interval Systems for Babbitt's Lists, and for Schoenberg's String Trio." *Music Theory Spectrum* 17: 81–118.

———. 1997. "Conditions under Which, in a Commutative GIS, Two 3-Element Sets Can Span the Same Assortment of GIS-Intervals; Notes on the Non-Commutative GIS in This Connection." *Intégral* 11: 37–66.

———. 1998a. " Notes on the Opening of the F♯ minor Fugue from WTC I." *Journal of Music Theory* 42: 235–39.

———. 1998b. "The D Major Fugue Subject from WTCII: Spatial Saturation?" *Music Theory Online* 4.4. http://mto.societymusictheory.org/issues/mto.98.4.4/mto.98.4.4.lewin.html. Accessed December 7, 2009.

———. 2000–2001. "All Possible GZ-Related 4-Element Pairs of Sets, in All Possible Commutative Groups, Found and Categorized." *Intégral* 14/15: 77–120.

———. 2006. *Studies in Music with Text.* New York: Oxford University Press.

Lorenz, Alfred. 1924. *Das Geheimnis der Form bei Richard Wagner,* Band I: *Der Musikalische Aufbau des Bühnenfestspieles* Der Ring des Nibelungen. Berlin: Max Hesse.

———. 1933. *Das Geheimnis der Form bei Richard Wagner,* Band IV: *Der Musikalische Aufbau von Richard Wagners* Parsifal. Berlin: Max Hesse.

Mann, Alfred. 1958. *The Study of Fugue.* London: Faber and Faber.

McClary, Susan. 1991. *Feminine Endings: Music, Gender, and Sexuality.* Minneapolis: University of Minnesota Press.

———. 2001. *Conventional Wisdom: The Content of Musical Form.* Berkeley: University of California Press.

McGlathery, James. 1998. *Wagner's Operas and Desire.* New York: P. Lang.

Mooney, Michael Kevin. 1996. "The 'Table of Relations' and Music Psychology in Hugo Riemann's Harmonic Theory." Ph.D. diss., Columbia University.

Morgan, Robert. 1998. "Symmetrical Form and Common-Practice Tonality." *Music Theory Spectrum* 20: 1–47.

Moseley, Roger. 2010. "Brahms vs. Joachim: Irreconcilable Differences in the Double Concerto, op. 102." Unpublished MS.

Musgrave, Michael. 1985. *The Music of Brahms.* Boston: Routledge.

Narmour, Eugene. 1990. *The Analysis and Cognition of Basic Melodic Structures: The Implication-Realization Model.* Chicago: University of Chicago Press.

Nattiez, Jean-Jacques. 1990. *Music and Discourse: Toward a Semiology of Music.* Trans. Carolyn Abbate. Princeton: Princeton University Press.

Notley, Margaret. 1999. "Late-Nineteenth-Century Chamber Music and the Cult of the Classical Adagio." *19th Century Music* 23: 33–61.

Rahn, John. 2001. *Music Inside Out: Going Too Far in Musical Essays.* Amsterdam: G+B Arts International.

Rameau, Jean-Philippe. 1722. *Traité de l'harmonie.* Paris: Ballard.

———. 1737. *Génération harmonique ou traité de musique théorique et pratique.* Paris: Prault fils.

Rehding, Alexander. 2003. *Hugo Riemann and the Birth of Modern Musical Thought.* Cambridge: Cambridge University Press.

Reilly, Edward R. 1982. *Gustav Mahler and Guido Adler: Records of a Friendship.* Cambridge: Cambridge University Press.

Renwick, William. 1995. *Analyzing Fugue: A Schenkerian Approach.* Stuyvesant, NY: Pendragon.

Riemann, Hugo. 1880. *Skizze einer neuen Methode der Harmonielehre.* Leipzig: Breitkopf & Härtel.

———. 1882. "Die Natur der Harmonik." *Waldersees Sammlung musikalischer Vorträge* 4: 159–90.

———. 1893. *Harmony Simplified.* London: Augener.

———. 1917. *Handbuch der Harmonielehre.* 6th ed. Leipzig: Breitkopf & Härtel.

———. 1920. *Ludwig van Beethovens sämtliche Klavier-Solosonaten,* vol. III. Berlin: Max Hesse.

———. 1967. *Präludien und Studien I–III.* Hildesheim: Georg Olms.

Rings, Steven. 2006. "Tonality and Transformation." Ph.D. diss., Yale University.

———. 2007. "Perspectives on Tonality and Transformation in Schubert's Impromptu in E♭ major, D. 899, no. 2." *Journal of Schenkerian Studies* 2: 33–63.

———. 2011a. "Riemannian Analytical Values, Paleo- and Neo-." In *The Oxford Handbook of Neo-Riemannian Music Theories,* ed. Alexander Rehding and Edward Gollin. New York: Oxford University Press.

———. 2011b. "The Learned Self: Artifice in Brahms's Late Intermezzi." In *Expressive Intersections in Brahms: Essays in Analysis and Meaning,* ed. Heather Platt and Peter Smith. Bloomington: Indiana University Press.

Roeder, John. 2009. "Constructing Transformational Signification: Gesture and Agency in Bartók's Scherzo, op. 14, no. 2, measures 1–32." *Music Theory Online* 15.1. http://mto.societymusictheory.org/issues/mto.09.15.1/mto.09.15.1.roeder_signification.html. Accessed December 7, 2009.

Rosen, Charles. 1997. *The Classical Style.* Exp. ed. New York: Norton.

———. 2004. *Piano Notes: The World of the Pianist.* New York: Simon and Schuster.

Rothfarb, Lee A. 2002. "Energetics." In the *Cambridge History of Western Music Theory*, ed. Thomas Christensen, pp. 927–55. Cambridge: Cambridge University Press.

Rothstein, William. 1981. "Rhythm and the Theory of Structural Levels." Ph.D. diss., Yale University.

———. 1991. "On Implied Tones." *Music Analysis* 10: 289–321.

———. 2001. Review of articles on Schenkerian theory in the *New Grove Dictionary of Music and Musicians*, 2nd ed., ed. Stanley Sadie. *Journal of Music Theory* 45: 204–27.

Samarotto, Frank. 2003. "Treading the Limits of Tonal Coherence: Transformation vs. Prolongation in Selected Works of Johannes Brahms." Paper presented at the annual meeting of the Society for Music Theory, Madison, WI.

———. 2005. "Schenker's 'Free Forms of Interruption' and the Strict: Toward a General Theory of Interruption." Paper presented at the annual meeting of the Society for Music Theory, Boston, MA.

Sárosi, Bálint. 1978. *Gypsy Music.* Budapest: Corvina.

Satyendra, Ramon. 2004. "An Informal Introduction to Some Formal Concepts from Lewin's Transformational Theory." *Journal of Music Theory* 48: 99–141.

Schachter, Carl. 1999. *Unfoldings: Essays in Schenkerian Theory and Analysis.* Ed. Joseph N. Straus. New York: Oxford University Press.

Schenker, Heinrich. 1926. *Das Meisterwerk in der Musik*, vol. I. Munich: Drei Masken.

———. 1954. *Harmony.* Trans. Elizabeth Mann Borgese. Chicago: University of Chicago Press.

———. 1956. *Der freie Satz.* 2nd ed. Ed. Oswald Jonas. Vienna: Universal Edition.

———. 1969. *Five Graphic Music Analyses.* New York: Dover.

———. 1979. *Free Composition.* Trans. and ed. of Schenker 1956 by Ernst Oster. New York: Schirmer.

———. 1987. *Counterpoint*, vols. I and II. Trans. John Rothgeb and Jürgen Thym, ed. John Rothgeb. Ann Arbor, MI: Musicalia.

———. 1996. *Masterwork in Music*, vol. II. Ed. William Drabkin. English translations of Schenker 1926. Cambridge: Cambridge University Press.

Schoenberg, Arnold. 1978. *Theory of Harmony.* Trans. Roy E. Carter. Berkeley: University of California Press.

Siciliano, Michael. 2002. "Neo-Riemannian Transformations and the Harmony of Franz Schubert." Ph.D. diss., University of Chicago.

Sisman, Elaine. 1990. "Brahms and the Variation Canon." *19th Century Music* 14: 132–53.

Smith, Peter. 1997. "Brahms and Motivic 6/3 Chords." *Music Analysis* 16: 175–217.

———. 2000. "Outer-Voice Conflicts: Their Analytical Challenges and Artistic Consequences." *Journal of Music Theory* 44: 1–43.

———. 2006. "You Reap What You Sow: Some Instances of Rhythmic and Harmonic Ambiguity in Brahms." *Music Theory Spectrum* 28: 57–97.

Snarrenberg, Robert. 1997. *Schenker's Interpretive Practice.* Cambridge: Cambridge University Press.

Sokolowski, Robert. 2000. *Introduction to Phenomenology.* Cambridge: Cambridge University Press.

Straus, Joseph N. 2005. *Introduction to Post-Tonal Theory.* 3rd ed. Upper Saddle River, NJ: Pearson.

Swafford, Jan. 1998. *Johannes Brahms.* New York: Vintage.

Taruskin, Richard. 1997. *Defining Russia Musically: Historical and Hermeneutical Essays.* Princeton: Princeton University Press.

Temperley, David. 1999. "The Question of Purpose in Music Theory." *Current Musicology* 66: 66–85.

Thomson, William. 1999. *Tonality in Music: A General Theory.* San Marino, CA: Everett.

Tovey, Donald Francis. 1949. *The Main Stream of Music and Other Essays*. New York: Oxford University Press.

Trudeau, Richard J. 1993. *Introduction to Graph Theory*. New York: Dover.

Tymoczko, Dmitri. 2006. "The Geometry of Musical Chords." *Science* 313: 72–74.

———. 2008. "Lewin, Intervals, and Transformations: A Comment on Hook." *Music Theory Spectrum* 30: 164–68.

———. 2009. "Generalizing Musical Intervals." *Journal of Music Theory* 53: 227–54.

———. 2011. *A Geometry of Music: Harmony and Counterpoint in the Extended Common Practice*. New York: Oxford University Press.

Vos, Piet. 2000. "Tonality Induction: Theoretical Problems and Dilemmas." *Music Perception* 17: 403–16.

Wen, Eric. 1999. "Bass-Line Articulations of the *Urlinie*." In *Schenker Studies 2*, ed. Carl Schachter and Hedi Siegel, pp. 276–97. Cambridge: Cambridge University Press.

Whitehead, Alfred North. 1967. *Adventures of Ideas*. New York: Simon and Schuster.

Wollenberg, Susan. 1975. "The Jupiter Theme: New Light on Its Creation." *Musical Times* 116: 781–83.

Wright, Edmond, ed. 2008. *The Case for Qualia*. Cambridge, MA: MIT Press.

Zbikowski, Lawrence M. 2002. *Conceptualizing Music: Cognitive Structure, Theory, and Analysis*. Cambridge: Cambridge University Press.

Žižek, Slavoj, and Mladen Dolar. 2002. *Opera's Second Death*. New York: Routledge.

Zuckerkandl, Victor. 1956. *Sound and Symbol*. New York: Pantheon.

INDEX

absolute pitch, 42n1, 94, 117
addition, 32–33
    and GISes, 19, 21, 23, 29
    and intervals, 12–13, 15
Adorno, Theodor W., 222
Agawu, Kofi, 2n8, 218–20
Agmon, Eytan, 45, 47n15, 48n18
apperceptions, 4, 41–44, 49, 220–21
    and analysis, 36–40, 125
    and culture, 17–19, 41, 222
    and Lewin's "intuition," 17–19
    improbable, 53–54, 74
    multiplicity of, 20–25, 46, 76–78,
        87–88, 125
    See also intention, tonal; qualia, tonal
arrows, 11, 16, 99, 103–5
    in digraphs, 110–15
    in event networks, 141–42
    spanning, 144–46
    and the transformational attitude,
        24–27
associativity (in groups), 13, 27
atonality, 1–2, 28, 43, 89, 114

Bach, Johann Sebastian
    Art of the Fugue, BWV 1080, 89–90
    Cello Suite no. 1 in G major, BWV
        1007, 21–24, 35–36
    Fugue in C minor, WTC I, BWV 847,
        157–58
    Fugue in C♯ minor, WTC I, BWV 849,
        48, 74–5, 153
    Fugue in D♯ minor, WTC I, BWV
        853, 64–65
    Fugue in E major, WTC II, BWV 878,
        142–43, 151–69
    Goldberg Variations, BWV 988,
        68–69

    key areas in, 152–53
    Prelude in C major, WTC I, BWV 846,
        48, 74
    Prelude in D minor, WTC I,
        BWV 851, 157
Bamberger, Jeanne, 140
Bartók, Béla, 20–21
Beethoven, Ludwig van
    Piano Concerto no. 3 in C minor, op.
        37, 64–66
    Piano Sonata no. 21 "Waldstein" in C
        major, op. 53, 102, 121
    Piano Sonata no. 23 "Appassionata" in
        F minor, op. 57, 102
    Piano Sonata no. 32 in C minor, op.
        111, 54
    Symphony no. 5 in C minor, op. 67, 20
    Symphony no. 9 in D minor, op. 125,
        128
Bellman, Jonathan, 204, 209
binary composition, 12, 27
Brahms, Johannes, 1, 5–6, 148
    Intermezzo in A major, op. 118, no. 2,
        185–202
    Intermezzo in B♭ minor, op. 117, no. 2,
        81n50, 94
    Intermezzo in E minor, op. 119, no. 2,
        129–34
    Piano Concerto in D minor, op. 15,
        124–25, 127–28
    String Quintet in G major, op. 111,
        203–20
    Symphony no. 4 in E minor, op. 98, 53
Brinkman, Alexander, 45, 47n15, 82n15
Burnham, Scott, 174n5, 181, 182n10

Cadwallader, Allen, 185, 198n11, 199n12
Callender, Clifton, 1n3, 11n4

Caplin, William, 34n49, 173
cartesian product, 15
Cavell, Stanley, 18
centers, tonal, 3, 5, 107–10, 144
    and networks, 113–14, 122–23
    and Riemannian functions, 117
Chopin, Frédéric
    Preludes, op. 28, 62, 146–47
    See also intention, tonal; networks,
        oriented; tonality
chords, 66, 87–88, 123, 175–80
    and sets, 55–56, 94
    and tonal hearing, 107, 109, 117
chroma, pitch, 44–46
    and key, 71
    and pivots, 58, 66, 78–80
    and qualia, 64, 78–80, 192
closure (in groups), 12, 27
Clough, John, ixn1, 45, 153n5
cognition, 41n1, 42–43, 106, 119.
        See also apperception
Cohn, Richard, 1, 78n48, 83n54, 88n59,
        228
commutativity, 14
consonance, 3, 47, 56, 79
    apparent, 119, 121, 130
culture. *See* apperception

Da Ponte, Lorenzo, 171, 173–74, 181–82,
        184
Debussy, Claude, 20–21
descriptive (and suggestive) theory, 43.
        See also pluralism, methodological
digraphs, oriented, 110–16, 142–44
    tonal interpretation of, 113–14,
        117–19
Dolar, Mladen, 184
double emploi (Rameau), 102, 105
Douthett, Jack, 45, 121n36
Dubiel, Joseph, 124n39, 145n61

Emerson, Ralph Waldo, 18
enharmonicism, 44, 47–49. *See also*
        pivot
esthesic level, 3, 36–39. *See also*
        apperception

Ferrando (Così fan tutte), 171, 177,
        181–84
Fétis, François-Joseph, 2n8, 117

ficta, 155, 161–62
Fischer, J.C.F., 151–52, 166n16
Forte, Allen, 56
Froberger, Johann Jacob, 151–52, 156
functions, 15–16, 25, 51
    Riemannian (*See* Riemannian theory)
fundamental bass, 190–96
Fux, Johann Joseph, 151–52, 156, 161

gamelan, 20–21, 152
generalized interval systems (GISes),
        10–24, 36–37
    and Cartesian dualism, 16–17, 24
    and distance, 13–14, 28–29
    formal limitations, 19–20
    GIS statements, 11–12, 15–16, 21,
        28, 74
    for heard scale degrees, 44–99, 104
        formal definition, 74
    and oriented networks, 122–25
    introduction to, 11–16
    and transformation networks, 25,
        27–29
geometrical music theory, 1, 11n4, 20, 52
Gjerdingen, Robert, 43, 158n11
Gollin, Edward, 14n15, 54n23, 110n20,
        141
graphs, transformation, 25, 98–99,
        115–16
    operation, 25, 115–21
    oriented, 110–16
    realizability, 99, 115, 119
    See also digraphs; networks,
        kinetic aspects
groups, 10, 12–14, 110
    canonical, 93–95
    commutative and noncommutative, 14
    direct product group, 47
    isomorphic, 14
    shape, 14, 23n36
Guidonian theory, 45, 158

Harrison, Daniel, 13, 76n45, 136–38
    and accumulative analysis, 86n58
    and harmonic "attitude," 114n26
    and Riemannian syntax, 116n31
    and transformational
        methodology, 104n6
    and voice-leading
        accompaniments, 76n47

hexachordal mutation. *See* Guidonian
  theory
hexatonicism, 83–84, 121–22
Hook, Julian, 22n34, 72n41, 99
  and path-consistency condition,
    99n73, 113n23, 115, 119
  skepticism regarding transformational
    attitude, 10n3, 104n6
  See also Uniform triadic transformations
Huron, David, 10n3, 41n1, 42
Hyer, Brian, 1–3, 101n1, 106n10,
  108n14

Identity element (in groups), 12–13, 27
IFUNC, 56–57
Inganno, Fuxian, 157
intention, tonal, 5, 43, 104–10, 218–20
  asymmetry of, 111–12
  and graphs/networks, 113–14, 122–25,
    144
  historical resonances, 107–10
  vs. qualia, 124–25
  and Riemannian functions, 116–21
  and Schenkerian theory, 144–48
  See also apperception
intervals, 2, 19, 46–49, 122
  directed, 12, 50–54
  generalized, 11–16, 19–21
  as group elements, 10, 13, 17, 23, 45,
    53, 93
  intervallic vs. transformational
    attitude, 10–11, 16–17, 27–29
  just, 23, 192
  modulatory, 66–71
  multiplicity of, 20–24, 37
  as paths, 51–54, 186–88
  simple and compound, 52–54
  size and direction of, 13–14
  See also generalized interval system;
    IFUNC; inverse; pivots
intuitions, 17–19, 21
  kinetic, 101, 104, 131–33, 147, 186–88
  See also apperception
inverse
  in groups, 13, 26–27
  interval labels, 50–54, 60
inversions, 89–95, 98–99, 198–99, 206–9,
  218–19
  definitions, 89
  durational, 164

James, William, 18n26
Kerman, Joseph, 152, 166, 184
key, 71–76
  modally mixed, 75–76
Kirnberger, Johann Philipp, 175
Kittler, Friedrich, 136
Klumpenhouwer, Henry, 17n22, 27–28,
  116n31
Krebs, Harald, 193, 196
Kurth, Ernst, 78n48, 88, 104

Lewin, David, 10, 12, 14, 142
  on Cartesian dualism, 16–17, 24,
    27–28, 104
  on formal/figural networks, 140
  on intuitions, 17–19, 21
  on musical space, 24, 37, 104
  and neo-Riemannian theory,
    1, 101
  See also transformational attitude;
    transformational theory
Liszt, Franz, 55, 209
  Il penseroso, 78–81, 192
Littera/vox pairing. *See* Guidonian
  theory
Lorenz, Alfred, 87, 138n51

Mahler, Gustav
  Das Lied von der Erde, 95–98
mapping. *See* function
Mendelssohn, Felix
  Lied ohne Worte, op. 19b, no. 1,
    90–93, 99
mind, philosophy of, 18n26, 41, 43.
    See also apperception
mode, 74–76
modulation, 58–71. *See also* interval,
    modulatory; pivot
Molino, Jean, 36
Mozart, Wolfgang Amadeus, 148
  Così fan tutte, 171–84
  The Magic Flute, 50–52
  Piano Sonata in B♭ major, K. 333,
    62–64
  Piano Sonata in C major, K. 309,
    122–26
  String Quartet "Dissonance" in C
    major, K. 465, 102
Myerson, Gerald, 45, 153n5

Nattiez, Jean-Jacques, 3, 36
Neo-Riemannian theory, 1–2, 4, 14n16,
    19–20, 35
    analysis of Liszt, 78–79
    analysis of Wagner, 83–84
    and network design, 104, 141 (*See also*
        networks, event; networks, spatial)
    and Riemannian theory, 119, 121,
        128–30
    and tonal concepts, 88, 101
networks, transformational, 11, 25, 27,
    98–99
    additive and proportional, 32–34
    event, 102, 121, 140–44
    figural (*See* networks, event)
    formal (*See* networks, spatial)
    and GIS statements, 27–29
    kinetic aspects, 103, 111, 114–15, 128,
        133, 156, 165–66, 206
    Klumpenhouwer, 28
    oriented, 110–16, 122–25, 218–19
        examples, 145, 178, 193
    and temporality, 113, 142, 207 (*See
        also* networks, event)
    spatial, 140–44, 153–54, 210, 214–17
Nietzsche, Friedrich, 136
Node, 140–41
    barbell, 142–44
    classes and tonal attitudes, 114–15,
        123
    long, 142
    node/arrow system (*See* digraphs)
    root, 101–2, 107, 111, 113–15, 123,
        144

operations, 25–26, 115–18
    diatonic and chromatic, 98–99
    dominant and subdominant, 101–5
    See also graphs, operation
ordered pair, 12, 15, 44–47, 72n42
Oster, Ernst, 147–48

Palestrina, Giovanni Pierluigi da, 18, 156
Passus duriusculus, 160–61
paths. *See* interval
perception. *See* apperception; cognition
pluralism, methodological, 4, 35–40,
    221–22
pivots, 58–66, 137–38, 190
    skewed, 66–68, 162

qualia, tonal, 41–49, 56, 88, 214
    and chroma, 64, 78–80, 192
    vs. intention, 124–25
    and key, 71
    shifting, 48, 59–60, 66, 76, 159–60, 189
    See also apperception; pivot
Quinn, Ian, 1n3, 11n4

Rahn, John, 36
Rameau, Jean-Philippe, 102, 104, 192,
    194, 211
    on tonality, 107–8
Rehding, Alexander, 107n13, 108,
    116n31, 117
relational hearing, 10, 20, 105. *See also*
    intention, tonal
Rémenyi, Ede, 209
resolution. *See* transformations,
    resolving
Riemann, Hugo, 66, 84n55, 107–9
Riemannian theory, 106–9
    analysis of Brahms, 129–34, 205–7
    harmonic functions, 66, 116–22
    and neo-Riemannian theory, 129–30,
        141
Roeder, John, 140

Samarotto, Frank, 2n5, 146–47
Sárosi, Bálint, 204
Satyendra, Ramon, 9, 28, 29n40, 104n6,
    224
scale degree
    GIS for, 44–99
    as heard, 41–43, 122–26 (*See also*
        intention, tonal; qualia, tonal)
    inversions, 89
    and key, 71
    paths in scale-degree space, 51–52, 54
Schachter, Carl, 107–10
Scheinkonsonanzen. *See* consonance,
    apparent
Schenker, Heinrich, 144–48, 158n12,
    185–86
Schenkerian theory, 1–2, 4, 35–40, 142,
    157
    analysis of Brahms, 185–86, 199–200,
        205–6, 213–14
    analysis of Liszt, 78–79
    analysis of Mozart, 173–82
    and tonal intentions, 144–48, 186

Schoenberg, Arnold, 20
Schubert, Franz, 1
  Piano Sonata in A, D. 664, 29–34,
    39–40, 127–28
Schumann, Robert
  Piano Sonata no. 1 in F# minor, op. 11,
    66–67
semigroups, 10–11, 27, 99, 110, 116
sets, 12, 55–58, 93–98
  set types, 93–95
simple transitivity, 16, 28–29
Sisman, Elaine, 203
Smith, Peter
  analysis of Schubert's Piano Sonata in A,
    D. 664, 29n42, 32n44, 35, 39n57,
  analysis of Brahms's Quintet in G,
    op. 111, 204n4, 204n5, 206n7,
    213, 220n16
  and Brahms's six-three chords, 124n39
Sokolowski, Robert, 106
space, 12–15, 19–21
  multiplicity of, 45–46
Strauss, Richard
  "Zueignung," op. 10, no. 1, 128–29
style hongrois, 203–20
subgroups, 14, 98. See also groups
suggestive (and descriptive) theory, 43.
    See also pluralism,
    methodological

Tchaikovsky, Pyotr Il'yich
  Eugene Onegin, 50–52, 76–77
Temperley, David, 43
temporality. See networks
tetrachords
  diatonic, 153–55
  gypsy, 209–12
Thomson, William, 3
tonality, 101–10, 117
  definitions, 2–3
  See also qualia, tonal; intention, tonal;
    centers, tonal
Tonnetze, 121n6, 141
torus, 45–46, 121n36
transformational attitude, 24–25, 104–5,
    109
transformational theory
  introduction to, 9–11

and Schenkerian theory, 35–40
  and tonal music, 1–5, 34–35
transformations
  durational, 32–34
  kinetic implications of, 25, 31, 90, 101,
    103–4, 112
  vs. intervals, 10–11, 24, 27–29
  introduction to, 24–34
  vs. operations, 25–27, 116, 126
  resolving, 25–28, 125–29, 189
  tonic-directed, 101–4
transitivity. See simple transitivity
transposition, 81–88, 93–95, 98–99
  definitions, 81–83
  real, 64, 81
Tymoczko, Dmitri
  criticisms of Lewinian theory, 13–15,
    20, 51–54
  and definitions of tonality, 3n11
  and geometrical music theory, 1n3,
    11n4
  and interval size, 22n34,
  and tangent spaces, 32n47

uniform triadic transformations, 115n28,
    206n8

Verdi, Giuseppe
  Don Carlos, 60–62
  Falstaff, 59–60
  Il trovatore, 70–71, 74
  La traviata, 60–62
voice leading, parsimonious, 66–67,
    83–88

Wagner, Richard, 1
  Das Rheingold, 77n48, 134–40
  Götterdämmerung, 58–59
  Parsifal, 83–88, 99
  Tristan und Isolde, 62n33
Webern, Anton
  pieces for String Quartet, op. 5, no. 2,
    142–43
Whitehead, Alfred North, 5

Zarlino, Gioseffo, 23
Žižek, Slavoj, 184
Zuckerkandl, Victor, 107–9, 112